Focus on Community College Success

with Planner

Second Edition

Constance Staley

CENGAGE
Learning

Australia • Brazil • Japan • Korea • Mexico • Singapore • Spain • United Kingdom • United States

CENGAGE
Learning™

Focus on Community College Success: with
Planner, Second Edition

FOCUS on Community College Success, 2nd Edition
Constance Staley

© 2012 Cengage Learning. All rights reserved.

Executive Editors:
Maureen Staudt
Michael Stranz

Senior Project Development Manager:
Linda deStefano

Marketing Specialist:
Courtney Sheldon

Senior Production/Manufacturing Manager:
Donna M. Brown

PreMedia Manager:
Joel Brennecke

Sr. Rights Acquisition Account Manager:
Todd Osborne

Cover Image:
Getty Images*

*Unless otherwise noted, all cover images used by Custom
Solutions, a part of Cengage Learning, have been supplied
courtesy of Getty Images with the exception of the Earthview
cover image, which has been supplied by the National
Aeronautics and Space Administration (NASA).

For product information and technology assistance, contact us at
Cengage Learning Customer & Sales Support, 1-800-354-9706

For permission to use material from this text or product,
submit all requests online at **cengage.com/permissions**
Further permissions questions can be emailed to
permissionrequest@cengage.com

This book contains select works from existing Cengage Learning resources and
was produced by Cengage Learning Custom Solutions for collegiate use. As such,
those adopting and/or contributing to this work are responsible for editorial
content accuracy, continuity and completeness.

Compilation © 2011 Cengage Learning
ISBN-13: 978-1-133-06854-9

ISBN-10: 1-133-06854-5

Cengage Learning
5191 Natorp Boulevard
Mason, Ohio 45040
USA
Cengage Learning is a leading provider of customized learning solutions with
office locations around the globe, including Singapore, the United Kingdom,
Australia, Mexico, Brazil, and Japan. Locate your local office at:
international.cengage.com/region.

Cengage Learning products are represented in Canada by Nelson Education, Ltd.
For your lifelong learning solutions, visit **www.cengage.com/custom.**
Visit our corporate website at **www.cengage.com.**

Printed in the United States of America

Brief Contents

Acknowledgments   x
Meet the Cast   xii
Introduction to Students   xix
FOCUS Entrance Interview   xxi

1 Getting the Right Start.. 1

2 Building Dreams, Setting Goals 25

3 Learning about Learning... 47

4 Managing Your Time, Energy, and Money 73

5 Thinking Critically and Creatively 103

6 Developing Technology, Research,
and Information Literacy Skills...................................... 127

7 Engaging, Listening, and Note-Taking in Class 155

8 Developing Your Memory 185

9 Reading and Studying.. 207

10 Taking Tests.. 235

11 Building Relationships, Valuing Diversity 265

12 Choosing a College Major and Career 297

13 Creating Your Future 315

FOCUS Exit Interview   339
Appendix: Additional Time Monitors   342
Notes   344
Index   354

Contents

Acknowledgments   x
Meet the Cast   xii
Introduction to Students   xix
FOCUS Entrance Interview   xxi

chapter 1 Getting the Right Start — 1

Readiness Check   1
FOCUS Challenge Case: Darnell Williams   2
What Do *You* Think?   4

You're in College Now   4
Exercise 1.1 We'd Like to Get to Know You...   6

Earning a Two-Year Degree   7

How College Works: Being "In the Know"   7
Develop a Degree Plan and Plan Your Coursework   9
Exercise 1.2 Why Do I Have to Take This Class?   11
Be Advised! Advising Mistakes Students Make   12
Make the Grade: Computing Your GPA   13
Realize the Value of Remediation   14
Master the Syllabus   15

Box 1.1 Analyzing a Syllabus   16
Avoid the PCP Syndrome: Use Campus Resources   17
Exercise 1.3 Top Ten Resources Your Campus Offers   19

Toughing It Out: What College Takes   20
The Good News and the Bad News (Benefits and Obstacles)   20
This Course Has a Proven Track Record   22

How Do I Want to Be Different When I'm Done?   23
Now What Do You Think?   23
Your Plans for Change   24
Reality Check   24

chapter 2 Building Dreams, Setting Goals — 25

Readiness Check   25
FOCUS Challenge Case: Gloria Gonzales   26
What Do *You* Think?   28

Who Are You? And What Do You Want?   28

Spending Time "in the System"   29
Exercise 2.1 How Do You "Spend" Your Time?   31

How Motivated *Are* You and *How* Are You Motivated?   32
Exercise 2.2 Academic Intrinsic Motivation Self-Assessment   32
Exercise 2.3 The Ideal Student   36

Give Yourself an Attitude Adjustment   36
Six Ways to Adjust Your Attitude   37

Box 2.1 Statements That Ought to Be Outlawed in College . . . and Why   38
Exercise 2.4 Your Academic Autobiography   38

Ability versus Effort: What's More Important?   38
Exercise 2.5 Theories of Intelligence Scale   39
CONTROL Your Toughest Task   40

What Drives You? Values, Dreams, and Goals   41
Exercise 2.6 Core Values Self-Assessment   41
Values at the Core   41
Dreams versus Goals   42
CURIOSITY Know Thyself! How Hard Can That Be?   43
Now What Do You Think?   45
Your Plans for Change   45
Reality Check   46

chapter 3 Learning about Learning 47

Readiness Check 47
FOCUS Challenge Case: Tammy Ko 48
What Do *You* Think? 50

Go to the Head of the Class: Learning and the Brain 50
Exercise 3.1 What Is Learning? 50
Use It or Lose It 50
Ask Questions and Hardwire Your Connections 51

Take Charge and Create the Best Conditions for Learning 51
CONTROL Your Learning 56

Multiple Intelligences: *How* Are You Smart? 57
Exercise 3.2 Multiple Intelligences Self-Assessment 57
Translate Content into Your Own Intelligences 59
Use Intelligence-Oriented Study Techniques 61
Develop Your Weaker Intelligences 62

How Do You Perceive and Process Information? 63
Exercise 3.3 VARK Learning Styles Assessment 64
Using Your Sensory Preferences 66

What Role Does Your Personality Play? 68
Now What Do You Think? 71
Your Plans for Change 71
Reality Check 72

chapter 4 Managing Your Time, Energy, and Money 73

Readiness Check 73
FOCUS Challenge Case: Derek Johnson 74
What Do *You* Think? 76

Time Management Isn't Enough 76

Energy, Our Most Precious Resource 77
Get Physically Energized 79
Get Emotionally Connected 80

"I'll Study in My Free Time" ... and When Is That? 81
Exercise 4.1 Where Did the Time Go? 81
Box 4.1 Lame Excuses for Blowing Off Class 82

Schedule Your Way to Success 83
Exercise 4.2 Time Monitor 83
CURIOSITY Choose to Choose! 84
Exercise 4.3 Term on a Page 85

To Do or Not to Do? There *Is* No Question 88

Exercise 4.4 So Much to Do—So Little Time 90
How Time Flies! 90
Exercise 4.5 Are you a Preemptive, People-pleasing, Perfectionistic Procrastinator? 92

The P Word. Read This Section *Now!* ... or Maybe Tomorrow ... or ... 92
Exercise 4.6 Who, Me, Procrastinate? 93

Beyond Juggling: *Realistically* Manage Work, School, and Personal Life 95

Time Is Money! 97
Exercise 4.7 How Fiscally Fit Are You? 97
Exercise 4.8 Create a Spending Log 98
The Perils of Plastic 99
Box 4.2 Top Ten Financial Aid FAQs 100
Now What Do You Think? 102
Your Plans for Change 102
Reality Check 102

chapter 5 Thinking Critically and Creatively 103

Readiness Check 103
FOCUS Challenge Case: Desiree Moore 104
What Do *You* Think? 106

Rethinking Thinking 106

What Is Critical Thinking? 107
Exercise 5.1 And Just Why Is Critical Thinking Important? 108

A Four-Part Model of Critical Thinking 108

I. Reasoning: The Foundation of Critical Thinking 109

Exercise 5.2 Aspen Commons Apartment Complex Case Study 115

II. Problem Solving: The Basic How-To's 116

Exercise 5.3 Problem Solving for Yourself 119

III. Decision Making: What's Your Style? 120

IV. Thinking about Your Thinking 121

Becoming a Better Critical Thinker 121

Creativity: "Thinking Outside the ... Book" 122

Ten Ways to Become a More Creative Thinker 124

CONTROL Your Toughest Class 125

Now What Do You Think? 126

Your Plans for Change 126

Reality Check 126

chapter 6 Developing Technology, Research, and Information Literacy Skills 127

Readiness Check 127

FOCUS **Challenge Case:** Dario Jones 128

What Do *You* Think? 130

Technology Skills: Wireless, Windowed, Webbed, and Wikied 130

The Internet: The Good, the Bad, and the Ugly 130

CURIOSITY Are You Caught in the Net? 134

Use Technology to Your Academic Advantage 134

Exercise 6.1 How Tech-Savvy Are You? 136

Box 6.1 Other Need-to-Know Technology Definitions 138

Netiquette: Online Manners Matter 138

Exercise 6.2 How *Not* to Win Friends and Influence People Online 139

Taking Online Classes: E-Learning versus C-Learning 139

Research Skills and Your College Success 142

Navigating the Library 143

Information Literacy and Your College Success 144

Step 1. Define 145

Step 2. Locate 146

Step 3. Select 146

Exercise 6.3 Critical Searching on the Internet 147

Step 4. Organize 147

Step 5. Write and Present 148

Box 6.2 PowerPoint or PowerPointless? Five Ways to Make Your Presentations Stand Out 150

Exercise 6.4 Technology Project: Group Ad 151

Downloading Your Workload: The Easy Way Out? 151

Exercise 6.5 Plagiarism Survey 151

Exercise 6.6 Plagiarism or Not? 153

Now What Do You Think? 154

Your Plans for Change 154

Reality Check 154

chapter 7 Engaging, Listening, and Note-Taking in Class 155

Readiness Check 155

FOCUS **Challenge Case:** Rachel White 156

What Do *You* Think? 158

Get Engaged in Class 158

Dare to Prepare 158

Follow the Rules of Engagement 160

Listening with Focus 161

"Easy Listening" Is for Elevators—Focused Listening Is for Classrooms 161

Listen Hard! 162

Get Wired for Sound 164

Box 7.1 Listening Tips if English Is Your Second Language 164

Identify Lecture Styles So You Can Modify Listening Styles 165

CONTROL Your Learning 167

Turn Listening Skills into Note-Taking Skills 168

Exercise 7.1 How Well Do You Listen? 168

Different Strokes for Different Folks: Note-Taking by the System and Subject 169

Outlining 172

The Cornell System 173

Mind Maps 174

Note-Taking on Instructor-Provided Handouts   175
Note-Taking by the Book   177
Note-Taking by the Subject   177
Exercise 7.2 "Focused" Multitasking   179
Ask and You Shall Receive   179
Exercise 7.3 How Much Does Asking Questions Help?   180

Using Lecture Notes   181
Exercise 7.4 Note-Taking 4-M   182
Now What Do You Think?   184
Your Plans for Change   184
Reality Check   184

chapter 8 Developing Your Memory 185

Readiness Check   185
FOCUS Challenge Case: Kevin Baxter   186
What Do You Think?   188

Memory: The Long and Short of It   188
Exercise 8.1 Subjective Memory Test   188
Exercise 8.2 Test Your Memory   190

The Three R's of Remembering: Record, Retain, Retrieve   190
Your Sensory Memory: Focus   191
Your Working Memory: Record   192
Your Long-Term Memory: Retain and Retrieve   194

Twenty Ways to Master Your Memory   195
Make It Stick   195
Make It Meaningful   197
Make It Mnemonic   198
CURIOSITY Act on Your Memory!   199
Manipulate It   200
Make It Funny   201

How Our Memories (uh...hmmm...) Fail Us   202

Deepen Your Memory   204
Now What Do You Think?   205
Your Plans for Change   205
Reality Check   206

chapter 9 Reading and Studying 207

Readiness Check   207
FOCUS Challenge Case: Katie Alexander   208
What Do You Think?   210

Who Needs to Read?   210

Read Right!   211
Exercise 9.1 Keeping a Reading Log   212
Exercise 9.2 Marginal Notes   214

"Elementary, My Dear Watson": Build Your Reading Skills   217
Put English under the Magnifying Glass   218
CURIOSITY Reading When English Is Your Second Language   219
Exercise 9.3 Word Hunt   220
Search for Clues: Develop Your Skills of Detection   220
Exercise 9.4 Two-Way Inferences   221

Stay on the Case: Put Clues Together   221
Exercise 9.5 Paragraph Analysis   222
Box 9.1 Learning Disability? Five Ways to Help Yourself   223

Meta-what? Metacognition, Reading, and Studying   224
Exercise 9.6 Do You Know How to Study?   224

Becoming an Intentional Learner: Make a Master Study Plan   225
Exercise 9.7 "Disciplined" Studying   228

Sprinting to the Finish Line: How to Study when the Heat Is On   231

A Final Word about Reading and Studying   232
Now What Do You Think?   233
Your Plans for Change   233
Reality Check   234

chapter 10 Taking Tests   235

Readiness Check   235
FOCUS Challenge Case: Joe Cloud   236
What Do *You* Think?   238

Testing 1, 2, 3…*Show* What You *Know*   238

Before the Test: Prepare Carefully   239
Cramming: Does "All or Nothing" Really Work?   241
Test-Taking: High Anxiety?   243
Exercise 10.1 Test Anxiety Survey   243
Reduce Math Anxiety and *Increase* Your Test Scores   245

During the Test: Focus and Work Hard   247

Taking Objective Tests   250
True-False: Truly a 50–50 Chance of Getting It Right?   250

Multiple *Choice* or Multiple *Guess*? Taking the Guesswork Out   251
Exercise 10.2 Multiple-Choice Test   254
Short-Answer, Fill in the Blank, and Matching Tests   254

Taking Subjective Essay Tests   255
Exercise 10.3 Understanding "Verb-age"   256
CONTROL Your Learning   257

Don't Cheat Yourself!   258

After the Test: Continue to Learn   261
Now What Do You Think?   263
Your Plans for Change   263
Reality Check   264

chapter 11 Building Relationships, Valuing Diversity   265

Readiness Check   265
FOCUS Challenge Case: Kia Washington   266
What Do *You* Think?   268

The Heart of College Success   268
Exercise 11.1 How Would You Respond?   268

What Is Emotional Intelligence?   269

Can Emotional Intelligence Be Improved?   271
Box 11.1 What Is This Thing Called Love?   274
CURIOSITY Build Relationships One Drop at a Time   275

Communicating in Important Relationships   275

Managing Conflict: Life Is Not a Sitcom   279
Exercise 11.2 What's Your Conflict Style?   280
Exercise 11.3 25 Things We Have in Common   283

Diversity Makes a Difference   283
Exercise 11.4 Your Views on Diversity   283
Exercise 11.5 Facing the Race Issue   285

Appreciate the American Mosaic   287
Exercise 11.6 What's the Difference?   288
Exercise 11.7 Circles of Awareness   288

What's Your CQ?   290
Exercise 11.8 Diagnosing Your Cultural Intelligence   290

Think Globally; Act Locally   293
Box 11.2 Service-Learning: Learning by Serving   294
Now What Do You Think?   295
Your Plans for Change   295
Reality Check   296

chapter 12 Choosing a College Major and Career   297

Readiness Check   297
FOCUS Challenge Case: Ethan Cole   298
What Do *You* Think?   300

What's the Connection?   300

College in a Box?   300
How Do the Disciplines Connect?   301
CONTROL Your Learning   302

How to Choose a Major and a Career   303

Step 1: Follow Your Bliss   304

Step 2: Conduct Preliminary Research   305

Step 3: Take a Good Look at Yourself   306

Exercise 12.1 What Are Your Job Preferences?   306

Step 4: Consider Your Major
versus Your Career   308

Exercise 12.2 Get a Job!   313

Now What Do You Think?   313

Your Plans for Change   314

Reality Check   314

chapter

13   Creating Your Future   315

Readiness Check   315

***FOCUS* Challenge Case:** Anthony Lopez   316

What Do *You* Think?   318

What's the Next Step?   318

CURIOSITY Focus Your I's!   319

Launching a Career: Plan Your Work and Work Your Plan   320

Exercise 13.1 Career Auction   320

Try on a Career for Size   321

Exercise 13.2 Group Résumé   324

Build a Portfolio of Your Best Work   324

Network, Network, Network!   325

Write the Right Résumé   325

Exercise 13.3 Cover Letter Critique   328

Interview at Your Best   328

Continuing Your Education   330

Exercise 13.4 Circling the Right Career   332

Put What You've Learned to Good Use: Ten Things Employers Hope You Will Learn in College   333

What Ifs   336

What If College Isn't Right for You?   336

What If You Can't Finish a Degree Now?   336

My, How You've Grown! Goodbye and Good Luck!   337

Now What Do You Think?   338

Your Plans for Change   338

Reality Check   338

FOCUS *Exit Interview   339*

Appendix: Additional Time Monitors   342

Notes   344

Index   354

Acknowledgments

It's been said that "Achievement is a *we* thing, not a *me* thing, always the product of many heads and hands." Certainly that's true of the monumental effort involved in writing a new edition textbook. There are so many people to thank that this acknowledgments section could be as long as a chapter of *FOCUS on Community College Success*! However, here I'll at least mention those who have contributed the most, including all the students over the last 30-plus years who have taught me more than I've ever taught them.

Family Let me start at the center of my life. My deepest thanks go to Steve, my Sean-Connery-look-alike husband (How do I put up with it?), who almost forgot what I looked like over the last few years. As I *FOCUS*ed away in my attic office day after day and night after night, he brought me too many cups of tea to count. I cherish his devotion. My daughters Shannon and Stephanie helped bring some much-needed balance to my life, and aside from being the most adorable children on the planet, my grandtwins Aidan and Ailie have been a living learning laboratory for me. As little children mastering one new thing after another, they truly have taught me about of the pure joy of learning. And to my beautiful 80-something Mom, who lovingly alternated between urging me to "slow down and relax" and "hurry up and finish," thanks for all your motherly love.

Reviewers The list of reviewers who have contributed their insights and expertise to *FOCUS on Community College Success* is long. I'd like to especially thank Regina Lewis of Pikes Peak Community College for her willingness to serve as consulting editor of *FOCUS on Community College Success*. And my heartfelt thanks to the reviewers who helped inform the second edition revisions: Beverly Brucks, Illinois Central University; Colleen Courtney, Palm Beach State College; Myra Cox, City Colleges of Chicago, Harold Washington; Traci-Dale Crawford, Thomas Nelson Community College; Gregory Dieringer, University of Akron; Sammie Dortch, City Colleges of Chicago, Harold Washington; Evelyn Green, City Colleges of Chicago, Harry Truman; Lois Lawson-Bridell, Gloucester County College; Cherie Meador, Daley College; Bob Noyes, Tidewater Community College; Janet Sims, Cleveland Community College; Camilla Swain-Ledoux, Ivy Technical College; Ivanhoe Tejeda, City Colleges of Chicago, Harold Washington; Carrie Tomko, University of Akron.

I'd be remiss to ignore the valuable input gained from reviewers of the first edition of *FOCUS on Community College Success* that helped shape this book: Lynda Bennett, Blue Mountain Community College; Susannah Chewning, Union County Community College; Jean M. Davis, Florida Community College at Jacksonville; Melanie Deffendall, Delgado Community College; Anne Dickens, Lee College; Michael Discello, Pittsburgh Technical Institute; Shirley Flor, San Diego Mesa College; Wendy Grace, Holmes Community College; Laurene M. Grimes, Lorain County Community College; Anne M. Gupton, Mott Community College; William Hysell, Mohawk Valley Community College; Cynthia S. Johnson, Palm Beach Community College; Benjamin G. Kramer, New River Community College; Joseph Kornoski, Montgomery County Community College; Judy

Kronenberger, Sinclair Community College; Carol Kushner, Dutchess Community College; Christine Landrum, Mineral Area College; Amelia Leighton, Jackson Community College; Jeanine Long, Southwest Georgia Technical College; Sandra Mahon, Community College of Allegheny County; Michael G. McCreary, Florida Community College at Jacksonville; Mark A. Mills, Florida Community College at Jacksonville; Jennifer D. Morrison, J. Sargeant Reynolds Community College; Mita Noor, Los Angeles Pierce College; Bonnie Porter Pajka, Luzerne County Community College; Kate Pandolpho, Ocean County College; Patricia Parma, Palo Alto College; Richard Patete, Keiser University; Gail Platt, South Plains College; Mary Poole, Madisonville Community College; Cristina Rodriguez, Los Angeles Pierce College; Karla Thompson, New Mexico State University Carlsbad; Janice Woods, Mohave Community College.

The Wadsworth Team No book, of course, gets very far without a publisher, and *FOCUS* has had the best publishing team imaginable: the dynamic, highly people-skilled Annie Todd, Director of College Success; the meticulous, multi-talented Marita Sermolins, Development Editor; the energetic, industrious Kirsten Stoller, Marketing Manager; a true professional who combed the first pages and probably did more than I'll ever know, Alison Eigel Zade, Content Project Manager; and Annie Beck, Project Manager at Lachina Publishing Services. I'd like to especially thank Larry Harwood, the master photographer who spent a long, hard weekend clicking photos of the *FOCUS* cast on the University of Colorado at Colorado Springs campus. And heartfelt thanks to Wadsworth's Annie Mitchell and Sean Wakely, who believed in this project from the very start; Sylvia Shepherd, whose creative vision shaped much of this book, and Lauren Larsen, whose wit and wisdom formed the basis for several of the early chapters.

Other Contributors I'd also particularly like to thank the "*FOCUS* All-Stars," as I call them, who modeled for the photo shoots and starred in the "Inside the *FOCUS* Studio" videos. They followed artistic direction like pros, and they make this book unique. I'd also like to thank the Career Outlook interviewees and my colleagues at UCCS who have helped me develop many of the ideas in this book, whether they know it or not— all the Freshman Seminar faculty past and present. I also can't go without thanking the many authors who granted me permission to use their work and three essential scholars who allowed me to use, apply, and extend their instruments throughout the book: Neil Fleming, Brian French, and John Bransford. And thanks to my expert student research assistants; to John Cowles and Ric Undershile, my expert Instructor's Resource Manual co-authors; and to Aren Moore, who worked with me to create the "props" for each chapter's opening case study, and the dynamic, ground-breaking, multimedia FOCUS-points for each chapter. And finally, I'd like to thank Matt McClain, the comedy writer who brought his innovative humor to the learning process through podcast summaries of the chapters and television scripts for the website TV shows. He took the "big ideas" from *FOCUS* chapters and made them memorable to students by using their own best-loved media.

Above all, *FOCUS* has taught me truly to focus. Writing a book takes the same kind of endurance and determination that it takes to get a college degree. My empathy level for my students has, if anything, increased—and I am thankful for all I've learned while writing. It has been a cathartic experience to see what has filled each computer screen as I've tapped, tapped, tapped away. Ultimately, what I have chosen to put into each chapter has told me a great deal about who I am, what I know (and don't), and what I value. There's no doubt: I am a better teacher for having written this book. May all my readers grow through their *FOCUS* experience, too.

Meet the Cast

©Larry Harwood Photography. Property of Cengage Learning.

Chapter 1: Darnell Williams / Calil

Hometown: Colorado Springs, Colorado

Major: History with a secondary education emphasis

Lessons Learned: Calil noticed many similarities between himself and the FOCUS Challenge Case character he portrayed, besides playing football and watching movies. Calil, too, had problems with the transition from high school to college. He admits he was a student who "coasted" through his senior year of high school, which made his first year of college more difficult.

Toughest First-Year Class: English, like Darnell, because he wasn't fully aware of the instructor's expectations.

Advice to New Students: "Determination is the key to success. If you are determined, there is nothing in the world that can stop you."

©Larry Harwood Photography. Property of Cengage Learning.

Chapter 2: Gloria Gonzales / Debbie

Hometown: Saguache, Colorado

Major: Business with a minor in Communication

Lessons Learned: Debbie learned through her first-year seminar course that it takes time and effort to establish great relationships. She got involved in intramural sports, which helped her meet new people and make friends. Although she's doing well now, she wishes she'd studied more her first term.

Toughest First-Year Class: Microeconomics because it was an entirely new subject for her.

Advice to New Students: "Get your priorities straight; college is a great place to be, so get a great start by setting good study habits, and I HIGHLY recommend a planner because you will be surprised at how fast your time can become occupied."

Chapter 3: Tammy Ko / Jessica

Hometown: Manitou Springs, Colorado

Major: Marketing

Lessons Learned: Juggling a part-time job while in school, Jessica loved meeting new people, but she regretted not talking to other students about which instructors and courses to take towards her marketing major. In order to succeed, she says, you've "gotta give it all you've got!"

Toughest First-Year Class: Microeconomics because it wasn't like high school courses that just required memorizing a lot of facts.

Advice to New Students: "Talk to other students to learn about the best instructors, and make sure you are studying something that you are interested in."

Chapter 4: Derek Johnson / Derrick

Hometown: Colorado Springs, Colorado

Major: Communications/Recording Arts

Lessons Learned: Even though he's not married and has no children, Derrick and his case study character have much in common—too much to do and too little time! Derrick felt his biggest mistake in college was not asking enough questions in class. He knows now he should ask for clarity on content or assignments he doesn't understand.

Toughest First-Year Class: English because he and his instructor had differing opinions, but he communicated through the tough spots and earned an "A".

Advice to New Students: "Surround yourself with positive people. As the saying goes, 'you are the company you keep.' I've seen many of my friends drop out because the people they called friends were holding them back from their full potential."

Free Time: composing music and producing films

Chapter 5: Desiree Moore / Regina

Hometown: Colorado Springs, Colorado

Major: M.A. Communication

Lessons Learned: Organization, time management, study groups, and note cards.

Toughest First-Year Course: Psychology because in this class I had to be very organized to keep my notes in order. There were only two exams in this class during the entire semester. I did not organize my notes or my time very well.

Advice to New Students: "Get to know your professors, ask questions, and have a study buddy."

Free Time: In my free time, I work out at the gym. I also spend quality time with my son.

Chapter 6: Dario Jones / Orlando

Hometown: Fountain, Colorado

Major: MA, Communication

Lessons Learned: Start strong, work hard, and finish strong

Toughest First-Year Course: Math 099

Advice to New Students: "Get to know your instructors and fellow classmates. Ask questions in class when you're not sure about something."

Free Time: What free time? To relax, I listen to jazz or classical music, or I'll channel surf until I find something interesting to watch.

Chapter 7: Rachel White / Shannon

Hometown: Denver, Colorado

Major: Philosophy

Lessons Learned: Go to class!

Toughest First-Year Course: Intro to Geography (it might have been easier if I'd gone to class)

Advice to New Students: "Balance fun and schoolwork, so you don't get burned out on either one!"

Free Time: Acting and improv

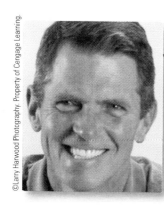

Chapter 8: Kevin Baxter / Dave

Hometown: St. Paul, Minnesota

Background: Portraying a student returning to school after fifteen-plus years in the working world, Dave is currently a professor of chemistry at University of Colorado at Colorado Springs.

College Memories: Dave remembers how much he liked the different social environment college provided after graduating from high school.

Toughest First-Year Course: English Composition since writing wasn't exactly his forte.

Advice to New Students: "Study hard, and use your time wisely."

Free Time: woodworking, hiking, and climbing

Chapter 9: Katie Alexander / Christina

Hometown: Colorado Springs, Colorado. Since she went to college in her hometown, Christina really enjoyed the opportunity college provided to meet new people.

Major: Nursing

Lessons Learned: Spending her free time with her friends watching movies, going bowling or dancing, and just hanging out, Christina found that like her *FOCUS* Challenge Case character, she, too, would make up excuses to get out of studying and doing her homework. She quickly learned the importance of reading and taking notes. "As weird as it may sound, reading cuts your end study time by more than half. Reading the material ahead of time helps you understand everything so much better."

Advice to New Students: "Stay motivated. College is going to FLY by! If you stay motivated and get good grades, it really will be over before you know it."

Chapter 10: Joe Cloud / Alvin

Hometown: Ganado, Arizona (Navajo Nation)

Major: Business

Toughest First-Year Course: Spanish because he comes from a place where no other languages are ever spoken.

Lessons Learned: President of the American Indian Science and Engineering Society on campus, Alvin identifies closely with his *FOCUS* Challenge Case character. He, too, is one of a minority of Native Americans in higher education, so a lot of people in his hometown are carefully watching his academic success. Alvin admits his biggest mistake in his first term was not opening up to people—he came to school for class and left without trying to meet new people. But he learned from his mistakes and eventually came to value meeting all sorts of different people through activities on campus.

Advice to New Students: "Learn from *my* mistakes: Be open to try new things, get out of your comfort zone, and be free to be silly—everyone is at some point. You meet a lot of new people that way and it makes your first year the experience of a lifetime."

Chapter 11: Kia Washington / Charmaine

Hometown: Colorado Springs, Colorado

Major: Psychology and Sociology

Toughest First-Year Course: General psychology because there was so much to learn in such a short period of time.

Lessons Learned: Charmaine learned how to manage her time more effectively, as well as the necessity of keeping yourself healthy in mind, body, and spirit, something she felt her *FOCUS* Challenge Case character could have benefited from.

Advice to New Students: "Remember to have fun in everything that you do, both academically and otherwise. Take care of yourself first and don't feel as though you have to do everything all the time; sometimes the best parts of life come during moments of down time. This is where you are able to truly reflect on what it is you're doing and remember why you're doing it in the first place!"

©Larry Harwood Photography. Property of Cengage Learning.

Chapter 12: Ethan Cole / Josh

Hometown: Fort Morgan, Colorado

Major: Sociology

Lessons Learned: Like his *FOCUS* Challenge Case character, Josh noticed that he, too, didn't always push himself to reach his potential. But he learned through his first-year seminar course that he is responsible for himself and that instructors aren't like high school teachers. They will let you fail a class if you don't do what you need to. It's up to you.

Advice to New Students: "Not only did getting involved on campus help me have more fun in school, but it has also helped me academically. It has taught me how to manage my time and has made it so much easier for me to participate with confidence in class. Just make sure you get what you need to do done, and you will enjoy your college experience so much more."

Free Time: "Free time? What's that?! I'm too busy to have free time!" (But he secretly admits he snowboards, plays guitar, draws, and spends time with friends.)

©Larry Harwood Photography. Property of Cengage Learning.

Chapter 13: Anthony Lopez / Luis

Hometown: Aguascalientes, Mexico

Major: Spanish with an emphasis on secondary education

Lessons Learned: Luis is extremely involved on campus and within his community—he is President of the Association of Future Teachers, sings with his church choir, plays intramural soccer, and works for the Air Force on weekends. Luis thinks one mistake he made in his first term was that he procrastinated with homework because his new freedom let him think he could have fun first and study later, but he quickly learned he was wrong.

Advice to New Students: "Be smart and be involved, but always do your homework first. If you are involved on campus, you will meet people that will help make your college experience easier and more fun."

MEET THE AUTHOR: Constance Staley

Hometown: Pittsburgh, Pennsylvania (although she never actually lived there. Instead, she lived all over the world and went to ten schools in twelve years.)

Background: Connie has taught at the University of Colorado at Colorado Springs for more than 30 years after getting a bachelor's degree in education, a master's degree in linguistics, and a Ph.D. in communication.

College Memories: Connie remembers loving her public speaking class as a first-year student and having tons of friends, but being extremely homesick for her family.

Advice to New Students: "Earning a college degree is hard work, takes a long time, and requires a substantial investment of your time, energy, and resources. But it's the best investment you can make in your own future—one you'll never regret."

Free Time: Spending time with her husband, her two daughters, and her boy-girl grandtwins; relaxing at her cabin in the mountains; and traveling around the country to speak to other instructors who also care about their first-year students and their success.

Introduction to Students

Dear Reader,

This book is different. It won't coerce, coddle, caution, or coax you. Instead, it will give *you* the tools you need to coach yourself. Ultimately, this book is about you, your college career, and your career beyond college. It's about the future you will create for yourself.

FOCUS on Community College Success stars a cast of my own students (several colleagues, and one of my daughters), like a stage play. One student "actor" is featured in each chapter's opening case study. All thirteen cast members reappear throughout the book, so that you'll get to know them as you read. I've been teaching for more than 30 years now and worked with thousands of students. Each case study is about a real student (with a fictitious name) that I've worked with or a mixture of several students. You may find you have some things in common with them. But whether you do or not, I hope they will make this book come to life for you. You'll also be able to meet these "actors" electronically in *FOCUS TV* videos on the book's CourseMate website.

I love what I do, and I care deeply about students. I hope that comes through to you as a reader. You'll see that I've inserted some of my personality, had a bit of fun at times, and tried to create a new kind of textbook for you. In my view, learning should be engaging, personal, memorable, challenging, and fun.

Most importantly, I know that these next few years hold the key to unlock much of what you want from your life. And from all my years of experience and research, I can tell you straightforwardly that what you read in this book works. It gets results. It can turn you into a better, faster learner. *Really?* you ask. Really! The only thing you have to do is put all the words in this book into action. That's where the challenge comes in.

Becoming an educated person takes time, energy, resources, and focus. At times, it may mean shutting down the six windows you have open on your computer, and directing all your attention to one thing in laser-like fashion. It may mean disciplining yourself to dig in and stick with something until you've nailed it. Can you do it? I'm betting you can, or I wouldn't have written this book. Invest yourself fully in what you read here, and then decide to incorporate it into your life. If there's one secret to college success, that's it.

So, you're off! You're about to begin one of the most fascinating, liberating, challenging, and adventure-filled times of your life. I may not be able to meet each one of you personally, but I *can* wish you well, wherever you are. I hope this book helps you on your journey.

Constance Staley

Answers to the back cover questions are 1) b; 2) d; 3) b; 4) a; 5) a.

Take a look at this poem, written by a community college graduate who continued on for a bachelor's degree. He wrote this poem as he finished his associate's degree, and now he has an important job in an organization that provides scholarships, grants, and funding that make a difference in people's lives.

Passion in Action

By Jason Gaulden

There's no such thing as an answer
to a question that is not asked.
And there's no way to find yourself
until you take off the mask.
And get rid of all of those thoughts
about chasing your dreams.
And start having some thoughts
of catching every one of those things.

There's a world of opportunity
that is waiting for you.
But it's passion in action
that makes dreams come true.

It is by grace,
and by faith,
and by fate
that at this time,
at this place,
we've crossed paths.
This fork in the road is great
because this intersection
is a marketplace for life lessons.
You've seen things on your path
that I didn't see on mine.
I've seen things on my path
that you didn't see on yours.
These are my expressions of pain
and pleasure, risk and reward.
This is the formula that made me.
Just like your experiences made you.

Now, we're all on a journey
and we've all come a long way
but today is that day
that marks in a significant way
that what is behind you
is behind you.
In some ways that bind you
into a state of reminiscence and reflection.

A state of introspection.
That's a good place to visit
but you do not want to stay there.

For what is before you is before you
and I implore you
to experience the magnitude of this moment.
Today is the link between potential and promise.

This moment is yours for the making.
Success is yours for the taking.
And the future is yours for the shaping.

The world is yours.
If these things seem too much for you,
realize that today is the bridge between dreams
and dreams come true.

I don't know how you define success,
but it has something to do with moving
from where you are
to where you want to be.
So let's be about the business
of transforming dreams into reality.

To accept or reject the mission
you have to choose between the two,
but it's passion in action
that makes dreams come true.

There are countless complexities
for you to get through,
but it's passion in action
that makes dreams come true.

To the bottom or to the top,
it's all up to you,
but it's passion in action
that makes dreams come true.

There's absolutely nothing wrong
with having something to prove,
but it's passion in action
that makes dreams come true.

So believe in yourself
and know that the determination within you
is greater than the past that is chasing you.
Greater than the obstacles in front of you.
Greater than the pressures that surround you.

They are no match
for who you are destined to be.
They are no match
for what you are destined to do.
Because it's passion in action that makes dreams come true.
Put your passion in action
and make your dreams come true.

FOCUS Entrance Interview

Although you may not have experienced life as a new college student for long, we're interested in how you expect to spend your time, what challenges you think you'll face, and your general views of what you think college will be like. Please answer thoughtfully.

INFORMATION ABOUT YOU

Name _____

Student Number _____ Course/Section _____

Instructor _____

Gender _____ Age _____

1. **Ethnic Identification (check all that apply):**
   ____ American Indian or Alaska Native   ____ Native Hawaiian or Other Pacific Islander
   ____ Asian   ____ Hispanic/Latino
   ____ Black or African American   ____ White   ____ Prefer not to answer

2. **Is English your first (native) language?**
   ____ yes   ____ no

3. **Where are you living this term?**
   ____ with my immediate family   ____ on my own
   ____ with a relative other than my immediate family   ____ other (please explain)_____

4. **Did your parents graduate from college?**
   ____ yes, both   ____ neither
   ____ yes, father only   ____ not sure
   ____ yes, mother only

5. **How many credit hours are you taking this term?**
   ____ 6 or fewer   ____ 15-16
   ____ 7-11   ____ 17 or more
   ____ 12-14

6. **Did you start college elsewhere before attending this school?**
   ____ yes   ____ no

7. **In addition to going to college, do you expect to work for pay at a job (or jobs) this term?**
   ____ yes   ____ no

8. **If so, how many hours per week do you expect to work?**
   ____ 1-10   ____ 31-40
   ____ 11-20   ____ 40+
   ____ 21-30

9. **Which of the following describes why you are working for pay this term? (Mark all that apply.)**
   ____ to pay for college tuition   ____ to pay for child care
   ____ to pay for basic expenses that I need (rent, housing, food, etc.)   ____ to pay for textbooks
   ____ to pay for extra expenses that I want (clothes, entertainment, etc.)   ____ to save money for the future
   ____ to buy a car   ____ to see how much I can make
   ____ to support a family   ____ other (please explain)
   _____

10. **How will you pay for your college expenses? (Check all that apply.)**

___ my own earnings   ___ scholarships and grants

___ my parents' contributions   ___ loans

___ my spouse or partner's contributions   ___ other (please explain)_____

___ my employer's contributions

11. **If you plan to work for pay, where will you work?**

___ on campus   ___ off campus   ___ at more than one job

12. **If you are entering college soon after completing high school, on average, how many total hours per week did you spend studying outside of class in high school?**

___ 0–5   ___ 26–30

___ 6–10   ___ 31–35

___ 11–15   ___ 36–40

___ 16–20   ___ 40+

___ 21–25   ___ I am a returning student and attended high school some time ago.

13. **What was your high school grade point average?**

___ A+   ___ C+

___ A   ___ C

___ A−   ___ C−

___ B+   ___ D or lower

___ B   ___ I don't remember.

___ B−

INFORMATION ABOUT YOUR COLLEGE EXPECTATIONS

14. **How do you expect to learn best in college? (Check all that apply.)**

___ by looking at charts, maps, graphs   ___ by reading books

___ by looking at color-coded information   ___ by writing papers

___ by looking at symbols and graphics   ___ by taking notes

___ by listening to instructors' lectures   ___ by going on field trips

___ by listening to other students during an in-class discussion   ___ by engaging in activities

___ by talking about course content with friends or roommates   ___ by actually doing things

15. **For each of the following pairs of descriptors, which set sounds most like you? (Please choose between the two options on each line and place a checkmark by your choice.)**

___ Extraverted and outgoing   or   ___ Introverted and quiet

___ Detail-oriented and practical   or   ___ Big-picture and future-oriented

___ Rational and truthful   or   ___ People-oriented and tactful

___ Organized and self-disciplined   or   ___ Spontaneous and flexible

16. *FOCUS* **is about 13 different aspects of college life. Which are you most interested in? Which may contain information you expect to find most challenging to apply in your own life? (Check all that apply.)**

Most interested in	Most challenging to apply to myself	Most interested in	Most challenging to apply to myself
___	___ Getting the right start	___	___ Engaging, listening, and note-taking in class
___	___ Building dreams, setting goals	___	___ Developing your memory
___	___ Learning to learn	___	___ Reading and studying
___	___ Managing time and energy	___	___ Taking tests
___	___ Thinking critically and creatively	___	___ Building relationships, valuing diversity
___	___ Developing technology, research, and information literacy skills	___	___ Choosing a major and career
		___	___ Creating your future

17. **Which one of your current classes do you expect to find most challenging this term and why?**

Which class? (course title *or* department and course number) _____

Why? _____

Do you expect to succeed in this course? ___ yes ___ no

Perhaps (please explain): _____

18. How many total hours per week do you expect to spend outside of class studying for your college courses this term?

___ 0-5   ___ 26-30
___ 6-10   ___ 31-35
___ 11-15   ___ 36-40
___ 16-20   ___ 40+
___ 21-25

19. Which of the following on-campus resources do you plan to use once or more this term? (Please check all that apply.)

___ library

___ campus learning centers (whatever is available on your campus, such as a Writing Center, Math Learning Center, etc.)

___ computer labs

___ the Student Success Center or New Student Center, if one is available

___ the Counseling Center, if one is available

___ instructors' office hours for individual meetings/conferences/help

___ student clubs or organizations

___ none

20. For the following sets of opposite descriptive phrases, put a checkmark on the line between the two that best represent your response.

I expect my first term of college to:

challenge me academically	___ ___ ___ ___ ___	be easy
be very different from high school	___ ___ ___ ___ ___	be a lot like high school
be exciting	___ ___ ___ ___ ___	be dull
be interesting	___ ___ ___ ___ ___	be uninteresting
motivate me to continue	___ ___ ___ ___ ___	discourage me
be fun	___ ___ ___ ___ ___	be boring
help me feel a part of this campus	___ ___ ___ ___ ___	make me feel alienated

21. Please mark your *top three areas of concern* relating to your first term of college by placing 1, 2, and 3 next to the items you choose.

___ I might not fit in.

___ I might have difficulty making friends.

___ I might not be academically successful.

___ My performance might disappoint my family.

___ My personal life might interfere with my studies.

___ My studies might interfere with my personal life.

___ I might have financial difficulties.

___ My job might interfere with my studies.

___ My studies might interfere with my job.

___ My social life might interfere with my studies.

___ My studies might interfere with my social life.

___ My instructors might not care about me as an individual.

___ I might not finish my degree.

___ I might not manage my time well.

___ I might be bored in my classes.

___ I might feel intimidated by my instructors.

___ I might feel overwhelmed by all I have to do.

___ other (please explain)_____

22. Broadly speaking, which area do you expect to major in?

___ General Studies

___ An associate's degree in_____ .

___ A certificate in _____ .

___ Other (please explain) _____

23. How certain are you now of a chosen major? (1 = totally sure, 5 = totally unsure) ____

24. How certain are you now that you will complete your degree or certificate? (1 = totally sure, 5 = totally unsure) ____

25. How certain are you now that you will complete your degree or certificate at this school? (1 = totally sure, 5 = totally unsure) ____

26. How certain are you now of your intended career choice? (1 = totally sure, 5 = totally unsure) ____

27. How certain are you now about whether you'll transfer to a four-year school? (1 = totally sure, 5 = totally unsure) ____

28. What do you expect your grade point average to be at the end of your first term of college?

___ A+   ___ B+   ___ C+   ___ D or lower
___ A   ___ B   ___ C
___ A−   ___ B−   ___ C−

29. **All college students develop expectations of what college will be like from various sources. How did you develop your expectations of what college might be like? (Mark your top three information sources with 1, 2, and 3.)**

_____ TV and movies   _____ talks with my family
_____ friends/siblings who have already gone to college   _____ talks with my friends who are also now starting college
_____ discussions with teachers/counselors in high school   _____ the Internet
_____ information I received from colleges in the mail   _____ other (please explain) _____

30. **How confident are you in yourself in each of the following areas? (1 = very confident, 5 = not at all confident)**

_____ overall academic ability   _____ technology skills
_____ mathematical skills   _____ physical well being
_____ leadership ability   _____ writing skills
_____ reading skills   _____ social skills
_____ public speaking skills   _____ emotional well being
_____ study skills   _____ teamwork skills

31. **Why did you take the course for which you are using this textbook? (Mark your top three reasons with 1, 2, and 3.)**

_____ It was required.   _____ My advisor recommended it.
_____ It sounded interesting.   _____ A high school teacher/counselor recommended it.
_____ I thought it would help make my transition to college easier.   _____ The information I received in campus mailings convinced me.
_____ I thought it would help me learn about the campus.   _____ The materials I received at freshman orientation convinced me.
_____ I thought it would help me make friends.   _____ A friend/sibling who'd taken this course recommended it.
_____ I thought it would help me academically.   _____ other (please explain) _____
_____ My parent(s) or other family member(s) thought it was a good idea.

32. **What is the most important reason you decided to attend this school? (Check one)**

_____ Recommendation of friend(s) who attended here   _____ Financial aid I was offered
_____ Reasonable cost   _____ Recommendation of high school teachers/counselors
_____ Reputation of the school   _____ Campus website
_____ Location of the school   _____ other (please explain) _____
_____ Availability of academic programs I'm interested in

33. **Was this school your first choice among the colleges you considered?** _____ yes _____ no

34. **Why did you decide to go to college? (Check all that apply)**

_____ Because I want to build a better life for myself.   _____ Because it was expected of me.
_____ Because I want to build a better life for my family. _____ Because I was recruited for athletics.
_____ Because I want to be very well off financially in the future.   _____ Because I want to continue learning.
_____ Because I need a college education to achieve my dreams.   _____ Because the career I am pursuing requires a degree.
_____ Because my friends were going to college.   _____ Because I was unsure of what I might do instead.
_____ Because my family encouraged me to go.   _____ other (please explain) _____

35. **Looking ahead, how satisfied do you expect to be with your decision to attend this school?**

_____ very satisfied   _____ somewhat dissatisfied
_____ satisfied   _____ very dissatisfied
_____ not sure

36. **What are you most looking forward to in college?** _____
_____

37. **How would you describe the best outcomes you hope for at the end of this term? Why are they important to you?** _____
_____

38. **Do you expect to achieve these outcomes? Why or why not?** _____
_____

chapter 1

Getting the Right Start

YOU'RE ABOUT TO DISCOVER . .

- ✔ Who goes to community colleges and why
- ✔ How to be a PROFESSIONAL student
- ✔ What different types of degrees are available
- ✔ How to master a syllabus
- ✔ Why developmental courses are important
- ✔ Why college success courses work

©Larry Harwood Photography. Property of Cengage Learning.

READINESS CHECK — What do you **Know?**

Before beginning this chapter, take a moment to answer these questions. Your answers will help you assess how ready you are to focus.

1 = not very/not much/very little/low   5 = very/a lot/very much/high

How much do you *already* know?

Rate your current level of knowledge about topics covered in this chapter.

The characteristics of students who go to community colleges

1 2 3 4 5

The difference between certificate and associate degrees

1 2 3 4 5

The expectations of community college instructors

1 2 3 4 5

The success rates of college success courses

1 2 3 4 5

How motivated are you to learn *more*?

In general, how motivated are you to learn the material in this chapter?

1 2 3 4 5

How much do you think this information might affect your college success?

1 2 3 4 5

How much do you think this information might affect your career success after college?

1 2 3 4 5

How ready are you to read *now*?

How ready are you to focus on this chapter—physically, intellectually, and emotionally? Which of these three areas is most challenging for you right now? Circle a number to represent it.

1 2 3 4 5

If any of your answers is below a 3, consider addressing the issue before reading. Then, read the chapter carefully, while looking for ways to improve your focus.

Finally, how long do you think it will take you to complete this chapter? If you start and stop, keep track of the overall time.

_____ Hour(s) _____ Minutes

©Larry Harwood Photography. Property of Cengage Learning.

Darnell Williams

Quite honestly, Darnell Williams hadn't found high school all that challenging. Playing football his last two years had made it bearable. But at his school, if you showed up and had a pulse, you could count on passing your courses. There wasn't anything in particular he really wanted to do after high school, so he didn't do much of anything except hang out with friends, watch movies, and play an occasional game of football. But that got boring fast, and after a year had gone by, his friends started getting jobs and had less time to hang out with him. So Darnell decided to go to the community college in his hometown. Maybe something there would appeal to him.

But after two weeks, Darnell admitted that he didn't find his classes all that engaging. Although he was strong physically from working out for football, he knew he was out of shape academically. He didn't do any homework in high school, but how much would he have to do here? Since Darnell had no idea which classes to take, he figured he'd just get some required courses out of the way during his first term. He'd always heard people say, "College is about your communication skills, like writing and speaking. If your basic skills are good, and you're willing to work hard, you'll do fine." Based on that advice, he'd enrolled in two courses: English Composition and Public Speaking.

Earlier that morning, Darnell had received an e-mail from his best friend, Curtis, at the large state university two hours from home. It read like this:

Man, I hope I can make it here! The competition is stiff, and I wish I'd taken more college prep courses. Remember how we had lots of tests in our high school classes—every couple of weeks? If we just memorized a few things, like math formulas, even if we didn't understand them, we could do well on tests. And since there were so many tests, one low grade didn't matter. Here, there's a midterm and a final exam. If I blow one of those, I'm in big trouble. How long B4 midterms 4 you? AFAIK, I'm already off to a rough start. I gotta just T+. GTG 8 :-) Curtis

© Laurin Rinder, 2009/Used under license from Shutterstock.com

CINEMA
Good Only Date Sold
ADMIT ONE
048107 048107
© belle23, 2009/Used under license from Shutterstock.com

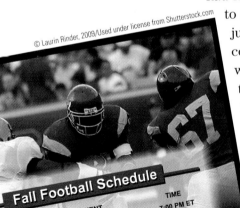

Fall Football Schedule

DATE	OPPONENT	TIME
September 6	Colorado State	7:00 PM ET
September 11	at Toledo	9:00 PM ET
September 19	Wyoming	3:30 PM ET
October 1	at West Virginia	7:30 PM ET
October 10	at Texas	7:00 PM ET
October 17	Kansas	9:00 PM ET
October 24	at Kansas State	3:30 PM ET
October 31	Missouri	9:00 PM ET
November 7	Texas A&M	3:30 PM ET
	at Iowa State	9:00 PM ET
	Oklahoma State	7:30 PM ET
		3:30 PM ET

© Cengage Lea

Course Schedule
Main Campus
FALL SEMESTER
Williams, Darnell

Course Title	Hrs	Days	Meeting Times	Bldg	Room	Meeting Dates

Toward the end of the message, Darnell noticed that Curtis had slipped into the usual e-mail abbreviations like T+ for "think positively" and AFAIK for "as far as I know." *I wish I could write like that in my composition class,* Darnell thought. *In e-mails, texts, and IMs, you can be informal, and no one worries about it. That's an easier way to write.* But he knew that kind of informality wouldn't fly with his teacher, Professor Monroe. But one particular aspect of the e-mail caught Darnell's attention. Even though they were at different schools, both he and Curtis noticed a big difference between high school and college. Looking back, high school seemed like a piece of cake. In college, you actually had to work for your grades by getting assignments done on time and paying attention to the instructor's high standards.

Darnell wondered if he'd be more motivated in college if he could have signed up for some courses he'd actually been interested in, like Sports in Society or Modern American Cinema. Sports and movies were two of his favorite things. At the moment, Darnell had absolutely no idea what to major in. He was—as his college put it—an "undecided" student.

Professor Monroe had already begun when Darnell walked into class, and she shot a scowl in his direction. As he sat down at his computer station in the writing lab and pulled up the course website, his mind went totally blank. In high school, he hadn't been required to write anything longer than a few paragraphs. *I'm going to blame this stress on my senior-year English teacher, Mr. Forester. This is his fault. He should have done a better job of preparing us for college,* Darnell decided.

Just then, Professor Monroe was reminding the students that they'd get back their first graded essays today. "I have to be honest with you, class," she'd warned, "I expected more from you, and frankly, I'm disappointed in your work. We have a lot of work to do this term!" *Ouch!* Darnell thought to himself. *I hope she's not talking about me!*

Darnell held his breath as he looked at the paper she handed him, and then he saw it. At the top there was no grade at all—nothing but the teacher's note that said, "See me." What could that possibly mean? *This college thing is going to be more challenging than I thought,* he said to himself. One thing was clear to him: If he wanted to do well, he'd probably have to cut back on movies and sports now that he was in college.

Jeremy Edwards/ Istockphoto.com & Copyright Sergiy Zavgorodny, 2010; Andresr, 2010; bikeriderlondon, 2010; © Lorelyn Medina, 2010 Used under license from Shutterstock.com.

© Cengage Learning

© Cengage Learning

EAST HIGH SCHOOL
OFFICIAL TRANSCRIPT

STUDENT INFORMATION

: Darnell Williams
UARDIAN: Michael and Joan Williams

ACADEMIC RECORD

R: 2005–2006	GRADE LEVEL: 9th		SCHOOL YEAR: 2006–2007	GRA
	Credit Earned	Final Grade	Course Title	
s I	1.0	B	English II	
lab	1.0	C		

1. Do you have anything in common with Darnell? If so, what steps are you taking to help make sure you're successful?
2. Why do you think the instructor didn't give Darnell a grade? Would a teacher's note on a paper that says "See me" always indicate a problem?
3. In your experience, what are some of the main **academic** differences between high school and college? How did you read and study in high school, and how do you think that will change in college?

academic having to do with education

You're in College Now

Congratulations! You're in college. You've just started a new chapter of your life! As the saying goes, "The first step toward getting somewhere is to decide that you are not going to stay where you are." In choosing to go to community college, that's what you've decided. You're *not* going to stay where you are. Your journey has begun. This chapter will launch you on your journey by covering the basics. You may already know much of this information, but not everyone does. So, let's start at the beginning.

Why do people go to community college? Generally, people go to a community college to improve their skills or gain completely new ones. Many community college students differ from four-year college students in ways like these: they attend school part-time, support themselves, work full-time, are single parents, waited to go on to college, or got their high school degrees in nonstandard ways.[1] (In fact, if you don't yet have a high school diploma or **GED**, your community college may be able to help you with that.)

GED stands for **g**eneral **e**ducation **d**evelopment; passing these tests is an alternative to earning a traditional high school diploma

> **Reason 1: Transitioning from High School to College.** If you just finished high school, you may see college as the obvious next step. Like Darnell, you'll find college to be a very different game. Think of it this way: Darnell arrived at college, playing what he thought was a decent game of checkers. But he quickly discovered that his instructors expected him to play chess. He'd been successful

©Larry Harwood Photography. Property of Cengage Learning.

> 66 99
>
> **First say to yourself what you would be; and then do what you have to do.**
>
> *Epictetus, Greek philosopher, 55–135 a.d.*

> **The road to success is lined with many tempting parking spaces.**
>
> *Traditional proverb*

in high school, and to the inexperienced eye, college looked like the same game board. After all, school is school, right? Wrong! Darnell quickly discovered that college is a new game with different rules!

Other students you know may have gone off to college somewhere else. But you considered things like cost and convenience and chose a college in your own community. A community college is a *real* college—a **marketplace of ideas**, where you can try out all kinds of new things. According to one study, more community college students than students at four-year schools report more opportunities to speak in class and get to know their instructors. A community college that focuses on teaching—and on you—can be a good place to be.[2]

marketplace of ideas a place where many ideas are exchanged freely

A community college can also be a great place to test the waters. Before plunging into a university setting (often with higher tuition rates), you want to see if college is right for you. After you get into the rhythm of your classes, you may decide you've made a good decision. Or you may decide to wait until your life is less complicated or your head is in the right place.

> **Reason 2: Going Back to School after a Break.** Perhaps you've tried college before and quit. But now you've decided to get back on the road to success. Maybe you're absolutely committed to making it this time, so you're more motivated. Something may have changed in your life, or you worked to save up for college for a while, or you've been a stay-at-home mom, or you have an employer now who will help foot your tuition bill.

One of the most interesting things about community colleges is the amazing mix of students from all walks of life. You're just as likely to be sitting beside a grandmother who's decided it's her turn now, a soldier who's just come back from overseas, or a businessman gaining credentials for a promotion. Adult community college students are practical, self-directed learners who want to build on their past experiences and apply what they learn to their everyday lives. Does that describe you?[3]

Or perhaps you're returning to school to gear up with a select course or two. For example, maybe you have a new job that requires giving presentations, and the thought of it terrifies you. So you take a course to help you overcome your fear of public speaking. You don't necessarily want a

degree; you just want to take a course or two. There's probably no better place than a community college to meet those kinds of focused needs.

Who goes to community college? Take a look at these statistics:

> 48 percent of all college students nationwide attend community colleges.

> 46 percent of community college students are 25 or older. The average age is 29 years old.

> 58 percent are female.

> 33 percent are parents.

> 45 percent are the first in their families to go to college.

> 85 percent work full- or part-time.

> 33 percent are minority students, with the Latino population increasing most rapidly.[4]

EXERCISE 1.1

We'd Like to Get to Know You…

Take a few minutes to finish the following statements. Think about what each sentence says about you. Use your responses to introduce yourself to the class or form pairs, talk over your responses together, and use your partner's answers to introduce him or her to the class.

1. I'm happiest when _____.

2. If I had an extra $100, I'd _____.

3. The thing I'm most proud of is _____.

4. Once people get to know me, they're probably surprised to find I'm _____.

5. I've been known to consume large quantities of _____.

6. I'd rather be _____ than _____.

7. My best quality is _____.

8. My worst quality is _____.

9. The academic skill I'd most like to develop is _____.

10. One thing I'd like to figure out about myself is _____.

People go to a community college like yours at a particular point in their lives for a variety of reasons. As you discuss this exercise in class, explore these additional questions: What is your background and why are you here?

Earning a Two-Year Degree

If you're in college to earn a degree, an associate's degree will prepare you to go one of two ways in a relatively short amount of time: (1) into a career or (2) on to further education. If you want a career-oriented associate's degree, in two years you can train for one of the fastest-growing jobs in the economy by taking approximately twenty classes. The best jobs for the future requiring a two-year degree include becoming a nurse, environmental technician, paralegal, fashion designer, dental hygienist, occupational therapist, or radiologic technologist.[5] If you prefer hands-on coursework and a career like one of these is your goal, a community college is exactly the right place for you. (It's also quite possible that you couldn't prepare for some of these specific degrees at a four-year institution.)

Instead of a career-oriented associate's degree, you may want to earn a fairly general two-year degree to apply toward a bachelor's degree at a university near you. Part of the coursework you'll complete to get an associate's degree will consist of core requirements or general education courses, like writing and speaking, that apply to any career field. If those are your plans, you'll leave your community college with transferable courses when the time comes.[6]

Perhaps instead of a two-year associate's degree, you want to specialize even further, and finish your coursework sooner, so instead, you opt for a certificate. Certificates generally require fifteen to as many as fifty credits, and you'll most likely only take courses that apply specifically to the career field you're preparing for. You set your sights on a target and finish your certificate program in as little as one year, sometimes less.[7]

One of the biggest differences between an associate's degree and a certificate is that the courses you take for an associate's degree usually transfer to a four-year school and include core requirements, general courses like speaking, writing, and math.[8] That may not be true of certificate programs. So if you think you may want to earn a bachelor's degree at some point, choose an associate's degree. It's up to you. How soon do you need a job? What interests you? How hands-on do you want your course of study to be?[9]

How College Works: Being "In the Know"

This chapter is about the advice that the Greek philosopher Epictetus offered centuries ago: "Do what you have to do." But exactly what are those things?

One of the first ways to demonstrate you're "in the know," is to understand that your community college instructors will expect you to be a professional student. Here is a list of ten suggestions that are important to them, and therefore to you:

1. **Don't just pile on.** If you want to be successful in college, you may have to give something up to give it all you've got. Some people hope they'll

If everyone is moving forward together, then success takes care of itself.

Henry Ford, American industrialist (1863–1947)

be able to just add college to an already-long list of obligations. But when they add one more thing, the entire stack crumbles. Something in your life will need adjusting to make room for coursework. You may need to reduce your hours at work temporarily, or tell your aunt that you can't watch her kids on Thursday nights so she can go to class, because you have to go to class, too.

priority something considered to be particularly important

2. **Reserve class time as a top priority.** Let's face it: Life is complicated. Your boss wants a piece of you, your kids (if you have any) disturb your attempts to study, your friend wants to go to the movies the night before your mid-term exam, the bills keep mounting, and on and on. Because some students see college as just one more commitment, they decide to miss class for less important tasks: to pick up a relative at the airport or shop with a friend who's in town, for example. Sometimes true emergencies in your personal life will interfere with your academic life. But your instructors will expect you to plan nonemergencies around your already scheduled (and paid-for!) classes. Many things in your life are important—it's true—but while you're in school, coming to class and doing your coursework should be at the top of your list. Unfortunately, many community college students sabotage themselves within the first few weeks of classes by skipping class (25 percent), turning in an assignment late (33 percent), or not turning an assignment in at all (24 percent). Don't allow yourself to become one of these statistics![10]

conscientiously responsibly paying attention to detail

3. **Complete your assignments conscientiously and on time.** In high school, your teachers may have cut you some slack. Remember that teacher who dropped your lowest quiz grade, forgave a homework assignment that didn't get done, and curved the test if the whole class didn't do well? Your college instructors aren't likely to do that. This is college, and college is the big leagues. Your instructors are preparing you, not only for a job, but for life, and they have your long-term, best interests in mind.

4. **Don't come late and don't leave early.** One thing instructors dislike is getting a sense from students that school isn't a top priority. When you breeze in late or sneak out early, you're communicating that you don't value school, your instructor, and your classmates, whether you realize it or not.

5. **Dress like a professional student.** Dress like you're a serious student who's there to learn. Leave the muscle tanks and halter tops for truly informal occasions. You're not in college to score fashion points, draw attention to your tattoos, or define your personality with your baseball cap. That doesn't mean you can't be yourself, but it does mean that you should use good judgment. Always remember why you're there: To learn.

6. **Ask questions if things are unclear.** Even though you may be afraid to speak up or not want to admit that you're fuzzy about something, your instructors will rely on *you* to let them know that. They aren't mind readers.

7. **Come prepared.** Get ready for class beforehand, and then jump in once you're there. Bring your books, notebook, and pen, and sit up straight, too, just like mom always used to say. College isn't a place to just slide by or wing it. It's a place to put your best foot forward.

8. **Learn to work in groups.** Your instructors know the value of teamwork later in your career, so they'll expect you to work with your classmates in class, outside of class, or online. They may even think it's important enough to assign points for group projects in the course syllabus. Even though you may prefer to work alone, teamwork skills are highly valued in today's workplace, and you'll learn things from other students that you might not learn from your instructor.[11]

9. **Take charge.** Sometimes new students don't realize that *they're* supposed to be in charge. They wait to be told what to do, and if no one tells them, they don't do whatever needs to get done. If you want to know how to study for a test, ask your instructor. If you're unclear about the homework directions, ask your instructor. It's much better to take responsibility than it is to hope for the best. As the advertising slogan goes, "Just do it."

10. **Engage!** Students who soak up all they can enjoy college most. When they're in class, they're tuned in. Sure, Professor Whoever may not be quite as entertaining as your favorite TV star, and going to class isn't as much fun as going to the movies. But college is about becoming an *educated* person, not an *entertained* one.

Any time you start something new, there's a **learning curve** involved. The best thing to do is to admit it, decide what to do, and start climbing! Beyond conducting yourself as a professional student, what other things will help you be in the know? Here's a basic list of essentials.

learning curve a measure of how long it takes you to learn something and how hard it is

Develop a Degree Plan and Plan Your Coursework

In some ways, college is like a journey with parts of the itinerary planned for you. You can't just hitchhike wherever you like. It's more like a guided tour planned by experts in the areas you'd like to explore. You can choose to go left or right at particular moments, but much of the trip is planned in

If you don't know where you are going, you might wind up someplace else.

Yogi Berra, major league baseball player and manager

Rhienna Cutler/iStockphoto.com

How **FULL** is your plate?

> **There is one thing we can do, and the happiest people are those who can do it to the limit of their ability. We can be completely present. We can be all here. We can . . . give all our attention to the opportunity before us.**
>
> —MARK VAN DOREN, PULITZER PRIZE–WINNING
> POET (1894–1972)

One reason many of us are overwhelmed by all we have to do is because we do the right things, but we do them at the wrong times. We aren't truly present. If you're a morning person, and math is your toughest course, study math in the mornings! The same goes for night owls. In order to be completely present for challenging tasks, ready to give all our attention, we must know ourselves and our own natural rhythms.

Stefan Glebowski/Shutterstock.com

advance.[12] If you'd like to become a nurse, for example, your coursework will be prescribed for you. However, everyone appreciates the focused knowledge of nurses when they need one!

Some courses will count toward your major or area of **concentration**, and some will satisfy **core** requirements. Core requirements often make students wonder: "I'm never going to be another Stephen King. Why do I have to suffer through writing courses I'll never use?" The key words in that last sentence are *never use*. You'll speak and write and think and solve problems in any career. Even though you're in college to prepare for a career, becoming a more knowledgeable person in general should be a big part of your mission.

Most community colleges will ask you to fill out a degree plan up front. You'll plan your coursework for each semester or quarter from now until you've finished. Not only do you end up taking the right courses, but you can watch your progress as you go.

If you decide to transfer to a four-year institution later to get a bachelor's degree, it's likely you can bring many of your associate's degree credits (up to 60 credit hours or half the credits you'll need for a four-year degree) from your community college courses with you. That wouldn't be true unless community colleges were considered to be **real** colleges and coursework was seen as equivalent. However, it is your responsibility to know what courses will transfer to the particular transfer institution you may have in mind. Do some digging on your own by calling an advisor at that school for information that will help you with your planning now. Find out **exactly** which courses will transfer into the major you're considering. And remember that there's a difference between whether a course will **transfer** (for general credit) or **count** (toward a specific degree).

concentration focused effort; specialization

core basic

Why Do I Have to Take This Class?

Here is a road map, or a sample degree plan, for Darnell, assuming he decides to get a general Associate of Arts Degree at his community college. (The requirements at your community college will be different from this example.)

GREAT BLUFFS COMMUNITY COLLEGE
DEGREE TRACKING WORKSHEET ←

> Many community colleges, yours included, use a worksheet or degree plan, like this one of Darnell's, to help you stay on course and track your progress as you earn your degree. Check with an advisor to see what aids like this your campus provides.

NAME___Darnell Williams___   EMAIL ADDRESS___dwilliams@gbcc.edu___
STUDENT NUMBER___123-45-6789___   PHONE___555-9876___

GENERAL STUDIES
Associate of Arts Degree

> In the "Notes" column, Darnell can keep track of his thoughts about each course and things to keep in mind when registering for the next term.

Program Course #	Course Title	Term (to be) Taken	Term Hours	Grade A = 4 B = 3 C = 2 D = 1 F = 0	Notes ←
ENGL 101	English Composition I	Fall 2011	3	?	
HIST 103	United States History I		3		
	Foreign Language		5		
GBCC 100	College Success		3		
SPE 115	Public Speaking	Fall 2011	3	?	
ENGL 102	English Composition II		3		
HIST 104	United States History II		3		
	Foreign Language (must be the same language)		5		
	Humanities		3		
PSC 205	United States Government		3		
	Literature		3		
	Visual and Performing Arts		3		
SOC 103	Introduction to Sociology		3		
	Mathematics		3		
	Humanities		3		
PSC 206	State and Local Government		3		
	Natural Science I		3–4		
	Natural Science II		3–4		
	Unrestricted Elective		3		
	Unrestricted Elective		3		

> The courses with department abbreviations and numbers listed are required for Darnell's degree plan. The open categories are places where he can choose from a list of possible courses. His advisor will help him know his options.

(Adapted from Austin Community College website. Available at www3.austincc.edu/catalog/fy2008/deggens01.rtf)

To complete this activity, visit your academic advisor to get a degree plan for the associate degree or certificate program you're most interested in now. (You may change your mind later.) Fill it in with the help of your advisor, looking ahead to which courses you'll take, semester (or quarter) by semester. Use this degree plan as a working document as you progress through your program.

Be Advised! Advising Mistakes Students Make

One of the most important relationships you'll have as a community college student is the one you build with your academic advisor. On your campus, this person may be an advisor, a counselor, or a faculty member who can steer you toward courses you can handle and instructors you can learn best from. An advisor can keep you from taking classes that bog you down academically or unnecessary ones that take you extra time to earn your degree. Here's a list of advising mistakes students make from real advisors who work with college students every day.

1. **Not using the campus advising office or your faculty advisor.** If you don't get regular advice from an advisor, counselor, or a designated faculty member who's serving as your advisor, your degree may take longer and cost more money. It's that simple. It's your college career, after all, and it's important that you and your advisor work as partners.

2. **Not planning ahead.** Some students walk into the advising office or e-mail an advisor and expect help right away, and sometimes that works. However, planning ahead is a better option. Planning ahead includes making an appointment, looking through the course offerings, making a list of questions to ask, and thinking in advance about which days you can attend classes based on your work schedule, how many classes you can take, and on which days of the week. And, if you're leaving your advisor a voice-mail, remember to include all of this important information. What's wrong with this message? "Hi, this is Tony. I have a question about my schedule. Please call me back, OK?" Tony who? And what's his phone number? Or how about an e-mail like this from hotchick13@email.com? "Do I need to take English 090? Please let me know." Exactly who is "hotchick13"?

3. **Procrastinating.** It's important not to put off advising appointments. To drop a class, you may need to meet a deadline. Or you may need help from an advisor to solve a problem with a faculty member, but by the time you get around to it, the instructor has already left campus for the summer. If you deal with problems right away, while they're small, they may be reversible. (And it's always a good idea to discuss dropping a class with the instructor first.)

4. **Skipping prerequisites.** Some students want to skip the required **prerequisites**. They think they can handle the work. They think prereqs are a waste of time and money when, actually, they're in place because hundreds of students before you have proven that these classes help you succeed. And in some cases, students who haven't taken a prereq are actually disenrolled from the course that requires it.

5. **Choosing the wrong major.** Sometimes students lock on to a major because someone else thinks it's a good idea or because a particular career field pays well, not because they enjoy the subject and are suited for it. Staying motivated is hard when you're not interested in something. Advisors can help you figure out which major is right for you.

6. **Taking too many credits or too few.** Some students are overly optimistic and think they can handle a heavier course load than the other factors in

their lives will permit. Other students may underestimate the number of courses they should take, which increases the time it takes them to finish school. An advisor can help you stay on target.

7. **Ignoring problems.** If you run into difficulty and end up on academic probation, for example, an advisor or college official will work with you to get you back on track. But you must agree to that bargain and accept the help, possibly by signing a contract of steps you must take to reverse the situation.

8. **Being afraid to drop a course.** Sometimes, when you've tried everything (for example, tutoring, extra help sessions, and the campus learning center), but you're still not succeeding in a course, the best thing to do may be to drop the course by filling out a drop form (online or on paper) and submitting it. Then retake the course later. That option is better than just not going to class and assuming by not coming, you've dropped the course. Colleges require deliberate action from you. It's always best to know your school's rules and talk with your instructor first. *And beware that dropping a course may affect your financial aid.*[13]

Make the Grade: Computing Your GPA

One of the most important things to learn as a new college student—and fast—is what grade point averages (**GPAs**) are and how they work. Your GPA is an indication of how well you're doing, and you keep track of it over time, term by term. Your academic record will follow you for the rest of your life! Some students don't realize how grade points add up. They end up on academic probation, even if they only have one failing grade. Let's say you're taking four courses this term, and you earn the following grades:

GPA an average of all your grades for a single semester or a running average across all your coursework

Course	Credits	Final Grade	Grade Point Value
English Composition	3 credits	C (2 points)	6
College Algebra	3 credits	F (0 points)	0
College Success	3 credits	B (3 points)	9
Public Speaking	3 credits	D (1 point)	3
TOTAL	**12 credits**		**18 grade points**

You may look at this record and think, *Not bad. I passed three of my four courses.* But divide that Grade Point Value column total (18) by the total number of credits (12), and you get 1.5.

GPA = Grade Point Value ÷ Total Number of Credits

At most schools, a 1.5 GPA puts you on academic probation, and eventually, you may be facing suspension. That can be a discouraging way to start, and digging yourself out of a GPA hole once you're there takes a very long time, like paying off credit card debt.

Not only is it important to keep track of your grades over the whole term, but it's also important to keep track of your grade in each course. If you stop going to your math class because it's too hard or because you don't like the teacher, your grade will suffer. If an assignment is worth 25 percent of your grade, and you don't turn it in, the highest grade you can possibly earn, even if you do everything else perfectly, is a 75 percent or "C." You may think, *but it's only one assignment.* It is only one assignment, but it counts as one-quarter of your grade. In college, everything counts. The typical grading scale in college is:

A = 90–100%   B = 80–89%   C = 70–79%   D = 60–69%   F = 59% and below

Realize the Value of Remediation

As a rule, community colleges have what's called an open-door admissions policy. That means that anyone who wants to get an education is invited in. You don't have to get a certain score on the SAT or ACT standardized national tests, and you don't have to have a particular GPA in high school to be admitted. That's a good thing. As a nation, we are opening the doors of education to everyone, and our society as a whole benefits in many ways. Education improves the quality of life.[14]

developmental designed to develop or improve a skill

But when restrictions are removed, more variety is a natural result, right? Think of it this way: If every student at your community college had to be over six feet tall to be admitted, then you and all your classmates would tower over the general public. But if anyone of any height could attend, you'd see a range from very short to very tall. Some people would need steps to reach high places, and others would have to duck under low ceilings. But variety presents challenges. Community colleges are characterized by variety, and they've devised ways to make it work. Here's how.

New community college students bring standardized test scores or take placement tests that help schools know where to *place* them. If you're "short" on some necessary skills for success, like reading, writing, or math, they'll place you in a **developmental** (sometimes called *remedial*) class to help you catch up fast. Some students see these courses negatively, thinking they're a waste of time or money. Not so! Don't get discouraged if you're in one or more of these classes. They're insurance that you grow into the skills you'll need.

If you're enrolled in a developmental class, you're in good company. In one study of 35 community colleges

Photoservice/iStockphoto.com

66

Problems are only opportunities in work clothes.

Henry J. Kaiser, American industrialist (1882–1967)

> Your current safe boundaries were once unknown frontiers.
>
> *Anonymous*

that are all part of a proposal to increase student success, 37 percent of incoming students required one remedial course, 26 percent required two courses, and 22 percent required three courses—for a total of 85 percent. And note this piece of good news: In a related study, students who earned a C or better in a developmental course during their first semester were, from that point forward, more likely to stay in school and succeed than students who weren't required to take a developmental course in the first place![15] In another study, students who took a developmental writing course earned higher English grades in later courses and higher GPAs overall than students who did not.[16] If you're enrolled in a developmental class, perhaps you're beginning to see its value *now*. If you don't see the value yet, chances are you'll greatly appreciate what it did for you *later*.

Master the Syllabus

You'll get a syllabus (or course schedule) for most all of the college classes you'll take. If the syllabi (plural of syllabus) for your courses are available online, check them often to keep up with any changes in the schedule or new assignments. If you have a hard copy, keep it handy and refer to it often. Think of a syllabus as:

> a preview of what to expect during every class

> a road map for where the course will take you

> a contract between you and your instructor

> a summary of all the assignments and how much they count toward your grade

> a tool that lists reading and homework to help you prepare for class

> evidence of an instructor's standards, grading system, and values

BOX 1.1 Analyzing a Syllabus

Take a look at this example syllabus and see what you think. What is this professor like? Do you get a sense of her standards and values from her syllabus? Will this be a challenging course? Take a close look at a syllabus from one of your current classes. Analyze it, just as this one has been analyzed, and make a list of things you learn about specific aspects of the syllabus that can help you be successful.

Some community colleges have a syllabus template or standard format, so that your syllabus for each class will look basically the same and contain similar kinds of information.

Send the instructor an e-mail the first week of class, introducing yourself and discussing your thoughts about how this class will help you. Remember, however, that in college, you must use good grammar and correct spelling in ALL your writing, including e-mails.

GREAT BLUFFS COMMUNITY COLLEGE
COURSE SYLLABUS

It's appropriate to ask the instructor what she prefers to be called: Regina, Ms. Lewis, Professor Lewis, etc.

Course ID: SPE 115
Term: Fall 2011
Instructor: Regina Lewis
Office: Vail Hall 501
Office Hours: MW 10:00–11:00 a.m., TR 2:00–3:00 p.m., by appointment only

Course Title: Public Speaking
Credit Hours: 3
E-mail Address: regina.lewis@gbcc.edu
Office Phone: 555-1234

Pay attention to the course description. It's a summary of what you can expect.

Course Description: This course combines the theory of speech communication with oral performance skills. Emphasis is on researching, organizing, and preparing speeches and analyzing the needs and interests of your particular audience. Although this is primarily a performance class, you will also build your writing and researching skills.

Prerequisites/Co-Requisites: ENG 090, REA 090

You can buy the textbook from your college bookstore or order it online. But often textbooks are "customized" with portions inserted from different books or material that pertains to your own campus. You must buy those books from your campus bookstore. Even though textbooks cost money, they are a critical investment. Trying to get by without one puts you at a disadvantage right from the start.

Course Textbook: *Speak Out! A Public Speaker's Guide to Success,* 2011.

Professional Conduct in Class: Students are responsible for knowing and abiding by the "Standards of Conduct" listed in the 2011–2012 GBCC Catalog (beginning on page 10). Your cell phone or pager should be turned off, set to vibrate only, or left at home. Eating, sleeping, social discussions, or doing reading or homework for other classes are distracting behaviors and communicate indifference and disrespect for this learning environment and subject matter. Children should not be brought to class. Getting up and coming in and out during class (unless you are sick, of course) is distracting to your classmates. These activities are unacceptable in academic environments and qualify as examples of inappropriate conduct in class, which may result in your academic withdrawal from the class.

The instructor has devoted a substantial portion of the syllabus to this topic, and she has spelled out her expectations in detail. Professional conduct must be important to her.

Online Course Management System (CMS): e-CC (pronounced EASY). All students have access to the materials posted on the CMS website through the Internet from a campus computer lab or from home.

Attendance: If you must miss a class for an emergency, you must still submit assigned work by the due date. Please provide documentation to indicate that the absence was due to a situation beyond your control. There are no excused absences without documentation. In order to receive credit for attendance, you must attend the ENTIRE class period. IF YOU MISS A CLASS, IT IS YOUR RESPONSIBILITY TO CONTACT A CLASSMATE FOR NOTES AND ASSIGNMENTS. NO MAKEUP WORK IS ALLOWED.

Grading: Assignments must be turned in on time and speeches must be presented on schedule. Grades for makeup speeches are automatically reduced by 20 percent. Only one makeup day will be scheduled for speeches missed due to emergencies! THERE ARE NO MAKEUP EXAMS OR WRITTEN ASSIGNMENTS.

Americans with Disabilities Act (ADA): Any student eligible for academic accommodations because of a learning or physical disability should speak with the instructor during the first week of class and contact the Office of Support Services.

This syllabus actually continues on for several more pages and includes three other things: 1) a campus statement about academic honesty and plagiarism, 2) due dates for each assignment, and 3) specific information on how speeches will be graded.

Speeches: You will be required to give a minimum of five speeches.
· SP 1: Informative 5 mins. (+ or −1 min.) (1 visual aid) Prep and speaking outline required.
· SP 2: Career (Impromptu) Speaking on the spot!
· SP 3: Ceremonial 3 mins. (+ or −1 min.) (1 quote) Prep and speaking outline required.
· SP 4: Persuasive 7 mins. (+ or −1 min.) (2 visual aids and 2 sources) Prep and speaking outline required. You must have a partner for the opposition.
· SP 5: Public Speaking Outside the Box 10 mins. (+ or −2 mins.) (Poster, flyer, 2 visual aids) Presented in TV studio.

Source: Regina Lewis, Pikes Peak Community College. Used by permission.

Avoid the PCP Syndrome: Use Campus Resources

The convenience of community college can also be a drawback. Since you're going to college in your own community, it's easy to develop a drive-through mentality. You show up for classes and then hightail it for work or home right away. Some experts describe this phenomenon as the "PCP Syndrome: Parking Lot, Class, Parking Lot." What's wrong with that? you ask. When you've finished grocery shopping, you get back in your car and go home, right? You don't cruise the aisles and hang around.

But going to college is very different from shopping for groceries. Your campus has many things available for you to take advantage of: student clubs, special presentations, musical events, and learning resource centers, for example. You may never find out about these "free samples" if you're not there. You won't make new friends or get to know your instructors. The danger is that when the going gets rough, which can happen during exam time, you may be tempted to retreat to what you're most familiar with—your life before college—and abandon your efforts. Whatever the problem, there's a place to go for help on campus. Even if your campus doesn't have every possible kind of support center right there, your advisors or instructors can always direct you to services off campus.

Remember that "HELP" is not a four-letter word. Getting help when you need it isn't a stigma; it's smart. Take this example: In 1979, Diana Nyad achieved the record for open-water swimming a distance of 102.5 miles. But it took 51 other people to help her reach her goal (guides to check winds and currents, divers to look for sharks, and NASA nutrition experts to keep her from losing more than the 29 pounds she lost during that one swim).[17] Your campus has all kinds of resources available for the taking, but you must take them. They won't come to you. Here are some of the FAQs new college students often ask:

> **How can I meet other students?** Take advantage of favorite gathering spots on campus. If you're finding it hard to meet people, could it be because you're not around? To meet people, it helps to be where they are.

> **What if I need help with a challenging course?** Many campuses have support centers: a science learning center or a math learning center, for example. Or particular courses may offer what's called supplemental instruction, extra help beyond class sessions with basic course materials or homework assignments. You may be able to work with a tutor, too—a student who's extra-good at math, for example. Check out whatever options are available to you, and use them, rather than struggle on your own if you're not getting results.

> **I'm thinking of dropping a class. How do I do it?** The Office of the Registrar or Office of Admissions and Records is where to go. They also help with things like transferring credits and getting transcripts if you've attended college somewhere before or plan to transfer. Think through the results of dropping a class, however. Will doing so change your financial aid status, for example?

> **What if I need a counselor?** College is a time of change. Your relationships may be affected or you may suffer from symptoms of stress. If your

campus has a counseling center and you need to use its services, do so. And if you find yourself in the middle of a real crisis, call the campus hotline for immediate help.

> **How can I find out if I have a learning disability?** Check to see if your campus has a learning center or a special office that helps with learning disabilities. You can work with a specialist there who can help. If you've been diagnosed with a learning disability before, bring your documentation to that office for their records and let your instructors know. They can help, too.

> **What if I have a technology crisis?** Your campus probably has a computer help desk, where techies can often solve what sounds like a complicated problem with simple advice. Also, use the campus computer labs. They may have better computers than yours at home, and you can make good use of blocks of time between classes.

> **Are health services available to students?** Many campuses have a student health center where you can find a range of free or inexpensive services—everything from flu shots to strep throat tests to birth control advice if you're sexually active.

> **What do I want to be when I grow up?** Thinking ahead to a career when you finish college is sometimes hard when so much is going on at the moment. What do you like to do? What people skills do you have? Visit your campus's career center. Experts there can help you discover a major and career that will work for you.

> **Is child care available?** Many campuses have inexpensive child care available. Being able to drop off a child in the morning right on campus and pick him up after your classes are over can be a real help.

> **Where can I buy my books?** Textbooks are a big investment these days, and it's important to buy the right editions for your classes. Should you buy them from your campus bookstore or order online? Buying books online may save you money, although you'll have to wait for shipment. The bookstore is a much quicker option, and it's a good idea to find out where it is, no matter where you buy your books. You'll most likely need it for other school supplies. Renting your books or buying an e-book that you can read online may be an option, too.

wallik/iStockphoto.com

❝   **❞**

One hundred percent of the shots you don't take don't go in.

Wayne Gretzky, called the greatest ice hockey player of all time

> **Where can I get other pieces of information I may need?** Try your campus website, the school bulletin or catalog, the student handbook, and the school newspaper.

> **What if I need the help of Campus Security?** If you feel unsafe walking to your car late at night or you need information about parking permits on campus, check with the Campus Security or Public Safety Office. They're there for your protection.

What's the bottom line? Get to know your campus and its full range of offerings—and take advantage of everything that's in place to help you be as academically successful as possible.

EXERCISE 1.3

Top Ten Resources Your Campus Offers

Make a list of ten resources your campus offers that can help you succeed in your coursework. For example, does your campus have a health center, a day care center, or a learning center? Visit each location, and identify specific ways you will use each office or service.

	Name of office/service	Contact information	How will I use this resource?
1.			
2.			
3.			
4.			
5.			
6.			
7.			
8.			
9.			
10.			

Toughing It Out: What College Takes

What does it mean to succeed? Actually, success is difficult to define, and different people define success differently. Right now in college, you may think of success in terms of the money you'll make after you finish. But is success just about money? Is it about fame? Status? According to motivational author Robert Collier, "Success is the sum of small efforts, repeated day in and day out." Perhaps to you, success is somewhere off in the distant future, and it happens more or less suddenly, like winning the lottery.

Actually, success begins right now. You should be the one to define what success will look like in your life, but generally, success is *setting out to do something that means something to you, and then being fully engaged while doing it.* It's that simple. And it applies to your college experience as well. It starts now.

In order to understand your own definition of success in college, first you need to ask yourself why you're here. Why *did* you come—or return—to college, anyway? Do you want to develop into a more interesting, well-rounded, educated human being? Are you working toward a degree that leads to a specific career? Do you have children and want an education in order to give them a better life? This book will provide you with an honest look at what that takes, including plenty of opportunities to ask yourself questions about these things. It will also offer you tools you can use throughout your college courses and in your life beyond college.

Some students think going to college is like any other financial transaction: buying a gallon of milk, for example. You pay the cashier the money, and the milk now belongs to you. They think if they pay tuition, the college credits should be theirs. Not so. There's much more to it than that. A college education requires more than a financial commitment. It requires you to invest your ability, your intellect, your drive, your effort—and yourself. College has to do with more than the brain matter found between your ears.

The Good News and the Bad News (Benefits and Obstacles)

What's the good news about going to college? The benefits are wide-reaching and long-lasting. Think about how this list applies to you.

1. **Higher earning potential.** College increases your potential to earn money. It's that simple. On average, people with associate's degrees earn 20 to 30 percent more than those with a high school diploma only. Experts say that one-third of new job growth from 2008 until 2018 will require some education after high school.[18] And there's some evidence that jobs requiring certificates or associate's degrees will grow at an even faster rate than jobs requiring a four-year degree.[19] Sixty percent of jobs right now are held by people with post–high school education or training.[20]

2. **Lower unemployment rates.** College decreases your risk of unemployment. This is especially helpful when the economy takes a downturn.

> **Always bear in mind that your own resolution to succeed is more important than any one thing.**
>
> *Abraham Lincoln, 16th President of the United States (1809–1875)*

3. **Wisdom.** College gives you opportunities to gain understanding about many things—politics, people, and current affairs to name a few. Beyond theories, facts, and dates, well-educated people know how to think critically, contribute to society, and manage their lives.

4. **Insight.** College students have the opportunity to understand themselves better as they learn different ways of doing things.

5. **Lifelong learning.** College students are prepared to become lifelong learners. It's not just about grades. It's about becoming the best student-learner you can be—inside or outside of the classroom. This one benefit will stay with you through the rest of your life.

What's the bad news? What obstacles may stand in your path? Darnell Williams isn't quite sure why he's in college. Will he be successful? It depends, doesn't it? Here's some evidence on what "it" consists of.

Some experts say that fewer than half of community college students reach their educational goals.[21] But who goes, who finishes later, and who transfers to another school are hard things to track. The risk factors for dropping out of college include working more than thirty hours per week, going to school part-time, being a single parent or having children at home, and being a first-generation college student.[22] However, more than 70 percent of community college students have at least one of these characteristics, and half have two or more.[23] It's true that going to college is "A Whole 'Nother World," as one major report's title says. Juggling a job, family, friends, transportation, tuition, and all the things that are impacted by the energy and effort it takes to go to college can be overwhelming. If you're a first-generation college student, you may not have a role model at home that can help you, because your parents didn't go to college. (That's why it's important to make connections with your classmates, instructors, and advisors who can guide you.)[24] Even though college may be more challenging for first-generation students, you can still be highly successful. Perhaps the most famous current example is Michelle Obama, who went from first-generation college student to First Lady.[25]

The important thing to keep in mind as you think about risk factors is that they alone cannot determine your ultimate level of success. Don't throw in the towel now if you had a child at age sixteen or are working thirty-five hours per week. These factors are presented merely as information to assist you on your journey. They are simply **predictors**—not *determiners*. Only you can determine your outcomes in life, and that includes college.

predictors something that indicates something in the future may happen

Plenty of people who have achieved great things in their lives got their start at a community college. Look at this impressive list:[26]

> Queen Latifah, rapper, actress, talk show host

> Gwendolyn Brooks, Pulitzer prize-winning poet

> Billy Crystal, actor and comedian

> Tom Hanks, actor

> Calvin Klein, designer

> Clint Eastwood, actor

> Joyce Luther Kennard, California Supreme Court justice

> Jim Lehrer, news anchor

> James Sinegal, CEO of Costco

Your effort, attitude, and willingness to get any help you need to succeed are all vital.

This Course Has a Proven Track Record

If you're reading this book, there's a good chance you're enrolled in a first-year seminar course, called something like First-Year Seminar, First-Year Experience, College Success, Learning Community, or any of a host of other names. These courses are designed to introduce you to college life, familiarize you with your own campus, and help you improve your academic skills. Do they work? According to experts, the answer is yes![27] Of course, you have to keep your part of the bargain, but in general, community college students who complete first-year seminars are much more successful. Take a look at the results of one major study in Figure 1.1.

FIGURE 1.1

Outcomes of Community College Students Completing a College Success Course and Those Who Did Not (1999–2000 through 2003–2004)

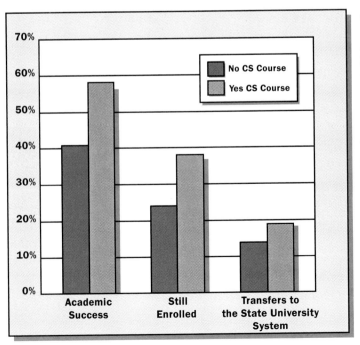

Zeidenberg, M., Jenkins, D., & Calcagno, J. C. (2007, June). Do student success courses actually help community college students succeed? Reprinted by permission of Teachers College, Columbia University and Data Trend #31, Florida Department of Education

> I am only one,
> But still I am one.
> I cannot do everything,
> But still I can do something;
> And because I cannot do everything
> I will not refuse to do the something that I can do.
>
> *Edward Everett Hale, American author*
> *(1822–1909)*

Students who completed a college success course were more likely to stay in school, succeed academically, and transfer to universities. And students who completed a college success course and also needed to take developmental courses in one to three subject areas were even more likely to achieve these results! That's what this course is about: your success. Your instructor and your classmates are rooting for you. Now it's up to you!

How Do I Want to Be Different When I'm Done?

One thing is sure: College will change you. Most every high-intensity experience full of opportunities does. Take advantage, meet new people, and stretch yourself. You may notice that as a result of your college experience, your old relationships may "fit" differently. Your romantic partner may brag about you or secretly envy you. Your family may praise your efforts or hardly notice. But you will. If you finish what you've begun, you will watch yourself become a more sophisticated, more knowledgeable, more confident person. You can't help but be. Ask yourself now, at the beginning of your college experience, just how you'd like to change, and make it happen.

step 3 INSIGHT *Now* What Do You Think?

At the beginning of this chapter, Darnell Williams faced a series of challenges as a new college student. Now after learning from this chapter, would you respond differently to any of the questions you answered about the "FOCUS Challenge Case"? Using what you learned in the chapter, write a paragraph ending Darnell's case study. What are some of the possible outcomes for Darnell?

1. Identify one new thing you learned in reading this chapter. Why did you select the one you've selected? How will it affect what you do in your college classes?

2. Why are you going to community college? How do you see your college experience impacting your future?

3. How do you want college to change you? Why?

REALITY CHECK | # What did you Learn?

On a scale of 1 to 5, answer these questions now that you've completed this chapter.

1 = not very/not much/very little/low   5 = very/a lot/very much/high

How much do you know *now*?

Now rate your current level of knowledge about topics covered in this chapter.

The characteristics of students who go to community colleges

       1 2 3 4 ⑤

The difference between certificate and associate degrees

       1 2 3 ④ 5

The expectations of community college instructors

       1 2 3 4 ⑤

The success rates of college success courses

       1 2 3 4 ⑤

How useful might the information in this chapter be to you?

How much do you think this information might affect your college success?

       1 2 ③ 4 5

How much do you think this information might affect your career success after college?

       1 2 ③ 4 5

How long did it actually take you to complete this chapter (both the reading and writing tasks)?

   4 Hour(s)   30 Minutes

  Challenge Yourself Online Quiz. To find out how much you've learned, access the CourseMate via www.cengagebrain.com/shop/ISBN/0495906433 to take the Challenge Yourself Online Quiz.

Compare these answers with your answers from the "Readiness Check" at the beginning of this chapter. How might the gaps between what you thought before starting the chapter and what you now think affect how you approach the next chapter?

chapter 2 Building Dreams, Setting Goals

You're About to Discover...

✔ How this book will help you learn

✔ What motivates you

✔ How your attitude can sabotage you

✔ Why you should distinguish between dreams and goals

✔ How to develop goals that work

©Larry Harwood Photography. Property of Cengage Learning.

READINESS CHECK What do you **Know?**

Before beginning this chapter, take a moment to answer these questions. Your answers will help you assess how ready you are to focus.

1 = not very/not much/very little/low   5 = very/a lot/very much/high

How much do you *already* know?

Rate your current level of knowledge about topics covered in this chapter.

How people learn

    1 2 3 4 5

Intrinsic versus extrinsic motivation

    1 2 3 4 5

Dreams versus goals

    1 2 3 4 5

FOCUSed goal-setting

    1 2 3 4 5

How motivated are you to learn *more*?

In general, how motivated are you to learn the material in this chapter?

    1 2 3 4 5

How much do you think this information might affect your college success?

    1 2 3 4 5

How much do you think this information might affect your career success after college?

    1 2 3 4 5

How ready are you to read *now*?

How ready are you to focus on this chapter—physically, intellectually, and emotionally? Which of these three areas is most challenging for you right now? Circle a number to represent it.

    1 2 3 4 5

If any of your answers is below a 3, consider addressing the issue before reading. Then, read the chapter carefully, while looking for ways to improve your focus.

Finally, how long do you think it will take you to complete this chapter? If you start and stop, keep track of the overall time.

_____ Hour(s) _____ Minutes

Gloria Gonzales

©Larry Harwood Photography. Property of Cengage Learning.

I t was her first day of college. As Gloria Gonzales walked to her first class, "College Success," from the parking lot, she had mixed feelings: excitement, anticipation, anxiety, and apprehension. She wondered if she'd meet any interesting people, if she'd like her instructor, and if she'd learn anything important in this class. After all, she'd gotten good grades in high school without even trying hard. If she just put in some effort, she thought, she'd be successful in college, too. *How can you study something like "College Success" for a whole term?* she asked herself.

Mom & Dad - last summer

© Andresr, 2009/Used under license from Shutterstock.com

To be honest, Gloria thought she probably already knew most of what there was to learn in this course, and if she didn't, so what? She knew what she had to do to get good grades—everyone does—but she didn't always choose to do it, that's all. School was part of her life, but it wasn't always her top priority. At least this course would probably be easier than her math course or her developmental writing course.

Gloria wasn't the first person in her family to go to college. Her sister had tried it, but she'd dropped out after her first term and gotten a job. "College, who needs it?" she'd exclaimed. "I want to start earning good money right away, not years from now!" There were times when Gloria thought her sister might be right. Her sister certainly seemed able to afford some of the things Gloria had always wanted herself. Was college really going to be worth all the time, effort, and expense? But everyone she knew was going to college; it was the right thing to do after high school, and everyone expected it of her.

Gloria's family didn't have much money. They were sacrificing to help finance her college education. She'd better perform, they'd said. They'd told her point-blank that her sister had set a bad example, and that her first-term grades had better not include anything lower than a B. Frankly, Gloria was beginning to feel a twinge of performance pressure. Of all the children in her family, her sister had always

Google, Inc.

been considered the smartest, and she'd given up after only one term. If her sister couldn't do it, how could Gloria? If she were to succeed, exactly what would it take?

Despite her worries as she walked down the hallway toward the classroom, Gloria was sure of one thing: She looked good today—really good. Her sister's skirt fit perfectly, the new red shirt was definitely her color, and thankfully it was a good hair day. Gloria had always been able to make heads turn. Beneath it all, Gloria knew what she wanted, anyway. She was going get a certificate in fashion merchandising at the community college she'd chosen, and eventually go into the fashion industry. She always watched all the fashion design TV shows, and she was hooked. She'd dreamed of that since she was ten years old. She wasn't sure exactly what she'd need to do to make it, but she'd worked in a clothing store at the mall all through high school, and she was good at it. In fact, the store kept trying to give her more hours because she had such amazing customer service skills. She thought she'd probably just work her college courses around her forty-five hours a week there. But she sensed that fitting everything in could be tough.

Gloria's parents wanted her to go to a four-year university and get a "real" degree in business, instead. They were always clipping articles about good jobs in business from the newspaper and giving them to her, but she kept telling them she had no interest. "There'll always be good jobs waiting for you, if you play your cards right," they said. She'd heard it so many times that her usual response now was "Yeah, whatever. . . ." While they talked of jobs in big companies, she dreamed of becoming a famous fashion designer with her own line of clothing. She was going to call it "Gloria." Her parents had named her after their favorite rock-and-roll song of all time, "G-L-O-R-I-A." Imagine—her own clothing label with her name on it!

As she reached for the classroom doorknob, Gloria couldn't help wondering about the two questions at the forefront of her mind: "Will I be successful?" and "How long will it take me to finish?" She took a deep breath as she opened the classroom door. *This is it*, she thought. Somehow, she felt as if she were outside herself, watching on the big screen—with Panavision and DTS sound. *This is real; this is me, starring in my own movie*, she said to herself. And even though it felt good, Gloria had to wonder about the ending. All she could do was hope for the best.

SDV 101: Academic Fit
Focus on College Suc

► CHECK IT OUT!

"Excellence is achieved by the mastery of fundamentals"
Vince Lombardi

Contacts:
Constance Staley

In this required

- Empower yourself
- Navigate School resources
- Network with professors and students
- and life

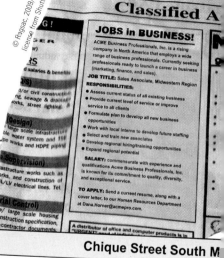

Classified A

JOBS in BUSINESS!

ACME Business Professionals, Inc. is a rising company in North America that employs a wide range of business professionals. Currently seeking professionals ready to launch a career in business (marketing, finance, and sales).

JOB TITLE: Sales Associate, Midwest Region

RESPONSIBILITIES:
- Assess current status of all existing business
- Provide current level of service or improve service to all clients
- Formulate plan to develop all new business opportunities
- Work with local interns to develop future staffing
- Select and train new associates
- Develop regional hiring/training opportunities
- Expand regional potential

SALARY: commensurate with experience and qualifications Acme Business Professionals, Inc. is known for its commitment to quality, diversity, and exceptional service.

TO APPLY: Send a current resume, along with a cover letter, to our Human Resources Department at Dana.Horner@acmepro.com.

A distributor of office and computer products is in

Course Schedule
Main Campus

FALL SEMESTER

dent: Gonzales, Glori

se ID	Course Title		Meeting	Status	Ins
ch 100	INTRO TO PSYCH				
L 099	DEV ENGLISH				
101	COLLEGE SUCCE				

Work Schedule   Week # 46

Chique Street South M

	Sunday	Monday	Tuesday	Wedensday	Thursday	Friday	Saturda
Abel, Nora	8-5	2-CL			8-5	9-6	8-5
Collins, Becky	2-CL						
Gonzales, Gloria			9-6	2-CL			

1. Do you have anything in common with Gloria? If so, how are you managing the situation so that you can be successful?
2. Is Gloria a *learner* or a *performer*? Does she think college is mostly about *effort* or *ability*? What do you think?
3. Is Gloria's vision of becoming a fashion designer a goal or a dream? Why?
4. Identify three things (attitudes, beliefs, fears, and so on) that do not show focus and might cause Gloria to make poor life management choices.
5. Identify three things that do show focus and might help Gloria make good life management choices.

Who Are You? And What Do You Want?

Imagine this voicemail greeting: "Hi. At the tone, please answer two of life's most important questions. Who are you? And what do you want?" Beep. Can you answer these questions right now? How much do you really know about yourself and what you want from this life of yours?

Don't worry. These aren't trick questions and there are no wrong answers. But there are some answers that are more right for you than others. College is a great time to think about who you are and what you want. In addition to learning about biology or history or business, college will be a time to learn about yourself: your motivation, values, dreams, and goals. You may make some of the most important choices of your life. Which major will you choose? Which career will you aim for? From this point on, it's up to you. Have you ever heard this phrase with ten two-letter words: "If it is to be, it is up to me"? It's true.

Think about it: a college education is one of the best investments you can make. Once you've earned a college degree, it's yours forever. Someone can steal your car or walk away with your cell phone, but once you've earned a college degree, no one can ever take it from you. Your choice to go to college will pay off in many ways. So even if you aren't sure exactly how you want to spend the rest of your life right now, you can't go wrong by investing in your future.

This book starts with the big picture: managing your life. Notice the phrase is "managing your life"—not *controlling* your life. Let's face it: Many things in life are beyond our control. But you can manage your life by making smart choices, setting goals you can work toward, paying attention to your time and energy, and motivating yourself. As the title of this book states boldly, it's about focus.

> "What is important is to keep learning, to enjoy challenge, and to tolerate ambiguity. In the end there are no certain answers.
>
> *Martina Horner, former President of Radcliffe College*

For many of us, focusing is a challenge. We work too many hours, crowd our lives with obligations, and rush from one thing to the next. We think we're good at **multitasking**. We can surf the Internet, text our friends, watch a DVD, and read this chapter—all at the same time! The truth is multitasking causes us

multitasking doing many different things at once

to sacrifice some of the self-discipline we need to focus and study. Multitasking may make us **feel** highly productive, but learning to focus is what most college students need.[1]

Of course, some people achieve success without a college degree, but by and large, they're the exception. Even Steven Spielberg, self-made billionaire in the film industry and winner of Academy Awards for *Schindler's List* and *Saving Private Ryan*, felt the need to finish the college degree he had started more than thirty years before. "I wanted to accomplish this for many years as a 'thank you' to my parents for giving me the opportunity for an education and a career, and as a personal note for my own family—and young people everywhere—about the importance of achieving their college education goals," he said. "But I hope they get there quicker than I did. Completing the requirements for my degree 33 years after finishing my principal education marks my longest post-production schedule."[2]

If you read this book carefully and follow its advice, it will help you become the best student you can possibly be. It will give you practical tools to help you manage your life. It will take you into your next level of education or into your career. And most of all, it will encourage you to become a true learner. That is this book's challenge to you as you begin your college experience.

Spending Time "in the System"

Spending time "in the system"? No, being in college isn't like being in jail—far from it. "The system" is the approach used in this book to help you learn: the Challenge → Reaction → Insight → Action system. It is based on the work of Dr. John Bransford and his colleagues, who together wrote an influential book called *How People Learn* (2000).

Bransford believes learning is a chain reaction that might look something like this:

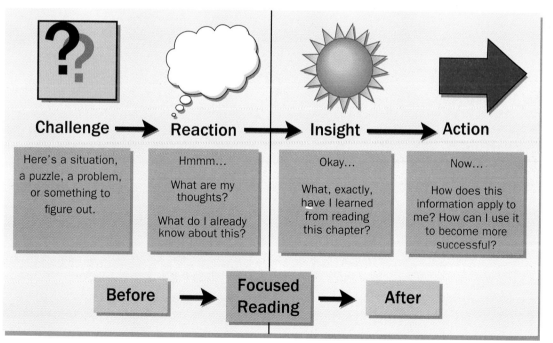

FIGURE 2.1

CRIA System: How People Learn

Source: Based on J. Bransford, et al. (2000). How People Learn: Brain, Mind, Experience, and School. Washington, DC: National Academy Press.

This Challenge → Reaction → Insight → Action learning chain reaction is integrated into *FOCUS* to help you learn. Each chapter takes you through "the system" by walking you through four steps:

STEP 1: Challenge. Whenever you're learning something new, the best place to start is by identifying what you think you already know. For example, each chapter's "Readiness Check" will ask you how much you think you already know about what you're about to read. Then you'll continue by reading a case study about a new college student who's facing problems related to the topics in the chapter. Research shows that people generally learn more from examples of things going wrong than they can from examples of things going right. The challenges are real ones many students face. Perhaps you (or a classmate you know) are facing similar issues yourself. Read the case studies carefully and think about solutions that would help these students—before you read the chapter's content. Every chapter begins with a challenge as the first step of the learning chain reaction.

STEP 2: Reaction. After you read the case study, you are asked for your reaction by answering a few questions about it. What is the student in the case study doing wrong or right? What should the student do differently? Your instructor may ask you to discuss your reaction in class or answer the questions in writing. This step of the learning process shows you how much you already know—before you begin reading. It also shows you what you don't know and what you can learn by reading. The goal of

Surround yourself with people who take their work seriously, but not themselves, those who work hard and play hard.

Colin Powell, former U.S. Secretary of State

this book is help you become a deep learner, as opposed to someone who skims the surface and simply rushes on to the next assignment and the next course. It will ask you to pause, take stock, focus, and think.

deep learner someone who learns everything they can about a topic

take stock evaluate your progress

STEP 3: Insight. At the end of each chapter, you'll be asked to revisit the "Reality Check's" same knowledge questions you were asked about in the chapter's opening "Readiness Check." Comparing your responses on the two sets will help you gauge how much you've learned. You'll also be asked to revisit the chapter's opening case study. For example, when Gloria Gonzales and her challenge of turning her dreams into goals may have seemed simple, but after reading about it in the chapter, you might decide that you really hadn't thought about it very deeply and there's more to it than you originally thought. The difference between Step 2 (your immediate reaction) and Step 3 (the new insights you've gained from reading) demonstrate that you've learned! After reading the chapter and discussing it in class, you'll know some research on the subject, the chapter's suggestions, examples you can apply, and your instructor's thoughts about how the case study student handled the challenges. You'll also gain some insights about yourself, if you face any of these issues, too.

STEP 4: Action. The final step in this learning chain reaction is about action. What have you learned that will change how you face similar challenges? Learning takes place when it relates to you personally, and insights have no impact unless they lead to change. The bottom line is: You must use your insights to take action. Think of this comparison. One day you feel tired, you notice that your clothes are tight, and you are suddenly aware that you're out of shape. You realize that you must eat healthier food and exercise more. But if you don't take action, it won't happen. To become real, new knowledge must lead to personal insights that result in action. What you learned by reading relates to you, and you must use it!

If you follow the system built into this book and use it as you read all your textbooks, the learning chain reaction will become automatic for you.

EXERCISE 2.1

How Do You "Spend" Your Time?[3]

Add up the cost of going to college for an entire term: tuition for one semester/trimester/quarter, the total estimated cost of all the gas you will use to get to and from class for the term, books and supplies, a computer you may have bought, and childcare or any other expenses related to your going to school. Put down everything you can think of. Divide that grand total by the number of hours you are in school (number of weeks class is in session multiplied by the number of hours you are scheduled to be in class). For example, if you are taking two, three-hour classes for a 16-week semester, the number you divide your grand total by will be 96 (= 6 hours × 16 weeks). Completing this exercise will show you how much money each class session costs you—and the cost of missing class! Compare your "hourly rate" with that of your classmates and discuss the results as a group.

How Motivated *Are* You and *How Are You* Motivated?

Academic Intrinsic Motivation Self-Assessment

How intrinsically motivated are you? Read each of the following statements and circle the number beside each statement that most accurately represents your views about yourself.

	Completely Not True	Somewhat Not True	Neutral	Somewhat True	Completely True
1. I have academic goals.	1	2	3	4	5
2. I am confident I can complete my degree.	1	2	3	4	5
3. I determine my career goals.	1	2	3	4	5
4. I enjoy solving challenging, difficult problems.	1	2	3	4	5
5. I work on an assignment until I understand it.	1	2	3	4	5
6. I am confident I will finish a degree or certificate.	1	2	3	4	5
7. I determine the quality of my academic work.	1	2	3	4	5
8. I am pursuing college because I value education.	1	2	3	4	5
9. I feel good knowing that I determine how my academic career develops.	1	2	3	4	5
10. I have high standards for academic work.	1	2	3	4	5
11. Staying in college is my decision.	1	2	3	4	5
12. I study because I like to learn new things.	1	2	3	4	5
13. I enjoy doing outside readings in connection to my future coursework.	1	2	3	4	5
14. I am intrigued by the different topics introduced in my courses.	1	2	3	4	5
15. I study because I am curious.	1	2	3	4	5
16. I look forward to going to class.	1	2	3	4	5
17. I am excited to take more courses within my major.	1	2	3	4	5
18. I enjoy learning more within my field of study.	1	2	3	4	5
19. I like to find answers to questions about material I am learning.	1	2	3	4	5
20. I enjoy studying.	1	2	3	4	5
21. I have pictured myself in a career after college.	1	2	3	4	5
22. I am excited about the job opportunities I will have later.	1	2	3	4	5
23. I have pictured myself being successful in my chosen career.	1	2	3	4	5

	Completely Not True	Somewhat Not True	Neutral	Somewhat True	Completely True
24. I believe I will make a substantial contribution to my chosen profession.	1	2	3	4	5
25. I feel good knowing I will be a member of the professional community in my area of study.	1	2	3	4	5
Total each column, then add your scores across.	___ +	___ +	___ +	___ +	___ =

___ OVERALL SCORE

Continue reading to find out what your overall score means.

French, B. F., & Oakes, W. (2003). Measuring academic intrinsic motivation in the first year of college: Reliability and validity evidence for a new instrument. Journal of the First Year Experience 15(1), 83–102.

When it comes to getting a college education, where does motivation come into the picture? In general, motivation is your desire to put forth effort, even when the going gets rough. The word *motivation* comes from Medieval Latin, *motivus*, meaning "moving." What moves you to learn? There are many ways to define motivation, and different people are motivated by different things.

How motivated would you be to learn something difficult, like a new language, one you'd never studied before? Let's say that you were offered a chance to learn Finnish, a challenging language that is not related to English. For example, in Finnish *Kiitoksia oikein paljon* means "thank you very much." Finnish would be a challenge to learn. To determine your level of motivation, it would help to know your attitude toward Finland and Finnish people, whether you needed to learn Finnish for some reason, how you felt about learning it, if you thought you could learn it successfully, if you were rewarded in some way for learning it, and just how stimulating you found the learning process to be.[4] In other words, your motivation depends on many factors, right?

You'd probably be more motivated to learn Finnish if these sorts of things were part of the picture: (a) you were going to visit relatives in Finland and were excited about it, (b) you'd always been good at learning foreign languages and you expected to learn this one easily, (c) your boss was planning to transfer you to Helsinki as part of a big promotion, or (d) you enjoyed your Finnish language class, thought the instructor was a gifted teacher, and found the other students to be as motivated as you were. So, whose job is it to motivate you? Your instructor's? This book's? Yours? *Can* anyone else besides you motivate you? This book will ask you: how motivated *are* you to succeed in college? And *how* are you motivated?

To assess your own motivation, it's important to understand the difference between *extrinsic* and *intrinsic* motivation. People who are **extrinsically**, or externally, motivated learn in order to get a grade, earn credits, or complete a requirement, for example. They are motivated by things outside themselves. You could be motivated to learn Finnish to earn three credits or to get an A. People who are **intrinsically**, or internally, motivated learn

extrinsically outside yourself
intrinsically inside yourself

You are never given a wish without the power to make it come true. You may have to work for it, however.

Richard Bach, from Illusions

because they're curious, fascinated, or challenged, or because they truly want to master a subject. They are motivated from within. You could be motivated to learn Finnish for the challenge, because you're curious about it, or because you find it fascinating. Let's be realistic, however. Extrinsic motivation is real and important. You need to earn college credits, and you'd rather get A's than F's. But how intrinsically motivated you are in college will have a great deal to do with just how successful you are. The motivation to become truly educated must come from within you.

Extrinsic Motivation   **Intrinsic Motivation**

FIGURE 2.2

**Extrinsic versus
Intrinsic Motivation**

Grades   Credits   Curiosity   Mastery

Pay   Parents   Fascination   Challenge

CAREER OUTLOOK: *Saree Robinson, Fashion Merchandiser*

Q1: Why did you decide to pursue a career in fashion/fashion merchandising?

I always loved fashion and knew that in order to be truly happy, I had to work in a field that I felt passionate and excited about! Many people think "fashion career," and they automatically think of fashion designers. The truth is there are many, many different career paths in this field. Fashion careers require you to be ahead of the game in order to spot and set trends, and help determine the market's needs. Because I have a very analytical brain, I like to assess and track trends, so I found fashion merchandising to be the best choice for me. Merchandising encompasses a lot. I play a role in creating a visual story for any given season, helping determine what manufacturers produce, what styles will stock shelves, and how displays in stores will be assembled to heighten interest in the looks we are trying to sell.

Q2: Beyond going to college, what else helped prepare you for your career?

Work, work work—and interning!! The more experience you have, the more valuable you will be to a company. In this field everyone starts at the bottom, or close to the bottom. Basic retail experience is useful. Following and reading about style trends are also imperative to understanding what is going on in fashion.

Q3: What are the best and worst aspects of your career field?

Fashion jobs are rarely as glamorous as they may seem. There is a lot of hard work involved! The best part of my job is when I see a woman on the street rocking a look I had suggested in my trend analysis. The worst part of my job is horribly ugly trends, snotty people, and the occasional high stress levels.

a great writer." If you had really [...] have been able to say that. Tha[...] "self-handicapping."[9] Some college[...] this strategy. They exert little effo[...] in themselves or because they fea[...] don't do well.

EXERCISE 2.5

Theories of Intel[...]

What is intelligence? Are people [...] following scale, write in the num[...] are no right or wrong answers.

1	2
Strongly Agree	**Mostly Agree**

_____ 1. You have a certain amo[...]

_____ 2. You can learn new thin[...]

_____ 3. You can always substan[...]

_____ 4. No matter how much i[...]

Research shows that what you [...] *mindset*—can make a difference in [...] glance this statement seems absur[...] right? Wrong.

The scaled questions demonst[...] are two basic ways to define intelli[...] us are performers, who agree wit[...] and 2, while others of us are learn[...] more with statements 3 and 4. *Perf[...] that intelligence is a fixed trait t[...] changed. From the moment you're b[...] certain amount of intelligence that [...] and that's that. *Learners*, on the othe[...] you can grow your intelligence if [...] on opportunities to learn. Wheneve[...] tough challenge, you learn from it. [...] learn, the more intelligent you can b[...] standing which view of intelligence [...] will make a difference in how you [...] college classes, and how successful [...]

Students who are taught the va[...] ing mindset over a performance min[...] ally achieve more than students v[...] one study, college students' views [...]

You completed the Academic Intrinsic Motivation Scale (AIMS) in Exercise 2.2, which is designed to measure your intrinsic, or internal, motivation to succeed in college in terms of these four C-Factors:

1. **Curiosity.** Do you want to learn new things? Are you truly interested in what you're learning? Are you curious? Do you ask questions?

2. **Control.** Do you think working hard in your academic courses will pay off? Do you believe you can control how successful you'll be?

3. **Career outlook.** Are you goal oriented? Are you future oriented? Can you imagine yourself using what you learn in college to help you get a job you want?

4. **Challenge.** Does your college coursework challenge you? It is important that the level of challenge is right for you. Too much challenge can cause you to become frustrated and give up. Not enough challenge can cause you to lose interest.[5]

Think about it this way: If your overall score on the AIMS was 100–125, you're intrinsically motivated at a high level. If you scored between 75 and 99, you're intrinsically motivated at a moderate level, but increasing your intrinsic motivation may help you achieve more. If you scored below 75, a lack of intrinsic motivation could interfere with your college success. If you're intrinsically motivated, you'll use all the learning tools offered to you in *FOCUS*.

Q4: What's your advice to college students who'd like to get into fashion/ fashion merchandising/ buying?

Don't get into this field unless you adore everything about fashion. If you LIVE for it, you will love it! This is a job that doesn't just disappear when you leave the office—everyone is connected to fashion, whether they know it or not.

Q5: What if anything has surprised you about your career?

There are surprises every day!!

HOW WOULD *YOU* LIKE IT?

Have you ever considered a career as a fashion merchandiser?

Facts to Consider[6]

Academic preparation required: Many companies require buyers to have a degree in business or economics, and to become a top-level buyer, a master's degree is typically required. But regardless of your educational background, most employers require buyers to go through a training period of one to five years to learn the company.

Future workforce demand: No change in the hiring patterns for buyers or purchasing managers is predicted soon.

Work environment: Typically buyers work in comfortable offices and travel a few days each month. Hours can be long during peak sales periods, and buyers are expected to

keep up with the pressure and pace of the fashion market.

Essential skills: Confidence, analytical skills, and very strong organization skills are all-important traits in the buying world. Buyers must be able to use data to predict trends, meet supply demands, and keep track of their purchases. A lot of the organizational part of buying includes using computers, so an understanding of spreadsheets and data programs is a must.

Questions to Ponder

1. Do you have (or could you acquire) the skills this career requires?

2. Are you interested in a career like this? Why or why not?

For more career activities online, access the CourseMate via www.cengagebrain.com/shop/ ISBN/ 0495906433 to do the Team Career exercises.

BOX 2.1 Statements
College . . .

Since words reflect attitudes
ten for statements like these
They can negatively affect yo
your learning:

- **"I thought college cla esting than they are."** the beholder.
- **"I didn't learn a thing** search for what you ca even if it didn't quite m
- **"The textbook is reall it?"** Reading may not

EXERCISE 2.4

Your Academic Au

Write a three-paragraph academic a of your primary, middle, and high sc ing now in college? What do you thi at your academic self throughout yo college, then write your academic au questions for your classmates.

Ability versus Ef

Succe challe They requir Th

"

Ability is what you're capable of doi Motivation determines what you do. determines how well you do it.

Lou Holtz, former colleg and ESP

CONTROL: *YOUR TOUGHEST TASK*

In Class: Think about the courses you're enrolled in this term. Which one will be the toughest? Use the following chart to analyze your C-Factors for this course. Describe this course in terms of its *challenge* level, your *curiosity* about the subject, how much *control* you believe you have to succeed, and the way each class impacts your *career outlook*. Once you've determined the levels of challenge, curiosity, control, and career outlook, remember that it's *your* responsibility to adjust them.

- What is the relationship between the four C-Factors and your intrinsic motivation to learn? For example, if you don't feel you have much control over how well you do, how can you change that?
- What can you do to increase your intrinsic motivation and become more successful?

Look at Gloria's entry as a model.

On the Job: If you prefer, think about your toughest task on the job. Perhaps you've been assigned a new project, and you're not sure where to start. Use the bottom row to analyze the level of challenge, how much curiosity you have about figuring it out, how much control you think you have over how successful you'll be at it, and how learning from this experience might affect your targeted career. Finally, what can you do to adjust these factors, if you need to?

Course Title	Challenge	Curiosity	Control	Career Outlook	Adjustments Required
Develop-mental English	Very High: never been good at writing	Very Low: had a discouraging teacher in H.S.	Moderate: probably higher than it feels to me	Will need to know how to write in any job	Need to spend more time pre-writing and going to the campus Writing Center for help

Job Task	Challenge	Curiosity	Control	Career Outlook	Adjustments Required

predicted the goals students valued in college. *Performers* were more likely to want to give up in challenging situations; learners wanted to try harder.[11] In one study that measured the electrical activity in college students' brains as they performed a difficult task, brain activity showed that *performers* cared most about whether their answers were right or wrong, while *learners* were interested in follow-up information they could learn from.[12] Yet another study showed that *learners* are more likely to buckle down academically, even when they feel depressed.[13] It's clear: Believing you're a *learner* provides advantages in motivation, achievement, enjoyment, and commitment.

Regardless of what you believe about your precise intelligence level, the fact is this: *Intelligence can be cultivated through learning.* And people's theories about their intelligence levels can be shifted.

EXERCISE 2.6

Core Values Self-Assessment

What are your core values? What's most important to you—deep down inside? Review the following list and check off the items that you value. Don't spend too much time thinking about each one; just go with your initial gut reaction. For each item, ask yourself "Is this something that's important to me?"

_____ Health	_____ Physical Appearance	_____ Financial wealth
_____ Fitness/Physical strength	_____ Independence	_____ Commitment
_____ Loyalty	_____ Honesty	_____ Compassion
_____ Academic achievement	_____ Children	_____ Leisure time
_____ Success	_____ Leadership	_____ Balance
_____ Happiness	_____ Family	_____ Friendship
_____ Social life	_____ Marriage/Partnership	_____ Recognition
_____ Athletics	_____ Spirituality	_____ Status
_____ Creativity	_____ Variety	_____ Wisdom
_____ Meaningful work	_____ Challenge	_____ Time spent alone
_____ Adventure	_____ Personal growth	_____ Other (list here)

Now review all of the items you checked off and circle the five that are most important to you at this point in your life. Then rank them by putting a number next to each of the five circled values with number one as your top priority. Finally, take stock. Is this the person you want to be? Is there anything about your values that you would like to change? If so, what's keeping you from making this change?

Before tackling the big questions about what you want to create with your life, it's important to first take a close look in the mirror. Who are you? What makes you tick? What do you **value**? What are your **goals**? Where will your **dreams** take you?

dreams something you wish for

value something you think is important

goals something you make specific plans to achieve

Values at the Core

What do you value in life? By taking time to examine your personal values, managing your life will become easier and make more sense. Values can be things you can't exactly see or touch, like love or respect, or things that are visible and real, like family or money. Understanding how they motivate you isn't as simple as it might seem. Values can change as you go through life. For example, if you're single now, you may value the freedom to meet a variety of potential romantic partners. Later, however, you may want a committed relationship because you want stability in your life. For this reason, it's important to look at your values from time to time and rethink them.

Knowing others is intelligence; knowing yourself is true wisdom. Mastering others is strength; mastering yourself is true power.

Lao Tzu, Taoist philosopher

Self-knc

What you get by achieving your goals is not as important as what you become by achieving your goals.

Zig Ziglar, Motivational speaker, writer, and trainer

important part of the life management skills this book will help you develop. Your goals may not seem at all clear to you right now, but the important thing is to learn that there's a right way and a wrong way to set your goals. The best way to ensure that the goals you set will serve you well is to make sure you *FOCUS*. Here's a brief overview of what that means.

F **Fit.** Your goal must fit your values, your character, and who you are as a person. Goals that conflict with any of these things will not only be difficult to accomplish, but they just won't work. If your goal is to become a writer for a travel magazine because you love adventure, but flying in planes terrifies you, you're in trouble.

O **Ownership.** Own your goal: See it, taste it, want it! It must be your goal, not someone else's goal for you. Ask yourself: Does the thought of achieving this goal get me fired up? Do I genuinely own this goal or do I feel I ought to have this goal because it sounds good or makes someone else happy?

C **Concreteness.** For any goal to be effective, it must be real. In other words, you must be able to describe your goal in detail: "To run a mile in less than six minutes by March 4th" is much more concrete than "to eventually run faster." The more concrete, the better.

U **Usefulness.** Goals must be useful. They must serve a purpose, and that purpose should be tied to your long-term vision of the person you want to become. For example, if you want to work for an international hotel some day, it would be useful to begin studying a foreign language now.

S **Stretch.** In the business world, people talk about stretch goals. These are goals that require employees to stretch beyond their usual limits to achieve something more challenging. Goals must be based in reality, but also offer you a chance to grow beyond the person you currently are.

Your goals should include both short- and long-term goals. Once your long-term goals are set (though they may shift over time as *you* shift over time), you will then want to set some short-term goals, which act as in-between steps to achieving your long-term goals.

Long-Term Goals	Short-Term Goals
What do I want to accomplish . . .	**What do I want to accomplish...**
In my lifetime?	This year?
In the next twenty years?	This month?
In the next ten years?	This week?
In the next three to five years?	Today?

How **FULL** is your plate? ....

" **This constant, unproductive preoccupation with all the things we have to do is the single largest consumer of time and energy.** "

—KERRY GLEESON, TIME MANAGEMENT EXPERT

How much time do you spend worrying about how much is on your plate—as opposed to removing things one at a time in a systematic way? Sometimes the biggest enemy of time management is worry. We're stopped by our worries and fears. How true is that statement for you?

-A3K-/iStockphoto.com

TRY IT!

List the three items you worry about getting done most, and for each one, list three suggestions you should follow to improve your time management skills and your life.

step 3 INSIGHT *Now* What Do You Think?

At the beginning of this chapter, Gloria Gonzales faced a series of challenges as a new college student. Now after learning from this chapter, would you respond differently to any of the questions you answered about the "FOCUS Challenge Case"? Using what you learned in the chapter, write a paragraph ending to Gloria's case study. What are some of the possible outcomes for her?

step 4 ACTION Your Plans for Change

1. Identify one new thing you learned in reading this chapter. Why did you select the one you've selected? How will it affect what you do in your college classes?
2. Do you have some of the same questions Gloria does about your own level of motivation to achieve in college? How could you increase your motivation? How important might that be?
3. How do your own goals and dreams differ? How do you plan to turn your dreams into goals?

What did you **Learn?**

On a scale of 1 to 5, answer these questions now that you've completed this chapter.

1 = not very/not much/very little/low   5 = very/a lot/very much/high

How much do you know *now*?

Now rate your current level of knowledge about topics covered in this chapter.

How people learn

1   2   3   4   5

Intrinsic versus extrinsic motivation

1   2   3   4   5

Dreams versus goals

1   2   3   4   5

FOCUSed goal-setting

1   2   3   4   5

How useful might the information in this chapter be to you?

How much do you think this information might affect your college success?

1   2   3   4   5

How much do you think this information might affect your career success after college?

1   2   3   4   5

How long did it actually take you to complete this chapter (both the reading and writing tasks)?

_____ Hour(s) _____ Minutes

Challenge Yourself Online Quiz. To find out how much you've learned, access the CourseMate via www.cengagebrain.com/shop/ISBN/0495906433 to take the Challenge Yourself Online Quiz.

Compare these answers with your answers from the "Readiness Check" at the beginning of this chapter. How might the gaps between what you thought before starting the chapter and what you now think affect how you approach the next chapter?

chapter 3

Learning about Learning

You're About to Discover...

✔ How learning changes your brain
✔ How people are intelligent in different ways
✔ How you learn through your senses
✔ How to become a more efficient and effective learner
✔ How your personality type can affect your learning style

READINESS CHECK

What do you **Know?**

Before beginning this chapter, take a moment to answer these questions. Your answers will help you assess how ready you are to focus.

1 = not very/not much/very little/low   5 = very/a lot/very much/high

How much do you *already* know?

Rate your current level of knowledge about topics covered in this chapter.

Learning and the human brain

   1 2 3 4 5

Multiple intelligences

   1 2 3 4 5

Sensory preferences for learning

   1 2 3 4 5

Becoming a better learner

   1 2 3 4 5

How motivated are you to learn *more*?

In general, how motivated are you to learn the material in this chapter?

   1 2 3 4 5

How much do you think this information might affect your college success?

   1 2 3 4 5

How much do you think this information might affect your career success after college?

   1 2 3 4 5

How ready are you to read *now*?

How ready are you to focus on this chapter—physically, intellectually, and emotionally? Which of these three areas is most challenging for you right now? Circle a number to represent it.

   1 2 3 4 5

If any of your answers is below a 3, consider addressing the issue before reading. Then, read the chapter carefully, while looking for ways to improve your focus.

Finally, how long do you think it will take you to complete this chapter? If you start and stop, keep track of the overall time.

_____ Hour(s) _____ Minutes

Tammy Ko

NORTH RIVE
COMMUNITY C

ENR
NO

WWW.NORTHRIVERVIEWC

© Lori Howard, 2010. Used under license from Shutterstock.com

©Larry Harwood Photography. Property of Cengage Learning.

How depressing!" Tammy Ko whispered under her breath as she walked out of her "Introduction to Criminology" class on a dark, rainy Thursday afternoon. *What's with him, anyway?* she asked herself about the instructor.

© Cengage Learning

Program Description

Criminology

we think of criminology as a relatively new discipline, the foundations of criminology can be traced back over uries. Criminology is the "scientific study of the causes of crime and delinquency, crime control policies, ons designed to control crime, and media depictions of crime, criminals, and victims." Criminology draws from other disciplines, including: psychology, sociology, political science, economics, and others.

nology is a rapidly growing field of study, and has many possible career options, including: Federal Agent, selor, Drug Enforcement Agent, Probation Officer, Forensic Specialist, Victim Services Specialist, Litigation ager, etc.

First Year

CRIM 103 – Introduction to Criminolog
CRIM 105 – Research Methods for Sc
ENGL 130 – Scientific Writing
CHEM 106 – General Chemistry I
CHEM 108 – General Chemistry II
MATH 135 – Calculus I
MATH 136 – Calculus II
Elective – 3 credits

Second Year

15 – Advanced Criminology
318 – Juvenile Delinquency
320 – Capital Punishment
300 – Ethical Dilemmas in Criminal Justice
350 – The Correctional System
360 – The Judicial System
CH 310 – Abnormal Psychology
ctives – 6 credits

ELECTIVES
- CSI: Fact or Fantasy?
- Interview and Interrogat
- Professionalism and Et
- Investigation of Injury a
- Crime Scene & Crime
- Psychosociology of Co
- Legal Aspects of Crim

©Larry Harwood Photography. Property of Cengage Learning.

Tammy was a first-semester student at the large community college in the city where she grew up. Even though she found college life hectic because of all the hours she had to work to pay her own tuition, Tammy was excited about working on her associate's degree in criminal justice. She wanted to get into her state's police academy and specialize in forensics, and she knew a degree would help her chances. The crime shows on TV were her favorites. She watched them all each week. She rationalized how much time it took by thinking of it as career development. The fun was picturing herself as an investigator solving headline cases: "Man Slain, Found in City Park" or "Modern

Day 'Jack the Ripper' Terrorizes Las Vegas." She could envision herself hunched over laboratory equipment, testing for fibers or DNA, and actually breaking the case.

When she registered for classes, her academic advisor had told her that taking an "Introduction to Criminology" course would be the right place to start. "It'll teach you how to think," he'd said, "and it'll give you the background you need to understand the criminal mind. At the end of this class," he said, "you'll know if you really want to pursue a career in law enforcement." *Maybe it would teach me how to think*, Tammy thought to herself now that the term was underway, *if only I could understand the instructor. Forget understanding the criminal mind—I'd just like a glimpse into his!*

Mr. Caldwell was quiet and reserved, and he seemed a bit out of touch. He dressed as if he hadn't bought a new piece of clothing in twenty years. In class, he organized all his papers neatly on his desk and covered each day's material carefully, point by point. Tammy wished

POLICE LINE DO NOT CROSS

© Mike Red, 2009/Used under license from Shutterstock.com; © Loren Rodgers, 2009/Used under license from Shutterstock.com;

he'd depart from his notes occasionally to explore other interesting things. Tammy had always preferred teachers who created exciting things to do in class over teachers who went completely by the book. Tammy's biggest complaint about Mr. Caldwell was that he only talked about *theories* of criminology. When was he ever going to get to the hands-on part of the course? She couldn't help thinking, *When will we stop talking about theories and start working on real cases—like the ones on all those TV shows?*

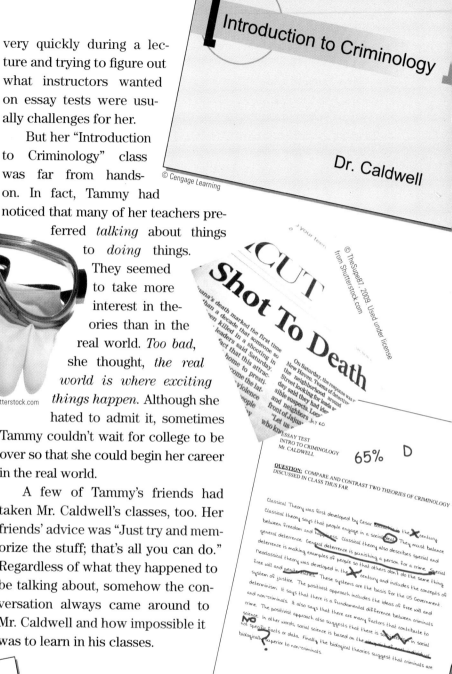

Michael J. Thompson/Shutterstock.com

To make matters worse, learning from lectures was not Tammy's strong suit. She hadn't done well on the first exam because she'd had to just memorize things that didn't make much sense to her, and her D grade showed it.

The entire exam consisted of one question: "Compare and contrast two theories of criminology discussed in class thus far." Tammy hated essay tests. She was at her best on tests with right or wrong answers, like true-false or multiple-choice questions. Making sense out of spoken words that go by

very quickly during a lecture and trying to figure out what instructors wanted on essay tests were usually challenges for her.

But her "Introduction to Criminology" class was far from hands-on. In fact, Tammy had noticed that many of her teachers preferred *talking* about things to *doing* things. They seemed to take more interest in theories than in the real world. *Too bad,* she thought, *the real world is where exciting things happen.* Although she hated to admit it, sometimes Tammy couldn't wait for college to be over so that she could begin her career in the real world.

A few of Tammy's friends had taken Mr. Caldwell's classes, too. Her friends' advice was "Just try and memorize the stuff; that's all you can do." Regardless of what they happened to be talking about, somehow the conversation always came around to Mr. Caldwell and how impossible it was to learn in his classes.

Introduction to Criminology

Dr. Caldwell

CUT
Shot To Death

65%   D

ESSAY TEST
INTRO TO CRIMINOLOGY
Mr. CALDWELL

QUESTION: COMPARE AND CONTRAST TWO THEORIES OF CRIMINOLOGY DISCUSSED IN CLASS THUS FAR

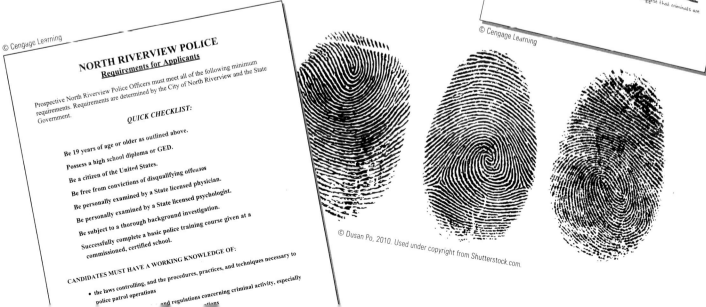

NORTH RIVERVIEW POLICE
Requirements for Applicants

Prospective North Riverview Police Officers must meet all of the following minimum requirements. Requirements are determined by the City of North Riverview and the State Government.

QUICK CHECKLIST:

Be 19 years of age or older as outlined above.
Possess a high school diploma or GED.
Be a citizen of the United States.
Be free from convictions of disqualifying offenses
Be personally examined by a State licensed physician.
Be personally examined by a State licensed psychologist.
Be subject to a thorough background investigation.
Successfully complete a basic police training course given at a commissioned, certified school.

CANDIDATES MUST HAVE A WORKING KNOWLEDGE OF:

- the laws controlling, and the procedures, practices, and techniques necessary to police patrol operations

and regulations concerning criminal activity, especially

2 REACTION What Do *You* Think?

1. Do you have anything in common with Tammy? If so, how are you managing the situation so that you can be successful?
2. Is Tammy smart? If so, in what ways? What is she particularly good at?
3. What sensory modality does Tammy prefer for taking in information? Does she learn best by viewing information through charts and graphs, for example, by talking and listening, by reading and writing, or by actually doing things?
4. What are the differences between Mr. Caldwell's teaching style and Tammy's learning style? How do these differences affect Tammy's learning?
5. What should Tammy do to become a better learner in Mr. Caldwell's class?

Go to the Head of the Class: Learning and the Brain

EXERCISE 3.1

What Is Learning?

*The following statements represent common student views on learning. Think about each statement, and mark it **true** or **false** based on your honest opinion.*

_____ 1. Learning is often hard work and really not all that enjoyable.

_____ 2. Memorization and learning are basically the same thing.

_____ 3. The learning done in school is often gone in a few weeks or months.

_____ 4. In college, most learning takes place in class.

_____ 5. Learning is usually the result of listening to an instructor lecture or reading a textbook.

_____ 6. The best way to learn is by working alone.

_____ 7. Most students know intuitively how they learn best.

_____ 8. Teachers control what students learn.

_____ 9. Learning only deals with subjects taught in school.

_____ 10. The learning pace is controlled by the slowest learner in the class.

You probably noticed that many of these statements attempt to put learning in a negative light. How many did you mark true? This chapter will help you understand more about learning as a process and about yourself as a learner. As you read, your goal should be to use the insights you gain to become a better learner.

Let's start our exploration of the learning process close to home—in our own heads. What's going on up there, anyway? While your hands are busy manipulating test tubes in chemistry lab, or your eyes are watching your psychology instructor's PowerPoint presentation, what's your brain up to? The answer? Plenty.

Use It or Lose It

The human brain consists of a complex web of connections between neurons or nerve cells. This web grows in complexity as it incorporates new knowledge.

But if the connections are not reinforced frequently, you lose them. As you learn new things, you work to hardwire these connections, making them less likely to deteriorate. When your instructors repeat portions of the previous week's lecture or assign homework so you can practice material covered in class, they're helping you to form connections in your brain by using and reusing them—or, in other words, to learn. Repetition is vital to learning. You must use and reuse information in order to hardwire it.

American humorist Will Rogers once said, "You know, you've got to exercise your *brain* just like your muscles." He was right. Giving your brain the exercise it needs—now and in your years after college—will help you form connections between neurons that, if you keep using them, will last a lifetime. From a biological point of view, that's what being a lifelong learner means. The age-old advice "use it or lose it" is true when it comes to learning.

Ask Questions and Hardwire Your Connections

Your instructors have been studying their disciplines for years, perhaps decades. They have developed extensive hardwired connections between their brain neurons. They are *experts*.

By contrast, you are a *novice* or newcomer to whatever discipline you're studying. You've not yet developed the brain wiring that your instructors have developed. That can lead to a potential problem. Sometimes instructors are so familiar with what they already know from years of traveling the same pathways in their brains that what you're learning for the first time seems obvious to them. Without even realizing it, they can expect what is *familiar* to them to be *obvious* to you. Think of how challenging it is when you try to teach something that you understand thoroughly to another person who doesn't, like teaching someone who has never used a computer before how to upload an assignment.

Since you're a novice, you may not understand everything your instructors say. Ask questions, check, clarify, probe, and persist until you do understand. Sometimes your confusion is not due to a lack of knowledge, but a lack of the *correct* knowledge. For example, you may study for a test by doing only one thing—reading and rereading the textbook. Actually, it's important to be familiar with many different ways to study and then choose the ones that work best for you.

Think of it this way. Some of the brain wiring you brought with you to college is positive and useful, and some actually hurts more than it helps. When you learn, you not only add new connections, but you rewire some old connections. While you're in college, you're under construction![1]

Take Charge and Create the Best Conditions for Learning

Throughout this discussion, we've been talking about processes inside your brain. *Your* brain, not anyone else's. The bottom line is this: Learning must be *internally initiated*—by you. It can only be *externally encouraged*—by someone else. You're in charge of your own learning. Learning changes your brain.

© Colin Anderson/Blend Images/CORBIS

> When we come to know something, we have performed an act that is as biological as when we digest something.
>
> *Henry Plotkin,* Darwin Machines and the Nature of Knowledge *(1994)*

prerequisite something that must be completed before something else

Let's look at food as an analogy: If learning is a process that is as biological as digestion, then no one can learn for you, in the same way that no one can eat for you. The food in the refrigerator doesn't do you a bit of good unless you walk over, open the door, remove it, and start eating. It's there for the taking, but you must make that happen. To carry the analogy further, you eat on a daily basis, right? "No thanks, I ate last week" is a silly statement. Learning does for your brain what food does for your body. Nourish yourself!

Brain researchers tell us the best state for learning has ten conditions.

1. You're intrinsically motivated (from within yourself) to learn material that is appropriately challenging.

> **Examine where your motivation to learn comes from.** Are you *internally* motivated because you're curious about the subject and want to learn about it or *externally* motivated to get an A or avoid an F? Can you generate your own internal motivation? This book has built-in reminders to boost your intrinsic motivation. Use them to your advantage as a learner.

> **Adjust the level of challenge yourself.** If you're too challenged in a class, you become nervous. Make sure you're keeping up with the workload and that you've completed the **prerequisites**. In many classes, you must know the fundamentals before tackling more advanced concepts. If you're not challenged enough, you can become bored and tune out. Your instructor will provide one level of challenge for everyone in the class. But it's up to you to fine-tune that challenge for yourself. Get extra help if you aren't quite up to the task or bump up the challenge a notch or two if you're ahead of the game so that you're continually motivated to learn.

2. You're appropriately stressed, but generally relaxed.

> **Assess your stress.** According to researchers, you learn best in a state of *relaxed alertness*, a state of high challenge and low threat.[2] While relaxed alertness may sound impossible, it can be achieved. No stress at all is what you'd find in a no-brainer course. Some stress is useful; it helps you learn. Stress can heighten your alertness and help you focus. How stressed are you—and why—when you get to class? Are you overstressed because you've rushed from your last class, you're late because you missed your bus, or because you haven't done the reading and hope you won't be called on? Prepare for class so that you're ready to jump in. Or instead of too much stress, are you understressed because you don't value the course material? Consider how the information can be useful to you—perhaps in ways you've never even thought of. Here's the vital question to ask yourself: How much stress do I need in order to trigger my best effort?

> **Pay attention to your overall physical state.** Are you taking care of your physical needs so that you can stay alert, keep up with the lecture, and participate in the discussion?

Stressed Out?

> **Movement is a medicine for creating change in a person's physical, emotional, and mental states.**
>
> —CAROL WELCH

Research shows that just twenty minutes of exercise can help calm you for as long as twenty-four hours. Vigorous exercise helps you get rid of excess adrenaline and pumps in endorphins that block pain and anxiety.[3] Not only does exercise help you burn off cheeseburgers, recent brain-imaging and neurochemical studies indicate that "sweating makes you smart." Physical exercise helps reinforce existing connections and create new ones between brain wiring via a protein called BDNF (brain-derived neurotrophic factor). Brain wiring helps you process and store information. "Learning is taking signals that come in from your senses and embedding them into brain anatomy," according to Dr. Vassilis Koliatsos, a psychiatrist at Johns Hopkins University. BDNF affects memory and mood; it literally helps rewire your brain.[4]

TRY IT!

Keep an exercise log for a week. On a daily basis, record the type of physical activity, the length of time you do it, and the level of workout (mild, medium, or high exertion). Using an online exercise calculator, record the number of calories you burned. Finally, monitor your stress level to see if exercise helps lower it (1 = low, 10 = high).

Devon Stephens/iStockphoto.com

	Sunday	Monday	Tuesday	Wednesday	Thursday	Friday	Saturday	TOTAL
Activity								
Time								
Exertion Level								
Calories Burned								
Overall stress level for the day (1 = low; 10 = high)								

3. **You enter into a state researchers call "flow" when you're so totally absorbed in what you're doing that you lose track of everything else.[5]**

> **Identify the kinds of learning situations that help you "flow."** Do you get fully engaged by hands-on activities? Do you find that certain courses naturally capture your attention so much so that you're surprised when it's time for class to end? Understanding your own preferences and style as a learner are key here.

> **Think about what you can do as a learner to get yourself there.** Not all classes or subjects will naturally induce a flow state in you. Nevertheless, ask yourself what *you* can do to focus on learning and exclude distractions. How can you become more engrossed in what you're learning?

4. You're curious about what you're learning, and you look forward to learning it.

> **Get ready to learn by looking back and by looking ahead.** When you're about to cross the street, you must look both ways, right? Keep that image in mind because that's what you should do before each class. What did class consist of last time? Can you predict what it will consist of next time?

> **Focus on substance, not style.** Part of Tammy's bias against Mr. Caldwell focused on his appearance. Despite society's obsession with attractiveness, grooming, and fashion, a student's job is to ask: What can I learn from this person? Deciding an instructor isn't worth paying attention to because he doesn't dress well or because his hair style is outdated is just an excuse not to learn.

5. You're slightly confused, but only for a short time.[6]

> **Use confusion as a motivator.** You may not be getting the lecture's main points because you don't understand new terms used along the way. Look them up early on in the learning process. Ask yourself what background information would help things click—and find out the answers to those questions.

> **Ask questions!** To your professor, questions indicate *interest*, not *idiocy*. Don't be afraid to probe more deeply into the material. As they say, "The only stupid question is the one you don't ask."

6. You search for personal meaning and patterns.

> **Ask yourself: What's in it for me?** Why is knowing this important? How can I use this information in the future? Instead of dismissing material that appears unrelated to your life, try figuring out how it *could* relate. You may be surprised!

> **Think about how courses relate to one another.** How does this new knowledge relate to things you're learning in other courses? Does sociology have anything to do with history? Psychology with economics?

7. Your emotions are involved, not just your mind.

> **Evaluate your attitudes and feelings.** Do you like the subject matter? Do you admire the teacher? Remember your high school teacher, Mr. Brown, whose class you just couldn't stand? Not every class will be your favorite. That's natural. But if a class turns you off as a learner, instead of allowing your emotions to take over, ask why and whether your feelings are in your best interest.

> **Make a deliberate decision to change negative feelings.** Fortunately, feelings can be changed. Hating a course or disliking a professor can only build resentment and threaten your success. It's possible to do a one-eighty and transform your negative emotions into positive energy.

©Larry Harwood Photography. Property of Cengage Learning.

It is not the answer that enlightens, but the question.

Eugene Ionesco, Romanian and French playwright (1909–1994)

8. **You realize that as a learner you use what you already know in constructing new knowledge.**[7]

> **Remember that passive learning is impossible.** When it comes to learning, you are the construction foreman, building on what you already know to construct new knowledge. You're not just memorizing facts someone else wants you to learn. You're a full partner in the learning process!

> **Remind yourself that constructing knowledge takes work.** No one ever built a house by simply sitting back or just hanging out. Builders work hard, but in the end, they have something to show for their efforts. In your college courses, identify what you already know and blend new knowledge into the framework you've built in your mind. By constructing new knowledge, you are building yourself into a more sophisticated, more polished, and most certainly, more educated person.

" It is what we think we know already that often prevents us from learning. "

Claude Bernard, French physiologist (1813–1878)

9. **You understand that learning is both conscious and unconscious.**

> **Watch where your mind goes when it's off duty.** Does learning take place when you're not deliberately trying to learn? Some of what you learn will be immediately obvious to you, and some will dawn on you after class is over, while you're in the shower, or eating lunch, or falling asleep at night, for example. Pay attention to your *indirect* learning and move it into your line of vision.

> **Remember that both kinds of learning are important.** Both conscious learning and unconscious learning count. There are no rules about when and where learning can occur. Capitalize on both.

10. **You're given a degree of choice in terms of what you learn, how you do it, and feedback on how you're doing.**

> **Make the most of the choices you're given.** College isn't a free-for-all in which you can take any classes you like toward earning a degree. However, which electives you choose will be up to you. Or in a particular course, if your instructor allows you to write a paper or shoot a video, choose the option that will be more motivating for you. When you receive an assignment, select a topic that fires you up. It's easier to generate energy to put toward choices you've made yourself.

> **O! this learning, what a thing it is.**
>
> *William Shakespeare*

> **Use feedback to improve, and if feedback is not given, ask for it.** It's possible to get really good at doing something the wrong way. Take a golf swing or a swimming stroke, for example. Without someone intervening to give you feedback, it may be difficult to know how to improve. Your instructors will most likely write comments on your assignments to explain their grades. Evaluating your work is their job; it's what they must do to help you improve. Take their suggestions to heart and try them out.

All of us are already good learners in some situations. Let's say you're drawn to technology, for example. You're totally engrossed in computers and eagerly learn everything you can from books, classes, and online sources—and you sometimes totally lose yourself in a flow state as you're learning. No one has to force you to practice your technology skills or pick up an issue of *Wired* or *PC World.* You do it because you want to. In this case, you're self-motivated and therefore learning is easy. This chapter provides several different tools to help you understand your own personal profile as a learner so that you can try to learn at your best in *all* situations.

CONTROL: *YOUR LEARNING*

Reflect on yourself as a learner in your toughest class this term. How optimal are the conditions for learning? Put a check mark in the box if any of the following conditions are present. If not, beside each item, write in a suggestion to help create the condition and improve your own learning.

Ten Conditions for Optimal Learning   Course Title: _____

1. You're intrinsically motivated to learn material that is appropriately challenging. ☐ _____

2. You're appropriately stressed, but generally relaxed. ☐ _____

3. You enter into a state researchers call flow. ☐ _____

4. You're curious about what you're learning, and you look forward to learning it. ☐ _____

5. You're slightly confused, but only for a short time. ☐ _____

6. You search for personal meaning and patterns. ☐ _____

7. Your emotions are involved, not just your mind. ☐ _____

8. You realize that as a learner you use what you already know in constructing new knowledge. ☐ _____

9. You understand that learning is both conscious and unconscious. ☐ _____

10. You're given a degree of choice in terms of what you learn, how you do it, and feedback on how you're doing. ☐ _____

Multiple Intelligences: *How Are You Smart?*

EXERCISE 3.2

Multiple Intelligences Self-Assessment

Are people smart in different ways? How so? On each line, put check marks next to all the statements that best describe you.

Linguistic Intelligence: The capacity to use language to express what's on your mind and understand others ("word smart")

_____ I'm a good storyteller.

_____ I enjoy word games, puns, and tongue twisters.

_____ I'd rather listen to the radio than watch TV.

_____ I've recently written something I'm proud of.

_____ I can hear words in my head before I say or write them.

_____ When riding in the car, I sometimes pay more attention to words on billboards than I do to the scenery.

_____ In high school, I did better in English, history, or social studies than I did in math and science.

_____ I enjoy reading.

_____ TOTAL check marks

Logical-Mathematical Intelligence: The capacity to understand cause/effect relationships and to manipulate numbers ("number/reasoning smart")

_____ I can easily do math in my head.

_____ I enjoy brainteasers or puzzles.

_____ I like it when things can be counted or analyzed.

_____ I can easily find logical flaws in what others do or say.

_____ I think most things have rational explanations.

_____ Math and science were my favorite subjects in high school.

_____ I like to put things into categories.

_____ I'm interested in new scientific advances.

_____ TOTAL check marks

Spatial Intelligence: The capacity to represent the world visually or graphically ("picture smart")

_____ I like to take pictures of what I see around me.

_____ I'm sensitive to colors.

_____ My dreams at night are vivid.

_____ I like to doodle or draw.

_____ I'm good at navigating with a map.

_____ I can picture what something will look like before it's finished.

_____ In school, I preferred geometry to algebra.

_____ I often make my point by drawing a picture or diagram.

_____ TOTAL check marks

(continued)

Bodily-Kinesthetic Intelligence: The capacity to use your whole body or parts of it to solve a problem, make something, or put on a production ("body smart")

_____ I regularly engage in sports or physical activities.

_____ I get fidgety (tap my foot, etc.) when asked to sit for long periods of time.

_____ I get some of my best ideas while I'm engaged in a physical activity.

_____ I need to practice a skill in order to learn it, rather than just reading or watching a video about it.

_____ I enjoy being a daredevil.

_____ I'm a well-coordinated person.

_____ I like to think through things while I'm doing something else like running or walking.

_____ I like to spend my free time outdoors.

_____ TOTAL check marks

Musical Intelligence: The capacity to think in music, hear patterns and recognize, remember, and perhaps manipulate them ("music smart")

_____ I can tell when a musical note is flat or sharp.

_____ I play a musical instrument.

_____ I often hear music playing in my head.

_____ I can listen to a piece of music once or twice, and then sing it back accurately.

_____ I often sing or hum while working.

_____ I like music playing while I'm doing things.

_____ I'm good at keeping time to a piece of music.

_____ I consider music an important part of my life.

_____ TOTAL check marks

Interpersonal Intelligence: The capacity to understand other people ("people smart")

_____ I prefer group activities to solo activities.

_____ Others think of me as a leader.

_____ I enjoy the challenge of teaching others something I like to do.

_____ I like to get involved in social activities at school, church, or work.

_____ If I have a problem, I'm more likely to get help than tough it out alone.

_____ I feel comfortable in a crowd of people.

_____ I have several close friends.

_____ I'm the sort of person others come to for advice about their problems.

_____ TOTAL check marks

Intrapersonal Intelligence: The capacity to understand yourself, who you are, and what you can do ("self-smart")

_____ I like to spend time alone thinking about important questions in life.

_____ I have invested time in learning more about myself.

_____ I consider myself to be independent minded.

_____ I keep a journal of my inner thoughts.

_____ I'd rather spend a weekend alone than at a place with a lot of other people around.

_____ I've thought seriously about starting a business of my own.

_____ I'm realistic about my own strengths and weaknesses.

_____ I have goals for my life that I'm working on.

_____ TOTAL check marks

Naturalistic Intelligence: The capacity to discriminate between living things and show sensitivity toward the natural world ("nature smart")

_____ Environmental problems bother me.

_____ In school, I always enjoyed field trips to places in nature or away from class.

_____ I enjoy studying nature, plants, or animals.

_____ I've always done well on projects involving living systems.

_____ I enjoy pets.

_____ I notice signs of wildlife when I'm on a walk or hike.

_____ I can recognize types of plants, trees, rocks, birds, and so on.

_____ I enjoy learning about environmental issues.

_____ TOTAL check marks

Which intelligences have the most check marks? Write in the three intelligences in which you had the most number of check marks.

_____ _____ _____

Although this is an informal instrument, it can help you think about the concept of multiple intelligences, or MI. How are you smart?

Based on Armstrong, T. (1994). *Multiple intelligences in the classroom.* Alexandria, VA: Association for Supervision and Curriculum Development, pp. 18–20.

Have you ever noticed that people are smart in different ways? Consider the musical genius of Mozart, who published his first piano pieces at the age of five. Olympic Gold Medalist Lindsey Vonn started skiing at when she was two years old. Not many of us are as musically gifted as Mozart or as physically gifted as Lindsey Vonn, but we all have strengths. You may earn top grades in math, and not-so-top grades in English, and your best friend's grades may be just the opposite.

According to Harvard psychologist Howard Gardner, people can be smart in the eight different categories you saw in Exercise 3.2. Most schools focus on particular types of intelligence, linguistic and logical-mathematical intelligence, reflecting the three R's: reading, writing, and 'rithmetic. But Gardner claims there are many different types of intelligence. It can't be measured by traditional one-dimensional standardized IQ tests and represented by a three-digit number: 100 (average), 130+ (gifted), or 150+ (genius). Gardner defines intelligence as "the ability to find and solve problems and create products of value in one or more cultural setting."[8]

So instead of asking the traditional question "How smart are you?" a better question is "How are you smart?" The idea is to find out *how,* and then apply this understanding of yourself to your academic work in order to achieve your best results.

Translate Content into Your Own Intelligences

Do you sometimes wonder why you can't remember things for exams? Some learning experts believe that memory is intelligence-specific. You may have a

good memory for people's faces but a bad memory for their names. You may be able to remember the words of a country-western hit but not the dance steps that go with it. The Theory of Multiple Intelligences may explain why.[9]

Examine your own behaviors in class. If your instructors use their linguistic intelligence to teach, as many do, and your intelligences lie elsewhere, do you get frustrated? Instead of zeroing in on the lecture, do you fidget (bodily-kinesthetic), doodle (spatial), or socialize (interpersonal)? You may need to translate the information into your own personal intelligences, just as you would if your instructor speaks French and you speak English. This strategy might have worked for Tammy Ko from the "FOCUS Challenge Case." Mr. Caldwell's most developed intelligence is linguistic, whereas Tammy's are bodily-kinesthetic (manipulating test tubes) and interpersonal (interacting with people). Tammy's learning problems are partially due to a case of mismatched intelligences between Mr. Caldwell and herself.

Let's say one of your courses this term is "Introduction to Economics," and the current course topic is the Law of Supply and Demand. Basically, "the theory of supply and demand describes how prices vary as a result of a balance between product availability at each price (supply) and the desires of those with purchasing power at each price (demand)."[10] To understand this law, you could:

CAREER OUTLOOK: *Mark Brown, NYPD Police Officer*

© Creatas Images/Jupiter Images

Q1: Why did you decide to become a police officer?

My father was a cop and I always thought of him as a hero. It wasn't until I grew up that I really realized that being a cop was what I wanted to do. It just seemed so perfect to be able to become the thing that I always looked up to as a kid, like becoming superman or something.

Q2: Beyond going to college, what else helped prepare you for your career?

I grew up around cops, so that helped, and beyond that I'm an athlete, which doesn't hurt. People make a lot of jokes about cops and donuts, but when you're running at top speed, pursuing a suspect, you need to be in good physical shape. Besides that I'm a caring person. I feel good when I'm helping others, and that's what being a cop is all about.

Q3: What are the best and worst aspects of your job?

I have a family, so I'd say the worst part is the fact that every day I put my life on the line. I worry that if something happens to me, my kids will grow up without a father. The hours are tough to deal with, too. We work in shifts, so sometimes you work nights, but you get used to it. The best part is the excitement. Not just the excitement of what people think of when they think of law enforcement—high speed chase scenes and all

that—but also the excitement of never knowing what each day will bring. That's the best part—and also knowing that my kids feel about me the way I did about my dad. It feels good to be someone's hero.

Q4: What's your advice to college students who'd like to become cops?

My advice would be: Know what you're getting into.

- read the textbook (linguistic)
- study mathematical formulas (logical-mathematical)
- examine charts and graphs (spatial)
- observe the Law of Supply and Demand in the natural world, through the changing price of gasoline, for example (naturalistic)
- look at the way the Law of Supply and Demand is expressed in your own body, using food as a metaphor (bodily-kinesthetic)
- reflect on how and when you might be able to afford something you desperately want, like a certain model of car (intrapersonal)
- write (or find) a song that helps you understand the law (musical).

You don't have to try all eight ways, but it's intriguing to speculate about various ways to learn that may work for you, rather than assuming you're doomed because your intelligences don't match your instructor's.

Use Intelligence-Oriented Study Techniques

What if your strongest intelligence is different from the one through which course material is presented? What can you do about it? Take a look at the following techniques for studying using different intelligences. Tweaking the *way* you study may make a world of difference.

Being a policeman or woman isn't like what you see on TV and in the movies. It's real life, and it can be real dangerous. Being an officer of the law is a privilege in my opinion. Your badge means something, and you have to respect that.

HOW WOULD *YOU* LIKE IT?

Have you ever considered a career as a police officer?

Facts to Consider[11]

Academic preparation required: Applicants must have at least completed high school and in some cases are required to hold a college degree (associate's or bachelor's). Beyond academic schooling, individuals will have to go through rigorous training before earning their badges.

Future workforce demand: In the coming years, it's predicted that the demand for law enforcement officers will increase as our society is becoming more and more security conscious.

Work environment: Obviously police work isn't for the faint-hearted. Law officers are put in dangerous situations all the time, and though they will typically work 40-hour weeks, the hours change depending on shift assignments.

Essential skills: One must be very physically fit to meet the demands of being a police officer. One must also be mentally fit, as many situations are extremely stressful and challenging. Beyond the mental and physical demands of the job, it's very important that you enjoy interacting with people. It's your job to serve and protect the public, so you must be able to communicate effectively and make people feel comfortable.

Questions to Ponder

1. Do you have (or could you acquire) the skills this career requires?
2. Are you interested in a career like this? Why or why not?

For more career activities online, access the CourseMate via www.cengagebrain.com/shop/ISBN/0495906433 to do the Team Career exercises.

Linguistic --→	1. Rewrite your class notes. 2. Record yourself reading through your class notes and play it as you study. 3. Read the textbook chapter aloud.
Logical Mathematical --→	1. Create hypothetical conceptual problems to solve. 2. Organize chapter or lecture notes into a logical flow. 3. Analyze how the textbook chapter is organized and why.
Spatial --→	1. Draw a map that demonstrates your thinking on course material. 2. Illustrate your notes by drawing diagrams and charts. 3. Mark up your textbook to show relationships between concepts.
Bodily–Kinesthetic --→	1. Study course material while engaged in physical activity. 2. Practice skills introduced in class or in the text. 3. Act out a scene based on chapter content.
Musical --→	1. Create musical memory devices by putting words into well-known melodies. 2. Listen to music while you're studying. 3. Sing or hum as you work.
Interpersonal --→	1. Discuss course material with your classmates. 2. Organize a study group that meets regularly. 3. Meet a classmate before or after class for coffee and class conversation.
Intrapersonal --→	1. Keep a journal to track your personal reactions to course material. 2. Study alone and engage in internal dialogue about course content. 3. Coach yourself on how to best study for a challenging class.
Naturalistic --→	1. Search for applications of course content in the natural world. 2. Study outside (if weather permits and you can resist distractions). 3. Go to a physical location that exemplifies course material (for example, a park for your geology course).

Develop Your Weaker Intelligences

It's important to cultivate your weaker intelligences. Why? Because life isn't geared to one kind of intelligence. It's complex. A photo journalist for *National Geographic*, for example, might need linguistic intelligence, spatial intelligence, interpersonal intelligence, and naturalistic intelligence. Being well-rounded, as the expression goes, is truly a good thing. Artist Pablo Picasso once said, "I am always doing that which I cannot do, in order that I may learn how to do it."

Use your multiple intelligences to multiply your success. Remember that no one is naturally intelligent in all eight areas. Each individual is a unique blend of intelligences. But the Theory of Multiple Intelligences claims that we all have the capacity to develop all of our eight intelligences further. That's good news!

How Do You Perceive and Process Information?

Style—we all have it, right? What's yours? Baggy jeans and a T-shirt? Sandals, even in the middle of winter? A signature hairdo that defies gravity? When it comes to appearance, you have your own style. You know it, and so does everyone who knows you.

Think about how your mind works. For example, how do you decide what to wear in the morning? Do you turn on the radio or TV for the weather forecast? Stick your head out the front door? Ask someone else's opinion? Throw on whatever happens to be clean? We all have different styles, don't we?

So what's a learning style? A learning style is defined as your "characteristic and preferred ways of gathering, interpreting, organizing, recalling, and thinking about information."[12]

perceive become aware of

Here's one way of looking at things. The way you **perceive** information and the way you process it—your perceiving/processing preferences—are based in part on your senses. Which senses do you prefer to use to take in information—your eyes (visual-graphic or visual-words), your ears (aural), or all your senses using your whole body (kinesthetic)? Which type of information sinks in best? Which type of information do you most trust to be accurate?

To further understand your preferred sensory channel, let's take this hypothetical example. Assume a rich relative you didn't even know leaves you some money, and you decide to use it to buy a new car. You must first answer many questions: What kind of car do you want to buy—an SUV, a sedan, a sports car, a van, or a truck? What are the differences between various makes and models? How do prices, comfort, and safety compare? Who provides the best warranty? Which car do consumers rate highest? How would you go about learning the answers to all these questions?

Marcela Barsse/MarsBars/
iStockphoto.com

Visual. Some of us would **look**. We'd study charts and graphs comparing cars, mileage, fuel tank capacity, maintenance costs, and customer satisfaction. We learn through graphic representations that explain what could have been said in normal text format.

Johanna Goodyear/
Dreamstime.com

Aural. Some of us would **listen**. We'd ask all our friends what kind of cars they drive and what they've heard about cars from other people. We'd pay attention as showroom salespeople describe the features of various cars. We learn through sounds by listening.

“ ”

Learning how to learn is life's most important skill.

Tony Buzan,
memory expert

Nadezda Firsova/
iStockphoto.com

Read/Write. Some of us would **read** or **write**. We'd buy a copy of *Consumer Reports*, annual edition on automobiles, or copies of magazines such as *Car and Driver* or *Road and Track*, and write lists of each car's pros and cons. We learn through words by reading and writing.

Pascal Genest/iStockphoto.com

Kinesthetic. Some of us would want to **do it**. We'd go to the showroom and test drive a few cars to physically try them out. We learn through experience when all our senses are activated.

What would you do? Eventually, as you're deciding which vehicle to buy, you might do all these things, and do them more than once. But learning style theory says we all have preferences for how we perceive and process information.

EXERCISE 3.3

VARK Learning Styles Assessment

Choose the answer that best explains your preference and circle the letter. Please select more than one response if a single answer does not match your perception. **Leave blank any question that does not apply.**

1. You are helping someone who wants to go downtown, find your airport, or locate the bus station. You would:
   a) draw or give her a map.
   b) tell her the directions.
   c) write down the directions (without a map).
   d) go with her.

2. You are not sure whether a word should be spelled "dependent" or "dependant." You would:
   a) see the word in your mind and choose by the way different versions look.
   b) think about how each word sounds and choose one.
   c) find it in a dictionary.
   d) write both words on paper and choose one.

3. You are planning a group vacation. You want some feedback from your friends about your plans. You would:
   a) use a map or website to show them the places.
   b) phone, text, or email them.
   c) give them a copy of the printed itinerary.
   d) describe some of the highlights.

4. You are going to cook something as a special treat for your family. You would:
   a) look through the cookbook for ideas from the pictures.
   b) ask friends for suggestions.
   c) use a cookbook where you know there is a good recipe.
   d) cook something you know without the need for instructions.

5. A group of tourists want to learn about the parks or wildlife reserves in your area. You would:
   a) show them Internet pictures, photographs, or picture books.
   b) talk about, or arrange a talk for them about, parks or wildlife reserves.
   c) give them a book or pamphlets about the parks or wildlife reserves.
   d) take them to a park or wildlife reserve and walk with them.

6. You are about to purchase a digital camera or cell phone. Other than price, what would most influence your decision?
   a) Its attractive design that looks good.
   b) The salesperson telling me about its features.
   c) Reading the details about its features.
   d) Trying or testing it.

7. Remember a time when you learned how to do something new. Try to avoid choosing a physical skill, like riding a bike. You learned best by:
   a) diagrams and charts—visual clues.
   b) listening to somebody explaining it and asking questions.
   c) written instructions—for example, a manual or textbook.
   d) watching a demonstration.

8. You have a problem with your knee. You would prefer that the doctor:
   a) show you a diagram of what was wrong.
   b) describe what was wrong.
   c) give you a pamphlet to read about it.
   d) use a plastic model of a knee to show what was wrong.

9. You want to learn a new software program, skill, or game on a computer. You would:
   a) follow the diagrams in the book that came with it.
   b) talk with people who know about the program.
   c) read the written instructions that came with the program.
   d) use the controls or keyboard and try things out.

10. I like websites that have:
    a) interesting design and visual features.
    b) audio channels where I can hear music, radio programs or interviews.
    c) interesting written descriptions, lists and explanations.
    d) things I can click on or try out.

11. Other than price, what would most influence your decision to buy a new nonfiction book?
    a) The cover looks appealing.
    b) A friend talks about it and recommends it.
    c) You quickly read parts of it.
    d) It contains real-life stories, experiences, and examples.

12. You are using a book, CD, or website to learn how to take photos with your new digital camera. You would like to have:
    a) diagrams showing the camera and what each part does.
    b) a chance to ask questions and talk about the camera and its features.
    c) clear written instructions with lists and bullet points about what to do.
    d) many examples of good and poor photos and how to improve them.

13. Do you prefer a teacher or a presenter who uses:
    a) diagrams, charts, or graphs?
    b) question and answer, talk, group discussion, or guest speakers?
    c) handouts, books, or readings?
    d) demonstrations, models, field trips, role plays, or practical exercises?

14. You have finished a competition or test and would like some feedback. You would like to have feedback:
    a) using graphs showing what you achieved.
    b) from somebody who talks it through with you.
    c) in a written format, describing your results.
    d) using examples from what you have done.

15. You are going to choose food at a restaurant or cafe. You would:
    a) look at what others are eating or look at pictures of each dish.
    b) ask the server or friends to recommend choices.
    c) choose from the written descriptions in the menu.
    d) choose something that you have had there before.

16. You have to give an important speech at a conference or special occasion. You would:
    a) make diagrams or create graphs to help explain things.
    b) write a few key words and practice your speech over and over.
    c) write out your speech and learn from reading it over several times.
    d) gather many examples and stories to make the talk real and practical.

Source: N. Fleming. (2001–2010). VARK, a Guide to Learning Styles. Version 7.0. Available at http://www.vark-learn.com/english/page .asp?p=questionnaire. Adapted and used with permission from Neil Fleming.

Scoring the VARK

Let's tabulate your results.

Count your choices in each of the four VARK categories.	(a)	(b)	(c)	(d)
	Visual	Aural	Read/Write	Kinesthetic

Now that you've calculated your scores, do they match your perceptions of yourself as a learner? Could you have predicted them? The VARK's creators believe that *you* are best qualified to verify and interpret your own results.[13]

Using Your Sensory Preferences

Knowing your preferences can help you in your academic coursework. If your highest score (by 4 or 5 points) is in one of the four VARK modalities, that particular learning modality is your preferred one.[14] If your scores are more or less even between several or all four modalities, these scores mean that you don't have a strong preference for any single modality. A lower score in a preference simply means that you are more comfortable using other styles. If your VARK results contain a zero in a particular learning modality, you may realize that you do indeed dislike this mode or find it unhelpful. You might want to reflect on why you don't like to use this learning modality. To learn more about your results and suggestions for applying them, see Figure 3.1 for your preferred modality.

Most college classes emphasize reading and writing; however, if your lowest score is in the read/write modality, don't assume you're academically doomed. VARK can help you discover alternative, more productive ways to learn the same course material. You may learn to adapt naturally to a particular instructor or discipline's preferences, using a visual modality in your economics class to interpret graphs and a kinesthetic modality in your chemistry lab to conduct experiments.

However, you may also find that you need to deliberately and strategically reroute your learning methods in some of your classes, and knowing your VARK preferences can help you do that. Learning to capitalize on your preferences

	Everyday Study Strategies	Exam Preparation Strategies
VISUAL	• Convert your lecture notes to a visual format. • Study the placement of items, colors, and shapes in your textbook. • Put complex concepts into flowcharts or graphs. • Redraw ideas you create from memory.	• Practice turning your visuals back into words. • Practice writing out exam answers. • Recall the pictures you made of the pages you studied. • Use diagrams to answer exam questions, if your instructor will allow it.
AURAL	• Read your notes aloud. • Explain your notes to another auditory learner. • Ask others to "hear" your understanding of the material. • Record your notes or listen to your instructors' podcasts. • Realize that your lecture notes may be incomplete. You may have become so involved in listening that you stopped writing. Fill your notes in later by talking with other students or getting material from the textbook.	• Practice by speaking your answers aloud. • Listen to your own voice as you answer questions. • Opt for an oral exam if allowed. • Imagine you are talking with the teacher as you answer questions.
READ/WRITE	• Write out your lecture notes again and again. • Read your notes (silently) again and again. • Put ideas and principles into different words. • Translate diagrams, graphs, etc., into text. • Rearrange words and "play" with wording. • Turn diagrams and charts into words.	• Write out potential exam answers. • Practice creating and taking exams. • Type out your answers to potential test questions. • Organize your notes into lists or bullets. • Write practice paragraphs, particularly beginnings and endings.
KINESTHETIC	• Recall experiments, field trips, etc. Remember the real things that happened. • Talk over your notes with another "K" person. • Use photos and pictures that make ideas come to life. • Go back to the lab, your manual, or your notes that include real examples. • Remember that your lecture notes will have gaps if topics weren't concrete or relevant for you. • Use case studies to help you learn abstract principles.	• Role-play the exam situation in your room (or the actual classroom). • Put plenty of examples into your answers. • Write practice answers and sample paragraphs. • Give yourself practice tests.

(from top to bottom) Marcela Barsse/MarsBars/iStockphoto.com; Johanna Goodyear/Dreamstime.com; Nadezda Firsova/iStockphoto.com; Pascal Genest/iStockphoto.com

and translate challenging course material into your preferred modality may serve you well. Remember these suggestions about the VARK, and try them out to see if they improve your academic results.

FIGURE 3.1

Visual, Aural, Read/ Write, and Kinesthetic Learning Strategies

1. **VARK preferences are not necessarily strengths.** However, VARK is an excellent vehicle to help you reflect on how you learn and begin to reinforce the productive strategies you're already using or select ones that might work better.

2. **If you have a strong preference for a particular modality, practice multiple suggestions listed in Figure 3.1 for that particular modality.** Reinforce your learning by doing many things in that column.

3. **An estimated 60 percent of people are** multimodal**.** In a typical classroom of 30 students (based on VARK data):

   multimodal prefer to use more than one sense

   ≫ 17 students would be multimodal,

   ≫ 1 student would be visual,

> 1 student would be aural,

> 5 students would be read/write,

> 6 students would be kinesthetic,

and the teacher would most likely have a strong read/write preference![15]

4. **If you are multimodal, as most of us are, it may be necessary to use several of your modalities to boost your confidence in your learning.** Practice the suggestions for all of your preferred modalities.

5. **While in an ideal world, it would be good to try to strengthen lesser preferences, you may wish to save that goal for later in life.** Some experts suggest that college isn't the place to experiment. Grades count, and your continuing success will depend on how well you do. You may decide it's better to try to strengthen your current preferences now and work on expanding your lesser preferences later. This book will give you an opportunity to practice your VARK learning preferences—whatever they are—in each chapter. Ultimately, learning at your best is up to you.

Gaining the insights provided in this chapter and acting on them have the potential to greatly affect your college success. Understand yourself, capitalize on your preferences, build on them, focus, and learn!

What Role Does Your Personality Play?

One of the best things about college is having a chance to meet so many different types of people. At times you may find these differences intriguing. At other times, they may baffle you. Look around and listen to other students, and you'll start to notice. Have you heard students saying totally opposite things such as those listed here?

"There's no way I can study at home. It's way too noisy."

"There's no way I can study in the library. It's way too quiet."

"I'm so glad I've already decided on a major. Now I can go full steam ahead."

"I have no idea what to major in. I can think of six different majors I'd like to choose."

"My sociology instructor is great. She talks about all kinds of things in class, and her essay tests are actually fun!"

"My sociology instructor is so confusing. She talks about so many different things in class. How am I supposed to know what to study for her tests?"[16]

You're likely to run into all kinds of viewpoints and all types of people, but, differences make life much more interesting! We're each unique. Perhaps your friends comment on your personality by saying, "She's really quiet," or "He's a 'party animal'," or "He's incredibly logical," or "She trusts her gut feelings." What you may not know is how big a role your personality plays in how you prefer to learn.

The Myers-Briggs Type Indicator® (MBTI) is the most well-known personality assessment instrument in the world. Each year, approximately four million people worldwide get a look into their personalities, their career choices, their interaction with others, and their learning styles by completing it. If you are able to complete the full Myers-Briggs Type Indicator in the class for which you're using this textbook, or through your college counseling center or learning center, do so. You'll learn a great deal about yourself.

The Myers-Briggs Type Indicator shows you your preferences in four areas:

" **Each person is an exception to the rule.** "

Carl Jung, psychiatrist
(1875–1961)

1. **What energizes you and where do you direct energy?** Do you get energy from other people (**E**xtravert) or do you go within yourself to find strength (**I**ntrovert)?

2. **How do you gather information and what kind of information do you trust?** Do you trust your senses and factually based information (**S**ensor) or do you trust your gut feelings (i**N**tuition)?

3. **How do you make decisions, arrive at conclusions, and make judgments?** Do you think things through logically (**T**hinker) or do you care about how others react and feel (**F**eeler)?

4. **How do you relate to the outer world?** Do you prefer organization and structure (**J**udging) or do you like spontaneity and going with the flow (**P**erceiver)?

If you take the Myers-Briggs Type Indicator you should realize that it isn't about what you *can* do. It's about what you *prefer* to do. Here's an illustration. Write your name on the line first line.

_____

_____

Now put the pen in your other hand, and try writing your name on the second line. What was different the second time around? For most people, the second try takes longer, is messier, probably feels strange, and requires more concentration. But could you do it? Yes. It's just that you prefer doing it the first way. The first way is easier and more natural; the second way makes a simple task seem like hard work! It's possible that you might have to try "writing with your other hand" in college—doing things that don't come naturally.

In the "FOCUS Challenge Case," Tammy was described as outgoing (**E**xtraverted) and hands-on (**S**ensing) while Mr. Caldwell was described as reserved

(**I**ntroverted) and theoretical (i**N**tuitive). It's unlikely that Mr. Caldwell will change his teaching style, and even if he did, students in his class have a variety of learning styles. Whose style would he try to match? Both Tammy's personality and Mr. Caldwell's are similar to the most common types found in college classrooms. Although you couldn't be sure without looking at actual MBTI scores, you'd expect Tammy to be an ESFP. ESFP's are outgoing, like facts as opposed to theories, pay attention to the feelings of others, and prefer exploring options to following a structure. Based on the clues in the "FOCUS Challenge Case," you'd also expect Mr. Caldwell to be an INTJ—the opposite.

This chapter has covered learning from several different perspectives, and you now know more about yourself as a learner than you did before you read it. But you may be wondering: So how do Multiple Intelligences, VARK preferences, and personality traits (MBTI) work together to produce a unique learner? Although the three perspectives aren't intended to connect, let's look at this example to help you understand how each one would explain how people learn.

Let's say the person you sit by in your math class always asks you if you want to join his study group. Based on what you've learned in this chapter, you'd be more likely to say yes if you:

1. **MI:** have *interpersonal* (or social) intelligence

2. **VARK:** are an *aural* learner who likes to discuss things

3. **MBTI:** are *extroverted* (you get energy from other people).

The three perspectives don't overlap; they're different. That's why this chapter presents all three. Each perspective explains how people learn in a different way.

While simply knowing about these three perspectives is good, it's important to go further and act on that knowledge. As a single learner in a larger class, you will need to adjust to the teaching style of your instructor in ways such as the following:

> **Translate for maximum comfort.** The way to maximize your comfort as a learner is to find ways to translate from your instructor's preferences to yours. If you know that you prefer feeling over thinking, and your instructor's style is based on thinking, make the course material come alive by personalizing it. How does the topic relate to you, your lifestyle, your family, and your future choices?

> **Make strategic choices.** While learning preferences can help explain your academic successes, it's also important not to use them to rationalize your nonsuccesses. An introvert could say, "I could have aced that assignment if the instructor had let me work alone! I hate group projects." Become the best learner you can be at what you're naturally good at. But also realize that you'll need to become more versatile over time. In the workforce, you will not always be able to choose what you do and how you do it. Actively choose your learning strategies, rather than simply hoping for the best. Remember: No one can learn for you, just as no one can eat for you.

> **Take full advantage.** College will present you with an extensive menu of learning opportunities. You will also build on your learning as you

move beyond your general, introductory classes into courses in your chosen major—and across and between classes. Don't fall victim to the temptation to make excuses as some students do ("I could have been more successful in college if . . . I hadn't had to work so many hours . . . I hadn't had a family to support . . . my instructors had been more supportive. . . ." If, if, if. College may well be the most concentrated and potentially powerful learning opportunity you'll ever have. Ultimately, learning at your best is up to you.

VARK Activity

Complete the activity recommended for your preferred VARK learning style and bring it to class (or follow your instructor's instructions).

 Visual: Put together a collage of photos that represents how you learn. Post it on the course blog or website, assemble it on a posterboard, or make a PowerPoint slide show.

 Aural: Discuss your multiple intelligences and VARK preferences that affect learning with your friends or family. See if they can predict their own scores (generally). Access the CourseMate via www.cengagebrain.com/shop/ISBN/0495906433 to listen to the iAudio summary for this chapter.

 Read/Write: Write a one-paragraph summary of what you have learned about yourself as a result of reading this chapter.

 Kinesthetic: Use a variety of kinesthetic learning techniques to prepare for an upcoming quiz or exam in this class or another one. Did the techniques help you master the material? Report your results.

(from top to bottom) Marcela Barsse/MarsBars/iStockphoto.com; Johanna Goodyear/Dreamstime.com; Nadezda Firsova/iStockphoto.com; Pascal Genest/iStockphoto.com

step 3
INSIGHT *Now* What Do You Think?

At the beginning of this chapter, Tammy Ko faced a series of challenges as a new college student. Now after learning from this chapter, would you respond differently to any of the questions you answered about the "FOCUS Challenge Case"? Using what you learned in the chapter, write a paragraph ending to Tammy's case study. What are some of the possible outcomes for her?

step 4
ACTION Your Plans for Change

1. Identify one new thing you learned in reading this chapter. Why did you select the topic you've selected? How will it affect what you do in your college classes?

2. How will you put the information from this chapter to good use, not only in this class, but in any others you're enrolled in this term?

3. List your learning and personality preferences as you discovered them in this chapter here:

   Multiple Intelligences _____

   VARK _____

   MBTI _____

   What do you think these preferences reveal about you and how you learn?

What did you **Learn?**

On a scale of 1 to 5, answer these questions now that you've completed this chapter.

1 = not very/not much/very little/low   5 = very/a lot/very much/high

How much do you know *now*?

Now rate your current level of knowledge about topics covered in this chapter.

Learning and the human brain

        1 2 3 4 5

Multiple intelligences

        1 2 3 4 5

Sensory preferences for learning

        1 2 3 4 5

Becoming a better learner

        1 2 3 4 5

How useful might the information in this chapter be to you?

How much do you think this information might affect your college success?

        1 2 3 4 5

How much do you think this information might affect your career success after college?

        1 2 3 4 5

How long did it actually take you to complete this chapter (both the reading and writing tasks)?

_____ Hour(s) _____ Minutes

Challenge Yourself Online Quiz. To find out how much you've learned, access the CourseMate via www.cengagebrain.com/shop/ISBN/0495906433 to take the Challenge Yourself Online Quiz.

Compare these answers to your answers from the "Readiness Check" at the beginning of this chapter. How might the gaps between what you thought before starting the chapter and what you now think affect how you approach the next chapter?

chapter 4
Managing Your Time, Energy and Money

You're About to Discover...
- ✔ Why time management alone doesn't work
- ✔ How time management differs from energy management
- ✔ How to schedule your way to success
- ✔ How the P word can derail you
- ✔ How to realistically balance work, school, and personal life
- ✔ How to manage your money

©Larry Harwood Photography. Property of Cengage Learning

READINESS CHECK | What do you **Know?**

Before beginning this chapter, take a moment to answer these questions. Your answers will help you assess how ready you are to focus.

1 = not very/not much/very little/low   5 = very/a lot/very much/high

How much do you *already* know?

Rate your current level of knowledge about topics covered in this chapter.

Time management vs. energy management

    1 2 3 4 5

Procrastination

    1 2 3 4 5

Balancing work, school, and personal life

    1 2 3 4 5

Money management

    1 2 3 4 5

How motivated are you to learn *more*?

In general, how motivated are you to learn the material in this chapter?

    1 2 3 4 5

How much do you think this information might affect your college success?

    1 2 3 4 5

How much do you think this information might affect your career success after college?

    1 2 3 4 5

How ready are you to read *now*?

How ready are you to focus on this chapter—physically, intellectually, and emotionally? Which of these three areas is most challenging for you right now? Circle a number to represent it.

    1 2 3 4 5

If any of your answers is below a 3, consider addressing the issue before reading.

Then, read the chapter carefully, while looking for ways to improve your focus.

Finally, how long do you think it will take you to complete this chapter? If you start and stop, keep track of the overall time.

———— Hour(s) ———— Minutes

DEREK JOHNSON

As Derek Johnson walked out of his World History class on Wednesday evening, he felt panicked. The instructor had just assigned a twelve-page paper, due one month from today. How could she? Derek thought. *Doesn't she realize how busy most returning students are?* The syllabus had mentioned a paper, but twelve pages seemed downright excessive. He sent a tweet complaining about it from his phone on his way to his next class. Twitter was quickly becoming Derek's favorite way to communicate.

MAKE TO-DO LIST!?

REMEMBER TO BUY MOM A BIRTHDAY GIFT!!!

REMEMBER: COMPUTER TRAINING CLASS FOR WORK ON WEDNESDAY!

© Hintau Aliaksei, 2009/ Used under license from Shutterstock.com

Blackpixel/ Shutterstock.com

fotorro/ Shutterstock.com

When Derek had decided to go back to college five years after he graduated from high school, he hadn't quite realized what a juggling act it would require. First, there was his family—his wife, Justine, his four-year-old daughter, Taura, and another baby due before winter break. Then there was his job, which was really quite demanding for what he earned. He hoped that an associate's degree in accounting would help him get a job as an accounting assistant and possibly even move into the management ranks, where the salaries were higher. Money was tight, and they always seemed to run out before payday. Add to that singing in his church choir, coaching the youth soccer league, competing in cycling races, and working out every morning at the gym. Derek had been a high school athlete, and physical fitness was a priority for him.

His head began to swim as he thought about all his upcoming obligations: his mother's birthday next week, his dog's vet appointment, his brother's visit, the training class he was required to attend for work. Something had to go, but he couldn't think of anything he was willing to sacrifice to make time for a twelve-page paper. Maybe he'd have to break down and buy one of those planners, but weren't most people who use those slightly, well . . . compulsive?

Still, the paper was to count as 25 percent of his final grade in the course. He decided he'd try and think of a topic for the paper on his way home. But then he remembered that his wife had asked him to stop at the store to pick up groceries. Somewhere on aisle 12, between the frozen pizza and the frozen yogurt, Derek's thoughts about his research paper vanished.

Andresr/Shutterstock.com

Community Center Gym Schedule

Monday	Tuesday	Wednesday	Thursday	Friday
Open Gym 6:30-8:30	Open Gym 6:30-8:30	Open Gym 6:30-8:30	Open Gym 6:30-8:30	Open Gym 6:30-8:30
Cycling Class 9:00-10:00	Taekwondo Class 9:00-10:00	Taekwondo Class 9:00-10:00	Kick Boxing 9:00-10:00	Cycling Class 9:00-10:00
Taekwondo Class 12:00-1:00	Yoga Class 12:00-1:00	Yoga Class 12:00-1:00	Yoga Class 12:00-1:00	Taekwondo Class 12:00-1:00
Yoga Class 3:00-4:00	Kick Boxing	Cycling	Taekwond	

The following week, the instructor asked the students in the class how their papers were coming along. Some students gave long descriptions of their research progress, the amazing number of sources they'd found, and the detailed outlines they'd put together. Derek didn't raise his hand.

A whole week has gone by, Derek thought on his way back to his car after class. *I have to get going!* Writing had never exactly been Derek's strong suit. In fact, it was something he generally disliked doing. Through a great deal of hard work, he had managed to earn a 3.8 GPA in high school—a record he planned to continue. A course in World History—a general education class that was not even a part of his major—was *not* going to ruin things! The week had absolutely flown by, and there were plenty of good reasons why his paper was getting off to such a slow start. Derek rarely wasted time, except for occasionally watching his favorite TV shows. But then again, with such a jam-packed schedule, he really felt the need to unwind once in a while. Regardless, he rarely missed his nightly study time from 11:00 p.m. to 1:00 a.m. Those two hours were reserved for homework, no matter what.

At the end of class two weeks later, Derek noticed that several students lined up to show the instructor the first drafts of their papers. *That's it!* Derek thought to himself. *The paper is due next Wednesday. I'll spend Monday night, my only free night of the week, in the library. I can get there right after work and stay until 11:00 or so. That'll be five hours of concentrated time. I should be able to write it then.* Despite his good intentions, Derek didn't arrive at the library until nearly 8:00 p.m., and his work session wasn't all that productive. As he sat in his library stall, he found himself obsessing about things that were bothering him at work. His boss was being difficult, and his coworkers were fighting among themselves. Finally, when he glanced at his watch, he was shocked to see that it was already midnight! The library was closing, and he'd only written three pages. Where had the time gone?

On his way out to the car, his cell phone rang. It was Justine, wondering where he was. Taura was running a fever, and his boss had called about an emergency meeting at 7:00 a.m. *If one more thing goes wrong . . . ,* Derek thought to himself. His twelve-page paper was due in two days.

HISTORY PAPER OUTLINE

INTRO...

WORLD HISTORY

Fall Semester Syllabus

Instructor: Julia Alexander
Office: Main Hall 320
Email: Julia.Alexander@campusmail.edu
Phone: 555-3424
Office Hours: 12:30-3pm daily

red Textbook:
History, 6th Edition. By William J. Duiker and Jackson J. Spielvogel ISBN: 04955

Exam: 10 @ 10 points each
nalysis: 100pts
ay: 100pts
                                                      50pts
                                                      150pts
                                                      100pts

                                                      500pts

ivilization and the Fertile Crescent
ne: Agriculture and Mesopotamia
wo: The Nile Valley and the Near East

Civilizations
ee: The World of Homer
: Classical Greece and the Golden Age
Rome: The Rise of the Republic
mperial Rome
Rome: The Fall of the Empire
China and the Far East

Accounting Associate

Job Description

We are currently looking for a qualified Accounting As
educational, and industry experience. This is an entry
graduates are encouraged to apply.

Job Responsibilities

Ensure timely collection of vendor A/R
Review, correct, and update sub ledger transactions a
Transaction review
Vendor follow-up and research
Vendor disputes
Inventor

CampusLibrary

FALL SEMESTER HOURS

Monday – Thursday: 8 am – Midnight
Friday – Saturday: 8 am – 8 pm

1. What do you have in common with Derek? What time, energy, or money management issues are you experiencing in your life right now?
2. Describe the time-wasters that are a part of Derek's schedule. Do you think procrastination is an issue for Derek? What's behind his failure to make progress on his paper?
3. Suggest three realistic ways for Derek to balance work, school, and personal life.

Time Management Isn't Enough

Before diving into the details of time management skills, let's clarify one important point. There's a sense in which the phrase *time management* is misleading. Let's say you decide to spend an hour reading an assigned short story for your literature class. You may sit in the library with your book propped open in front of you from 3:00 to 4:00 p.m. on the dot. But you may not digest a single word you're reading. You may be going through the motions, reading on autopilot. Have you managed your time? Technically, yes. Your planner says, "Library, short story for Lit 101, 3:00–4:00 p.m." But did you get results? Time management expert Jeffrey Mayer asks provocatively in the title of his book: *If You Haven't Got the Time to Do It Right, When Will You Find the Time to Do It Over?*. Now that's a good question!

"Time management" is not just about managing your time, it's about managing your attention. Attention management is the ability to focus your attention, not just your time, on a designated activity so that you produce a desired result. Time management may get you through reading a chapter of your textbook, but attention management will make sure that you understand what you're reading. It's about *focus*. If you manage your attention during that hour, then you've managed your time productively. Without attention management, time management is pointless.

Succeeding in school, at work, and in life is not just about what you do. It's about what gets done. You can argue about the effort you put into an academic assignment all you want, but it's doubtful your professor will say, "You know what? You're right. You deserve an A just for staying up late last night working on this paper." Activity and accomplishment aren't the same thing. Neither are quantity and quality. Just because the assignment asked for five pages and you turned in five, doesn't mean that you automatically deserve an A. Results count. So don't confuse being busy with being successful. Staying busy isn't much of a challenge; being successful is.

Here's a list of preliminary academic time-saving tips. However, remember that these suggestions won't give you a surefire recipe for academic success. To manage your time, you must also manage yourself: your energy, your behavior, your attention, your attitudes, *you*. Once you know how to manage all that, managing your time begins to work.

> In truth, people can generally make time for what they choose to do; it is not really the time but the will that is lacking.
>
> *Sir John Lubbock, British banker, politician, and archaeologist (1834–1913)*

> Have a plan for your study session; include suggested time limits for each topic or task.

- Pay attention to what gets you off track. If you come to understand your patterns, you may be better able to control them.

- Turn off your phone or tell other people you live with that you don't want to be disturbed if a call comes in for you. Let them know what time they can tell callers to call you back.

- If you're working on your computer, work offline whenever possible. If you must be online to check sources, don't give in to the temptation to check your social networking account or e-mail every ten minutes.

- Take two minutes to organize your workspace before beginning. Having the resources you need at your fingertips makes the session go much more smoothly, and you won't waste time searching for things you need.

- If you are in a study group, make sure everyone is clear about assigned tasks for the next session. Not knowing who's supposed to do what is a big time-waster for study groups.

- Learn to say no. Saying no to someone, especially someone you care about, can feel awkward at first, but people close to you will understand that you can't do everything.

- Focus. You can't do anything if you try to do everything. Multitasking may work for simple matters, such as scheduling a doctor's appointment while heating up a snack in the microwave. But when it comes to tasks that require brainpower, such as studying or writing, you need a single-minded focus.

- Slow down. Working at something a million miles a minute will most likely result in mistakes. If you rush, you may run out of time and end up settling for less than your best. Try to avoid the "headless chicken" phenomenon.

- Monitor how your life works. There are different ways to manage time, and different ways work best for different people. Think of this analogy: Is time like ice or like water? A hard copy planner is a day-by-day record of solid blocks of time. But in today's world, solid blocks can melt away in seconds as events around us change. Managing time may be less like moving around ice cubes and more like "going with the flow." Many dynamic e-tools are available to help you on a minute-by-minute basis, if you stay on top of how time flows in your life.[1]

> **Don't confuse activity with accomplishment. 'Time = Success' is a myth.**
>
> *Dr. Constance Staley, University of Colorado at Colorado Springs*

multitasking doing two or more tasks at one time

Energy, Our Most Precious Resource

"We live in a digital time. Our rhythms are rushed, rapid-fire and relentless, our days carved up into bits and bytes. . . . We're wired up but we're melting down." So begins a bestselling book, *The Power of Full Engagement: Managing*

Performance, health and happiness are grounded in the skillful management of energy.

Jim Loehr and Tony Schwartz,
from The Power of Full Engagement

Energy, Not Time, Is the Key to High Performance and Personal Renewal. The authors, Jim Loehr and Tony Schwartz, have replaced the term *time management* with the term *energy management.* Their shift makes sense. Since most of us are running in overdrive most of the time, energy is our most precious resource.

Energy management experts say you can't control time—everyone has a fixed amount—but you can manage your energy. And in fact, it's your responsibility to do so. Once a day is gone, it's gone. But your energy can be renewed.

It's clear that some things are energy *drains:* bad news, illness, interpersonal conflict, time-consuming hassles, a heavy meal, rainy days. Likewise, some things are energy *gains* giving you a surge of freshness: a new job, good friends, music, laughter, fruit, coffee. It's a good idea to recognize your own personal energy drains and gains so that you know how and when to renew your supply.[2] Energy management experts say it's not just about *spending time,* it's about *expending energy:*

> physical energy

> emotional energy

> mental energy

> spiritual energy

Of the four dimensions of energy, let's take a closer look at the first two. To do your very best academically, it helps to be *physically* energized and *emotionally* connected. Physical energy is measured in terms of *quantity.* How much energy do you have—a lot or a little? Emotional energy, on the other hand, is measured by *quality.* What kind of energy do you have—positive or negative? If you put them together into a two-dimensional chart with *quantity* as the vertical axis and *quality* as the horizontal axis, you get something like Figure 4.1.

FIGURE 4.1

The Dynamics of Energy[3]

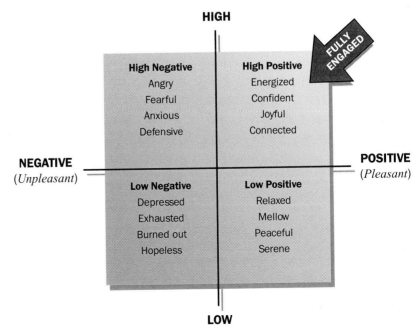

When you're operating in the upper right quarter of the chart with high, positive energy, you're most productive, which makes sense. The question is: How do you get there? How do you make certain you're physically energized and emotionally connected so that you can do your best, academically?

Get Physically Energized

To make sure you're physically energized, try these suggestions.

1. **Snap to your body's rhythm.** Have you noticed times of the day when it's easier to concentrate than others? Perhaps you regularly crash in the middle of the afternoon, for example, so you go for a chocolate fix, or a coffee pick-me-up. Everyone has a biological clock. Paying attention to your body's natural rhythms is important. Plan to do activities that require you to be alert during your natural productivity peaks. That's better than plodding through a tough assignment when the energy just isn't there. Use low energy times to take care of mindless chores that require little to no brainpower.[4]

2. **Up and at 'em.** What about 8:00 a.m. classes? Don't use your body's natural rhythms as an excuse to sleep through class! ("I'm just not a morning person. . . .") If you're truly not a morning person, don't sign up for early morning classes. If you are coming off working a night shift, you may need some rest first. Sleeping through your obligations won't do much for your success—and you'll be playing a continual game of catch-up, which takes even more time. Some experts advise that you start your day as early as possible. Marking six items off your to-do list before lunch can give you a real high.[5]

3. **Sleep at night, study during the day.** Burning the midnight oil and pulling all-nighters aren't the best ideas, either. It only takes one all-nighter to help you realize that a lack of sleep translates into a drop in performance. Without proper sleep, your ability to understand and remember course material is impaired. Research shows that the average adult requires seven to eight hours of sleep each night. If you can't get that much for whatever reason, take a short afternoon nap. Did you know that the Three Mile Island nuclear meltdown in Pennsylvania in 1979 and the Chernobyl disaster in the Ukraine in 1986 took place at 4 a.m. and 1:23 a.m., respectively? Experts believe it's no coincidence that both these events took place when workers would normally be sleeping.[6]

4. **"Burn premium fuel."** You've heard it before: Food is the fuel that makes us run. The better the fuel, the smoother we run. It's that simple. A solid diet of carbs—pizza, chips, and cookies—jammed into the fuel tank of your car would certainly gum up the works! When the demands on your energy are high, such as exam week, use premium fuel. If you don't believe it, think about how many people you know get sick during time of high stress. Watch how many of your classmates are hacking and coughing their way through exams—or in bed missing them altogether.

Get Emotionally Connected

Physical needs count, to be sure, but emotional connections are part of the picture too. See if you agree with these suggestions.

1. **Communicate like it matters.** Sometimes we save our best communicating for people we think we have to impress: teachers, bosses, or clients, for example. But what about the people we care about most in our lives? Sometimes these people get the leftovers after all the "important" communicating has been done for the day. Sometimes we're so comfortable with these people that we think we can let it all hang out, even when doing so is *not* a pretty sight. Communicate as if everything you said would actually come true—"Just drop dead," for instance—and watch the difference! Communicating productively with people we care about is one of the best ways to replenish our energy.

2. **Choose how you renew.** Finish this comparison: Junk food is to physical energy as _____ is to emotional energy. If you answered "TV," you're absolutely right. Most people use television as their primary form of emotional renewal, but, like junk food, it's not that nutritious and it's easy to consume

Stressed Out?

> **There is more to life than increasing its speed.**
> —MOHANDAS K. GANDHI, INDIAN SPIRITUAL LEADER
> (1869–1948)

What does the word *spirituality* mean to you? Do you picture a church, respond with the name of an organized religion, or think about looking inward or examining your life? According to a national study of 112,232 college students, four out of five first-year students are interested in spirituality, and nearly three-fourths report feeling a sense of connection with a higher power. Nearly half believe that college should help encourage their expression of spirituality.[7] Can college help you examine your values, find inner direction, ponder the meaning of life, and possibly lower your stress level?

Devon Stephens/iStockphoto.com

TRY IT!

Do you think paying attention to your spiritual health has the potential to lower your stress level? To help you think about your answer to this question, respond to the items below:

1. It's easy to get caught up in day-to-day details, like kids, jobs, and bills. But many experts believe that you can lower your stress level by taking time out to consider "life's bigger picture"—through yoga, meditation, prayer, or exercise, for example. Do you practice any of these? Do they help you manage stress?

2. Think about your college classes. Does "big picture" thinking come up (directly or indirectly) in any of them? If so, which class—and where has your thinking led you?

3. Sometimes spirituality is simply about freeing up your mind and slowing down long enough to think more deeply than usual. Make a promise to yourself to find time to do that this week, and then pay attention to the results. What were they?

too much. Try more engaging activities that affirm you: singing or reading or playing a sport.[8]

3. **Let others renew you.** Remember that people don't just make demands on your time, they can provide emotional renewal. There's pure joy in a child's laugh, a friend's smile, a father's pat on the back. These small pleasures in life are priceless—prize them!

We've focused on physical and emotional energy here, but remember that all four dimensions of energy—physical, emotional, mental, and spiritual—are interconnected. If you subtract one from the equation, you'll be firing on less than four cylinders. If you are fully engaged and living life to the fullest, all four dimensions of your energy equation will be in balance.

"I'll Study in My Free Time" ... and When Is That?

EXERCISE 4.1

Where Did the Time Go?

How do you spend your time? Complete this self-assessment to find out how you spend your time. Fill in the number of hours you spend doing each of the following, then multiply your answer by the number given (7 or 5 to figure weekly amounts) where appropriate.

	Number of hours per day
Sleeping:	_____ × 7 = _____
Personal grooming (for example, showering, shaving, putting on makeup):	_____ × 7 = _____
Eating (meals and snacks; include preparation or driving time):	_____ × 7 = _____
Commuting Monday thru Friday (to school and work):	_____ × 5 = _____
Doing errands and chores:	_____ × 7 = _____
Spending time with family (parents, children, or spouse):	_____ × 7 = _____
Spending time with boyfriend or girlfriend:	_____ × 7 = _____

	Number of hours per week
At work:	_____
In classes:	_____
At regularly scheduled functions (church, clubs, etc.):	_____
Socializing, hanging out, watching TV, talking on the phone, etc.:	_____

Now add up all the numbers in the far right column, and subtract your total from 168, the number of hours in a week.

168 – _____ = _____. *This is the total number of hours you have remaining in your week for that ever-important task of studying. You may wish to revise how much time you spend on other activities of your life, based on whether or not you're already short on hours without studying factored in.*

Ask ten students when they study, and chances are at least eight will reply, "in my free time." The strange thing about this statement is that if you actually waited until you had free time to study, you probably never would. Truthfully, some students are amazed at how easily a day can race by without ever thinking about cracking a book. This is why you should actually *schedule* your study time, but to do that, you should first be aware of how you're currently spending those twenty-four hours of each day.

Notice that Exercise 4.1 places studying at the bottom of the list, even though it's vital to your success in college. The exercise reflects a common attitude among college students, namely that studying is what takes place after everything else gets done. Where does schoolwork rank on *your* list of priorities?

If succeeding in college is a top priority for you, then make sure that you're devoting adequate time to schoolwork outside the classroom. Most instructors expect you to study two to three hours outside of class for every hour spent in class. If it's a particularly challenging class, you may need even more study time. You can use the following chart to calculate the total number of hours you ought to expect to study—effectively—each week:

Credit hours for less demanding classes: _____ × 2 hours = _____ hours

Credit hours for typical/average classes: _____ × 3 hours = _____ hours

Credit hours for more challenging classes: _____ × 4 hours = _____ hours

Expected total study time per week = _____ hours

Remember, just putting in the time won't guarantee that you'll truly *understand* what you're studying. You need to ensure that your study time is productive by focusing your attention and strategically selecting study techniques that work best for you.

BOX 4.1

Lame Excuses for Blowing Off Class

Do you find yourself skipping class at times in order to do something else: getting an oil change for your car, soaking up the sun's rays, or socializing with a friend on the phone? If so, ask yourself this: Would you walk into a gas station, put a $50 bill down on the counter to prepay for a tank of gas, and then put in a dollar's worth and drive off? Absolutely not, you say?

Would you buy a $10 movie ticket and then just toss it in the trash because you decided there was something else you'd rather do on the spur of the moment? No way!

Why, then, would you purchase much more expensive "tickets" to class—the average cost of an hour in class may be as high as $100, $150, or $200 or more—and then toss them in the trash by not attending? Don't you value your money more than that? More importantly, don't you value yourself more than that?

The next time you're tempted to opt out of your scheduled classes, ask yourself if you really want to throw away money, in addition to the opportunity. Check your priorities, then put one foot in front of the other and walk into that classroom. In the long run, it's the best investment in your own future.

Schedule Your Way to Success

Time Monitor

Can you remember how you spent all your time yesterday? Using the following Time Monitor, fill in as much as you can remember about how you spent your time yesterday for the complete 24-hour period. Be as detailed as possible, right down to thirty-minute segments.

7:00 A.M. _____	3:00 _____	11:00 _____
7:30 _____	3:30 _____	11:30 _____
8:00 _____	4:00 _____	12:00 A.M. _____
8:30 _____	4:30 _____	12:30 _____
9:00 _____	5:00 _____	1:00 _____
9:30 _____	5:30 _____	1:30 _____
10:00 _____	6:00 _____	2:00 _____
10:30 _____	6:30 _____	2:30 _____
11:00 _____	7:00 _____	3:00 _____
11:30 _____	7:30 _____	3:30 _____
12:00 P.M. _____	8:00 _____	4:00 _____
12:30 _____	8:30 _____	4:30 _____
1:00 _____	9:00 _____	5:00 _____
1:30 _____	9:30 _____	5:30 _____
2:00 _____	10:00 _____	6:00 _____
2:30 _____	10:30 _____	6:30 _____

Now monitor how you use your time today (or tomorrow if you're reading this at night), or your instructor may have you complete this Time Monitor for a several days. You can use the additional Time Monitor available in the appendix or create your own on a piece of paper. Again, be very specific. You will refer back to this exercise later in this chapter. At the conclusion of your record-keeping for this exercise, go back to Exercise 4.1 and check to see how accurate your estimates were.

There is no one right way to schedule your time, but if you experiment with the system presented in this book, you'll be on the right path. Eventually, you can tweak the system to make it uniquely your own. Try these eight steps, and schedule your way to success!

Have you ever thought about how many dozens, if not hundreds, of choices you make each day? From the second you wake up, you're making decisions, even about the simplest things, like whether to order a cappuccino or a latté; decaf, half-caf, or high-octane; nonfat, two-percent, or the real deal.

Psychologist and professor Barry Schwartz, in his book, *The Paradox of Choice: Why More Is Less*, believes that making non-stop choices can actually cause us to "invest time, energy, and no small amount of self-doubt, and dread." Choosing a new cell phone plan can take some people weeks while they research models of cell phones, minutes available, quotas of text messages, and Internet access, not to mention the fine print. Simply put: Being flooded with choices, while it feels luxurious, can be stressful and even unrewarding. Paralysis, anxiety, and stress rather than happiness, satisfaction, and perfection can be the result of too much "more."

Some of us, Schwartz says, are "maximizers"; we don't rest until we find the best. Others of us are "satisficers"; we're satisfied with what's good enough, based on our most important criteria. Of course, we all do some "maximizing" and some "satisficing," but generally, which are you?

Here are Schwartz's recommendations to lower our stress levels in a society where more can actually give us less, especially in terms of quality of life:

1. **Choose to choose**. Some decisions are worth lengthy deliberation; others aren't. Be conscious of the choices you make and whether they're worth the return on your investment. "Maximize" when it counts and "satisfice" when it doesn't.

2. **Remember that there's always greener grass somewhere**. Someone will always have a better job than you do, a nicer apartment, or a more attractive romantic partner. Regret or envy can eat away at you, and second-guessing can bring unsettling dissatisfaction.

3. **Regret less and appreciate more**. While green grass does abound, so do sandpits and bumpy roads. That's an important realization, too! Value the good things you already have going for you.

4. **Build bridges, not walls**. Think about the ways in which the dozens of choices you've already made as a new college student give you your own unique profile or "choice-print": where you live, which classes you take, clubs you join, campus events you attend, your small circle of friends, and on and on. Remember that, and make conscious choices that will best help you succeed.[9]

STEP 1: Fill Out a "Term on a Page" Calendar. Right up front, create a "Term on a Page" calendar that shows the entire school term on one page. (See Exercise 4.3.) This calendar allows you to see the big picture. You will need to have the syllabus from each of your classes and your school's course schedule to do this step properly. The following items should be transferred onto your "Term on a Page" calendar:

> Holidays when your school is closed

> Exam and quiz dates from your syllabi

> Project or paper deadlines from your syllabi

> Relevant administrative deadlines (e.g., registration for the next term, drop dates)

> Birthdays and anniversaries to remember

> Important out-of-town travel

> Dates that pertain to other family members, such as days that your children's school is closed or that your spouse is out of town for a conference—anything that will impact your ability to attend classes or study

Take care of your minutes, and the hours will take care of themselves.

Lord Chesterfield, British statesman and diplomat (1694–1773)

EXERCISE 4.3

Term on a Page

Take a few minutes right now to create your own Term on a Page using the charts in Figure 4.2.

Term ______ Year ______

FIGURE 4.2

Term on a Page

Month:	Sunday	Monday	Tuesday	Wednesday	Thursday	Friday	Saturday

Month:	Sunday	Monday	Tuesday	Wednesday	Thursday	Friday	Saturday

Month:	Sunday	Monday	Tuesday	Wednesday	Thursday	Friday	Saturday

Month:	Sunday	Monday	Tuesday	Wednesday	Thursday	Friday	Saturday

Month:	Sunday	Monday	Tuesday	Wednesday	Thursday	Friday	Saturday

STEP 2: Invest in a Planner. While it's good to have the big picture, you must also develop an ongoing scheduling system that works for you. Using the "It's all right up here in my head" method is a surefire way to miss an important appointment, fly past the deadline for your term paper without a clue, or lose track of the time you have left to complete multiple projects.

Although your instructor will typically provide you with a class syllabus that lists test dates and assignment deadlines, trying to juggle multiple syllabi—not to mention your personal and work commitments—is enough to drive you crazy. You need *one* central place for all of your important deadlines, appointments, and commitments. This central place is a planner—a calendar book with space to write in each day. Derek Johnson in the "FOCUS Challenge Case" expressed his view that planners are for nerds and worry warts. Not true! Most every successful person on the planet uses one.

When you go planner shopping, remember that you don't have to break the bank unless you want to. Many new college students find that an ordinary paper-and-pencil daily calendar from an office supply store works best. Having a full page for each day means you can write your daily to-do list right in your planner (more on to-do lists later), and that can be a huge help. Using an online calendar, like Google calendar, can work, too. But remember that unless you have a smart cell phone with Internet access, an online calendar won't be portable, and you'll have to remember to enter events later.

CAREER OUTLOOK: *Shaun Moreno, Accountant*

© Monkey Business Images/Shutterstock

Q1: Why did you decide to pursue a career in accounting?

I was good with numbers and had an interest in understanding how businesses worked, both from an operational and a financial point of view. Being an accountant helps you understand these things. I've also always wanted to eventually own my own business, or at least be the CEO of one some day. Understanding the financial side of things is key to positions of leadership.

Q2: Beyond going to college, what else helped prepare you for your career?

Believe it or not, I would say retail experience, customer service, and even food service helped me understand business as a process. It helped me understand money, what it takes to make a profit, and why the human side of business is so important.

Q3: What are the best and worst aspects of your career field?

At some points during the year that are related to the fiscal calendar, your job may demand more of your time, and you work longer and harder. Unless you enter governmental accounting where hours are mandated or restricted, there may be some times when you feel like all you do is work. The best parts of my work are job security and advancement opportunities. Companies always need accountants, and today there's increasing demand

for companies to be more open about their business dealings. Companies must comply with particular regulations, and accountants help them do that.

Q4: What if anything has surprised you about your career?

I didn't know the field of accounting had so many specialty areas. I had always thought all accountants were

STEP 3: Transfer Important Dates. The next step is to transfer important dates for the whole term from your "Term on a Page" overview to the appropriate days in your planner. This may seem repetitious, but there's a method to the madness. While it's important to be able to see all of your due dates together to create a big picture, it's equally important to have these dates recorded in your actual planner because you will use it more regularly—as the final authority on your schedule.

STEP 4: Set Intermediate Deadlines. After recording the important dates for the entire academic term, look at the individual due dates for major projects or papers that are assigned. Then set intermediate stepping-stone goals that will ultimately help you accomplish your final goals. Working backward from the due date, choose and record deadlines for completing certain chunks of the work. For example, if you have a research paper due, you could set an intermediate deadline for completing all of your initial research and other deadlines for the prewriting, writing, and rewriting steps for the paper.

STEP 5: Schedule Fixed Activities for the Entire Term. Next you'll want to schedule in all fixed activities throughout the entire term: class meeting times and reading assignments, religious services you regularly attend, club meetings, and family activities. It's also a great idea to schedule brief review sessions for your classes. Of course, sometimes you'll be going directly into

the same, debits and credits, and that's it. But accountants can do many different things: preparing and filing tax returns, preparing and filing Security Exchange Commission documents, calculating the profitability of a job or project, working on mergers and acquisitions, or being internal or external auditors. The list goes on and on, but that was what surprised me most, the endless number of ways to be an accountant.

HOW WOULD *YOU* LIKE IT?

Have you ever considered a career in accounting?

Facts to Consider[10]

Academic preparation required: Most accounting positions require at least a bachelor's degree in accounting or a related field. Accounting assistant positions require an associate's degree, but formal training at the college level in accounting is imperative.

Future workforce demand: With stricter accounting regulations being put on corporations, the job market for accountants is expected to grow significantly in the coming years.

Work environment: Typically accountants work in professional office environments, but in some cases they may work from home or other remote locations. Oftentimes accountants travel to client's offices to perform work, as well.

Essential skills: To be an accounting assistant, you must be extremely organized, good with numbers, and pay very close attention to detail. Computer skills such as knowing how to do spreadsheets and working with book-keeping software programs are essential as well. Also, you must be a strong communicator as the information you will be communicating is absolutely crucial to the company you're working for.

Questions to Ponder

1. Do you have (or could you acquire) the skills this career requires?
2. Are you interested in a career like this? Why or why not?

For more career activities online, access the CourseMate via www.cengagebrain.com/shop/ISBN/0495906433 to do the Team Career exercises.

© PhotodiSc/Getty Images

Nothing is so fatiguing as the eternal hanging on of an uncompleted task.

William James, American psychologist and philosopher (1842–1910)

another class, but ten-minute segments of time before and after each class to review your notes helps prepare you for any surprise quizzes and dramatically improves your ability to understand and remember the material.

STEP 6: Check for Schedule Conflicts. Now, take a final look at your planner. Do you notice any major scheduling conflicts, such as a planned business trip smack dab in the middle of midterm exam week? Look for these conflicts now, when there's plenty of time to adjust your plans and talk with your instructor to see what you can work out.

STEP 7: Schedule Flextime. In all the scheduling of important dates, checking and double-checking, don't forget one thing. You do need personal time for eating, sleeping, exercising, and other regular activities that don't have a set time frame. Despite your planner, life will happen. If you get a toothache, you'll need to see a dentist right away. Several times each week, you can count on something coming up that will offer you a chance (or force you) to revise your schedule. The decision of how high the item ranks on your priority list rests with you, but the point is to leave some wiggle room in your schedule.

STEP 8: Monitor Your Schedule Every Day. At this point, you've developed a working time management system. Now it's important to monitor your use of that system on a daily basis. Each night, take three minutes to review the day's activities. How well did you stick to your schedule? Did you accomplish the tasks you set out to do? Do you need to revise your schedule for the rest of the week based on something that happened—or didn't happen—today? This simple process will help you better schedule your time in the future and give you a sense of accomplishment—or of the need for more discipline—for tasks completed, hours worked, and classes attended.

To Do or Not to Do? There *Is* No Question

Part of your personal time management system should be keeping an ongoing to-do list. While the concept of a to-do list sounds relatively simple, here are a few tricks of the trade.

Before the beginning of each school week, brainstorm all the things that you want or need to get done in the upcoming week. Using this random list of to-do items, assign a priority level next to each one. The A-B-C method is simple and easy to use:

A = must get this done; highest priority

B = very important, but not absolutely necessary to get done immediately

C = not terribly important, but should be done right away (time-sensitive)

The two factors to consider when assigning a priority level to a to-do item are *importance* and **urgency**, creating four time zones. Use Figure 4.3 as a guide.[11]

urgency in need of immediate attention

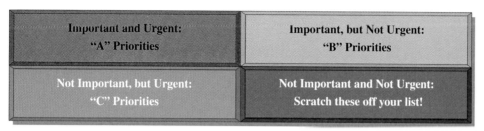

FIGURE 4.3

Time Zones

After you've assigned a time zone to each item, review your list of A and B priorities and ask yourself:

1. **Do any of the items fit best with a particular day of the week?** For example, donating blood may be a high priority task for you, yet you don't want to do it on a day when you have a sports event planned. That might leave you with two available days in the upcoming week that you can donate blood.

2. **Can any items be grouped together to make things easier?** For example, you may have three errands to run downtown on your to-do list, so grouping them together will save you from making three separate trips.

3. **Do any A and B priorities qualify as floating tasks that can be completed anytime, anywhere?** For example, perhaps you were assigned an extra long reading assignment for one of your classes. It's both important and urgent, an A priority item. Bring your book to read while waiting at the dentist's office for your appointment, a B priority. Planning ahead can really help save time.

4. **Do any priorities need to be shifted?** As the days pass, some of your B priorities will become A priorities due to the urgency factor increasing. Or maybe an A priority will become a C priority because something changed about the task. This is normal.

Items you've marked with a C must be decided on a case-by-case basis. But don't let their urgency convince you that you should do them before you accomplish items on your A and B lists. As for those not important and not urgent to-do items, scratch them off the list right now. Life is too short to waste time on unimportant tasks. Give yourself permission to focus on what's important. Since time is a limited resource, one of the best ways to guarantee a successful college experience is to use it wisely. If you don't already use these tools on a regular basis, give them a shot. What do you have to lose except time?

So Much to Do—So Little Time

Assume this is your to-do list for today (Monday). Assign each item one of the four time zones described earlier: A, B, C (and strike through any items that are not urgent and not important). Finally, renumber the items to indicate which you would do first, which second, and so forth.

Start time: 9:00 a.m., Monday morning, during the second week of the fall term.

1. _____ Return Professor Jordan's call before class tomorrow. He left a message saying he wants to talk to you about some problems with the assignment you turned in.
2. _____ Pick up your paycheck and get to the bank before it closes at 5:00 p.m. this afternoon.
3. _____ Call your mother to find out how grandma is doing in the hospital.
4. _____ Start figuring out how to go about your new assignment at work. Your boss seems nervous about it.
5. _____ Call your favorite aunt. She lives overseas in a time zone seven hours ahead of yours. Today is her fiftieth birthday.
6. _____ Stop by the Health Center to take advantage of free meningitis vaccinations today only.
7. _____ Listen to the new music you downloaded yesterday.
8. _____ Leave a note asking your boy- or girlfriend/sibling/child to please stop leaving messes everywhere. It's really aggravating.
9. _____ Read the two chapters in your history textbook for the in-class quiz on Wednesday.
10. _____ Watch the first episode of the new reality TV show you've been waiting for at 9 p.m. tonight.
11. _____ Write a rough draft of the essay due in your composition class on Thursday.
12. _____ Invite an out-of-town friend to spend the weekend.
13. _____ Return the three library books that are a week overdue.
14. _____ Call your math Teaching Assistant and leave a message asking for an appointment during her office hours to get help with the homework due on Wednesday. Nearly everyone is confused about the assignment.
15. _____ Meet your best friend for dinner for his or her birthday at 6 p.m.

Outline the criteria you used for making your decisions. For example, did you base your answers on personal priorities, locations (combining tasks based on where you need to be to do them), urgency/importance, or some other principle? (Note that this exercise asks you to put these tasks in order, according to whatever principles from this chapter you choose—not to figure out how to multitask and accomplish several at once!)

How Time Flies!

According to efficiency expert Michael Fortino, in a lifetime, the average American will spend:

> Seven years in the bathroom
> Six years eating
> Five years waiting in line
> Three years in meetings

> Two years playing telephone tag
> Eight months opening junk mail
> And six months waiting at red lights[12]

What a waste of time! We can't do much about some of these items, but what *can* we do about other time-wasters? Plan—schedule—organize! Think about the issue of control in time management, and write in examples for the following:

1. Things you think you can't control, and you can't: _____

2. Things you think you can't control, but you can: _____

3. Things you think you can control, but you can't: _____

4. Things you think you can control, but you don't: _____

5. Things you think you can control, and you can: _____

Perhaps you wrote in something like *medical emergencies* for (1). You could have written in *family or friends bothering you while you study* for (2). For (4), maybe you could control how much *time you waste online*, but you don't. And for (5), perhaps you wrote in *your attention*. You're absolutely right. But what about (3)? Did anything fit there? Are there things you think you can control, but you can't? Try and think of something that would fit into (3), and then think of creative ways you really could control this situation if you tried.[13] Have you ever thought about how much the issues of "control" and "time management" are related?

According to experts, there are four kinds of common problematic time management "Ps" in the world. When it comes to time management, control is generally a good thing. You take control and become more productive. But take a look at these four "P's." They exert control in way that can bring counterproductive results!

> **The Preemptive.** Preemptives believe they are doing their best; in fact, they are continuously ahead of the game. They constantly, compulsively play "beat the clock." They're always way ahead of schedule. So what's wrong with that? Sometimes, nothing. But preemptives can gain a reputation of being non-team players, only out for themselves. They look like they're trying to impress everyone—or someone in particular, like the boss or teacher.

> **The People Pleaser.** People pleasers have the best of intentions, but they take on too much and sabotage their own effectiveness by trying to make others happy. Always saying yes to everyone may mean that there's no time left for their own work. Over time, they can even come to resent the very people they're trying to please and vice versa.

> **The Perfectionist.** Nothing is ever good enough for perfectionists. In effect, what they do is make other people play a waiting game, while they continue to tinker with their projects to make them into some ideal they may never reach. They're control freaks, and they lead anxiety-ridden lives.

> **The Procrastinator.** Procrastinators are adrenaline junkies. They put things off until the 11th hour and then make a mad dash for the finish line, trailing a long list of excuses. Often, the root cause of procrastination is fear. While the perfectionist will only accept an A+, the procrastinator is secretly afraid of not ever being able to achieve an A+. If he doesn't turn in an assignment, he can't find out just how good (or not) he is.[14]

Are you a Preemptive, People-pleasing, Perfectionistic Procrastinator?

Do you know people who fit into each of these four problematic time management "P" categories? Do you? Work in groups or as a class to brainstorm ways of helping these people improve their time management skills. What advice would you give each type?

Preemptive

People Pleaser

Perfectionist

Procrastinator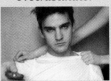

Photos.com

The P Word. Read This Section Now!... or Maybe Tomorrow...or...

Picture this: You sit down to work on a challenging homework assignment. After a few minutes, you think, *Man, I'm thirsty*, so you get up and get a soda. Then you sit back down to continue your work. A few minutes later, you decide that some chips would go nicely with your soda and you head to the kitchen. Again, you sit down to face the task before you, as you concentrate more on eating than on working. Ten minutes go by and a nagging thought starts taking over: *Must do laundry*. Up you go again and throw a load of clothes in the washer. Before long you're wondering where all the time went. Since you only have an hour left before class, you think, *Why bother getting started now? Doing this project will take much more time than that, so I'll just start it tomorrow.* Despite good intentions at the beginning of your work session, you've just succeeded in accomplishing zip, nada, nothing.

Congratulations! You—like thousands of other college students—have just successfully procrastinated! Researchers define procrastination as "needlessly delaying tasks to the point of experiencing subjective discomfort."[15] And according to researchers, 70 percent of college students admit to procrastinating on their assignments.[16]

You may be in the majority, but alas, in this case, there's no safety in numbers! Academic procrastination is a major threat to your ability to succeed in college. And procrastination in the working world can actually bring your job, and ultimately your career, to a screeching halt. Plenty of people try to rationalize their procrastination by claiming that they work better under pressure. However, the challenge in college is that during some weeks of the term, every class you're taking will have an assignment or test due, all at once, and if you procrastinate, you'll not only generate tremendous anxiety for yourself, but you'll lower your chances of succeeding on any of them.

Who, Me, Procrastinate?

Procrastination is a habit. It may show up as not getting around to doing your homework (if you don't turn it in, you can't get a bad grade on it—which almost guarantees that you'll get a bad grade on it), not vacuuming the carpet because it takes too much energy to lug the machine around, or not getting to work on time because your job is boring. What about you? Think about the following ten situations, and put a check mark next to each one to indicate the degree to which you normally procrastinate:

	Always	Sometimes	Never
1. Doing homework	____	____	____
2. Writing a paper	____	____	____
3. Studying for tests	____	____	____
4. Reading class material	____	____	____
5. Meeting with your academic advisor	____	____	____
6. Texting/e-mailing a friend	____	____	____
7. Playing a game/hanging out	____	____	____
8. Going to see a movie you've heard about	____	____	____
9. Meeting someone for dinner at a restaurant	____	____	____
10. Watching TV	____	____	____

If you are like many students, you checked "always" or "sometimes" more often for the first five items than you did for the last five items. But procrastination isn't as simple as not procrastinating when you want to do something and procrastinating when you don't. You may actually hate vacuuming but decide to vacuum the entire house so that you don't have to face studying for a test. There are "layers" of procrastination and many reasons why people procrastinate. Which of these apply to you?

____ Avoiding something you see as unpleasant

____ Feeling overwhelmed by all you have to do

____ Being intimidated by the task itself

____ Fearing failure

____ Fearing success

____ Not realizing how important the task is

____ Reacting to your own internal conflict

____ Protecting your self-esteem

____ Waiting for a last-minute adrenaline rush

____ Just plain not wanting to

Before you can control the procrastination monster in your life, it's important to understand *why* you procrastinate. Think about all the instances in which you don't procrastinate: meeting your friends for dinner, returning a phone call from a friend, going to the store. Why are those things easy to do, but getting started on an assignment is difficult until you feel the jaws of a deadline closing down on you?[17] The reasons for procrastinating vary from person to person, but once you know your own reasons for putting things off, you'll be in a better position to address the problem from its root cause.

The next time you find yourself procrastinating, ask yourself why. Procrastination hurts your chances for success and gives you ready-made excuses if you don't succeed: "It's like running a full race with a knapsack full of bricks on your back. When you don't win, you can say it's not that you're not a good runner, it's just that you had this sack of bricks on your back."[18] In addition to understanding why you procrastinate, try these ten procrastination busters to help you kick the habit.

1. **Keep track (of your excuses).** Write them down consistently, and soon you'll be able to recognize them for what they are. Own your responsibilities—in school and in the rest of your life.

2. **Break down.** Break your project into its smaller components. A term paper, for example, can be broken down into the following smaller parts: prospectus, thesis, research, outline, small chunks of writing, and bibliography. Completing smaller tasks along the way is much easier than facing a threatening monster of a project.

3. **Trick yourself.** When you feel like procrastinating, pick some aspect of the project that's easy and that you would have to do anyway. If the thought of an entire paper is overwhelming you, for example, work on the bibliography to start. Starting with something—*anything*—will get you into the rhythm of the work.

4. **Resolve issues.** If something's eating away at you, making it difficult to concentrate, take care of it. Sometimes you must deal with a bossy friend, your kids vying for your attention, or something equally intrusive. Then get down to work.

5. **Get real.** Set realistic goals for yourself. If you declare that you're going to finish a twelve-page paper in five hours, you're already doomed. Procrastinators are sometimes overly optimistic. They underestimate how much time something will take. Make it a habit to keep track of how long assignments take you in all your courses so that you can be increasingly realistic over time.

"Things which matter most should never be at the mercy of things which matter least.

Johann Wolfgang von Goethe, German writer and scholar (1749–1832)

6. **Be specific.** Instead of writing, "Finish chapter 10" in your planner, write exactly what you need to do, "Finish reading chapter 10, answer the discussion questions at the end, and e-mail my responses to my professor."

7. **Make a deal with yourself.** Even if it's only spending fifteen minutes on a task that day, do it so that you can see progress.

8. **Overcome fear.** Many of the reasons for procrastinating have to do with our personal fears. We may fear not doing something perfectly, or failing completely—or even the responsibility that comes with success to keep succeeding.

But as Susan Jeffers, author and lecturer, states, "Feel the fear, and do it anyway!"

9. **Get tough.** Sometimes projects simply require discipline. The best way to complete a tough task is to simply dig in. Become your own taskmaster; "crack the whip" and force yourself to focus on those things that are high priorities, but perhaps not your idea of fun.

10. **Acknowledge accomplishment.** We're not talking major shopping sprees at Neiman Marcus here. We're talking reasonable, meaningful rewards that match up with how much effort you invested. Go buy yourself a small treat, call your best friend in another state, take a relaxing soak in the bathtub, or do something to celebrate your accomplishments—big and small—along the way. Acknowledgment, from yourself or others, is a great motivator for tackling future projects.

Beyond Juggling: *Realistically* Manage Work, School, and Personal Life*

Your personal time management needs depend on who you are and how many obligations you have. Today's college students are more diverse than ever. Increasing numbers of college students are also parents, part-time employees or full-time professionals, husbands or wives, community volunteers, soccer coaches, or Sunday school teachers. How on earth can you possibly juggle it all?

The answer? You can't. According to work-life balance expert Dawn Carlson, juggling is a knee-jerk coping mechanism—the default setting when time gets tight and it seems that nothing can be put on the back burner. If you, like millions of others, feel overworked, overcommitted, and exhausted at every turn, you may have already learned that you can't juggle your way to a balanced life. It's impossible.[19]

Now for the good news. Balance among work, school, and personal life is possible. All of us have three primary areas of our lives that should be in balance, ideally—meaningful work (including school), satisfying relationships, and a healthy lifestyle. In addition to work and relationships, we all need to take care of ourselves. See what you think of these five rebalancing strategies. The idea is you can't have it all, but you can have it better than you do now.

1. **Alternating.** If you use this strategy, your work-life balance comes in separate, concentrated doses. You may throw yourself into your career with abandon, and then cut back or quit work altogether and focus intensely on your family. You may give your job 110 percent during the week, but devote Saturdays to physical fitness or to your kids or to running all the errands you've saved up during the week. Or you save Tuesdays and Thursdays for homework, and go to classes Mondays, Wednesdays, and Fridays. People who use this strategy alternate between important things, and it works for

*Adapted from Sandholtz, K., Derr, B., Buckner, K., & Carlson, D. (2002). Beyond juggling: Rebalancing your busy life. San Francisco: Berrett-Koehler Publishing.

The trouble with the rat race is that even if you win, you're still a rat.

Lily Tomlin, comedian

them. An alternator's motto is "I want to have it all, but just not all at once."

2. **Outsourcing.** Outsourcing, or paying someone else to do something for you, is another solution. An outsourcer's motto might be "I want to have it all, not do it all." This strategy helps you achieve work-life balance by giving someone else some of your responsibilities—usually in your personal life—to free up time for the tasks you care about most. If you have enough money, hire someone to clean the house or mow the lawn. If you don't, trade these jobs among family, friends, or neighbors who band together to help each other. Of course, there are ways this strategy could be misused by college students. Don't even think about outsourcing your research papers by having someone else write them or downloading them from the Internet with a charge card! Warning: This practice will definitely be hazardous to your academic health! In fact, your college career may be over!

3. **Bundling.** Bundling is efficient because it allows you to do two things at once. Examine your busy life and look for areas in which you can double dip, such as combining exercising with socializing. If your social life is suffering because you have too much to do, take walks with a friend so that you can talk along the way. A bundler's motto is "I want to get more mileage out of the things I do by combining activities."

4. **Techflexing.** Technology allows us to work from almost anywhere, anytime, using technology. If you telecommute from home several days a week for your job, you might get up early, spend some time on e-mail, go out for a run, have breakfast with your family, and then get back on your computer. In the office, you use instant messaging to stay connected to family members or a cell phone to call home while commuting to a business meeting. Chances are you can telecommute to your campus library and do research online, register for classes online, and pay all your bills online, including tuition. Use technology, and the flexibility it gives you, to your advantage to merge important aspects of your life.

5. **Simplifying.** People who use this strategy have decided they don't want it all. They've reached a point where they make a permanent commitment to stop the craziness in their lives. The benefit of simplifying is greater

freedom from details, stress, and the rat race. But there are trade-offs, of course. They may have to take a significant cut in pay in order to work fewer hours or at a less demanding job. But for them, it's worth it.[20]

These five strategies, used separately or in combination, have helped many people who are dealing with work, school, and family commitments at the same time. They all require certain trade-offs. None of these strategies is a magic solution.

But the alternative to rebalancing is more stress, more physical and emotional exhaustion, more frustration, and much less personal satisfaction. If you focus on rebalancing your life—making conscious choices and course corrections as you go—small changes can have a big impact. Work–life balance isn't an all-or-nothing proposition. It's an ever-changing journey. So take it one step at a time.

Time Is Money!

EXERCISE 4.7

How Fiscally Fit Are You?

Have you ever heard the phrase "time is money"? Before leaving the subjects of time and energy management, let's look at how you manage your money as well. How good are you at managing your finances? Check one of the three boxes for each statement to get a sense of how financially savvy you are.

	Always true of me	Sometimes true of me	Never true of me
1. At any given moment in time, I know the balance of my checking account.			
2. I use my credit card for particular types of purchases only, such as gas or food.			
3. I pay off my bills in full every month.			
4. I know the interest rate on my credit cards.			
5. I resist impulse buying and only spend when I need things.			
6. I have a budget and I follow it.			
7. I put money aside to save each month.			
8. When I get a pay raise, I increase the proportion of money I save.			
9. I keep track of my spending on a daily or weekly basis.			
10. I don't allow myself to get pressured by others into buying things I don't really need.			

Look over your responses. If you have more checks in the "Never true of me" column than you do in either of the two others, you may be able to put the information you're about to read to good use!

People say that "time is money." It's true. If you're so efficient with your time that you can call more customers or sell more products, then time does equal money. If your company is the first to introduce a hot new kind of cell phone or a zippy fuel-efficient car, you win. Even if better models come out next year, they may fall flat because people have already invested.

Both time management and money management are key to your college success.

Studies show that working too many hours for pay increases your chances of dropping out of college.[21] Many students find themselves working more so that they can spend more, which in turn takes time away from their studies. They may take a semester off from college to make a pile of money and then never come back. While there's evidence that working a moderate amount can help you polish your time and energy management skills, the real secret to financial responsibility in college is to track your habits and gain the knowledge you need to make sound financial decisions.

"I'd say it's been my biggest problem all my life . . . it's money. It takes a lot of money to make these dreams come true."

Walt Disney, American animator, entrepreneur, and philanthropist (1901–1966)

EXERCISE 4.8

Create a Spending Log

Take a look at this student's spending log, then complete one for yourself. Money has a way of slipping through our fingers. Choose one entire day that is representative of your spending, and use the chart on the next page to keep track of how you spend money. Write down everything from seemingly small, insignificant items to major purchases, and explain why you made that purchase. Your log may look something like this student's:

TIME	ITEM	LOCATION	AMOUNT	REASON
8–9 a.m.	coffee and bagel	convenience store	$3.50	overslept!
9–10 a.m.	computer paper	office supply store	$2.50	English paper due
10–11 a.m.	gas fill-up	gas station	$65.00	running on fumes!
11 a.m.– 12 p.m.	burger and fries	fast-food restaurant	$6.00	lunch on the run
12–1 p.m.	toiletries, etc.	drugstore	$18.00	out of stock
1–2 p.m.	bottled water	convenience store	$2.50	forgot to bring
2–3 p.m.	supplies	bookstore	$12.00	forgot to get earlier
3–7 p.m.	WORK			
7-8 p.m.	pizza	pizza place	$12.00	meet friends
8-9 p.m.	week's groceries	grocery store	$61.50	cupboard is bare!
9–10 p.m.	laundry	laundromat	$5.00	washer broken
10–11 p.m.	STUDY TIME			
11 p.m.– 12 a.m.	weekend movie, online tickets, DVDs, cell phone upgrade	Internet retail websites, phone service	$129.00 $20.00	friend's recommendations, need more minutes

This student has spent $337 today without doing anything special! When you analyze his expenditures, you can find patterns. He seems to (1) forget to plan, so he spends money continuously throughout the day, (2) spend relatively large amounts of money online, (3) be particularly vulnerable late at night, and (4) spend money grabbing food on the run. These are patterns he should be aware of if he wants to control his spending. He could pack food from home to save a significant amount of money, for example. Now create your own chart.

TIME	ITEM	LOCATION	AMOUNT	REASON
8–9 a.m.				
9–10 a.m.				
10–11 a.m.				
11 a.m. – 12 p.m.				
12–1 p.m.				
1–2 p.m.				
2–3 p.m.				
3–4 p.m.				
4–5 p.m.				
5–6 p.m.				
6–7 p.m.				
7–8 p.m.				
8–9 p.m.				
9–10 p.m.				
10–11 p.m.				
11 p.m.–12 a.m.				

What patterns do you notice about your spending? What kinds of changes will you try to make to curb any unnecessary spending?

The Perils of Plastic

The "newly minted" Credit Card Act of 2009 has changed some things about how credit cards work. In 2008 before the law went into effect, college students carried a balance of $3,173 (a ten-year high), and a full 82 percent kept paying on a balance every month.[22] Under the new law, credit cards cannot be issued to people under the age of 21 unless they have an adult co-signer or can show proof that they have enough income. College students will need permission from parents/guardians to increase their credit limits. And those under 21 will be protected from "sneaky" credit card offers unless they opt to get them. Read up on credible internet sites about the new law and the protections and restrictions it provides. If you already have a credit card or plan to get one, however, keep this general advice in mind.

3 INSIGHT *Now* What Do You Think?

At the beginning of this chapter, Derek Johnson, a frustrated and disgruntled student, faced a challenge. Now after reading this chapter, would you respond differently to any of the questions you answered about the "FOCUS Challenge Case"? Using what you learned in the chapter, write a paragraph ending to Derek's case study. What are some of the possible outcomes for Derek?

4 ACTION Your Plans for Change

1. What's the most important thing you learned in reading this chapter?
2. How will you apply the information you've learned to yourself to improve your time, energy, and money management?

REALITY CHECK | What did you **Learn?**

On a scale of 1 to 5, answer these questions now that you've completed this chapter.

1 = not very/not much/very little/low   5 = very/a lot/very much/high

How much do you know *now*?

Now rate your current level of knowledge about topics covered in this chapter.

Time management vs. energy management

    1 2 3 4 5

Procrastination

    1 2 3 4 5

Balancing work, school, and personal life

    1 2 3 4 5

Money management

    1 2 3 4 5

How useful might the information in this chapter be to you?

How much do you think this information might affect your college success?

    1 2 3 4 5

How much do you think this information might affect your career success after college?

    1 2 3 4 5

How long did it actually take you to complete this chapter (both the reading and writing tasks)?

_____ Hour(s) _____ Minutes

Challenge Yourself Online Quiz. To find out how much you've learned, access the CourseMate via www.cengagebrain.com/shop/ISBN/0495906433 to take the Challenge Yourself Online Quiz.

Compare these answers to your answers from the "Readiness Check" at the beginning of this chapter. How might the gaps between what you thought before starting the chapter and what you now think affect how you approach the next chapter?

chapter 5

Thinking Critically and Creatively

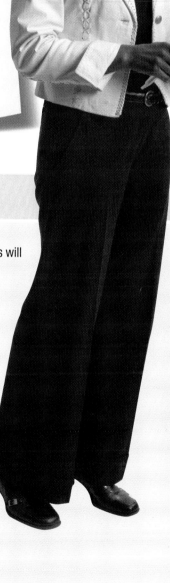

©Larry Harwood Photography.
Property of Cengage Learning.

You're About to Discover...

✔ How focused thinking, critical thinking, and creative thinking are defined
✔ How a four-part model of critical thinking works
✔ How to analyze arguments, assess assumptions, and consider claims
✔ How to avoid mistakes in reasoning
✔ What metacognition is and why it's important
✔ How to become a more creative thinker

READINESS CHECK

What do you **Know?**

Before beginning this chapter, take a moment to answer these questions. Your answers will help you assess how ready you are to focus.

1 = not very/not much/very little/low   5 = very/a lot/very much/high

How much do you *already* know?

Rate your current level of knowledge about topics covered in this chapter.

Focused thinking

1   2   3   4   5

Four-part model of critical thinking

1   2   3   4   5

Arguments, assumptions, claims

1   2   3   4   5

Critical versus *creative* thinking

1   2   3   4   5

How motivated are you to learn *more*?

In general, how motivated are you to learn the material in this chapter?

1   2   3   4   5

How much do you think this information might affect your college success?

1   2   3   4   5

How much do you think this information might affect your career success after college?

1   2   3   4   5

How ready are you to read *now*?

How ready are you to focus on this chapter—physically, intellectually, and emotionally? Which of these three areas is most challenging for you right now? Circle a number to represent it.

1   2   3   4   5

If any of your answers is below a 3, consider addressing the issue before reading. Then, read the chapter carefully, while looking for ways to improve your focus.

Finally, how long do you think it will take you to complete this chapter? If you start and stop, keep track of the overall time.

_____ Hour(s) _____ Minutes

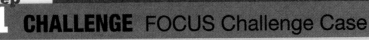
©Larry Harwood Photography. Property of Cengage Learning.

Desiree Moore

imply put: Desiree Moore was a perfectionist. Her friends said she was "detail-oriented." Her family said she was compulsive. Truthfully, though, she hadn't been all that successful in high school because her assignments were always turned in late, if at all, because they were never "finished." She'd always ask her teachers how long a paper should be and what topic she should write about. She wanted to get things right. Her teachers always advised her to stop "tweaking": "You spend so much time revising your assignments that nothing ever gets done." But she found it hard to take their advice.

High school had been so stressful that when she graduated, she took the first job that came along as a receptionist for a small law firm. When the two lawyers announced they were going to retire, she started to job hunt immediately. She found another job as a telemarketer. But being hung up on all day wasn't all that much fun, so eventually she quit. She tried waiting tables and cleaning houses, but those jobs didn't hold much appeal either. Before she knew it, more than a few years had gone by, and Desiree realized she didn't have much to show for it. She needed more specialized skills in order to get a better job. When she

thought back over all the jobs she'd had since high school, she realized that working with the two lawyers had been her favorite. So, Desiree decided to become a paralegal by earning a two-year degree at the big community college in town. She would be the first person in her family to go to college! It was a good career field, and she could investigate legal cases, draft documents, and do research working alongside an attorney.

Her first semester consisted of two night classes: "Introduction to Paralegal Careers" and "Paralegal Ethics." But "Paralegal Ethics" was a very challenging course. The instructor, Mr. Courtney, a retired lawyer himself, had announced on the first day of class that he believed in the Socratic method of teaching, by asking questions of students instead of lecturing. "Socrates, perhaps the greatest philos-

© Cengage Learning

Paralegal Associate's Degree Program

Courses offered:

- Introduction to the Law

- Torts & Personal Injury
- Contracts
- Legal Research, Writing & Civil Litigation
- Paralegal Ethics

- Criminal Law
- Business Law & Bankruptcy
- Constitutional L

Paralegal Ethics Syllabus

Instructor: Samuel Courtney
Email Address: S.Courtney@campusmail.edu
Office Hours: MWF 8am–10am
Office Location: Main Hall 1020
Text: *Legal Ethics for Paralegals and the Law Office* (1st Edition) by Laura Morrison

Class Content:
- Understand ethical issues that paralegals may face
- Review the universal concepts of professional responsibility and ethical practices
- Define the roles of paralegals versus attorneys
- Recognize what activities constitute the
- Discuss possible solutions to ethical dilemmas

Class Method: Since philosophy is an important part of law, for our class method we will turn to one of the founding fathers of critical and philosophical thinking: Socrates. Consequently, we will be using the "Socratic method" when approaching course material. This means that instead of giving a lecture, I will ask you, the students, questions in order to create a lively discussion.

Grading: This course will include 3 exams, each worth 20% of your overall grade. There will also be 5 quizzes during the semester, all of which contribute to another 20% of your grade. Finally, class participation will count for the final 20% of your grade. It is imperative that you attend every class session, and that you are actively participating in class discussions.

Course Outline:
This course covers the basic principles governing the ethical practice of law for paralegals. Subjects explored include the unauthorized practice of law, confidentiality, paralegal-client relations, conflicts of interest, disciplinary procedures, advertising, fee splitting, billing, and
　　duct in the law office.

opher of all time," he announced the first day, "is the 'father' of critical thinking. In this class, you'll learn to think critically. *Learning to think* is what college is all about." Mr. Courtney began every class session with a hypothetical story, and he always randomly chose a student to respond. His openings went something like this:

> An attorney has just finished law school and opens a law office. He hires a legal assistant, just out of college. He is eager to begin his new career, but he is also nervous because he's starting from scratch.
>
> The lawyer's specialty is civil law, and several weeks go by before the phone even rings. His first potential client has a big problem. He wants to sue his next door neighbor for keeping old cars, junk, and trash in his front yard. When he's asked the neighbor nicely to clean up his property, the neighbor has refused in threatening tones. The teenage sons who live in the home have ties to local gangs and other neighbors are afraid. They all suspect the teenage boys of a series of unsolved robberies in the neighborhood. The neighborhood is getting a bad reputation, and home values in the area have fallen dramatically.
>
> The lawyer, who desperately needs the work, decides to take the case. However, when the client fills out the contract, his legal assistant notices that the client's zip code is the same as her boss's. In fact, she recognizes the street name as one that's in the subdivision

where the lawyer himself lives. Is this a problem? Would you say the lawyer has a "conflict of interest"? What should our legal assistant do?

One student responded with, "Yes, the lawyer lives in the same neighborhood as his client. He doesn't want his own property value to fall. According to our textbook, that's a conflict of interest." Another student said, "But the legal assistant should keep quiet and just do her job. She needs a paycheck. She shouldn't tell her boss what to do. It's none of her business." Mr. Courtney continued, "But what if the new client discovers that he and his lawyer live in the same neighborhood? Would the client see that as a possible conflict of interest? Could this damage the lawyer's legal career? What would *you* do if the legal assistant were you?" Mr. Courtney's questions seemed endless. Her best friend suggested that she look him up on ratemyprofessors.com, but when she did, she found that students wrote about how much they had learned from him.

"What's important in college is thinking through problems," he said. "There aren't always clear right and wrong answers. The process of learning to think can be just as important as the answer itself."

Frankly, that explanation didn't sit well with Desiree. *If there aren't right answers, why go to college? The instructor knows the right answers. Why doesn't he just tell us?* Perfectionists like Desiree were always most comfortable when things were straightforward. Without fail, she always left Mr. Courtney's class with a headache from thinking so hard.

New attorney opens office
- civil law

Potential client:
- wants to sue neighbor
- won't clean trash in yard
- possible gang connections

Attorney takes case
- but, attorney lives in same neighborhood!

PROBLEM!?

RATE MY PROFESSORS

Over 6,000 Schools,
1 million professors, 10 million opinions

Home | Forum | Tell a F

Enter keywords (e.g. Sam Sm

About this site

Find a professor   Find your school
Search for a school by entering its name here...
United States ▾   (Search)
Hide Map
Or click the school's state below.

1. Do you have anything in common with Desiree, like an instructor who teaches in a way you find difficult to understand? What specific steps are you taking to help yourself succeed?
2. Do you agree with Mr. Courtney's statement that "there aren't always right answers"? If that's true, why is getting a college education so important?
3. Identify three things Desiree should do to get the most from Mr. Courtney's class.

Rethinking Thinking

Thinking is a natural, ongoing, everyday process we all engage in. In fact, we can't really turn it off, even if we try. We're always on. Everyone thinks all the time. We talk to ourselves in our heads. However, some experts say school teaches us how to just regurgitate what we've memorized, not how to think. Learning to think is what counts, and *focused thinking*—thinking critically and creatively—is what this chapter is about.

Picture this: You're in the library. It's late, and you're tired. You're supposed to be studying for your political science test, but instead of thinking about foreign policy, your mind begins drifting toward the vacation you took last summer, the great food you ate, and how much fun it was to be with your friends or family.

Would the mental process you're engaging in while sitting in the library be called *thinking*? For our purposes in this chapter, the answer is no. Here thinking is defined as a focused mental activity you engage in on purpose. You direct your thoughts toward a particular topic. You're the *active* thinker, not the *passive* daydreamer who is the victim of a wandering mind. Focused thinking involves zeroing in and managing your attention. It's deliberate, not accidental. You choose to do it for a reason.

Focused thinking is like a two-sided coin. Sometimes when you think, you *produce* ideas. That's what this chapter calls *creative thinking*, and that's something we'll deal with later. The other side of thinking requires you to *evaluate* ideas—your own or someone else's. That's *critical thinking*. The word *critical* comes from the Greek word for *critic* (*kritikos*), meaning "to question or analyze." You focus on something, sort through the information, and decide which ideas are most sensible, logical, or useful. When you're thinking critically, you're asking questions, analyzing arguments, assessing assumptions, considering

©Larry Harwood Photography. Property of Cengage Learning.

"
'Knowledge is power.' Rather, knowledge is happiness. To have knowledge, deep broad knowledge, is to know truth from false and lofty things from low.
"

Helen Keller, American author, activist, and lecturer (1880–1968)

claims, avoiding mistakes in reasoning, problem solving, decision making, and all the while, thinking about your thinking.

What Is Critical Thinking?

Critical thinking is a particular kind of focused thinking. It is purposeful, reasoned, and goal-directed. It's thinking that aims to solve problems, calculate likelihood, weigh evidence, and make decisions.[1] In that sense, movie critics are critical thinkers because they look at a variety of standards (screenplay, acting, production quality, costumes, and so forth) and then decide how a movie measures up. When you're thinking critically, you're not just being critical. You're on the lookout for both faults and strengths. You're looking at how things measure up.[2]

> " What we need is not the will to believe, but the will to find out.
>
> *Bertrand Russell, British philosopher, logician, and mathematician (1872–1970)*

Critical thinkers develop standards they can use to judge advertisements, political speeches, sales pitches, movies—you name it.[3] Critical thinking is not jumping to conclusions; buying arguments lock, stock, and barrel; accepting controversial ideas no matter what; or ignoring the facts.

Unfortunately, some people are noncritical thinkers. They may be biased or closed-minded. Other people are *selective* critical thinkers. When it comes to one particular subject, they shut down their minds. They can't explain their views, they're emotional about them, and they refuse to acknowledge any other position. Why do they believe these things? Only if they understand the *why*, can they explain their views to someone else or defend them under fire. The importance of *why* can't be overstated. Some people, of course, have already thought through their beliefs, and they understand their positions and the reasons for them very well. Arriving at that point is the goal of anyone who wants to become a better critical thinker.

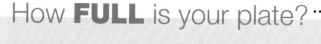
How **FULL** is your plate?

> " Blessed are the flexible, for they shall not be bent out of shape. "
>
> —MICHAEL MCGRIFFY, M.D.

When your plate is as full as yours probably is, sometimes you must *decide* to be flexible. You may not be able to do everything perfectly, as Desiree in the FOCUS Challenge Case wanted to. For her, procrastination was a way of giving herself permission to do a less than perfect job on a task that didn't require a perfect job in the first place.[4] For people like Desiree, developing flexibility can be a key to college success.

PhotostoGO.com

TRY IT!

Choose one item on your "to-do" list this week that can be shifted down the list, and one item that should be shifted up. What's *really* important? In class, discuss whether perfectionism is a problem for you, and if so, what you can do about it.

And Just Why Is Critical Thinking Important?

Here is a list of reasons why it's important to improve your critical thinking skills. Beside each entry, mark the degree to which you'd like to refine your critical thinking skills in each area. How important are each of these items to you? On a scale from 1 to 5 with 5 representing the highest degree, would you like to:

1. _____ **Become a more successful college student**? Most college courses require you to think critically (in answering essay questions, for example). In one study of over 1,100 college students, higher scores on critical thinking skills tests correlated highly with better grades.[5] Critical thinkers, for example, can ask better questions in class. There's even evidence that interaction with other students in activities outside of class can help you develop as a critical thinker.[6]

2. _____ **Become a better citizen**? Critical thinking is the foundation of a strong democracy. Voters must think critically about candidates' messages and whether they're likely to keep their campaign promises. It's easy to talk about balancing the budget, or lowering taxes, but the truth is these highly complex tasks are very challenging to carry out. The American public must sift through information and examine politicians' arguments in order to keep our democracy strong.

3. _____ **Become a better employee**? A workforce of critical—and creative—thinkers helps the American economy thrive and individuals become more successful. The U.S. Department of Labor reports that today's jobs require employees who can deal with complex issues, learn and perform multiple tasks, analyze and deal with a wide variety of options, identify problems, perceive alternative approaches, and select the best approach.[7] Employers are "practically begging" for employees who can "think, collaborate, communicate, coordinate, and create."[8]

4. _____ **Become a smarter consumer**? In today's world, everyone wants your money. If you bought everything advertised in magazines or on television, you'd run out of money very quickly. Critical thinking will help you evaluate offers, avoid slick come-ons, and buy responsibly.

5. _____ **Build stronger relationships**? Critical thinking helps us understand our own and others' actions and become more responsible communicators. Whether with friends or romantic partners, relationships take work. Sometimes you have to listen between the lines for important clues to figure out what your partner really means. Actually, critical thinking is at the heart of every relationship you care about.

6. _____ **Become a lifelong learner**? Your education doesn't end when you get your diploma. In many ways the real exams begin afterward when you put your classroom learning to the test on the job. And in today's world you must continue to learn as you transition through jobs—personally and professionally. You'll need to keep expanding your skills, no matter what your career is.

Look over your responses to these six items. Now rank them with one as your highest priority at this particular point in your life. Be prepared to explain how you rank ordered these six items in class.

A Four-Part Model of Critical Thinking

Now that we've defined critical thinking, let's ask an important related question: How do you do it? We'll look at the four primary components of critical thinking, and at the end of this chapter, we'll use a realistic news story, one that could take place near any community college campus, to allow you to apply what you've learned through a memorable example.

Take a look at Figure 5.1 to preview the four-part model of critical thinking. You'll see right away that your reasoning skills underlie everything. They are

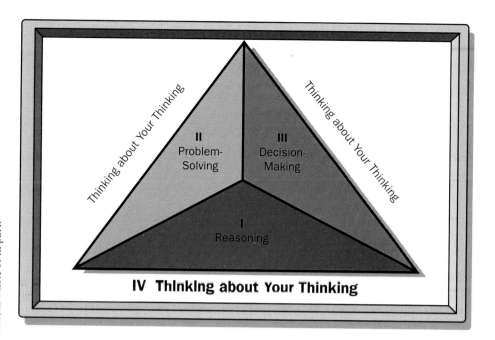

FIGURE 5.1

Critical Thinking Is Focused

Here's a four-part model of critical thinking. Your reasoning skills underlie everything. They are the foundation upon which your problem-solving and decision-making skills rest, and your metacognitive skills, or thinking about your thinking, surround all the focused thinking you do.

the foundation upon which your problem-solving and decision-making skills rest, and your metacognitive skills, or thinking about your thinking, surround all the focused thinking you do.

I. Reasoning: The Foundation of Critical Thinking

Reasoning, the foundation of critical thinking, is the ability to reach a conclusion from one or more arguments. A strong argument is convincing because it offers **evidence** to back up its claim. If no one would disagree with what you're saying, it's not an argument. It's obvious. "Grass is green" is not an argument. But "Cows that are grass-fed make the best meat" is (if supporting evidence is provided). Do you see the difference?

evidence reasons why something is true, based on statistics, expert testimony, or examples

Think about your reasoning skills. How good are you at creating a sound argument? Let's say that you're trying to convince your friend that her cell phone conversation is making it difficult for you to study for a major exam. What evidence would you use to convince her? What's the likelihood of your success? Or how about this: How good are you at evaluating someone else's argument? For example, you're trying to decide whether an online discount is really a good deal. Would you take the advertiser's word for it or would you compare prices on your own?

Throughout the rest of this chapter, ask yourself: Are there ways I can improve my reasoning skills? As you think about your own skills, consider these reasoning nuts and bolts that are essential parts of creating and evaluating arguments.

Analyzing Arguments Have you ever seen the *Monty Python Flying Circus* "Argument Sketch"? In this bizarre skit a man comes to an "argument clinic" to buy an argument. The two arguers—"professional" and customer—engage in a long, "yes, it is" "no, it isn't" squabble.

Critical thinking is about arguments. But most of us think of an argument as a back-and-forth disagreement. In the middle of the "Argument Clinic" sketch, however, the customer actually makes an important point. He says that they're not really arguing; they're just contradicting each other. He continues, "An argument is a connected series of statements intended to establish a proposition." That's the kind of argument that's related to critical thinking.

Critical thinking is about an argument that *one* person puts forth, not a squabble between two people. An op-ed piece in the newspaper contains an argument. (Op-ed stands for the page "opposite the editorial page" that features signed articles expressing personal viewpoints.) Both attorneys—prosecution and defense—put forth their closing arguments at the end of a trial.

Arguments are said to be inductive or deductive. *Inductive* arguments go from specific observations to general conclusions. In criminal trials, the prosecution puts together individual pieces of evidence to prove that the defendant is guilty: eyewitnesses put him at the scene, the gun store salesman remembers selling him a pistol, and his fingerprints are on the weapon. Therefore, the prosecutor argues that the defendant is guilty. Other arguments are said to be *deductive*, meaning they go from broad generalizations to specific conclusions. All serial killers have a particular psychological profile. The defendant has this psychological profile. Therefore the defendant is the killer.

What do arguments do? They propose a line of reasoning. They try to persuade. Arguments contain clear reasons to believe someone or something. Arguments say A plus B equals C. Once you understand what an argument is, you must also understand that arguments can be sound or unsound. If I tell you that two plus two equals four, chances are good that you'll believe me. If, on the other hand, I tell you two plus two equals five, you'll flatly deny it. If I say "Cats have fur." "Dogs have fur." "Therefore dogs are cats," you'll tell me I'm crazy—because it's an unsound argument.

The standard we use to test the soundness of arguments is logic, which is a fairly extensive topic. Let's just say for our purposes here that arguments are sound when the evidence for them is reasonable, more reasonable than the evidence against them. The important point is that a sound argument provides at least one good reason to believe. Let's look at an example:

Few people think more than two or three times a year. I have made an international reputation for myself by thinking once or twice a week.

George Bernard Shaw, Irish literary critic, playwright, and essayist, 1925 Nobel Prize for Literature (1856–1950)

I don't see why all students have to take an introductory writing course. It's a free country. Students shouldn't have to take courses they don't want to take.

Based on our definition, is this example an argument? Why or why not? Is the statement "It's a free country" relevant? What does living in a free country have to do with courses that community college students are required to take? Nothing. *Relevancy* is a condition needed for a sound argument.

Now look at this example:

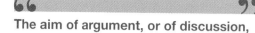

> *I don't see why all first-year students have to take an introductory writing course. Many students have developed good writing skills in high school, and their entrance test scores are high.*

Is this second example an argument? Why or why not? The first example doesn't give you a good reason to believe the argument; the second example does. A true argument must contain at least one reason for you to believe it.

Here's another warning. Not everything that sounds like an argument is one. Look at this example:

> *Everyone taking Math 100 failed the test last Friday. I took the test last Friday. Therefore, I will probably get an F in the course.*

Is that a sound argument—or is something missing? Even though all three statements may be true, when you put them together they don't make a sound argument. What grade has this student earned on earlier math tests? How many tests are left in the course? What other assignments figure into students' grades? The information present may not be adequate to predict an F in the course. *Adequacy* is another condition needed for a sound argument. This alternative, on the other hand, is a sound argument:

> *Everyone taking Math 100 failed the test last Friday. I took the test last Friday. Therefore, I earned an F on the test.*

When you're assessing the soundness of an argument, you must look for two things: *relevance* and *adequacy*.[9]

Not all arguments are sound. Have you ever heard this story? A scientist came up with a new study to find out what makes people drunk, using himself in the experiment. The study went like this. On Monday night, he drank three tall glasses of scotch and water, mixed in equal amounts. The next morning, he recorded his results: intoxication. On Tuesday night, he drank three tall glasses of whiskey and water. On Wednesday night, he drank three tall glasses of rum and water. On Thursday night, he drank three tall glasses of vodka and water. Each morning, his recorded results were the same. He had become drunk. His totally wrong conclusion? Water makes people drunk.

Not only is it important to be able to construct sound arguments, but it's also important to be able to recognize them. As a consumer in today's information society, you must know when to buy into an argument, and when not to.

Assessing Assumptions When you're thinking critically, one of the most important kinds of questions you can ask is about the *assumptions* you or someone else is making, perhaps without even realizing it. Assumptions are things you take for granted, and they can limit your thinking. Consider this well-known puzzle, and afterward, examine how the assumptions you brought with you interfered with solving it.

One day Kerry celebrated her birthday. Two days later her older twin brother, Harry, celebrated his birthday. How could that be?

You may have solved this puzzle if you were willing to question the underlying assumptions that were holding you back. (The answer is upside down at the bottom of this page.)

People reveal their basic assumptions in what they say. If you listen carefully, you can uncover them. "Go on for a bachelor's degree after I finish here? No way! As soon as I get my associate's degree, I'm done!" This student's underlying assumption is that college itself isn't as important as what comes afterward (like making money). This student may sit through her classes without getting engaged in the subject matter, and she checks off requirements as quickly as she can. Too bad.

Considering Claims Evaluating claims is one of the most basic aspects of reasoning. A claim is a statement that can be true or false, but not both. This is different from a fact, which cannot be disputed. What's the difference between a *fact* and a *claim*? Facts can't be disputed; claims can be true or false, but they must be one or the other, not both.

> *FACT: Ronald Reagan, George H. Bush, and Bill Clinton have been presidents of the United States during the last thirty years.*
> *CLAIM: Bill Clinton was the most popular American president in the last thirty years.*

The fact is obvious. The claim needs evidence to support it. As a critical thinker, it's important to use your reasoning skills to evaluate the evidence. Generally speaking, be wary of claims that

> - are supported by unidentified sources ("Experts claim . . . ").
> - are made by a person or company who stands to gain ("Brought to you by the makers of . . .").
> - come from a a single person claiming his experience as the norm ("I tried it and it worked for me!").
> - use a bandwagon appeal ("Everybody's doing it.").
> - mislead with statistics ("over half" when it's really only 50.5 percent).

On the other hand, we must also keep an open mind and be flexible in our thinking. If you get good evidence to support a view that contradicts yours, be willing to change your ideas. One way to evaluate the validity of claims is to use the Critical Thinking Pyramid (Figure 5.2). Consider claims by asking these four key questions: "who?" "what?" "why?" and "how?" Figure 5.2 shows how the questions progress from level 1 to 3.

Great minds discuss ideas. Average minds discuss events. Small minds discuss people.

Eleanor Roosevelt, First Lady of the United States (1884–1962)

Kerry and Harry are not twins, Harry and his brother are twins, and they are older than Kerry.

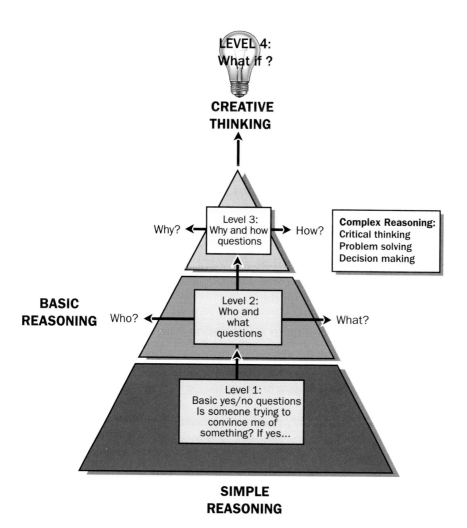

FIGURE 5.2

The Critical Thinking Pyramid

Source: Adapted from Hellyer, R., Robinson, C., & Sherwood, P. (1998). Study skills for learning power. New York: Houghton Mifflin, 18.

Avoiding Faulty Reasoning Although we can certainly improve our critical-thinking skills, it's impossible to be perfect critical thinkers 100 percent of the time. As thinkers, we make mistakes, and sometimes others try to trick us with bad arguments. It's important to cultivate both types of critical thinking skills: your *productive* skills, which you use as a speaker and writer when you "produce" ideas, and your *receptive* skills, which you use as a reader and listener when you "receive" others' ideas. As responsible communicators, we must understand what a sound argument is and know how to construct one ourselves. We must also understand what a defective argument is so that we avoid getting sucked in when we shouldn't.

Here is a top-ten list of logical fallacies, or false logic strategies, we can slip into—or others can use against us—if we're not careful. For each of the ten types, read through the example and then see if you can come up with one of your own.

1. **False cause and effect** (assuming one cause for something when other causes are possible, too)

   I moved back home from my own apartment last month. I've failed every exam I've taken since. Living at home is blowing my GPA!

> To treat your facts with imagination is one thing, but to imagine your facts is another.
>
> *John Burroughs, writer on ecology (1837–1921)*

A Four-Part Model of Critical Thinking   **113**

III. Decision Making: What's Your Style?

The kinds of arguments we're discussing in this chapter lead to decisions, and it's important to make good ones! After you've evaluated an argument, you must often do something about it. Before you know it, you'll be deciding on a major if you haven't already, a career field, a place to live, a romantic partner—you name it.

When you have an important decision to make, your critical thinking skills should kick into action. The more important the decision, the more thoughtful the process of deciding should be. But people make decisions in different ways.

Alan J. Rowe and Richard O. Mason wrote a book called *Managing with Style* about four basic decision-making styles used by managers. Although you may not be a manager now, think about what your style may be when you do have a position of responsibility. Here are the four styles they describe. See which one sounds as if it might describe you.

©Hemera Technologies/
PhotoObjects.net/Jupiter Images

> **Directive.** This decision-making style emphasizes the here and now. Directives prefer structure and using practical data to make decisions. They look for speed, efficiency, and results, and focus on short-term fixes. Directive decision makers base their decisions on experience, facts, procedures, and rules, and they have energy and drive to get things done. On the down side, because they work quickly, they are sometimes satisfied with simple solutions when something else might work better.

© Ian Scott, 2009. Used under license from Shutterstock.com

> **Analytical.** This decision-making style emphasizes a logical approach. Analyticals search carefully for the best decision, and they sometimes get hung up with overanalyzing things and take too long to finally make a decision. They are sometimes considered to be impersonal because they may be more interested in the problem than in the people who have it. But they are good at working with data and doing careful analysis.

©Hemera
Technologies/
PhotoObjects.net/Jupiter Images

> **Conceptual.** This decision-making style emphasizes the big picture. Conceptuals are adaptable, insightful, and flexible, and they look for interesting, new solutions. They are sometimes too idealistic, but they take risks and are very creative.

Ron Chapple/Open Index/
PhotostoGO.com

> **Behavioral.** This decision-making style emphasizes people. Behaviorals enjoy people and the social aspects of work. They use their feelings to assess situations, communicate well, and are supportive of others. On the other hand, they are sometimes seen as wishy-washy or are criticized because they can't make hard decisions or can't say no.

Whether you're in college to prepare for a career field or retool for a new one, eventually, you will have to make important decisions on a daily basis. It's useful to begin thinking about your decision-making style now.

IV. Thinking about Your Thinking

One of the most important aspects of critical thinking is that it evaluates itself. As you're solving problems, for example, you're thinking about how you're thinking. You're assessing your progress as you go, analyzing the strengths and weaknesses in your thinking, and perhaps even coming up with better ways to do it. We call that metacognition.

Novice or new learners don't stop to evaluate their thinking and make revisions. Expert or experienced learners do. Actually, whenever you're faced with learning something new, metacognition involves three elements. Ultimately, these elements should become the foundation of all your learning experiences so that you improve your metacognitive skills as you go.

And how is education supposed to make me feel smarter?

Homer Simpson, television cartoon character, The Simpsons

> **Before: Develop a plan of action.** Ask yourself what you already know that can help you learn something new. What direction do you want to go in your thinking? What should be your first task? How much time should you give yourself? Talk through your plan with someone else.

> **During: Monitor your plan.** While you're working, ask yourself how you're doing. Are you staying on track? Are you moving in the right direction? Should you slow down or speed up? What should you do if you don't understand what you're doing? Keep track of what works for you and what doesn't. Assume responsibility for your own thinking and learning.

metacognition thinking about your thinking and learning about your learning

> **After: Evaluate the plan.** How well did you do? Did you do better than expected or not as well as you expected? What could you have done differently? Can you apply what you just did here to future tasks? Give yourself some feedback.[11]

Becoming a Better Critical Thinker

Sharpening your critical thinking skills is vital because these skills underlie all the others in your academic toolkit. If you think well, you will be a better writer, a better presenter, a better listener, and a better reader. You will be more likely to engage more fully in your academic tasks because you will question, dig, analyze, and monitor yourself as you learn. Here are some suggestions for improving your skills. As you read them, think about yourself and how you learn.

1. **Admit when you don't know.** If you don't know enough to think critically about something, admit it, and then find out more. With the volume of information available in today's world, we can't possibly know everything about anything. But the good news is that information is everywhere. All you need to do is read, listen, point, and click to be well informed on many issues.

If you have an apple and I have an apple and we exchange these apples, then you and I will still each have one apple. But if you have an idea and I have an idea and we exchange these ideas, then each of us will have two ideas.

George Bernard Shaw, Irish literary critic, playwright, and essayist, 1925 Nobel Prize for Literature (1856–1950)

2. **Realize you have buttons that can be pushed.** We all have issues we're emotional about. That's normal. It's natural to feel strongly about some things, but it's also important to understand the reasons why so that you can tell your views to someone else. And of course, realize that you're not the only one with buttons. Your teacher, best friend, significant other, boss, and everyone else has them, too.

3. **Learn more about the opposition.** Many times, it's more comfortable to avoid what we don't agree with and reinforce what we already believe. But part of being a well-educated person means learning about the history, backgrounds, values, and techniques of people you disagree with so that you can anticipate and deal with their arguments more effectively.

4. **Trust and verify.** During the cold war, President Ronald Reagan liked to quote an old Russian saying to his Soviet counterpart, Mikhail Gorbachev: "Doveryay, no proveryay," or "Trust, but verify." Being a good critical thinker means achieving a balance between blind faith and healthy questioning.

5. **Remember that critical thinking is the foundation of all academic achievement.** There's nothing more important than learning to think critically. In college and in life, the skills discussed in this chapter will make you a better college student, a better citizen, a better employee, a smarter consumer, a better relational partner, and a better lifelong learner.

Creativity: "Thinking Outside the ... Book"

Do you believe this statement? *Everyone has creative potential.* It's true. Most of us deny it, however. "Me, creative? Nah!" We're often unaware of the untapped ability we have to think creatively. Try this experiment. Look at the following list of words, and divide the list into two (and only two) different categories, using any rules you create. Take a few moments and see what you come up with.

dog, salad, book, grasshopper, kettle, paper, garbage, candle

Whenever this experiment is tried, people always come up with very creative categories. They may divide the words into things that you buy at a store (dog, salad, kettle, paper, candle), things that move on their own (dog, grasshopper), things that have a distinct smell (dog, candle, garbage), words that have two consonants, and so forth. People never say it can't be done; they always *invent* categories. Interesting, isn't it? Our minds are hungry for the stimulation of a creative challenge.

The fact is that intelligence has more to do with coming up with the right answer, and creative thinking has more to do with coming up with more than one right answer. Often we get so focused on the *right* answer that we rush to find it instead of exploring all the possibilities. Creative thinking is thinking out-

coloroftime/iStockphoto.com

> **A mind that is stretched to a new idea never returns to its original dimensions.**
>
> *Oliver Wendell Holmes, American poet*
> *(1809–1894)*

side the box, or in terms of getting an education, perhaps we should call it thinking outside the book. Going beyond the obvious and exploring possibilities are important parts of becoming an educated person. Employers report that many college graduates today have specific skills, but that what they rarely see "is the ability to use the right-hand side of the brain—creativity, working in a team."[12]

In Figure 5.2, we looked at the Critical Thinking Pyramid. Creative thinking is at the top of the pyramid: What if? It goes beyond critical thinking. It is predictive and multidimensional. It asks "What if ...?" questions. Here are some interesting ones: "What if everyone was allowed to tell one lie per day?" "What if no one could perceive colors?" "What if colleges didn't exist?" "If you looked up a word like *squallizmotex* in the dictionary, what might it mean?"[13]

According to creativity expert Alan Rowe, our creative intelligence demonstrates itself in four major styles. Each of us has aspects of all four styles of creativity.

> **Intuitive.** This creative style is best described as *resourceful*. If you are an Intuitive, you achieve goals, use common sense, and work to solve problems. You focus on results and rely on past experience to guide your actions. Managers, actors, and politicians are commonly Intuitives.

> **Innovative.** This creative style is best described as *curious*. Innovatives concentrate on problem solving, are organized, and rely on data. They use original approaches, are willing to experiment, and focus on step-by-step inquiry. Scientists, engineers, and inventors typically demonstrate the Innovative creative style.

> **Imaginative.** This creative style is best described as *insightful*. Imaginatives are willing to take risks, have leaps of imagination, and are independent thinkers. They are able to visualize opportunities, are artistic, enjoy writing, and think outside the box. Artists, musicians, writers, and charismatic leaders are often Imaginatives.

> **Inspirational.** This creative style is best described as *visionary*. Inspirationals respond to societal needs, willingly give of themselves, and have the courage of their convictions. They focus on social change and the giving of themselves toward achieving it. They are often educators, motivational leaders, and writers.[14]

Which do you think is your predominant style? Think about how you can make the best use of your natural style. How will your creativity affect the major or career you choose? Most people have more than one creative style. Remember that motivation, not just intelligence, is the key to creativity. You must be willing to tap your creative potential and challenge yourself to show it.[15] According to *New York Times* best-seller, *A Whole New Mind*, "The future belongs to a very different kind of person with a very different kind of mind—creators and empathizers, pattern recognizers, and meaning makers. These people—artists, inventors, designers, storytellers, caregivers, consolers, big picture thinkers—will now reap society's richest rewards and share its greatest joys." (p.1)

Ten Ways to Become a More Creative Thinker

Becoming a more creative thinker may mean you need to accept your creativity and cultivate it. Consider these suggestions on how to think more creatively.

FIGURE 5.3

The Pillow Method

Position 1—I'm right and you're wrong.

Position 2—You're right and I'm wrong.

Position 3—We're both right.

Position 4—We're both wrong.

1. **Find new eyes.** Find a new perspective on old issues. Here's an interesting example. Years ago, a group of Japanese schoolchildren came up with a new way to solve conflicts and build empathy for others' positions, called the Pillow Method. Figure 5.3 is an adaptation of it, based on the fact that a pillow has four sides and a middle, just like most problems. The middle or *mu* is the Zen expression for "it doesn't really matter." There is truth in all four positions. Try it: take a conflict you're having difficulty with at the moment, and write down all four sides and a middle.[16]

2. **Accept your creativity.** Many mindsets block creative thinking: "It can't be done!" "I'm just not the creative type." "I might look stupid!" Many people don't see themselves as creative. This perception can become a major stumbling block. If creativity isn't part of your self-image, you may need to change your image. Everyone has creative potential. You may just have to learn how to tap into yours.

3. **Make your thoughts visible.** For many of us, things become clear when we can see them, either in our mind's eye or displayed for us. Even Einstein, a scientist and mathematician, had a very visual mind. Sometimes if we write something down or sketch something out, we generate a new approach without really trying.

4. **Generate lots of ideas.** Thomas Edison held 1,093 patents, still the record. He gave himself idea goals. The rule he set for himself was that he had to come up with a major invention every six months and a minor invention every ten days.

5. **Don't overcomplexify.** In hindsight, many of the most creative discoveries are embarrassingly simple. Biologist Thomas Huxley said, after reading Darwin's explanation of evolution: "How extremely stupid not to have thought of that!" But sometimes the most simple solution is the best one.[17]

6. **Capitalize on your mistakes.** Remember that Thomas Edison tried anything he could think of for a filament for the incandescent lamp, including a whisker from his best friend's beard. All in all, he tried about 1,800 things before finding the right one. Afterward he said, "I've gained a lot of knowledge—I now know a thousand things that won't work."[18]

7. **Let it flow.** Mihaly Csikszentmihalyi, the author of *Flow: The Psychology of Optimal Experience* and many other books on creativity, discovered something interesting. For his doctoral thesis, he studied artists by taking pictures of them painting every three minutes. He was struck by how engaged they were in their work, so engaged that they seemed to forget everything around them. He began studying other "experts": rock

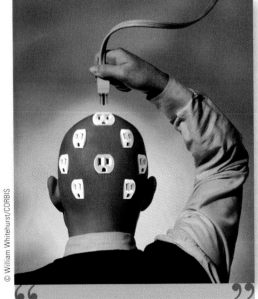

"A hunch is creativity trying to tell you something."

Frank Capra, Italian American film director (1897–1991)

climbers, chess players, dancers, musicians, surgeons. Regardless of the activity, these people forgot the time, themselves, and their problems. What did the activities have in common? Clear, high goals and immediate feedback. Athletes call it being in the zone. The zone is described as the ultimate human experience, where mind and body are united in purpose. Csikszentmihalyi's suggestions for achieving flow are these: Pick an enjoyable activity that is at or slightly above your ability level, screen out distractions, focus all your senses and emotions, and look for regular feedback on how you're doing.[19]

I can't understand why people are frightened by new ideas. I'm frightened by the old ones.

John Cage, American composer
(1912–1992)

8. **Bounce ideas off others.** One good way to become more creative is to use your family or friends as sounding boards. Sometimes just saying something out loud helps you understand more about it. Each person who provides a critique will give you a new perspective, possibly worth considering.

9. **Stop searching for the "right" answer.** This advice doesn't pertain to your upcoming math exam. But it does to apply to situations in which there are many ways to solve a problem. There may be more than one acceptable solution. A fear of making mistakes can hold you back.

10. **Detach your self-concept.** For most of us, creativity is often linked to self-concept. An idea is your brainchild, and you want it to win people over. You've invested part of yourself in giving birth to it. But there's nothing like self-criticism to shut down your creative juices. Your idea may not succeed on its own, but it may feed into someone else's idea and improve it. Or an idea you have about this problem may inform the next problem that challenges you. In the end, in addition to finding a workable solution, what's important is engaging in the creative process with others.

CONTROL: *YOUR TOUGHEST CLASS*

Look over the "10 Ways to Become a More Creative Thinker" in this chapter and choose one of these items to write about. Which piece of advice will be most useful to you? Is there a way you can use your natural creativity to improve your chances in your toughest class? For example, item 6 might be a good idea to use in your math class. When you get an exam back, look it over, analyze your mistakes, and then come up with creative new ideas to improve your score next time—now that you know what didn't work last time. Item 10 might be something to work on if you always fear the essays you write for your composition class won't measure up.

1. Find new eyes.
2. Accept your creativity.
3. Make your thoughts visible.
4. Generate lots of ideas.
5. Don't overcomplexify.

6. Capitalize on your mistakes.
7. Let it flow.
8. Bounce ideas off others.
9. Stop searching for the right answer.
10. Detach your self-concept.

At the beginning of this chapter, Desiree Moore, a frustrated student, faced a challenge. Now after reading this chapter, would you respond differently to any of the questions you answered about the "FOCUS Challenge Case"? Using what you learned in the chapter, write a paragraph ending to Desiree's case study. What are some of the possible outcomes for Desiree?

step

4 ACTION Your Plans for Change

1. What's the most important thing you learned in reading this chapter? Why did it have an impact on you?
2. What will you change about the way you try to learn in your classes or perform on the job as a result of reading it?

REALITY CHECK

What did you **Learn?**

On a scale of 1 to 5, answer these questions now that you've completed this chapter.

1 = not very/not much/very little/low   5 = very/a lot/very much/high

How much do you know *now*?

Now rate your current level of knowledge about topics covered in this chapter.

Focused thinking

1 2 3 4 5

Four-part model of critical thinking

1 2 3 4 5

Arguments, assumptions, claims

1 2 3 4 5

Critical versus *creative* thinking

1 2 3 4 5

How useful might the information in this chapter be to you?

How much do you think this information might affect your college success?

1 2 3 4 5

How much do you think this information might affect your career success after college?

1 2 3 4 5

How long did it actually take you to complete this chapter (both the reading and writing tasks)?

_____ Hour(s) _____ Minutes

 Challenge Yourself Online Quiz. To find out how much you've learned, access the CourseMate via www.cengagebrain.com/shop/ISBN/0495906433 to take the Challenge Yourself Online Quiz.

Compare these answers with your answers from the "Readiness Check" at the beginning of this chapter. How might the gaps between what you thought before starting the chapter and what you now think affect how you approach the next chapter?

chapter 6

Developing Technology, Research, and Information Literacy Skills

©Larry Harwood Photography. Property of Cengage Learning.

YOU'RE ABOUT TO DISCOVER...

✔ HOW TECHNOLOGY IMPACTS OUR LIVES

✔ HOW TO USE TECHNOLOGY TO BE MORE ACADEMICALLY SUCCESSFUL

✔ HOW E-LEARNING (ONLINE) IS DIFFERENT FROM C-LEARNING (CLASSROOM)

✔ HOW TO CULTIVATE YOUR RESEARCH SKILLS

✔ WHAT INFORMATION LITERACY SKILLS ARE AND WHY THEY'RE IMPORTANT

✔ WHAT PLAGIARISM IS AND HOW TO AVOID IT

READINESS CHECK   What do you **Know?**

Before beginning this chapter, take a moment to answer these questions. Your answers will help you assess how ready you are to focus.

1 = not very/not much/very little/low   5 = very/a lot/very much/high

How much do you *already* know?

Rate your current level of knowledge about topics covered in this chapter.

Academic uses of technology

1 2 3 4 5

E-learning techniques

1 2 3 4 5

Information literacy/research skills

1 2 3 4 5

Plagiarism

1 2 3 4 5

How motivated are you to learn *more*?

In general, how motivated are you to learn the material in this chapter?

1 2 3 4 5

How much do you think this information might affect your college success?

1 2 3 4 5

How much do you think this information might affect your career success after college?

1 2 3 4 5

How ready are you to read *now*?

How ready are you to focus on this chapter—physically, intellectually, and emotionally? Which of these three areas is most challenging for you right now? Circle a number to represent it.

1 2 3 4 5

If any of your answers is below a 3, consider addressing the issue before reading. Then, read the chapter carefully, while looking for ways to improve your focus.

Finally, how long do you think it will take you to complete this chapter? If you start and stop, keep track of the overall time.

_____ Hour(s) _____ Minutes

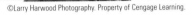

Dario Jones

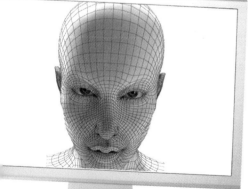

Mike Margol/PhotoEdit

Ever since grade school, Dario Jones had been called a geek. It was a label he hated, but, honestly, most people probably thought of him that way. As a kid, Dario lived for computer games. He played them nearly every waking hour. In the morning, he'd shower in record time, throw on whatever clean clothes he could find, and use any spare minutes for computer games. When he got home, he'd log right back on again. His Dad tried threatening him: "You'll lose your eyesight and flunk out of school." Once he faked a sore throat and played World of Warcraft at home for a week, while his parents were at work. As he got older, his Dad warned: "You'll never get a date." But Dario wasn't worried. Second Life relationships were enough. Real-life relationships were too much trouble. Even now that he had been on his own for several years, his cyber life was much more exciting than his real life. Dario spent more time—even sacrificing precious hours of sleep—surfing the Internet, envisioning how he could improve websites, and grooming his MySpace page than he spent talking to any living being.

Then one day the obvious truth dawned on him. Why was he wasting his time woring in his Dad's auto body shop? The world of cars didn't really interest him. The world of cyberspace did. But somehow after high school, he hadn't thought about it much and went to work for his Dad because it was easy.

Eventually, Dario made a decision. Even though it had been a while since he had been in school, he needed to change his life. Being a web designer

was the right career for him. He drove to the community college campus across town and parked in the parking lot. He sat in his car for a while, and then bit the bullet, walked through a big door, and talked with someone. As it turned out, that was the last official day to enroll for the semester. So with the help of a friendly advisor, who took him to the Financial Aid office and helped him fill out the application, Dario was in school again. He'd have to increase his hours at his Dad's auto body shop to afford tuition, but he thought it would be worth it.

But Dario quickly discovered that messing around with computers and studying computers were two very different things. His toughest class, required for his certificate program in web design, was a class called Fundamentals of Internet Business. Right off the bat, he discovered the course required a research paper. The assigned topic was Globalization and Internet Commerce. Even though he had always considered himself to be a technology expert, frankly, he didn't know where to start. *Step one*, Dario thought to himself, *is to Google*. He always Googled everything: the directions to a new Mexican restaurant—his favorite food—or some little-known fact that he wondered about, like how many Chihuahuas were sold in the United States last year. (He had just bought one.) But when he Googled "Internet Commerce," he got 22 million hits. *Better regroup*, he advised himself.

But how? Should he go to the library on campus, or try to do his research online in the comfort of his own apartment? Physically going to the library seemed unnecessary when so much information was available online. Then he had a flash of inspiration: Wikipedia. He found a page on "Electronic Commerce." At least that was a start—that is, until he looked at his instructor's handout on the assignment. Students were discouraged from using Wikipedia as a primary research source. The handout said "Information literacy is required." He got another idea: He'd close Wikipedia and go back to Googling. This time he'd try "Electronic Commerce." *Ah, only 7 million hits this time*. He was on a roll. He plugged in "E-Commerce," "E-Business," and "Globalization." He tried "Global Issues," but before he knew it, he found himself knee-deep in articles about "Global Warming." He was so far afield now that he couldn't find his way back to his topic. Should he shut everything down and start over or just give up?

Dario's paper was due the following day. At the last minute, he panicked. He found a few useful things online, and in the interest of time, he cut and pasted from the Internet until he'd filled five pages. At least he had something to turn in. He wondered if this was the way to do research and whether he'd broken any rules. *Well, at least there will always be fender-benders*, he thought pessimistically. But to be honest, a career smoothing out dents in other people's cars wasn't at all what he wanted to do with his life.

Web Design Certifica

Learn How to Be
Website Wiz

Community College Program
Call 555- 4242

**Fundamentals of Internet Business
CS 112**

Research Paper Guidelines

TOPIC: Globalization and Internet Commerce

For this assignment you will write a 10 page research paper investigati relationship between globalization and Internet commerce. You shoul focus on how globalization has affected Internet commerce, but how t relationship may be a two-way street. In other words, look at how Int commerce has changed the pace of globalization in the 21st century.

POTENTIAL AREAS OF RESEARCH FOCUS:

- What is Globalization?
- Free Trade
- tional Corporations

Wikipedia.

http://en.wikipedia.org/wiki/Electronic_commerce

File Edit View Favorites Tools Help

W Electronic commerce - Wikipedia, the free encyclopedia

Help us provide free content to the world by donating today!

article | discussion | edit this page | history

Electronic commerce

From Wikipedia, the free encyclopedia

WIKIPEDIA

Electronic Commerce, commonly known as (electronic marketing) e-commerce or eC

**Fundamentals of Internet Business
CS 112**

Instructor: Dr. Greg Otis
Office: Hansford Hall 230
Office Hours: T, W 2:00-4:00 PM

Description:
The Internet has fundamenta

1. Do you have anything in common with Dario? Do you find doing research for papers like his to be easy or challenging?
2. The instructor's assignment required "information literacy." What is information literacy? Dario was tech-savvy, but did he have the right skills? Why or why not?
3. Did Dario plagiarize his paper—or did he simply find the sources he needed and use them? Give the reasons behind your answer.
4. In your view, is Dario addicted to technology? Can being too dependent on technology be a problem? Why?

Technology Skills: Wireless, Windowed, Webbed, and Wikied

Ah, technology . . . Does it make our lives simpler or more complicated? Like Dario, are you pulled into games like World of Warcraft? Do you live to text? Do you run, not walk, to any nearby computer to check your Facebook account? Or, on the other hand, do you hate the thought of facing your e-mail after you haven't had access for awhile? Did you find yourself answering "yes" to any of these questions—or maybe answering "yes" to all of them?

Many of us have a love-hate relationship with technology: We love the convenience but hate the dependence. But in college, your techno-skills will be another key to your success. You'll need to know things like how to produce an essay in Microsoft Word, how to give a PowerPoint presentation, and how to use course management systems like Blackboard. "Whoa! Wait a minute," you say. "I'm no expert at all of that!" You don't have to be an expert, but you do need to know the basics and be willing to learn more. Dario considered himself to be a technology expert, but his expertise was more about *entertainment* than *education*. In college, you'll be using technology to enhance your education.

Your community college may have invited you to enroll with a MySpace or Facebook invitation. Your school will provide you with an e-mail account and send you official college documents, like your tuition bill and weather alerts over e-mail. You will take entire courses or parts of courses online so that you can learn on your own time at your own pace. Many of your instructors will use course management systems, YouTube clips, streaming video, and websites in the classroom to increase your learning. (And the good news is that 70.4 percent of college students say it helps.[1]) So the time to start building your skills is now! Dario began researching his paper by Googling. Just how useful is the Internet to college students? The answer is: Just like anything else, the Internet has pros and cons.

The Internet: The Good, the Bad, and the Ugly

The Good Students who enter college right after high school are the leading consumers of digital technology in the United States.[2] In one study, 79 percent of college students reported that the Internet has had a positive impact on their

college academic experience.[3] For many of us, the Internet is how we get our news, our research, our entertainment, and our communication. When it comes to all the potential benefits of the Internet, think about advantages like these:

> **Currency.** While some of the information posted on the Internet isn't up to date, much of it is current. This is especially important during a crisis or a national emergency, for example, when it's important to get news fast. Reports, articles, and studies that might take months to publish in books or articles are available on the web as soon as they're written.

> **Availability.** The Internet never sleeps. If you can't sleep at 2:00 a.m., the Internet can keep you company. It can be a good friend to have. Unlike your real instructor who teaches other classes besides yours and attends marathon meetings, Professor Google is always in. For the most part, you can check your e-mail or log onto the Internet from anywhere, any time.

> **Scope.** You can find out virtually anything you want to know on the Internet from the recipe for the world's best chocolate chip cookie to medical advice on everything from **A**thlete's Foot to **Z**its. (Of course, real human beings are usually a better option for serious questions.)

> **Interactivity.** Unlike other media, the Internet lets you talk back. You can write a letter to the editor of a newspaper and wait for a reply, or you can push buttons on your phone in response to an endless list of menu questions ("If you want directions in English, press 1 . . .") and finally get to a real-live human being. But the Internet lets you communicate instantly and constantly. You can instant message to your heart's content, if you want to, add to your Facebook page daily, or edit a Wikipedia entry whenever you like.

> **Affordability.** As of December 2009, there were 1,802,330,457 Internet users worldwide; 234 million Americans are on the Net today.[4] For most of us, when it comes to the Internet, the price is right. After you buy a computer, and pay a monthly access fee, you get a great deal for your money.

The Bad Too much of a good thing—anything—can be bad. When anything becomes that central to our lives, it carries risks. Here are some Internet dangers worth thinking about:

> **Inaccuracy.** Often we take information presented to us at face value, without questioning it. But on many Internet sites, the responsibility for checking the accuracy of the information presented there is yours. Bob's Statistics Home Page and the U.S. Census Bureau's website are not equally valid. Not everything published online is true or right.

> **Laziness.** It's easy to allow the convenience of the Internet to make us lazy. Why go through the hassle of cooking dinner when you can just stop for a burger on the way home? The same thing applies to the Internet. Why not just do what Dario did and find information somebody else has already posted on the Internet and use it? What's wrong with that? For one thing, if you don't give the rightful author credit, that's plagiarism, which can give you a zero on an assignment, or even cause you to fail a course. But another thing worth considering is that the *how* of learning

If your computer is next to the TV or your kids are acting up to get attention, move to another location that's calm, well lit, and quiet.

7. **Use each login session as an opportunity to review.** Begin each online session by reviewing what you did or how much progress you made last time. Physically logging on can become a signal to take stock before moving forward with new course material.

8. **Call on your time management skills.** If your e-course is self-paced, you'll need to plan ahead, schedule due dates, and above all, discipline yourself to make continual progress. If you're sharing a computer with other family members, you'll need to create a master schedule. Remember that you may need to be online at particular times to engage in class chats or discussions.[21]

Research Skills and Your College Success

Many of your class assignments in college will require you to conduct research. Why? Aren't you in college to learn from your instructors? Why do they ask *you* to do research on your own?

There are unanswered questions all around us in everyday life. Some questions are simple; others are complex. How much time will it take to get across town to a doctor's appointment during rush hour? What can you expect college tuition to cost by the time your kids are old enough to go? What are the chances that someone you know who has cancer will survive for five years? Research isn't necessarily a mysterious thing that scientists in white coats do in laboratories. Research is simply finding answers to questions, either real questions you encounter every day or questions that are assigned to you in your classes. Doing research on your own can be a powerful way to learn, sometimes even more so than hearing answers from someone else, even if those people are your instructors. Going off to a research expedition in the library may sound like exhausting busywork, but the skills you stand to gain are well worth the effort.

Conducting research teaches you some important things about how to formulate a question and then find answers. And it's not just finding answers so that you can scratch a particular assignment off your to-do list. It's about learning an important process. When you get into the world of work, your instructors won't be there to supply answers, so knowing how to figure things out on your own will be key to your success. So, exactly what is college-level research?

66

99

Any occurrence requiring undivided attention will be accompanied by a compelling distraction.

Robert Bloch, American fiction writer, (1917–1994)

What Research Is *Not*	What Research Is
Research isn't just going on a "search and employ" mission. It's not just seeing what all you can find and then using it to check off an assignment on your to-do list.	**Research starts with a question.** If an assignment is broad, as Dario's was, you must come up with a specific question to research yourself. More about that later.
Research isn't just moving things from Point A (the library) to Point B (your paper).	**Research is a process with a plan.** A plan was something Dario lacked. He jumped in without a question—or a plan.
Research isn't random rummaging through real or virtual files to find out something.	**Research is goal-oriented.** You've formulated a question, developed a plan, and now you begin to find answers by using both online sources and ones that sit on your library's shelves.
Research isn't doing a quick Internet search. The cutting and pasting Dario did to fill up his five pages is actually plagiarism!	**Research often involves breaking a big question into several smaller ones.**[22]

Navigating the Library

You've probably heard this since you were a child: "The library is your friend." As a young child, it was exciting to go to the library, choose a book, check it out with your own library card, and bring it home to read. Now, being "exiled" to the library to do research for a paper may seem like torture that can ruin a perfectly good weekend. But if you look at things differently, it can be a mind-expanding trip into places unknown. The truth is: In college, the library should be more than just a friend. It should become your best friend! Beyond navigating the web to find research for your assignments, as many students do, it's important to learn your way around the actual, physical space of the library on your campus. The library has many useful resources, including real, very knowledgeable librarians who are there to help you. Asking a reference librarian for help can save you hours of unproductive digging on your own. Here are some of the resources your library offers and how you should use these resources when you're assigned a research project:

> **Card Catalog.** Explore your library's catalog that lists all of the books available to you. Card catalogs used to be actual cards in file cabinet drawers, but now most libraries put all the information about their holdings online. Go to your college's website, and from there, you can find your way to your college library's home page. Click on the library's catalog button. Let's say Dario follows these instructions and finds this book in his campus library's catalog: *The Global Internet Economy, edited by Bruce Kogut. Cambridge, MA: MIT Press, 2003.* The call number for the book is HC79. I55 G579, based on the Library of Congress classification system, which

> I find that a great part of the information I have was acquired by looking up something and finding something else on the way.
>
> *Franklin P. Adams, American journalist and radio personality (1881–1960)*

most college libraries use. (Some libraries, like your community's public library, may use the Dewey Decimal system. One advantage of the Library of Congress system is that books usually have the same number, no matter which library you find them in. That's not always true for the Dewey Decimal system.) The Library of Congress number identifies this item as a book about economics and information technology. Now, after identifying other possible useful books, Dario needs to make his way to campus and find the actual book on the shelf.

> **Databases.** If you go to your library's home page, you can link to the list of online databases it subscribes to. Databases identify articles from academic journals and sometimes contain entire articles online. Generally, different databases exist for different disciplines, for example:

Education	**ERIC** (Educational Resources Information Center)
Psychology	**PsycInfo**
Business	**Business Source Premier**

But more general databases also exist. Dario might want to search through:

Academic Search Premier

WilsonWeb OmniFile Full Text Mega

The key to making the most of databases is to find the right search words to plug into the database's search engine. That's where a short coaching session with a real reference librarian can be enormously helpful. You can have productive results or no results at all, just by slightly altering the search words you enter.

> **Stacks.** Physically walk through the stacks or collections of books and periodicals (journals, magazines, newspapers, and audiovisual resources, for example). Get to know the stacks in your library, and figure out how to find what you need. Look for the Library of Congress numbers posted on signs at the end of each row of books. When Dario finds the book he's looking for, he's likely to find other books in the library's "HC" section that would also be useful to him. That's why even though doing online research is convenient, there's no substitute for "being there."

Information Literacy and Your College Success

Much of the research you do for your college assignments will take place online. Information literacy is defined as knowing *when* you need information, *where* to find it, *what* it means, *whether* it's accurate, and *how* to use it. Simply put, it's "the ability to use technology to solve information problems." Information literacy includes five components, as seen in Figure 6.2. Think about them as a step-by-step process as we work through Dario's assignment.[23]

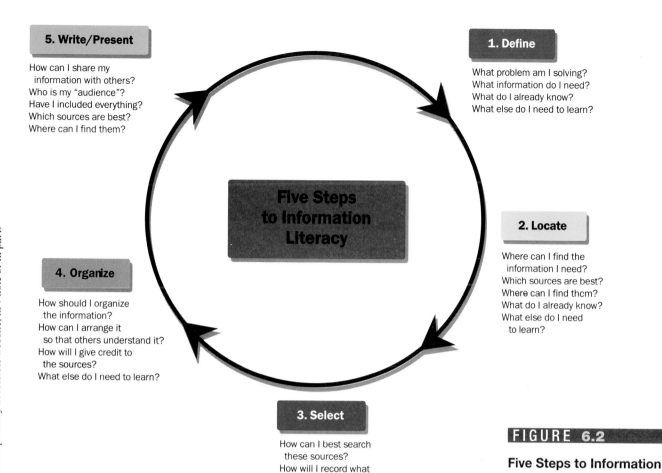

5. Write/Present

How can I share my
   information with others?
Who is my "audience"?
Have I included everything?
Which sources are best?
Where can I find them?

1. Define

What problem am I solving?
What information do I need?
What do I already know?
What else do I need to learn?

Five Steps to Information Literacy

2. Locate

Where can I find the
   information I need?
Which sources are best?
Where can I find them?
What do I already know?
What else do I need
   to learn?

4. Organize

How should I organize
   the information?
How can I arrange it
   so that others understand it?
How will I give credit to
   the sources?
What else do I need to learn?

3. Select

How can I best search
   these sources?
How will I record what
   I find?
How will I give credit to
   the sources?
What else do I need to learn?

FIGURE 6.2

Five Steps to Information Literacy

Source: Wood, G. (2004, April 9). Academic original sin: Plagiarism, the Internet, and librarians. The Journal of Academic Librarianship, 30(3), 237–242.

Step 1. Define

Define what the assignment requires of you. Dario was assigned a *research* paper. He wasn't being asked to **summarize** or *evaluate* a topic. He was asked to *find out about it*. But "Globalization and Internet Commerce" is a huge topic. He must narrow it down and decide which specific research question (or questions) he wants to focus on.

summarize condense a longer work into a few essential statements

If you were assigned the paper Dario was assigned, and you knew very little about "Globalization and Internet Commerce," you might start as he did, by Googling your topic to help you define it. But the Internet is huge and unstructured. There's really no way to organize that much information into simple, neat categories.[24] And how do you whittle down 22 million hits? According to a recent study, less than 1 percent of Google users look further than the first page of their Google results, regardless of how many hits they get![25]

If you don't know anything about the topic you need to research—absolutely nothing at all—the Internet is a great place to start. You can type in "globalization" and "Internet commerce," and within the blink of an eye, information appears. The problem is that you now have too much information, and the challenge is knowing what to do next. Your college instructors will insist you go beyond the Internet and avoid relying too much on encyclopedias and Wikipedia. College requires you to do more research than you've probably done before, and to do it differently.

Dario could have used the websites that Google brought up to help him *define* a specific research focus, instead of being overwhelmed by the number of hits. Consider these more focused research topics or questions, which Google or Wikipedia could have led him to:

1. **Five Reasons to Go Global with Your Website** (Why is it a good idea?)

2. **Online Retail Businesses Will Explode over the Next Ten Years** (Where will it go in the future?)

3. **Three Problems with Doing E-Business Internationally: Language, Shipping, and Money** (What are the challenges of trying to make it happen?)

Let's take that last focused topic and run with it. Suppose you have an online business and you want to attract customers from around the world to expand it. That's a good idea, but how will you deal with translating what's on your website to other languages? How will you ship your product overseas for a reasonable cost? How will you deal with the exchange rate between the U.S. dollar and the currency used in other countries? Now we've taken a big, broad topic ("Globalization and Internet Commerce") and broken it down into three specific questions or subtopics to research. Your preliminary Google and Wikipedia searches can help you identify what the smaller chunks of your topic could be.

But they can't do *all* the work for you, and you can't stop there, as Dario did. You have to know what to do next. (If you think this process is challenging, you're not alone. In one study, only 35 percent of college students knew how to narrow a Google search!)[26]

Step 2. Locate

If you've identified electronic sources, bookmark them in a file labeled with the name of your project. If they're print resources, physically find them in the library. If they're not available in your own campus library, see if it participates in an interlibrary loan agreement among libraries. Your own library may be able to borrow the resource from another library. (But be aware that this process may take up to two weeks or so. That's why it's important to start your research projects early!)

Step 3. Select

The Information Age surrounds us with huge amounts of data of all kinds. With so much information available, how do we know what to believe? Whether or not it's true, we tend to think that if something is on television or in a book or online, it must be important. But in any of these cases, we need to exercise our critical thinking skills and turn them into critical searching skills. Just because information is published doesn't automatically make it right or true. In particular, some of the so-called research you encounter online may be bogus, containing inaccuracies or bias. You must read, interpret, and evaluate research to decide whether to use it. Use these five criteria to evaluate any website you come across:

"Plans are only good intentions unless they immediately degenerate into hard work.

Peter Drucker, management expert (1909–2005)

bookmark a way to save and organize websites in your web browser

1. **Currency.** How up to date is the information? Some websites don't list a date at the bottom of the screen (where copyright information is often found). If you don't see one, try using other hints on the site to get at how old the information is ("According to a study published in 1995 . . ."). You may find that you need to search for something more up to date.

2. **Accuracy.** How accurate is the information presented? If a website makes an unbelievable claim ("Grow a new head of hair in just six weeks!") or presents shaky statistics to make a case, it's important to be skeptical. Take responsibility to validate the information elsewhere.

3. **Authority.** Does the sponsor of the website have the credentials to post the information you see? Chances are "Steve's Picks" or "myfavoritemovies .com" is a collection of one person's opinions. Compare that to a film reviewer's site with information compiled by a professional film critic for a major newspaper. Which one would you trust more? You may not agree with Steve or the professional film critic, but one has credentials, and the other doesn't.

4. **Objectivity.** Does the website sponsor have a reason to convince you of something, or is it presenting unbiased information? If the site wants you to order something online because it claims to have better products than those you can buy at a store, for example, you should be suspicious.

objectivity ability to not take sides, being neutral

5. **Coverage.** If a website just presents one side of an issue or a very small piece of a larger picture, check to make sure you're getting all the information you need. If you're left wondering, *but what about . . . ?* you're probably having the right reaction.

EXERCISE 6.3

Critical Searching on the Internet

With these five criteria in mind, choose one of the following two assignments to complete. Each one will ask you to use your critical searching skills.

Assignment 1: Create a list of three websites that pertain to your intended major. (If you're not sure of your major right now, choose one to explore anyway.) Evaluate the websites, using the five criteria, to see which ones seem most useful to you as a student.

Assignment 2: Compare websites with contradictory information. Choose a controversial subject such as abortion, the death penalty, religion, politics, or some other subject of interest. Find three websites on your topic and compare them on the five criteria. Which of the three websites gets the highest marks? Why?

Step 4. Organize

Now that you have located the information you need, using a variety of sources, and selected those that will be most useful to you in your research project, it's time to organize. Dario's paper will be easier to write now that he has created three subtopics: language, shipping, and money. He should begin taking notes on index cards or highlighting pieces of information he wants to quote

1. Do have anything in common with Rachel? If so, how are you managing the situation so that you can be successful?
2. List five mistakes Rachel is making.
3. Now list five things that Rachel should do immediately to improve her childhood development classroom experience.

Get Engaged in Class

engagement emotional and psychological commitment to a task

No, this chapter isn't about buying a ring and getting down on one knee. It's about your willingness to focus, listen, discuss, ask questions, take notes, and generally dive into your classes. It's about being a full participant in your learning, not just a spectator sitting on the sidelines. It's about not just memorizing information for exams and then forgetting it. You see, the secret to college success hinges on this one word: **engagement**.

Think about this analogy. How did you learn to swim? Did you watch swimming on TV? Did you get advice from your friends about swimming? Did you just Google it? No, you probably jumped in and got wet, right? The same thing is true with your college classes. The more willing you are to jump in and get wet, the more engaged you'll be in the learning process.

Dare to Prepare

If you want to get a head start on developing good academic habits in class, then start before you get there. Preparation separates students into two categories: those who excel at learning and those who don't. Although not all students see the value of preparation, do more than your classmates do—dare to prepare! Follow these suggestions and you'll find that it's easier to get engaged in class because you're ready.

1. **Look ahead.** By checking your course syllabus before class, you'll be prepared for the upcoming topic. You'll also avoid the "oops" factor of sitting down, looking around, and noticing that everyone else knows something you don't about what's supposed to happen today.

2. **Do the assigned reading.** If you have a reading assignment due for class, do it, and take notes as you read. Write in the margins of your textbook or on sticky notes. Or take notes using one of many convenient online note-taking tools while you read. Question what you're reading and enter into a mental conversation with the author. Having some background on the topic will allow you to listen more actively and participate more intelligently during any discussion: *Yes, I remember the chapter covering that topic*, you'll think when the instructor begins talking about something you recognize. Instead of hearing it for the first time, you'll *strengthen* what you've already read. According to one study, as few as one-third of your classmates will have done the assigned reading prior to class. That little known fact isn't a reason to excuse yourself from reading; instead it gives you insider information on how *you* can shine in class by comparison.[1]

> " When you can do the common things of life in an uncommon way, you will command the attention of the world.
>
> —*George Washington Carver, 1864–1943, horticulturist, chemist, and educator*

> " You cannot truly listen to anyone and do anything else at the same time. "
>
> *M. Scott Peck, American author, (1936–2005)*

3. **Show up physically.** Not only is attending class important for your overall understanding of the material, but it may move your grade up a few notches. Even if attendance isn't required by your instructor, require it of yourself. Research says that missing classes is definitely related to your academic performance. And once you give yourself permission to skip one single class, it becomes easier to do it the next time, and the time after that. Studies indicate that on any given day, approximately one-third of your classmates will miss class, and that most students think that several absences during a term is "the standard."[2] Exercise good judgment, even if your classmates don't!

4. **Show up mentally.** Showing up means more than just occupying a seat in the classroom. It means thinking about what you bring to the class as a learner on any particular day. Do a mental "Readiness Check" when you arrive in class. If you're not ready, what can you do to rally for the cause?

5. **Choose your seat strategically.** Imagine paying $150 for a concert ticket, just like everyone else, and then electing to sit in the nosebleed section as high up and far away from the action as you could get. Sitting in the back means you're more likely to let your mind wander and less likely to hear clearly. Sitting in the front means you'll keep yourself accountable by being in full view of the instructor and the rest of the class. What's the best spot for great concentration? Front and center, literally—the "T zone"! In one study, students who sat at the back of a large auditorium were six times more likely to fail the course, even though the instructor had assigned seats randomly![3]

6. **Bring your tools.** Bring a writing utensil and notebook with you to every class. Your instructor may also ask you to bring your textbook, calculator, a blue book or scantron form for an exam, or other necessary items. If so, do it. Question: How seriously would you take a carpenter who showed up to work without a hammer, nails, and screwdriver? Get the point?

7. **Don't sit by your best friend.** Resist the temptation to sit next to your best buddy in order to catch up during class. Of course, it's important to have friends, but class is hardly the best time to devote yourself to helping your friendship blossom.

8. **Posture counts!** Your parents may have told you more than once as a kid: "Sit up straight!" Sitting up straight in class will help you develop a healthy mind. It's hard to focus when you're slouched into a position that screams, "I could really use a power nap right about now!" When your body says, "I'm ready to learn," your mind follows suit.

9. **Maintain your health.** Being sick can take its toll on your ability to concentrate, listen well, and participate. Prevent that from happening by getting enough sleep, eating well, and exercising. Remember, *energy management* is key to your ability to focus.

10. **Focus.** After sitting down in class each day, take a moment to clear your head of all daydreams, to-do's, and worries. Take a deep breath and remind yourself of the opportunity to learn that lies ahead. Think of yourself as a reporter at a press conference, listening carefully because you'll be writing a story about what's going on. You *will* be writing a "story"—often in response to an essay question on an exam!

Follow the Rules of Engagement

Just as is the case with most places you can think of, college classrooms have rules about how to behave. You don't find people yelling in church or staring at other people in elevators or telling jokes at funerals. There are rules about how to behave in a variety of contexts, and college classrooms are no exception.

1. **Be aware that gab is not a gift.** In class, talking while others are speaking is inappropriate. And it's certainly not a gift—especially to your instructor. In fact, side conversations while your instructor is lecturing or your classmates are contributing to the discussion are downright rude. If you're seated next to a gabber, don't get sucked in. Use body language to communicate that you're there to learn, not to gab. If that's not enough, politely say something like, "I really need to pay attention right now. Let's talk more later, okay?" Don't let other students cheat you out of learning.

2. **Control your hunger.** If your class meets through a meal hour, get in the habit of eating before or after class. Crunching and munching in the classroom may get in the way of others' learning, not to mention the distraction caused by enticing smells. Instructors differ on their preferences here. It's a good idea to find out what your instructors' preferences are, and then abide by them.

3. **Turn off your cell phone, please!** There's a reason why people are asked to turn off their cell phones before concerts, athletic events, or movies. Imagine being in a jam-packed theater trying to follow the film's plot with cell phones going off every few seconds. You've paid good money to see a film. The same thing goes for your college classes.

4. **Better late than never?** Students arriving late and leaving early are annoying, not only to your instructor, but to your classmates. To them, it looks

like you don't value the other students or the class content. How would you like dinner guests to arrive an hour late, after you'd slaved over a hot stove all day? Your instructors have prepared for class, and they feel the same way. Build in time to find a parking place, hike to the building where class is held, or stop for a coffee. Do everything you can to avoid coming late and leaving early.

5. **Actively choose to engage, not disengage.** Engagement isn't something that just happens to you while you're not looking. It's a choice you make, and sometimes it's a difficult choice because the material isn't naturally appealing to you, or the course is a required one you didn't choose, or you're just in a bad mood. Choose to engage, anyway. Instead of actively choosing to disengage in class by sleeping through lectures, surfing the Internet, or texting friends, choose to engage by leaning forward, listening, finding your own ways to connect to the material, and thinking of questions to ask.

Listening with Focus

Listening with focus is more than just physically hearing words as they stream by. It's actually a complicated process that's hard work.

"Easy Listening" Is for Elevators—Focused Listening Is for Classrooms

Stores, restaurants, and elevators are known for their programmed, background easy listening music. Chances are you hardly notice it's there. Listening in class, however, requires actual skill, and you'll be doing a great deal of it as a college student. Experts estimate that the average student spends 80 percent of class time listening to lectures.[4]

Many of us think that listening is easy. If you happen to be around when there's something to listen to, you can't help but listen. Not so! Did you know that when you're listening at your best, your breathing rate, heartbeat, and body temperature all increase? Just as with physical exercise, your body works harder when you're engaged in focused listening. When all is said and done, listening is really about energy management. You can't listen well when your energy is zapped, when you've stayed up all night, or when your stomach is growling fiercely. Focused listening means that you are concentrating fully on what's going on in class.

Here are some techniques for improving your listening skills in the classroom. Read through the list, then go back and check off the ones you're willing to try harder to do in class this week.

> **Calm yourself.** Take a few deep breaths with your eyes closed to help you put all those nagging distractions out of your mind during class time.

> **Be open.** Keep an open mind and view your class as yet another opportunity to strengthen your intellect and learn something new. Wisdom comes from a broad understanding of many things, rather than from a consistently limited focus what's going on in your own world.

❝ ❞

Politeness is the art of choosing among one's real thoughts.

Adlai Stevenson II, U.S. Presidential candidate (1900–1965)

> **Don't make snap judgments.** Remember, you don't have to like your instructor's wardrobe to respect his knowledge. Focus on the content he's offering you, even if you don't agree with it. You may change your mind later when you learn more. Don't jump to conclusions about content *or* style.

> **Assume responsibility.** Speak up! Ask questions! Even if you have an instructor with an accent who's difficult to understand, the burden of understanding course content rests with you. You will interact with people with all sorts of accents, voices, and speech patterns throughout your life. It's up to you to improve the situation.

> **Watch for gestures that communicate "Here comes something important!"** Some typical examples include raising an index finger, turning to face the class, leaning forward from behind the lectern, walking up the aisle, or using specific facial expressions or gestures.

> **Listen for speech patterns that subtly communicate "Make sure you include this in your notes!"** For example, listen for changes in the rate, volume, or tone of speech, longer than usual pauses, or repeated information.

> **Uncover general themes or roadmaps for each lecture.** See if you can figure out where your instructor is taking you *while* he's taking you there. Always ask yourself, "Where's he going with this? What's he getting at? How does this relate to what was already said?"

> **Appreciate your instructor's prep time.** For every hour of lecture time, your teacher has worked for hours to prepare. Although she may make it look easy, her lecture has involved researching, organizing, creating a PowerPoint presentation, overheads, or a podcast, and preparing notes and handouts.

Listen Hard!

It's estimated that college students spend ten hours per week listening to lectures.[5] Instructors can speak 2,500–5,000 words during a fifty-minute lecture. That's a lot of words flying by at breakneck speed, so it's important to listen correctly. But what does *that* mean?

Think about the various situations in which you find yourself listening. You often listen to empty chit-chat on your way to class. "Hey, how's it going?" when you spot your best friend in the hallway is an example, right? Listening in this type of situation doesn't require a lot of brainpower. Although you wouldn't want to spend too much time on chit-chat, if you refused to engage in any at all, you'd probably be seen by others as odd, withdrawn, shy, or stuck up.

You also listen in challenging situations, some that are emotionally charged; for example, a friend needs to vent, relieve stress, or verbalize her anxieties. Most people who are blowing off steam aren't looking for you to fix their problems. They just want to be heard and hear you say something like "I understand" or "That's too bad."

How **FULL** is your plate?

> ❝ **Speed is the blessing (and the curse) of the modern age. It is our drug of choice.** ❞
>
> —EDWARD M. HALLOWELL, M.D., *CRAZY BUSY*

Are you a fast food fanatic, mostly because it's fast? Do your days whiz by as you rush from thing to thing? Time management expert, Edward Hallowell, writes, "We go fast not just because we're busy, but because speed is fun. Speed grips attention. Speed excites. Speed speeds you out of boredom. Nothing is boring if it's fast enough." But what's the down side of speed? What do we lose? Are our lives long on stress and short on satisfaction?

© Rafa Irusta/Shutterstock

The most basic way to connect ... person is to listen. Perhaps the ... tant thing we ev... other is our atte...

Rac...
ph...

Identify I... Listening

Regardless of h... college will requ... instructor. Some... information on ... ture as their pr... learner, listenin...

Chances are... And even if you... styles. But what... what class or wl... see if you recog...

© Sophie Louise Phelps, 2010. Used under license from Shutterstock.com

Listening to chit-chat and listening in emotionally charged situations require what are called **soft listening skills**. You must be accepting, sensitive, and nonjudgmental. You don't have to assess, analyze, or conclude. You just have to be there for someone else.

But these two types of listening situations don't describe all the kinds of listening you do. When you're listening to new information, as you do in your college classes, or when you're listening to someone trying to persuade you of something, you have to pay close attention, think critically, and ultimately make decisions about what you're hearing. Is something true or false? Right or wrong? How do you know? When you're listening to a person trying to inform you or to persuade you, you need **hard listening skills**. In situations like these you must evaluate, analyze, and decide.

One mistake many students make in class is listening the wrong way. They should be using their hard listening skills, rather than sitting back and letting information float over them. Soft listening skills don't help you in class. You must listen intently, think critically, and analyze carefully what you're hearing. It's important to note that neither listening mode is better than the other. They are each simply better suited to different situations. But soft listening won't get you the results you want in your classes. You don't need to be there for your instructor; you need to be there for yourself.[6]

You may find many of your classes to be naturally fascinating learning experiences. But for others, you will need to be convinced. Even if you don't find Intro to Whatever to be the most engaging subject in the world, you may find yourself fascinated by your instructor. Most people are interested in other people. What makes him tick? Why was she drawn to this field? If you find it hard to get interested in the material, trick yourself by paying attention to the person delivering the message. Sometimes focusing on something about the speaker can help you focus on the subject matter, too. And you may just find out that you actually do find this class to be valuable. While tricking yourself isn't always a good idea, it *can* work if you know what you're doing and why.

So what are the various note-taking methods? What are the steps involved in using each one? Knowing your options, developing your skills, and learning flexibility as a note-taker are keys to your success.

Outlining

Outlining is probably the oldest, and perhaps the most trusted form of taking notes. The problem, of course, is that not all instructors speak from an outline. Rachel's instructor probably did, and if Rachel had been able to focus, outlining may have worked well. Here's what Rachel's notes would have looked like. She'd listen for key points, like the five developmental milestones, and list examples beneath each one, like this:

BOX 7.1

Child Development 1, Week 4

1. Child development involves learning and mastering skills like sitting, walking, talking, skipping, and tying shoes.
    A. Developmental milestones are learned during predictable time periods.
    B. Children develop skills in five main areas of development:
        1. Cognitive development: ability to learn and solve problems.
            a. two-month-old baby learning to explore the environment with hands or eyes
            b. five-year-old learning how to do simple math problems
        2. Social/emotional development: ability to interact with others, including helping themselves and self-control.
            a. six-week-old baby smiling
            b. ten-month-old baby waving bye-bye
            c. five-year-old boy knowing how to take turns in games at school
        3. Speech/language development: ability to both understand and use language.
            a. 12-month-old baby saying his first words
            b. a two-year-old naming parts of her body
            c. a five-year-old learning to say "feet" instead of "foots"

She's listed the instructor's main points and several examples below each point to help her remember what it's about. At the end of the lecture, she could have included a **summary** of her notes. Summarizing is an excellent way to make sure you've understood the gist of all the information you've written down.

summary a condensed version of the main points

Summary:

Children reach developmental milestones in five areas at fairly predictable ages. These five areas are cognitive, social/emotional, speech/language, fine motor skills, and gross motor skills.

Of course, if your instructor's lecture is less organized, you can elect to use an informal variation of outlining, like listing bullets, and perhaps even color-coding them so they're easier to remember, as shown here:

Child Development 1, Week 4

Child development = learning & mastering skills
- *sitting*
- *walking*
- *talking*
- *skipping*
- *tying shoes*

Children develop skills in five main areas of development:
1. *Cognitive development: ability to learn and solve problems.*
2. *Social/emotional development: ability to interact with others, including helping themselves and self-control.*
3. *Speech/language development: ability to both understand and use language.*

Even if your instructor is flashing PowerPoint slides on the screen, don't count on your memory to do all the work. You have to take notes yourself to help the information stick.

The Cornell System

The Cornell system of note-taking, devised by educator Walter Pauk, suggests this. On each page of your notebook, draw a line from top to bottom about one and a half inches from the left edge of your paper. (Some notebook paper already has a red line there.) Take notes on the right side of the line. Your notes should include main ideas, examples, short phrases, and definitions, for example—almost like an outline.

Leave the left side blank to fill in later with key words or questions you'd like answered, as Rachel has done in Figure 7.1. After class as you review your notes, put your hand or a sheet of paper over the right side and use the words or questions you've written on the left side as prompts to see if you can remember what's on the right side.[17] By doing this to recall the lecture, you can get a good idea of how much of the information you've really understood.

Luck is what happens when preparation meets opportunity.

Darrell Royal, football coach

KEY WORDS AND QUESTIONS	SHORT PHRASES, EXAMPLES, DEFINITIONS
Child development	—Every child goes through.
	—learning and mastering skills (sitting, walking, talking, skipping, tying shoes, etc.)
Developmental milestones	— predictable time periods
Five main areas of development	1. Cognitive development
	Ability to learn and solve problems
	—two-month-old baby learning to explore the environment with hands or eyes
	—five-year-old learning to do simple math
Was it five main areas or six?	2. Social/emotional development
	Ability to interact with others, including helping themselves and self-control
	—six-week-old baby smiling
	—ten-month-old baby waving goodbye
	—five-year-old knowing how to take turns in games at school

FIGURE 7.1

Child Development Milestones: Cornell System Example

Mind Maps

An alternative to the Cornell system, or a way to expand on it, is to create mind maps. Mind maps use both sides of your brain: the logical, orderly left side and the visual, creative right side. What they're particularly good for is showing the relationship between ideas. Mind maps are also generally a good note-taking method for visual learners, and even the physical act of drawing one may help you remember the information, particularly if you're a kinesthetic learner. To give mind mapping a try, here are some useful suggestions:

1. **Use extra wide paper (11 × 17 or legal size).** You won't want to write vertically (which is hard to read) if you can help it.

2. **Write the main concept of the lecture in the center of the page.** Draw related concepts coming from the center.

3. **Limit your labels to key words so that your mind map is visually clear.**

4. **Use colors, symbols, and images to make your mind map livelier and more memorable.**

5. **Consider using software such as MindManager, MindManuals, Mind-Plugs, MindMapper, or MindGenius, which are all powerful brainstorming and organizing tools.** As you type, these programs will anticipate relationships and help you draw a mind map on screen.

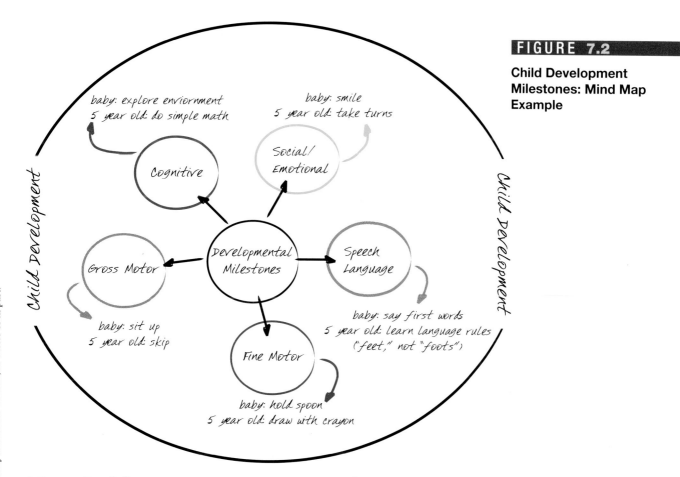

FIGURE 7.2

Child Development Milestones: Mind Map Example

Note-Taking on Instructor-Provided Handouts

PowerPoint Miniatures. Some instructors provide full-text lecture notes on-line or copies of their PowerPoint slides (three or six miniatures on a page). Instructors may hand out PowerPoint miniatures in class before the lecture, so you can follow along, hand them out after the lecture so that you still have to take your own notes but have the print outs of the miniatures as back-up, or e-mail them as attachments (see Figure 7.3). If you have copies of the Power-Point slides to use during class, write in specifics on the lines provided next to each slide miniature, more or less as you would if you were using the Cornell System. Put down examples that are discussed in class but don't appear on the slide, or a story that will help you remember a main point on a slide. If they're

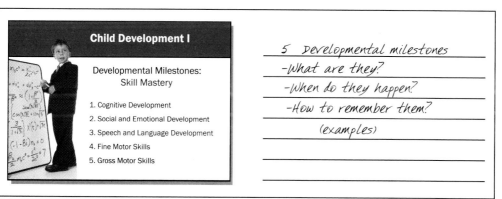

Photos.com

FIGURE 7.3

Child Development Milestones: PowerPoint Miniatures Example

> I make progress by having people around me who are smarter than I am and listening to them. And I assume that everyone is smarter about something than I am.
>
> *Henry J. Kaiser, American industrialist (1882–1967)*

handed out after class, transfer your own notes to the PowerPoint fill-in lines. If they're e-mailed to you before or after class, make sure you use them. They're "insurance" that you have access to what appeared in class on the screen. Tools such as these can be a valuable resource, if you remember to use them. Don't rely on PowerPoints your instructors provide to the extent that you skip taking notes yourself in class altogether. Although it's helpful to have them available as a tool, you still need to take notes on your own to help you process the information you're listening to in class.

Guided Notes. Your instructor may actually help you to pay attention in class by providing what are called "Guided Notes," or copies of lecture outlines or PowerPoint miniatures with key words missing, so that you must listen closely to "fill in the blanks." In one study, students in a college algebra class who used guided notes with problem sets they worked out together in groups liked their math class and did much better than comparable students who weren't using guided notes.[18]

Parallel Note-Taking. Because many instructors today provide e-support for lectures, either through web notes, hard copies of onscreen slides, lecture outlines, or a full transcript, parallel note-taking may be particularly useful, if you go about it in the right way.[19] Here's how it works, ideally.

If they're available, print out lecture notes before class and bring them with you, preferably in a ring binder. As your instructor lectures, use the back (blank) side of each page to record your own notes as the notes from the ongoing, real-time lecture face you. You can parallel what you're hearing from your instructor with your own on-the-spot, self-recorded notes, using a Cornell format on each blank page. It's the best of both worlds! You're reading, writing, and listening at the same time, fully immersing yourself in immediate and longer-lasting learning. Figure 7.4 illustrates how parallel note-taking might look for Rachel in her childhood development class.

FIGURE 7.4

Child Development Milestones: Parallel Note-Taking Example

[Fill in the blank page during actual lecture.] My In-Class Lecture Notes	[Print out instructor's notes and place in binder.] Instructor's Lecture Notes
Every child develops skills like learning to sit up, walk, talk, skip, and tie shoes. *These are called developmental milestones, and they happen to most children around the same age.* *Children learn skills in five main areas of development: cognitive, social/emotional, speech/language, fine, and gross motor skills:*	Child development is a process every child goes through. This process involves learning and mastering skills like sitting, walking, talking, skipping, and tying shoes. Children learn these skills, called developmental milestones, during predictable time periods. Children develop skills in five main areas of development: First, let's look at cognitive development. This is the child's ability to learn and solve problems. For example, this includes a two-month-old baby learning to explore the environment with hands or eyes or a five-year-old learning how to do simple math problems. Second, social/emotional development is the child's ability to interact with others, including helping themselves and self-control. Examples of this type of development would include a six-week-old baby smiling, a ten-month-old baby waving bye-bye, or a five-year-old boy knowing how to take turns in games at school.

Note-Taking by the Book

So far this chapter has discussed taking notes in class. What about taking notes as you read from a textbook? Is that important, too? The answer: absolutely! It's easy to go on auto-pilot as you read and have no idea what you read afterwards! Instead, take notes in the margins, on sticky notes, or better yet, keep a spiral-bound notebook next to you, and fill it with your own words as you read. Jot down questions, summarize main points, or use the Cornell System. Actually, the best thing to do is to read a section, close the book, and write down what you remember. You'll prove to yourself what you absorbed and what you didn't. Then you can dive back into the textbook again and clarify concepts that are still fuzzy.[20]

Note-Taking by the Subject

Beyond figuring out which note-taking style seems to "fit" you best, think about times when the subject dictates that you vary your note-taking style. In your American History class, it may make sense to take your notes along a timeline of the beginning of World War II, for example (see Figure 7.5). Since your instructor and your textbook report key events that took place during World War II chronologically, along a time line, you might want your notes to reflect that.

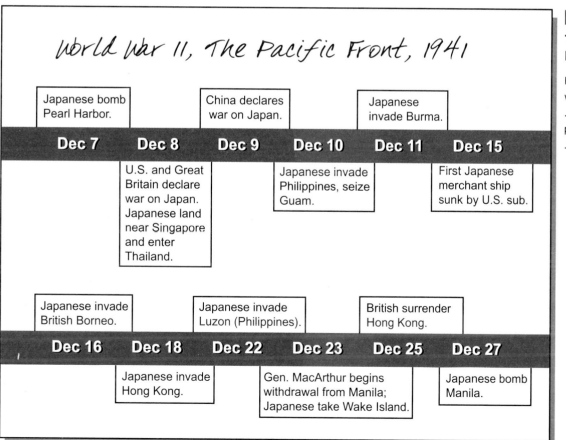

FIGURE 7.5

Timeline Example

Based on http://www.historyplace.com/unitedstates/pacificwar/timeline.htm

However, in your college algebra class, you may want to take notes very differently. Let's say, for example, that your instructor lectures by working problems on a white board or by projecting them on the screen. Then you are asked to work a problem and then talk it over with a classmate next to you. You may want to divide up your notes into columns by proposing a solution and then showing how you arrived at your answer. Having a record of how you worked a problem can be a valuable aid later when you're studying for a test that will probably contain algebra problems very much like the ones you solve regularly in class. Write everything down, and skip a few lines if there's something you want to fill in later (see Figure 7.6).

Mind mapping, on the other hand, is particularly useful in geology, physiology, biology, psychology, and education courses, where relationships between concepts are important.[21] Some students may make the mistake of thinking that mind maps are "scribbling," but the process of making connections on paper helps you make those same connections in your brain. Successful note-taking does mean "different strokes for different folks"—and different subjects. Be sure to make the right choices about which note-taking system makes the most sense for the course material being presented.

FIGURE 7.6

Math Note-Taking Example

From http://www.math.armstrong
.edu/MathTutorial/exerciseSoln/
LinearEqSoln/LinearEq1Soln/
13LinearEq1.html

Notes, College Algebra 100, Wednesday, Oct. 5

Determine which of the x values are solutions to the equation

$$x^4 + x^3 - 5x^2 + x - 6 = 0$$

a) $x = -3$,   b) $x = -2$,   c) $x = 1$,   d) $x = 2$

STEPS TO SOLUTION	CALCULATIONS	RESULTS
1) Try answer a Substitute -3 into the equation for x and see if the equation is satisfied.	$(-3)^4 + (-3)^3 - 5(-3)^2 + (-3) - 6 \stackrel{?}{=} 0$ $81 \quad -27 \quad -45 \quad -3 - 6 = 0$ $0 = 0$	YES since both sides are 0.
2) Try answer b Substitute -2 into the equation for x and see if the equation is satisfied.	$(-2)^4 + (-2)^3 - 5(-2)^2 + (-2) - 6 \stackrel{?}{=} 0$ $16 \quad -8 \quad -20 \quad -2 - 6 = 0$ $-20 \neq 0$	NO since the two sides are unequal.
3) Try answer c Substitute 1 into the equation for x and see if the equation is satisfied.	$(1)^4 + (1)^3 - 5(1)^2 + 1 - 6 \stackrel{?}{=} 0$ $1 \quad +1 \quad -5 \quad +1 - 6 = 0$ $-8 \neq 0$	NO since the two sides are unequal.
4) Try answer d Substitute 2 into the equation for x and see if the equation is satisfied.	$(2)^4 + (2)^3 - 5(2)^2 + 2 - 6 \stackrel{?}{=} 0$ $16 \quad +8 \quad -20 \quad +2 - 6 = 0$ $0 = 0$	YES since both sides are 0.

"Focused" Multitasking

One reason it's hard to focus in class is because of distractions. Like Rachel, you may be tempted to check your Facebook account or text someone about something that pops into your mind. Being pulled in different directions at once is what happens when you multitask. It breaks your concentration and disrupts your learning. Try this experiment instead. Let's call it "Focused Multitasking," meaning that all your attention is directed at one thing. Before you listen to an in-class lecture, divide into groups with each group trying out a different note-taking strategy presented in this chapter. For example, group 1 members should use outlines. Group 2 should use the Cornell System, Group 3 should create mind maps, etc. Then begin the lecture. The lecture could be your instructor lecturing about this chapter of FOCUS. Or it could be something different, like listening to an NPR podcast that the instructor or the whole class chooses. You are intentionally using all of your VARK preferences at once to focus on a single topic. After the lecture, take a quiz provided by your instructor and see which note-taking group's method earns the highest score!

Ask and You Shall Receive

Even if you listen carefully to every word your instructor utters, it's likely you won't understand them all. After all, your instructor is an expert in the subject you're studying, and you're new to it. At some point or other, you'll need to ask questions. Even though that makes sense, not all students feel comfortable asking questions in class. Why? See if you've excused yourself from asking questions for any of these reasons:

> I don't want to look stupid.

> I must be slow. Everyone else seems to be understanding.

> I'm too shy.

> I'll get the answer later from the textbook.

> I don't think my question is important enough.

> I don't want to interrupt the lecture. The instructor's on a roll.

> I'm sure the instructor knows what he's talking about. He must be right.

66 99

He who is ashamed of asking is ashamed of learning.

Danish Proverb

If any of these reasons for not asking questions in class applies to you, the good news is . . . you're in good company. Many students think this way. The bad news, of course, is that your question remains unasked, and therefore, unanswered.

The next time you find yourself in a situation where you don't understand something, consider these points.

1. **Remember that you're not in this alone.** Chances are you're probably not the only person in class who doesn't understand. Not only will you be doing yourself a favor by asking, but you'll also be helping someone else who's too shy to speak up.

2. **Ask academically relevant questions when the time is right.** As opposed to "Why do we need to know this?" or "Why did you make the test

5. Get help if you need to. If you have been diagnosed with ADHD, your brain is wired somewhat differently, affecting your memory and your ability to concentrate.[6] If you've not been diagnosed with a learning disability, but your attention appears be difficult to control and you're not sure why, get help from a counselor or learning specialist on campus.

Your Working Memory: Record

After you've focused your camera on your subject, you're ready to take a picture, right? But with a digital camera, you don't just click and walk away. You actually click and then review the picture on the small viewing screen to decide whether you want to save it or delete it.

Similarly, *recording* sensory impressions involves an evaluation process that takes place in your short-term or *working memory*. Your working memory is like a review screen, where you review recently acquired sensory impressions. In fact, your working memory is often involved in the focus process. In our example of you walking to class, which of these three specific sensations you just experienced are you likely to remember: the crowd, the car, or the billboard? To stay true to the camera **analogy**, which one would you take a picture of? It depends, right? You may remember the billboard because you plan to show it to someone else later, or the crowd because you hate crowded

analogy comparison

CAREER OUTLOOK: *Carlos Gomez, Computer Assisted Draftsman*

© Phase4Photography/Shutterstock

Q1: Why did you decide to get into drafting?

I became fascinated by the symbolism and precision of architectural drawings. In architecture much more goes on than just drafting. But drafting is the foundation, the design in a very pure form. This is what I love about it. I also love seeing a design through from drafting table to final product. It's very rewarding.

Q2: Beyond going to college, what else helped prepare you?

You have to be a visual person, learn how to closely observe things, and have

strong drawing skills. So much takes place on the computer nowadays, but if you don't know how to communicate things visually, then drafting can become that much more difficult. I've always been good with computers and visual communication, so I'd say that plus my observational skills served as a helpful foundation for my career.

Q3: What are the best and worst aspects of your career field?

The best thing about the career is that it is so respected. People need architecture, and even those who don't know a lot about

it can appreciate a beautiful structure. When someone likes a building I worked on it feels good: "Hey, I helped make that." One of the downfalls I believe is that people can become too isolated in their work stations and not communicate all aspects of a project with their teams. You can get sucked into your work and just assume people understand what you're trying to do. Again it comes back to being a good visual communicator but also being a good verbal communicator. If you don't work well as part of a team, I'd say this isn't a job for you.

Q4: What's your advice to college students who'd like to become CAD draftsmen?

The career offers many possibilities: You can design furniture, fashion, anything that requires specific drawings. At some point everything around us has been drawn. And thinking so analytically really develops your mind as well. I'd say start by paying attention. Look around you at everything you use from a pen to a bicycle. Pay attention to the buildings you inhabit and the cars

places, or the car horn because it scared you. Your working memory records something because it holds personal meaning for you.

The problem with working memory is that the length of time it can hold information is limited. You probably don't remember what you ate for dinner last Monday, do you? You'd have to reconstruct the memory based on other clues. Where was I? What was I doing? Who was I with?

The other problem with working memory is that it has limited capacity. It fills up quickly and then dumps what it doesn't need. If you look up a number in the campus directory, you can usually remember it long enough to walk over to the phone, right? A few minutes after you've dialed, however, the number is gone. Current estimates are that you can keep something in working memory for one to two minutes, giving your brain a chance to do a quick review, selecting what to save and what to delete.[7] Look at these letters and then close your eyes and try to repeat them back in order.

SAJANISMOELIHHEGNR

Can't do it? This task is virtually impossible because the string contains eighteen letters. Researchers believe that working memory can recall only seven pieces of information, plus or minus two.[8] (There's a reason why telephone numbers are prechunked for us.) Chunking these eighteen letters into five units helps considerably. Now look at the letters again and try to recall all eighteen.

you drive. Think about how you'd draw them. I'd also say get an internship. My internship gave me the practical experience I needed to be able to hunt for my first job with confidence. You learn things that you can't learn in school. This to me is invaluable. Internships are also a chance to prove yourself and impress the people you're working for. Even if there are no openings immediately, if they're impressed by your work, there's a good chance they'll keep you in mind for the future.

HOW WOULD *YOU* LIKE IT?

Have you ever considered a career as a computer aided draftsman?

Facts to Consider[9]

Academic preparation required: Most draftsmen have at least some training at a technical school. Employers will want to see not only samples of your work, but evidence that you've had some formal training after high school. An associate's degree or a bachelor's will give you a leg up when looking for work in this field.

Future workforce demand: CAD drafters will see a slowdown in job openings in the coming years due to overseas outsourcing. Since CAD files can be sent over the Internet, drafters here are seeing shrinking opportunities for work. However, the higher your level of training and experience, the more opportunities you'll find in this field.

Work environment: Typically CAD draftsmen can expect to spend most of their time in front of a computer in a professional office.

Essential skills: You must be artistically inclined as well as have a fundamental understanding of technical design and construction. Communication skills are very important since you'll constantly have to communicate your ideas and drawings to clients and supervisors.

Questions to Ponder

1. Do you have (or could you acquire) the skills this career requires?

2. Are you interested in a career like this? Why or why not?

For more career activities online, access the CourseMate via www.cengagebrain.com/shop/ISBN/0495906433 to do the Team Career exercises.

SAJA NISM OELI HHEG NR

If we rearrange the letters into recognizable units, it becomes even easier, right?

AN IS MAJOR ENGLISH HE

And if the words are rearranged to make perfect sense, the task becomes simple.

HE IS AN ENGLISH MAJOR

The principle of chunking is also used to move information from your working memory to your long-term memory bank, and it's used in memorization techniques described later in this chapter.

Your Long-Term Memory: Retain and Retrieve

Once your camera's memory card gets full, you probably transfer the photos to your computer, or you print them out and put them in photo albums or picture frames. However, before you do that, you generally review the photos, decide how to arrange them, where to put them, whether to print them, and so forth. In other words, you make the photos memorable by putting them into some kind of order or context.

Just as you must transfer photos from your camera's memory stick to a more permanent location with more storage room, you must transfer information from short-term, or working, memory to long-term memory. You *retain* the information by transferring it, and this transfer takes place if you review and use information in a way that makes it memorable. It is this review process that we use when we study for a test. You transfer information to long-term memory by putting the information into a context that has meaning for you, linking new information to old information, creating stories or using particular memory techniques, or organizing material so that it makes sense. You can frame material you're learning by putting a mental border around it, just as you put pictures into frames.

Your long-term memory is the computer in which you store new knowledge until you need to use it. However, while the memories in long-term memory aren't easily disturbed, they can be challenging to retrieve.[10] Ideally, you'd like your memories to be readily available when you want to retrieve them, just like the pictures or digital images that you have transferred to your computer or put in a photo album (Figure 8.1). You can click on them to view them again, arrange them into a slideshow or send them to your friends as attachments. If you just dump your photos onto your hard drive, or print them out and then put them into a box, with no organization or labeling system, how easy will it be to find a specific photo? Difficult, right? Retrieving information from your long-term memory can be equally challenging if you haven't organized your information, or created mental labels that will help you retrieve them later. Good recall often depends on having a good storage system. The remainder of this chapter will be about how to *retain* information by transferring it from working memory into long-term memory and how to *retrieve* information when you need to.

A memory is anything that happens and does not completely unhappen.

Edward de Bono, creative thinking expert and author of Lateral Thinking: Creativity Step by Step

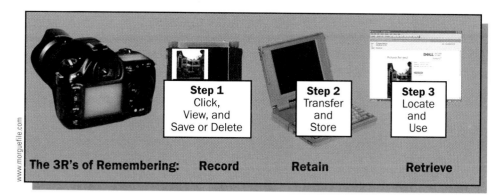

FIGURE 8.1

Your Memory as a Digital Camera

Twenty Ways to Master Your Memory

What can you do to sharpen your memory for the reading and test-taking you'll do in college? Try the following twenty techniques, grouped into five major categories (to help you remember them). These techniques are specifically designed to help you with the *retain* and *retrieve* parts of the memory process. As you consider each one, think about what you know about your own learning style.

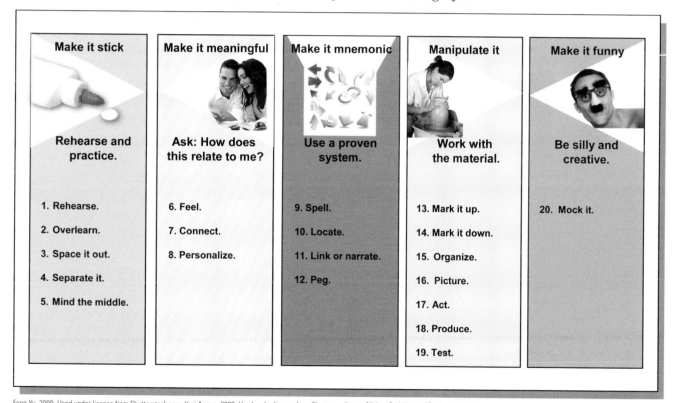

Feng Yu, 2009. Used under license from Shutterstock.com; Yuri Arcurs, 2009. Used under license from Shutterstock.com; Nishan Sothilingam/iStockphoto.com; IKO, 2009. Used under license from Shutterstock.com; Alex James Bramwell, 2009. Used under license from Shutterstock.com.

FIGURE 8.2

Twenty Ways to Master Your Memory

Make It Stick

How do you actually move material from your working memory to your long-term memory? What will work best for you? Some techniques are more effective than others, but the following suggestions are a good start.[11]

FIGURE 8.3

1. **Rehearse.** Although it's not the most powerful memorization strategy available to you, especially by itself, repeating information helps. Nothing gets stored in your memory for long without practice. How did you learn those multiplication tables in fourth grade? Probably not by just reading them over once or twice.

   Memory experts distinguish between *maintenance* (or shallow) rehearsal and *elaborative* rehearsal. Maintenance rehearsal helps you keep something in working memory for a short time. Repeating a phone number twenty times while you look for your cell phone might help you keep it there for several minutes, but will you remember it tomorrow when you need to call again? Shallow rehearsal didn't work for Kevin in the "FOCUS Challenge Case," who just kept rereading course material. Elaborative rehearsal—actually working with the information—helps transfer information to long-term memory more effectively. Most of the techniques described in this chapter will focus on elaborative rehearsal techniques. Typically, we remember the elaborate over the simple (Figure 8.3).

2. **Overlearn.** Overlearning helps you truly hardwire information, so that you can practically work in autopilot. When you think you've learned something, don't automatically assume it's time to move on. Keep working at it. The more you continue to work at it, the greater your degree of mastery.[12]

3. **Space it out.** Many studies show that studying for several hours at a time, as opposed to one long stretch, is much more effective. Clearing your entire day so that you can study algebra for six hours isn't the best idea. Your anxiety level would mount over that time, and you'd get tired, keeping you from maximizing your memory. Instead, study in shorter spurts for several days leading up to the exam. Cramming may work in the short run, but your working memory will most likely dump what you think you've mastered right after the exam.

4. **Separate it.** When you're tasked with learning similar, yet distinct, information, "bleeding" can occur. One body of knowledge can spill over into another. Imagine the confusion you'd experience if you tried to learn Spanish, French, Russian, and Chinese at the same time.

   Kevin from the "FOCUS Challenge Case" had trouble differentiating between Plato, Aristotle, and Socrates. He would have benefited from deliberately working to separate the three philosophers as he studied by making his own compare-and-contrast chart.

Interference presents a particular problem for college students because the subject matter in different courses often overlaps; one course may contain information that's similar to another's. Knowledge is interconnected; that's not the issue. It's the challenge of keeping knowledge bases separate for exams. If your sociology test is on Wednesday and your psychology test is on Friday, study sociology on Tuesday and psychology on Thursday. But if both tests are on Friday, separating the two bodies of information will be a challenge. Differentiate your study sessions as much as possible by studying for each test in a specific location or at a particular time of day, for example.[13]

5. **Mind the middle.** Perhaps you've heard of the serial-position effect. Research shows that we tend to remember what comes first because of the impression it makes on us, and what comes last because it's most recent. But what's in the middle sometimes tends to get lost.[14] That's an important principle for you to know. If you need to memorize a list of items, or a timeline, for example, pay particular attention to the middle.

Make It Meaningful

Sometimes we make the mistake of creating artificial distinctions between thoughts and feelings, when in fact, emotions and personal connections play an important role in learning.

6. **Feel.** Emotions and memories can team up in powerful ways. A piece of new information that makes you feel happy, angry, or sad lights up your amygdala, a small area of your brain that serves as your emotional center of operations. If a novel makes you cry or laugh or actually feel fear, you're likely to remember the story. If course content hooks into career goals you care about, you're likely to commit more of it to memory. Human beings care about other human beings and themselves, so the emotional side of new information (which you may have to create yourself) is a strong magnet for your memory.[15] All American adults remember where they were on September 11, 2001. Emotions enhance memory and recall.[16]

7. **Connect.** Create associations between what you're trying to commit to memory now and what you already know. That's why doing the reading assignment before class is so useful. During the lecture, you can think to yourself, *Oh, I remember that . . . and that . . . and that.* When you learn new information, it's almost as if you "file" it between other files already in place. If you know where to put it, instead of just stuffing it somewhere, that helps. Connecting it to previous knowledge also helps you retrieve the memory later.

8. **Personalize.** Find ways you can relate what you're memorizing to your own life. Okay, so you're thinking what do the plot and characters of *Pride and Prejudice*, a novel published by England's Jane Austen in 1813, possibly have to do with me now? Actually, there may be more similarities than you first think. Imagine the story taking place in your household. Do you have sisters? Does your mother worry about you marrying someone good enough for you? Do you have a close relationship with your father? Once

you start actively searching for overlap, you may be surprised. This task is easier with some course content than others, but the very act of trying to do this may be useful.

Make It Mnemonic

Some of the oldest ways to master your memory are through the use of mnemonic (pronounced *ne MON ik*) devices, verbal or visual memory aids, first used by Greek orators around 500 B.C. Imagine trying to remember a speech that goes on for hours; you'd need to devise specific ways to train your memory to keep working (without a teleprompter!). Although mnemonic devices can become complicated and aren't a solution to all memory challenges, for some students, these specialized elaborative rehearsal strategies can work well.

acronym a short word made up of the first letters of a longer phrase, such as radar (**ra**dio **d**etecting **a**nd **r**anging) or an abbreviation, like FBI for **F**ederal **B**ureau of **I**nvestigation

9. **Spell.** Acronyms are the simplest type of mnemonic device, words you create by putting together the first letters of what you want to memorize. Let's say, for example, that you want to learn the first five items in the list of random words in Exercise 8.2: theory, rehearsal, student, bone, and frostbite. You could create a bizarre acronym such as Ten rabbits' soup bowls fell. If you had vowels to work with, you may also be able to create an acronym you can pronounce, such as RAM for Random Access Memory.

10. **Locate.** The Loci (pronounced *LO si*) mnemonic system cues memory by using locations. Using the Loci system requires two steps. First, think of a familiar path, setting, or route. Perhaps you decide on the path from your apartment to the classroom where your exam will be given. On your way, you always pass distinct markers: the fountain in front of the big hotel, a tunnel that helps you bypass the freeway, the gym where you swim laps every morning, the hospital where someone you know had surgery, and the parking lot where you leave your car. Perhaps you want to use these five locations (fountain, tunnel, gym, hospital, and parking lot) to cue your memory to produce the first five items on our random list: theory, rehearsal, student, bone, and frostbite. You might picture saying hello to your science instructor, a "fountain" of knowledge who always says the word *theory* in class at least once. Then you might imagine conducting a *rehearsal* of a philharmonic orchestra in the tunnel, which would be a ridiculous sight and create a huge traffic jam. Then you envision *students* on a swim team thrashing about in the pool during a team practice. You know about a recent financial scandal involving the hospital so you imagine "skeletons" (*bones*) in the closet. And finally, you think of how terrible it would be to lose your apartment key and get a case of *frostbite* from spending the night in your car in the parking lot. Now without looking back, try it and see if it works for you. Of course, the optimal way the Loci system works is if the locations are familiar to *you*. Its main benefits are that it uses cues, connects things you already know about, and puts information in order, all of which aid in memory transfer and storage.[17] Or here's a simple example: perhaps you can remember the names of your classmates by simply paying attention to where they sit (the locations of their seats) each week.

Have you ever watched a movie, wondering how *do* actors learn all those lines? Do they have super-human memory powers? The average movie-goer assumes that actors simply repeat their lines over and over until they learn them. However, actors themselves say that's not all there is to it.[18]

Actually, what actors are most concerned with is convincing you that they're not playing a role. But actors' contracts require them to stick to the exact script, so how do they do it? Four of the techniques used by actors may also be useful to you as you try to commit course material to memory. Maybe you've even tried some of these techniques.

Chunking: Actors chunk their material into beats. For example, an actor might divide a half page of dialogue into three beats: to flirt, to sweet-talk, and to convince. In other words, the character would first flirt with the other actor, then sweet-talk him to lower his guard, and then convince him to do something he might not want to do. The results? Three chunks to remember instead of twelve lines of double-spaced text.

Goal Setting: Notice that the chunks are based on goals, a strategy that also works well while you're studying. Actors ask themselves goal-oriented questions such as: "Should I be flirting with him here?" In the same way, you can ask yourself, "Am I trying to learn the underlying formula so that I can work other problem sets?" or "Should I be coming up with my own reasons for why the play is considered to be Shakespeare's best comedy?" When you ask yourself goal-oriented questions while you study, you steer your actions toward learning.

Moving: Going through the motions while rehearsing their lines helps actors memorize them. Imagine the hypothetical actor whose goals were to flirt, to sweet-talk, and to convince, glancing toward the other actor from across the room, moving closer and smiling, and then touching his arm while making the persuasive case. The actor must know the meanings behind the movements to give meaning to the lines. The meanings are tied to the movements, which are tied to the lines, and the lines become committed to memory. Likewise, when you study, moving around may help you learn. Even if you're not primarily a kinesthetic learner, pieces of information become tied to motions in ways that help you recall information.

Meaning: "Say what you mean" and "mean what you say" was Lewis Carroll's advice in *Alice's Adventures in Wonderland*. Researchers use the term *active experiencing* to refer to what actors do when they use all their physical, mental, and emotional channels to communicate the meaning of their lines to someone else, real or imagined. As you study course material, do the same thing. Imagine you need to communicate the information to someone you know who needs it.

11. **Link or narrate.** Instead of a Loci system, you can create a linking mnemonic to help you memorize a list. To do this, you must connect item A to item B, item B to item C, and so forth. Consider again the list of words you were challenged to remember and write down: theory, rehearsal, student, bone, frostbite, camera, rose, calculus, and lecture. Your visual links might go like this: (1) (theory + rehearsal) You imagine a *theoretician* at a *rehearsal* dinner. (2) (rehearsal + student) The *rehearsal* dinner is attended by *student* friends of the bride and groom. (3) (student + bone) One *student* is in a leg cast because of a broken *bone*, and so forth.

12. Peg. The Peg system uses rhyming syllables modified by England's John Sambrook in 1879.[19] Remember the old nursery rhyme, "One, two, buckle my shoe"? The Peg system uses these rhyming pairs:

one—bun	six—sticks
two—shoe	seven—heaven
three—tree	eight—gate
four—door	nine—wine
five—hive	ten—hen

To use the Peg system, create *specific* images for yourself. To continue with our example, you'd picture a *theoretical* treatise stuffed between the hamburger *bun*, an image of a teenage girl's *rehearsal* of how to walk in her first pair of stiletto high-heeled *shoes*, a *student* sprawled out studying under a weeping willow *tree*, and so forth. Other types of Peg systems have been devised, but the rhyming system is the most common.

Manipulate It

Although some of us aren't kinesthetic learns, all of us can benefit from memory techniques with a kinesthetic basis. Actively doing something with information is a better way to commit it to memory than being passive. If you had three hours to study a textbook chapter that takes one hour to read, what should you do: Read the chapter three times, or work with the material after reading it once? The second option is generally more effective. So what kinds of things should you *do*?

13. Mark it up. Be an active reader; interact with the text. People who are used to reading complex material—your instructors, for example—read slowly, chew on each word, and make notes in the margins, arguing, questioning, summarizing, or explaining. Take notes as you read, "talk" with the author, and write out your reactions. Highlighting can be somewhat helpful, but it's often not enough. It certainly wasn't for Kevin from the "FOCUS Challenge Case." Every time you reach for your highlighter, ask yourself why you want to highlight that passage. Why is it important? To commit information to memory, you must go beyond simply coloring.[20]

14. Mark it down. If you want to give yourself a break, don't bother committing something unimportant to memory. Just write it down. (Of course, you still have to remember where you put that piece of paper.) Writing something down is an obvious memory alternative; save your memory for more important tasks. If it's something you do want to remember, however, the physical act of writing itself can help. Unless the exam is open-book, however, actually bringing your notes with you at exam time could be "hazardous to your [academic] health!"

15. Organize. Arrange and rearrange the material you're trying to memorize. Outline it—putting concepts into an order or pattern can help you figure out important relationships. If you're trying to learn the responsibilities of the

various branches of the government for your political science class, actually drawing a kind of written organizational chart is likely to help your essay answer flow better.

16. **Picture.** Drawings and mind maps can also be effective memory tools, particularly for visual learners. Think of drawing pictures to help you remember ridiculous visualizations or word associations. If you're trying to remember bones for your anatomy and physiology class, try Farsighted *Fibula*, Tempting *Tibia*, Party Girl *Patella*, Feathered *Femur*, and Pretty *Pelvis*.

17. **Act.** Consider putting motions to your memorizing. If you're trying to memorize a famous speech like Martin Luther King, Jr.'s "I Have a Dream," deliver it in front of a mirror. Write a short script and ask someone to play opposite you, if it helps you remember who said what to whom for an exam in history, or obviously, theater.

18. **Produce.** There's good evidence that putting things in your own words is highly beneficial to remembering.[21] Redeliver the instructor's lecture. Can you explain the concepts he explained, or do you stop after a few minutes because you are confused? Producing information requires you to dig deeper into your memory and benefits you and your memory beyond simple recognition tasks. One of the very best ways to produce is to teach something to someone else.

19. **Test.** Rather than assuming you remember something, test yourself. Create a multiple-choice, matching, or true-and-false test. Doing so requires you to ask what's important? Better yet, create essay questions that require you to organize and write what you know about a subject.

Make It Funny

Humor is an excellent memory-enhancing tool. Think about how easy it is to remember the plots of comedies you've seen at the movies or on television. For example, you may be able to remember conversations between *Friends* or *The Simpsons* cast members in shows you've watched once or twice, almost word for word, just because they tickled your funny bone.

20. **Mock it.** Experts on learning and the brain believe that the optimal condition for learning is *relaxed alertness*. Sounds like an oxymoron, doesn't it? How can you be relaxed and alert at the same time? Actually, it is possible when the challenge is high, but the threat is low—you're working hard, but you know you're learning.[22] What better way to create those conditions than to be a stand-up (or sit-down) comedian?

oxymoron combination of two words that mean opposite things

Think back to some of the funniest TV or movie scenes you've ever seen. They're probably still vivid in your memory. Ask yourself how you could apply your own humor to the material you're attempting to trigger your memory to learn. If you're having trouble separating Socrates and Plato, draw a picture of a crate full of socks next to Socrates' name and a can of PlayDoh® next to Plato's.

Create a David Letterman-like top-ten list of the reasons why Shakespeare's ten tragedies are tragic. Or put Shakespeare's *Romeo and Juliet* into

contemporary slang so that you can remember what it is about. Or if you can never remember which character is from the Montague family and which is a Capulet, write a silly limerick to help you remember:

There once was a girl named Cap

Who fell for a guy and was hap

But her family and his

Wouldn't stand for the biz

So they both ended up playing taps.

Set it to music. Be imaginative. We tend to remember what's bizarre, funny, or even obscene![23]

How Our Memories (uh...hmmm...) Fail Us

Imagine this: You meet someone at a school reception who says, "Hey, I know you! Remember? We met a year ago—it was October—at that Halloween party, and we even went out a few times. I've never forgotten you." You rack your brain. This person doesn't even look familiar. You wonder, *Am I being confused with someone else? Am I crazy? I have no recollection at all!* Later, you comb through your calendar to reconstruct that month. You weren't even attending your current school then. It couldn't have been you.

Digital cameras can malfunction, files we've saved can become corrupted, and sometimes our memories fail us, too. We forget things or change them in our thinking. Think of how many times you have had to e-mail someone for a password because you've forgotten your original one.

Here are seven ways our memories fail us from *The Seven Sins of Memory: How the Mind Forgets and Remembers*. See how many cause you to say "yes" because you've experienced them, and think about which ones particularly apply most to Kevin from the "FOCUS Challenge Case."

1. **Fading.** Memories fade over time. You probably remember what you wore yesterday, but how about on October 5 a year ago? As time goes by, memories generally weaken.

2. **Absentmindedness.** Sometimes there's a disconnect between your focus and your memory. You were doing several things at one time—talking to the girl next to you after class and checking your cell phone while stuffing your backpack—and now you have no idea what you did with your history textbook. It's not that the information is lost over time; it probably never registered in the first place because your attention was elsewhere.

3. **Blocking.** It's right on the tip of your tongue, but you just can't quite retrieve it. You can see the face, but you can't dig up the name. But later that day, without even trying, suddenly it comes to you. Psychologists call it TOT, the Tip of the Tongue phenomenon. You feel as if you're about to sneeze, but can't, and the word—whatever it is—just won't come to you.

4. **Mistaking.** You say to your friend, "Hey, that was an interesting story you told me about the new girl in our writing class." "What story?" your friend replies. Someone told you something, but you're wrong about who it was. Or you read a passage in one book, but think you've read it in another. Or you've dreamed about something for so long that the fantasy actually becomes real in your mind. Your memory deceives you by mistaking one source for another or tricks you by inventing a memory where none actually exists.

5. **Inventing.** Sometimes you retain bits of information that you think are memories, but they really aren't. Here's an example: Perhaps your mother has told you the cute story about yourself as a two-year-old toddler so many times that you can now envision it, and you think you remember it. You were actually too young to remember anything, but the event has become real at someone else's suggestion.

6. **Bias.** Sometimes we knowingly, or more often unknowingly, rewrite history. We insist on some detail that, if we had the ability to go back in time to verify it, is actually wrong. Perhaps someone has caught you in a trap in one of those instances by finding a piece of real evidence, and you've had to back down and admit that your memory is off a bit.

bias based on your own personal feeling or belief

7. **Persistence.** Another way that memory bothers us is by nagging. You'd really like to forget something, but you just can't. You wake up in a cold sweat at 3 a.m., remembering the embarrassing thing you did at work or said in class. You'd like to be able to push the memory away, but it won't budge.

persistence keeping at it; not letting go; continuing

While these seven memory faults are aggravating and inconvenient at times, they also have value. Persistence may serve as a reminder to be more careful next time. Fading is the result of memory efficiency. Why waste time recalling outdated, insignificant details we no longer need? Chances are you can't recall

How **FULL** is your plate?

" Make use of time, let not advantage slip. "
—WILLIAM SHAKESPEARE

When it comes to managing your time, perhaps the biggest challenge is actually doing it. That may sound like talking in a circle, but think about it: You buy a planner, fill in due dates, color code the level of priority of various items, and devote a substantial amount of time to getting yourself organized. Then you lose the planner, leave it in your car, or don't remember to take it out of your backpack when you get home. You can't find the time to actually use the planner you've planned to use. Follow through and remember Shakespeare's wisdom: "let not advantage slip"!

© Paul Maguire/Shutterstock

TRY IT!

Of course you're busy, but if you took five minutes—or even three—to review your planner before going to bed each night, time management might actually become a habit, rather than something you just can't find the time to do. Try it for one week and report your results in class.

On a scale of 1 to 5, answer these questions now that you've completed this chapter.

1 = not very/not much/very little/low   5 = very/a lot/very much/high

How much do you know *now*?

Now rate your current level of knowledge about topics covered in this chapter.

Short-term versus long-term memory

1 2 3 4 5

Memory as a process

1 2 3 4 5

Memory improvement techniques

1 2 3 4 5

Causes for memory failures

1 2 3 4 5

How useful might the information in this chapter be to you?

How much do you think this information might affect your college success?

1 2 3 4 5

How much do you think this information might affect your career success after college?

1 2 3 4 5

How long did it actually take you to complete this chapter (both the reading and writing tasks)?

_____ Hour(s) _____ Minutes

Challenge Yourself Online Quiz. To find out how much you've learned, access the CourseMate via www.cengagebrain.com/shop/ISBN/0495906433 to take the Challenge Yourself Online Quiz.

Compare these answers to your answers from the "Readiness Check" at the beginning of this chapter. How might the gaps between what you thought before starting the chapter and what you now think affect how you approach the next chapter?

chapter 9 Reading and Studying

You're about to Discover. . .

- ✔ Why reading is important
- ✔ How to engage in focused reading
- ✔ How to tackle reading assignments
- ✔ What metacognition is and how it can help you
- ✔ How to become an intentional learner and create a master study plan
- ✔ How to study when the heat is on

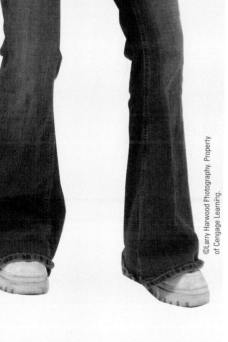

READINESS CHECK | What do you **Know?**

Before beginning this chapter, take a moment to answer these questions. Your answers will help you assess how ready you are to focus.

1 = not very/not much/very little/low   5 = very/a lot/very much/high

How much do you *already* know?

Rate your current level of knowledge about topics covered in this chapter.

Focused reading

     1   2   3   4   5

Study skills and techniques

     1   2   3   4   5

Metacognition

     1   2   3   4   5

Intentional learning

     1   2   3   4   5

How motivated are you to learn *more*?

In general, how motivated are you to learn the material in this chapter?

     1   2   3   4   5

How much do you think this information might affect your college success?

     1   2   3   4   5

How much do you think this information might affect your career success after college?

     1   2   3   4   5

How ready are you to read *now*?

How ready are you to focus on this chapter—physically, intellectually, and emotionally? Which of these three areas is most challenging for you right now? Circle a number to represent it.

     1   2   3   4   5

If any of your answers is below a 3, consider addressing the issue before reading. Then, read the chapter carefully, while looking for ways to improve your focus.

Finally, how long do you think it will take you to complete this chapter? If you start and stop, keep track of the overall time.

_____ Hour(s) _____ Minutes

Katie Alexander

College would be a lot more fun if it weren't for all the reading and studying required. That was Katie Alexander's take on things. She wasn't much of a reader; she much preferred playing softball or volleyball with her friends to sitting in one spot with a book propped open in front of her. Reading for fun wasn't something she'd ever even consider doing—at least not reading books. To Katie, reading 75 text messages a day was necessary; reading books was boring. *Anyway, why read the book when you can just watch the movie?* she always asked. Katie was an energetic, active, outgoing person, and "doing" and "socializing" were her things. Reading and studying definitely weren't.

Text Message:

Katie! are you still on campus? It's movie night tonight at 9... c u there!

Sept 6th, 8:10 pm

Actually, this was Katie's second attempt at college. She'd gone to a small liberal arts school right after high school, but the self-discipline required to read and study just wasn't there. A specialist at the college officially diagnosed dyslexia, a learning disability that affects reading skills, and Katie became discouraged and dropped out. Working as a server for two years at a restaurant in her neighborhood helped her earn enough money to go back to school. She loved the people part of her waitressing job, and thought a hospitality degree from the community college close to home would be the right choice for her. Besides, how much reading would she possibly have to do for a career like that?

Because of her dyslexia, reading and studying were hard work for Katie. She was smart enough to make it in college—she was sure of that—and this time around, she was more motivated. But reading a long assignment, page by page, made her fidgety, and after she read something, she found it hard to summarize what it had been about. Reading took her a long time, so long that her mind wandered wherever it seemed to want to go. She found it hard to focus, and things just didn't seem to stick. Before she knew it, she was off in some other world, thinking about her friends, or her schedule at

1027

9-13-10
DATE

Great Bluffs Community College $ 2159 00

thousand one hundred and fifty nine & 00/100
DOLLARS

FOR

ST# 34	OP#	TE#	TR#
	005749801035		3.38
	007065200750		2.97
	007065200750		2.97
	006025835503		14.96
	068113176369		4.97
	002340035457		0.93
	005963148202		3.87
	002340035458		0.93
	005920000731		0.93
	SUBTOTAL		35.91
	HST 15%		4.88
	TOTAL		40.79
	DEBIT TEND		40.79
	CHANGE DUE		0.00
GST/HST	RT		

Metro Sports Equipment

PURCHASE TRANSACTION RECORD
40.79
CHEQUING
RRN # :   ************

work, or everything else she had to do.

Back in grade school, Katie had been labeled as a slow reader. She was never in the top reading group, and although she resented the label, she didn't quite know what do to about it. The last time reading had actually been a subject in school was sixth grade. Now, eight years later, she was enrolled in a developmental reading class. Would it really help her?

Katie's best friend, Amanda, was an Elementary Education major who loved to read. In fact, that's all she ever seemed to do. Her best friend, Brittney, however, had a different strategy. "There's so much required reading in all my classes that I don't even know where to start," Brittney admitted, "so I just don't do it. I go to class, listen to the lectures, and write down what the instructor has said on the essay tests. Katie, just learn to 'play the game'!"

Besides her developmental reading class, Katie was enrolled in an introduction to psychology class. She knew she'd have plenty of reading to do there, and her friend Brittney's strategy definitely wasn't going to work. Professor Harris-Black had assigned a shocking number of chapters to read in their thick textbook for the first exam. She didn't even go over the reading in class, and her lectures were about all sorts of things, much of which wasn't even related to the reading. Whenever Katie sat down to read a chapter, she found what to her were unfamiliar words and long, complicated phrases. The instructor had suggested that students read with a dictionary at their sides, but who'd ever want to keep stopping to look up words? You'd never finish!

With a midterm exam coming up in her psychology class next week, Katie was beginning to panic. She'd only read one of the nine chapters assigned. In fact, she hadn't made it through the first chapter when she got discouraged and gave up. She knew the essay questions would be challenging. Winging it wouldn't work, and choosing to "watch the movie" instead of reading the book wasn't an option. Exactly what did psychology have to do with hospitality, she puzzled, and why did she have to take this course in the first place?

The night before the test, Katie decided to get serious. She sat down at her desk, armed with her yellow highlighter. As she began reading, however, she realized she didn't know exactly what to highlight since she didn't really understand what she was reading. Looking back at the page she had just finished, she saw that she had basically highlighted everything.

Exasperated, Katie told herself that she couldn't go to bed until she'd finished reading everything, no matter when that was. She started with the second chapter, since she'd read the first one, and by morning, she'd be as ready as possible. Anyway, whether or not she did well wasn't up to her—it was up to Professor Harris-Black. She was the one making up the test.

Getting a good grade on her Introduction to Psychology midterm exam was probably out of the question, but if she could just manage to pass, Katie knew she would have to settle for that. On the other hand, she secretly hoped that maybe she'd just luck out.

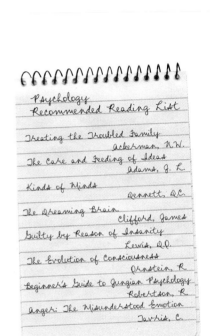

© Christoph Weihs, 2009/Used under license from Shutterstock.com

Psychology
Recommended Reading List

Treating the Troubled Family
Ackerman, N.W.
The Care and Feeding of Ideas
Adams, J. L.
Kinds of Minds
Dennett, D.C.
The Dreaming Brain
Clifford, James
Guilty by Reason of Insanity
Lewis, D.O.
The Evolution of Consciousness
Ornstein, R.
Beginner's Guide to Jungian Psychology
Robertson, R.
Anger: The Misunderstood Emotion
Tavris, C.

© delihayat, 2009/Used under license from Shutterstock.com

© Cengage Learning

Study Strategies for Students with Dysle[xia]

- Take advantage of multi-sensory learning meth[ods]
  Study diagrams, look at charts
  Listen to the instructor's words
  Combine sensory input to create a more complete picture

- Read through superficially first
  Look at the title page and intro
  Note the major headings and bullets
  Skim through the text to get the main ideas

- Read out loud
  Read out loud while highlighting, then read what you [...]
  Listen to your voice as you emphasize important poin[ts]

- Organize your workspace
  Categorize papers and books for each subject
  Color-code assignments and papers to make orga[...]

- Improve your work methods
  Brainstorm at the beginning of a project
  Set priorities and outline your work strategy

- Prepare for tests
  Be sure to attend all classes leading up to the [...]
  [...] try to determine the form [...]

© Adisa, 2009/Used under license from Shutterstock.com

1. Do you have anything in common with Katie? If so, in what ways, specifically?
2. Katie is probably an intelligent student, but she has decided that she dislikes reading and studying, so she avoids it. How important will these two skills be as she continues to pursue a college degree? Is she likely to succeed her second time around?
3. How would you characterize Katie as a student? Identify five specific problems described in this case study that could interfere with her college success.
4. Identify three specific things Katie should do to get her college career on track.

Who Needs to Read?

What's so important about reading? Teachers seem to think it's important, but times have changed, haven't they? Now you can just skim predigested information on websites, get a summary of the day's news from television, and watch movies for entertainment. Who needs to read? Look around the next time you're in a doctor or dentist's waiting room. You'll see some people staring at the TV screen mounted on the wall, others plugged into iPods, and still others working with their smart phones. A few may be skimming through magazines, but does anyone ever pick up a book to actually read it cover to cover anymore? Does it matter?

The answer, according to many experts, is a definite yes, it does matter![1] Reading helped create civilization as we know it and taught us particular ways of thinking.

One fairly predictable result of doing anything less often is that eventually you may not do it as well. Practice helps you improve. Even an Olympic athlete who doesn't stick with training gets rusty after a while. As students read less, their reading skills deteriorate and they don't enjoy doing it. On the other hand, the better you get at reading, the more you may enjoy it. Falling down every ten minutes the first time you get on skis isn't all that much fun, but once you can zip down the mountain like a pro, you begin to appreciate the sport.

Like Katie from the "FOCUS Challenge Case," reading may not be your favorite pastime. You may feel about reading like many people do about eating cauliflower. You know it's good for you, but you'd prefer to avoid it. However, this chapter wouldn't be worth its weight in trees if it didn't try to convince you otherwise. One aspect of reading Katie particularly dislikes is that reading is not a social or physical activity. You can read with someone else in the room, of course, or talk about what you read afterward with other people, but basically, reading is something you do alone.

© Tom McCarthy/PhotoEdit

❝ ❞

You don't have to burn books to destroy a culture. Just get people to stop reading them.

Ray Bradbury, science fiction writer

Stressed Out?

> **In times of great stress or adversity, it's always best to keep busy, to plow your anger and your energy into something positive.**
> —LEE IACOCCA, AMERICAN BUSINESSMAN (1924–)

Stress . . . it's all in your head. That's what some people say. Stress is what you feel when your mind reacts to tough challenges. They even say some stress is good for you. But when stress goes unchecked, there's always the possibility you'll blow up like Vesuvius. How can you tell when you're about to reach that point? Is it when the stress that was in your head spreads to other parts of your body? Your immune system goes haywire and you come down with the cold of the century? Your headache is debilitating or your back feels like six kids are jumping on it? *Feel* the stress!

Devon Stephens/iStockphoto.com

TRY IT!

Keep track of when your body tells you to deal with the stress in your life. Write down your top three symptoms here:

1. _____
2. _____
3. _____

Lee Iacocca says that the best way to deal with stress is to channel negative energy into something positive in your life, something you want to achieve, something you value—like getting a college education. This week, pay attention to symptoms of unchecked stress and take positive action!

It's a solitary activity that involves you, words on a page, an invisible author, and your brain. You need to do it with a minimum of physical movement. Reading while playing a game of volleyball would be tough to pull off.

If you enjoy reading, congratulations! When you settle in with an exciting novel, you can travel to the far corners of the Earth, turn back the clock to previous centuries, or fast-forward to a future that extends beyond your lifetime. Whether or not you enjoy reading, it will be one of the primary skills you need to cultivate in college. According to one study, 85 percent of the learning you'll do in college requires careful reading.[2] First-year students often need to read and comprehend 150–200 pages per week in order to complete their academic assignments.[3]

What's more, reading skills go hand in hand with writing skills, which makes them even more important. The better you get at reading, the more likely you are to achieve academic success. Many of your classes will require intensive reading of complex material, including **primary sources** by original authors and **scholarly research**. If you complete reading assignments, and your classmates don't, think about how much ahead of the nonreaders *you* will be! But how do you become a better reader?

primary sources works written by authors themselves, like the autobiography of Benjamin Franklin (that he wrote himself)

scholarly research articles in academic journals, like the studies about reading and college students, footnoted at the end of the last paragraph

Read Right!

What do we know about reading? How *should* you tackle your many reading assignments in college? Consider these twelve essential points:[4] As you read, put checkmarks next to items you see as potential areas of improvement for yourself as a reader.

> **It matters, if individuals are to retain any capacity to form their own judgments and opinions, that they continue to read for themselves.**
>
> *Harold Bloom, literary critic*

Paragraph Analysis

Here are three passages from Katie Alexander's psychology textbook. You will need to know the answers to these six questions by the time you finish reading each paragraph.

Paragraph A

1. What's the difference between a Type A personality and a Type B personality?
2. Which personality type is most beneficial to a person's health and well-being?

Paragraph B

3. What is learned helplessness?
4. Where does learned helplessness come from?

Paragraph C

5. What are the three personality characteristics that make up hardiness?
6. How can being hardy help college students?

(When you read assignments for your classes, skipping ahead to the questions that will be asked of you afterward can be a good way to make sure you read more closely.) Below each paragraph, list the main idea, the supporting evidence for the main idea, and any inferences you detect:

Paragraph A

Would you consider yourself more of a Type A personality, a person who is aggressive, competitive, and driven to achieve? Or do you characterize yourself as more of a Type B personality, a person who is more relaxed, easygoing, patient, and flexible? . . . Cardiologists Meyer Friedman and Ray Rosenman were the first to examine the connection between personality and heart disease. They suspected that personality or behavior patterns may play a role in the lives of men who were more likely to develop heart disease, and in men more likely to die from a heart attack. To test their idea, the researchers gathered a sample of 3,000 men between the ages of 35 and 59 with no known health problems. Each man was interviewed, and based on the man's behavior during the interview, each was designated as a Type A personality, a Type B personality, or somewhere in between. The majority of the sample fell somewhere in between, but in comparing the two types over the next decade, Friedman and Rosenman found that Type A personalities were two to three times more likely to have suffered a heart attack.

Topic: _____

Main idea: _____

Supporting evidence: _____

Inference: _____

Paragraph B

Research supports the notion that college students who feel helpless are less likely to persist, more likely to give up easily, and as a result earn poor grades and report unhappiness. Adults and adolescents who react to stress by feeling at a loss to do anything about the situation are more prone to depression and other stress problems. Learned helplessness also has been documented in children with a history of reading failure. It can develop in elderly people in nursing homes who are not given choices about their daily activities and routines. In all of these situations, the expectation of failure and lack of control are what influence one's perceived level of stress, one's subsequent response to stress, and ultimately, one's mental and physical health.

Topic: _____

Main idea: _____

Supporting evidence: _____

Inference: _____

Paragraph C

Do you view stressors as challenges rather than as threats? For example, if you try out for the soccer team one year and do not make it, do you try out again the next year or do you simply give up? Do you stay committed to the pursuit of your goals and values? If you fail an exam, do you go and get help, or do you just assume that you'll never understand the material and withdraw from the class—possibly spoiling your chance at a college degree? Do you believe that your actions influence the outcome of a situation? Your answers to these questions outline three factors that appear to be related to health: challenge, commitment, and control. . . . The "three Cs" taken together were labeled by psychologists Salvatore Maddi and Suzanne Kobasa as the hardy personality. This term resulted from Kobasa's research on upper-level executives and attorneys who had experienced considerable stress over a three-year period. Those who exemplified hardy traits were less likely to get ill during this time of stress. Even Type A people who scored high on measure of hardiness were less likely to get ill compared with Type A people who scored low on hardiness.

Topic: _____

Main idea: _____

Supporting evidence: _____

Inference: _____

Paragraphs adapted from Pastorina, E., & Doyle-Portillo, S. (2006). *What is psychology?* Belmont, CA: Thomson Wadsworth, p. 602–604.

BOX 9.1 Learning Disability? Five Ways to Help Yourself

Perhaps you were diagnosed with Attention-Deficit/Hyperactivity Disorder (ADHD) or dyslexia as a young child. If you're beginning your college career with a learning disability (LD), you're not alone. In a college or university with an enrollment of 25,000 students, for example, approximately 550 of those students have learning disabilities.[17] By some estimates, two-thirds of students with diagnosed LDs continue on to college after high school.[18] Does a learning disability mean all the odds are against you? No, but there are some important steps you must take to help yourself. Successful college students with LDs recognize, understand, and accept these steps, and develop compensating strategies to offset them.

1. If you've been previously diagnosed with a learning disability, bring a copy of your evaluation or Individualized Education Plan (IEP) with you to campus. Some schools require documentation in order to use the institution's support services.

2. Locate the support services office on your campus and use it. These services are free and can make all the difference in your success.

3. Learn more about your specific LD. Read about it. Visit credible websites. Understanding the ins and outs of what you're up against is important.

4. If you need special accommodations such as taking exams somewhere other than the classroom, schedule an appointment with your instructors early in the term to let them know. Having a learning disability doesn't mean you're required to do less work, but you'll get the support you need in order to do your best.

5. Remember that the advice in this book, which is helpful to all college students, can be even more useful to anyone with a learning disability. Time management strategies and study skills tailored to your specific LD are key.

Don't let fear of failure immobilize you. Instead, keep your eye on the goal and take charge of your own learning.[19]

Meta-what? Metacognition, Reading, and Studying

Do You Know How to Study?

To what extent do these ten statements apply to you? Write the number for each statement on the line preceeding it.

Never		Sometimes		Always
1	2	3	4	5

_____ 1. I keep going with things I have to learn, rather than skipping over what I don't understand.

_____ 2. When I'm studying something difficult, I realize when I'm stuck and ask for help.

_____ 3. I make a study plan and stick to it in order to master class material.

_____ 4. I quiz myself as I'm studying to see what I understand and what I don't.

_____ 5. I talk through my problems, understanding things while I study.

_____ 6. After I study something, I think about how well it went.

_____ 7. I know when I learn best: morning, afternoon, or evening, for example.

_____ 8. I know how I study best: alone, with one other person, in a group, etc.

_____ 9. I know where I study best: at home, at the library, at my computer, etc.

_____ 10. I believe I'm in control of my own learning.

Now tally your scores on this informal instrument. If you scored between 40 and 50 total points, you have excellent metacognitive skills. If you scored between 30 and 40 points, your skills are probably average. However, note any items you rated down in the 1 to 2 range, and then continue reading this section of the chapter carefully.

Talk about needing to use a dictionary! What does the word *metacognition* mean? *Meta* is an ancient Greek prefix that is often used to mean *about*. For example, metacommunication is communicating *about* the way you communicate. ("I feel humiliated when you tease me in front of other people. Can you *not* do that?")

Since cognition means thinking and learning, metacognition is thinking about your thinking and learning about your learning. It's about identifying your learning goals, monitoring your progress, backing up or getting help when you're stuck, forging ahead when you're in the groove, and evaluating your results. Metacognition is about knowing yourself as a learner and about your ability (and motivation) to control your own learning. Some things

> ❝ Force yourself to reflect on what you read, paragraph by paragraph. ❞
>
> *Samuel Taylor Coleridge, British poet (1772–1834)*

are easy for you to learn; others are hard. What do you know about yourself as a learner, and do you use that awareness *intentionally* to learn at your best?[20]

These questions may seem simple, but how do you know:

1. When you've finished a reading assignment?

2. When your paper is ready to turn in?

3. When you've finished studying for an exam?

When you're eating a meal, you know when you're full, right? But when it comes to academic work, how do you know when you're done? Some students resort to answers like this to the question, "How do you know when you're done?" Look at the range of students' answers:

> - I just do.
> - I trust in God.
> - My eyelids get too heavy.
> - I've been at it for a long time.
> - My mom tells me to go to bed.
> - I understand everything.
> - I can write everything down without looking at the textbook or my notes.
> - I've created a practice quiz for myself and get all the answers right.
> - When my wife or girlfriend drills me and I know all the answers.
> - When I can teach my husband everything I've learned.
> - When I've highlighted, recopied my notes, made flash cards, written sample questions, tested myself, etc.

You can see that their answers become increasingly reliable as you progress down the list.[21]

Metacognition is about having an "awareness of [your] own cognitive machinery and how the machinery works."[22] It's about knowing the limits of your own learning and memory capabilities, knowing how much you can accomplish within a certain amount of time, and knowing what learning strategies work for you.[23] Know your limits, but at the same time, stretch.

Becoming an Intentional Learner: Make a Master Study Plan

What's your favorite class this term? Or let's turn the question around: What's your least favorite class? Becoming an educated person may well require you to study things you wouldn't *choose* to study. Considering all you have to do, including your most and least favorite classes, what would making a master study plan look like? You've "been there, done that" all through your schooling, but do you *really* know how to study?

To begin, think about what you have to think about. What's your goal? Is it to finish your English essay by 10:00 P.M. so that you can start your algebra homework? Or is it to write the best essay you can possibly write? If you've allowed yourself one hour to read this chapter, but after an hour, you're still not finished, you have three choices: keep reading, finish later, or give up entirely. What's in your best interest, honestly? See if you find the following planning strategies helpful.

1. **Make sure you understand your assignments.** Understanding is critical to making a master plan. You can actually waste a great deal of time trying to read your instructor's mind after the fact: "Did she want us to *analyze* the play or *summarize* it?" When you leave class, make sure you're clear on what's been assigned.

2. **Schedule yourself to be three places at once.** Making a master plan requires you to think simultaneously about three different time zones:

   The past: Ask yourself what you already know. Is this a subject you've studied before? Have your study habits worked well for you in the past? How have you done your best work—in papers, on exams, on projects?

   The present: Ask yourself what you need to learn now. How interested are you in this material? How motivated are you to learn it? How much time will you devote to it?

   The future: Ask yourself how you'll go about learning it. Will you learn it using the strategies that work best for you? Which learning factors will you control? Will you do what you can to change what's not working?[24]

3. **Talk through your learning challenges.** There's good evidence that talking to yourself while you're studying is a good thing. Researchers find it helps you figure things out: *Okay, I understand the difference between a neurosis and a psychosis, but I'm not sure I can provide examples on my psychology test.* Once you've heard yourself admit that, you know where to focus your efforts next.[25]

4. **Be a stickler.** Sticklers pay attention to details. They want to make sure everything is absolutely right. Have you ever thought about how important accuracy is? For example, if you were 99 instead of 100 percent accurate, that would mean that:

   ➤ 500 airplanes in U.S. skies each day wouldn't be directed by air traffic controllers.[26] Disastrous!

No one can become really educated without having pursued some study in which he took no interest.

T. S. Eliot, American-born poet (1888–1965)

As you read and study, remember this example. Be thorough. Read the entire assignment. Pay attention to details. If you make a mistake, for example in solving a math problem, figure out exactly what went wrong, so that you don't hold on to a bad academic habit. Rework the problem at least twice, write a few

sentences describing the right way to solve it, and try another problem similar to it to see if you really understand.[27] Accuracy counts!

5. **Take study breaks.** The human attention span is limited, and according to some researchers, it's shrinking, rather than expanding.[28] Plan to take brief scheduled breaks to stretch, walk around, or grab a light snack every half hour during study sessions. Of course, it's important to sit down and get back to work again. Don't let a quick study break to get a snack multiply into several hours of television viewing that wasn't in the plan.

6. **Mix it up.** Put a little variety into your study sessions by switching from one subject to another, or from one mode of studying—for example, reading, self-quizzing, writing—to another. Variety helps you fight boredom and stay fresh (unless, of course, you're on the verge of a breakthrough).

7. **Review, review, review!** Review your course material often enough that you can retain and retrieve information at the level expected by your instructor. If you have to start fresh each time you come to class, trying to work from what you remember from the last class, you'll always feel behind.

8. **Find a study buddy.** Find a classmate who also values studying, and commit to keeping one another focused during study sessions. Go beyond just studying together. Create quizzes and hypothetical test questions for each other, and use your study partner to keep you on track.

9. **Estimate how long it will take.** Before starting an assignment, estimate the amount of time you will need to complete that assignment (just as you do at the start of each chapter of this book), and then compare that estimate with the actual amount of time the assignment took to complete. Getting into this habit helps you develop realistic schedules for future projects.

10. **Vary your study techniques by course content.** Studying productively is more than just learning a few general rules that apply to any type of subject matter. You need to zoom in on whatever subject or discipline it is that you're studying. Look over the pages of your textbook. Does the material synch with your learning style? Is it text-heavy (read/write)? Do graphs or charts explain the text and seem important? Are color-coding or bulleting used to call your attention to particular items (visual)? If the material isn't presented as you'd prefer, what can you do to "translate"? For example, if you're a kinesthetic learner, can you make flash cards? Can you create and complete practice tests? If you learn by listening, can you read the material aloud (aural)? And finally, what kind of exam (multiple-choice, essay, problem sets, etc.) does the material lend itself to? What are you likely to need to know and what will you be asked to do on an exam? When you study math, it's important to do more than read. Working problem sets helps you actually develop the skills you need. When you study history, you study differently. You might draw a timeline of the events leading up to World War I, for example.[29]

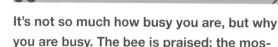

It's not so much how busy you are, but why you are busy. The bee is praised; the mosquito is swatted.

Marie O'Conner

"Disciplined" Studying

Assume you are taking three classes this term: calculus, psychology, and music. For the three textbook pages here, describe how you would go about studying the material, based on what the content in these three subjects requires. Among other things, which particular VARK learning style preferences should be used: V, A, R, and/or K? Fill in specifics about how you would study each subject's textbook page. After you're done, compare notes with your classmates.

---

2   **Chapter P**   Preparation for Calculus

P.1 Graphs and Models

- ■ Sketch the graph of an equation.
- ■ Find the intercepts of a graph.
- ■ Test a graph for symmetry with respect to an axis and the origin.
- ■ Find the points of intersection of two graphs.
- ■ Interpret mathematical models for real-life data.

The Graph of an Equation

RENÉ DESCARTES (1596–1650)

Descartes made many contributions to philosophy, science, and mathematics. The idea of representing points in the plane by pairs of real numbers and representing curves in the plane by equations was described by Descartes in his book *La Géométrie*, published in 1637.

In 1637 the French mathematician René Descartes revolutionized the study of mathematics by joining its two major fields—algebra and geometry. With Descartes's coordinate plane, geometric concepts could be formulated analytically and algebraic concepts could be viewed graphically. The power of this approach was such that within a century of its introduction, much of calculus had been developed.

The same approach can be followed in your study of calculus. That is, by viewing calculus from multiple perspectives—*graphically*, *analytically*, and *numerically*—you will increase your understanding of core concepts.

Consider the equation $3x + y = 7$. The point $(2, 1)$ is a **solution point** of the equation because the equation is satisfied (is true) when 2 is substituted for x and 1 is substituted for y. This equation has many other solutions, such as $(1, 4)$ and $(0, 7)$. To find other solutions systematically, solve the original equation for y.

$$y = 7 - 3x \qquad \text{Analytic approach}$$

Then construct a **table of values** by substituting several values of x.

x	0	1	2	3	4
y	7	4	1	-2	-5

Numerical approach

From the table, you can see that $(0, 7)$, $(1, 4)$, $(2, 1)$, $(3, -2)$, and $(4, -5)$ are solutions of the original equation $3x + y = 7$. Like many equations, this equation has an infinite number of solutions. The set of all solution points is the **graph** of the equation, as shown in Figure P.1.

NOTE Even though we refer to the sketch shown in Figure P.1 as the graph of $3x + y = 7$, it really represents only a *portion* of the graph. The entire graph would extend beyond the page. ■

Graphical approach: $3x + y = 7$
Figure P.1

In this course, you will study many sketching techniques. The simplest is point plotting—that is, you plot points until the basic shape of the graph seems apparent.

EXAMPLE 1   Sketching a Graph by Point Plotting

Sketch the graph of $y = x^2 - 2$.

Solution   First construct a table of values. Then plot the points shown in the table.

x	-2	-1	0	1	2	3
y	2	-1	-2	-1	2	7

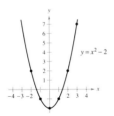

The parabola $y = x^2 - 2$
Figure P.2

Finally, connect the points with a *smooth curve*, as shown in Figure P.2. This graph is a **parabola**. It is one of the conics you will study in Chapter 10. ■

How would you study this? *Calculus, 9th Edition, by Ron Larson and Bruce H. Edwards*

VARK Activ

Visual: M
your cell p

Aural: Ac
iAudio sun

**Read/Wri
up in the d
classmates

Kinesthe
the Focus

(from top to bottom) Marcela Barsse/MarsBars,

step 3 INSIGHT

At the beginning of t
after reading this cha
Challenge Case"? U:
some of the possible

step 4 ACTION Y

1. What, in particular,
2. In what ways migh
   are you expecting

studies of the brain. Case studies lack formal control groups. This, of course, limits the conclusions that can be drawn from clinical observations.

Survey Method

Sometimes psychologists would like to ask everyone in the world a few well-chosen questions: "Do you drink coffee? How often per week?" "What form of discipline did your parents use when you were a child?" "What is the most dishonest thing you've done?" Honest answers to such questions can reveal much about people's behavior. But, because it is impossible to question everyone, doing a survey is often more practical.

In the **survey method,** public polling techniques are used to answer psychological questions (Tourangeau, 2004). Typically, people in a representative sample are asked a series of carefully worded questions. A **representative sample** is a small group that accurately reflects a larger population. A good sample must include the same proportion of men, women, young, old, professionals, blue-collar workers, Republicans, Democrats, whites, African Americans, Native Americans, Latinos, Asians, and so on as found in the population as a whole.

A *population* is an entire group of animals or people belonging to a particular category (for example, all college students or all single women). Ultimately, we are interested in entire populations. But by selecting a smaller sample, we can draw conclusions about the larger group without polling each and every person. Representative samples are often obtained by *randomly* selecting who will be included (▶▶ Figure 1.11). (Notice that this is similar to randomly assigning participants to groups in an experiment.)

How accurate is the survey method? Modern surveys like the Gallup and Harris polls are quite accurate. The Gallup poll has erred in its election predictions by only 1.5 percent since 1954. However, if a survey is based on a biased sample, it may paint a false picture. A *biased sample* does not accurately reflect the population from which it was drawn. Surveys done by magazines, websites, and online information services can be quite biased. Surveys on the use of guns done by *O: The Oprah Magazine* and *Guns and Ammo* magazine would probably produce very different results—neither of which would represent the general population. That's why psychologists using the survey method go to great lengths to ensure that their samples are representative. Fortunately, people can often be polled by telephone, which makes it easier to obtain large samples. Even if one person out of three refuses to answer survey questions, the results are still likely to be valid (Hutchinson, 2004).

Internet Surveys

Recently, psychologists have started doing surveys and experiments on the Internet. Web-based research can be a cost-effective way to reach very large groups of people. Internet studies have provided interesting information about topics such as anger, decision making,

Survey method The use of public polling techniques to answer psychological questions.

Representative sample A small, randomly selected part of a larger population that accurately reflects characteristics of the whole population.

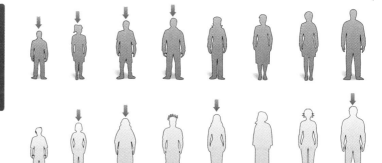

▶▶ **FIGURE 1.11** If you were conducting a survey in which a person's height might be an important variable, the upper, nonrandom sample would be very unrepresentative. The lower sample, selected using a table of random numbers, better represents the group as a whole.

44 CHAPTER ONE

How would you study this? *Psychology: A Journey, 4th Edition by Dennis Coon and John O. Mitterer*

(continued)

1. Do you have anything in common with Joe? If so, how are you managing the situation so that you can be successful?
2. What should Joe have done differently before, during, and after the exam?
3. Does Joe have test anxiety? Why or why not?
4. Does cramming work? Why or why not?
5. Do you think most students would have cheated to save their scholarships? Why or why not?

Testing 1, 2, 3...*Show* What You *Know*

Let's face it, life would be very different without grades in college, or time clocks on the job, or performance reviews throughout your career, wouldn't it? You wouldn't have to show up at work if you didn't feel like it, and you'd get a paycheck anyway. You wouldn't have to do a good job because no one would care. And you wouldn't have to write papers, or give presentations, or take tests in college. Not only would you benefit by having more free time, but your instructors wouldn't have to work their way through stacks of papers assigning grades, either. What a wonderful world that would be—or would it? Realistically, it would probably bring total chaos.

Accountability understanding the consequences of doing a good job or a poor one

Life's not like that. Results count. **Accountability** is the bottom line. Achievement is taken seriously. Like Joe in the "FOCUS Challenge Case," you may be thinking, "I'll never have to take another test once I get out of here," but exams are actually realistic representations of life's requirements. The experience of taking a test is similar to running a critical meeting or giving a high-stakes presentation on the job. You'll need to walk into the room, ready to show what you know, and answer unanticipated questions. Exams help you compare your progress with that of other students and to your instructor's set of expectations about what all students should know.[1] On the job, every day will be a test of your skills and abilities, and you'll get your "grade" when your supervisor gives you a review of your performance over the last six months or year. Tests are inevitable; so rather than complain about them, perhaps we should change the way we think about them.

The first step of test-taking, of course, is to make sure you're prepared. All of the information in this chapter is worthless if you haven't gone to class or read the textbook or taken good notes during lectures. Miracles, by their very definition, are in very short supply. Nothing can substitute for being **conscientious** about your work. Think about preparing for an exam as you would for an athletic event. Imagine running the 26 mile, 385 yard Boston Marathon. You'd have to work for months to develop the stamina you would need to finish successfully. You wouldn't want to just show up for kicks and wing it. If you did, at the very least, you'd probably pull a muscle. At the very worst, they'd carry you away on a stretcher.

conscientious dedicated to doing your best

The same principle holds true for exams in college. In order to have the stamina required and avoid the "injury" of not doing well, tests require this same kind of step-by-step, long-term preparation.

A Final Wo

Think about taking tests as a three-stage project with a beginning, middle, and end. What do you do *before* the test to get ready? What do you do *during* the test to do your best? What do you do *after* the test to ensure a productive learning experience you can use for future exams?

Before the Test: Prepare Carefully

Christina Ripp wins the 2003 Boston Marathon Women's Wheelchair Division

As you read the upcoming sections about *before*, *during*, and *after* a test, evaluate how many of these suggestions apply to you. Put a plus sign (+) in front of each item you already do regularly and a check mark (✓) in front of items you could start doing more regularly to improve your test-taking skills.

1. _____ **Begin preparing for an exam on the first day of class.** Nothing can replace consistent, regular study before and after each class. If you work along the way, then when it comes time for the exam, you will be much more ready and much less in need of last-minute heroics. Keep up with the reading, even if there are things you'd rather be doing.

2. _____ **Identify the days and times of all your exams for the whole term up front.** At the beginning of the term, record the days and times of all the exams in all your courses—even finals, which will seem very far off—in your planner, cell phone, or online calendar. You'll thank yourself many times over for completing this essential task.

3. _____ **Find out exactly what the test will cover.** There's nothing more terrifying than having a classmate next to you say something like this before the exam begins, "I can't believe this test covers the entire first six chapters," when you thought it only covered the first four chapters. Clarify whether handouts will be included, previous quiz questions—anything you're not sure of. Phone, text, or e-mail other students, or better yet, ask your instructor questions like these: How long will the test be? What material will it cover? Which topics are most important? It's also a good idea to ask about criteria that will be used in grading. Do punctuation and grammar count? Will you be asked to turn in your notes or draft so that the instructor can see your work? Will there be an in-class review? All these questions are usually fair game.

criteria standards

4. _____ **Understand that specific types of preparation are required for specific types of tests.** As described in later sections in this chapter, objective and subjective tests should be approached differently. Online tests require that you know the answers to important questions up front. For example, will the test time out? Must you complete the exam once you start, or can you save your answers and come back to finish later? Should you compose essay answers elsewhere and paste them into the online exam so that you don't lose all your work in case of a technology hiccup?

5. _____ **Make a study schedule.** How many days are left to study? What will you accomplish each day? Don't decide you'll use whatever time is left over to study for your test. Usually there isn't any time left over.

6. _____ **Begin serious reviewing several days before the test.** The best strategy is paying regular attention to class material, just as you take care of other things you care about, like your car or your dog. After each lecture, work with your notes, revising, organizing, or summarizing them. Then several days before the exam, step up your effort. Divide up the work by days or study blocks. Begin putting your lecture notes and reading notes together. Make flashcards, outlines, charts, summaries, tables, diagrams, whatever works for your learning style and fits the material.

7. _____ **Maximize your memory.** Research indicates that specific techniques help transfer information from short-term to long-term memory. Remember to "Make It Stick" (rehearse, overlearn, space it out, separate it, and mind the middle), "Make It Meaningful" (feel, connect, and personalize), "Make It Mnemonic" (spell, locate, link or narrate, and peg), "Manipulate It" (mark it up, mark it down, organize, picture, act, produce, and test), and "Make It Funny" (mock it).

8. _____ **Get everything ready the night before.** To calm your nerves, lay out your clothes the night before the exam and pack your book bag with things you'll need: several pencils, erasers, scrap paper, your calculator, and a watch that works. Remove as much hassle as you can from test day.

9. _____ **Manage your energy so that you're ready to focus and work quickly.** You've heard it before, but if you're exhausted or feverish, you're not as likely to "show what you know" as you will if you're healthy and rested. Don't resort to things like drinking cup after cup of coffee to stay awake. "All-nighters" are something students brag about, but they catch up with you, and they're a bad habit to get into. According to one expert, "for every hour of sleep we lose, we drop one IQ point."[2] A series of all-nighters during midterms or final exams can seriously impair your intellectual performance.

> If you would hit the mark, you must aim a little above it.

Henry Wadsworth Longfellow,
American poet (1807–1882)

10. _____ **Don't give in to a nonproductive, negative attitude.** Emotions are contagious. Stay away from other students who are freaked out or pessimistic about the exam. Think—and feel—for yourself. Make sure your self-coaching is productive ("I've studied this section for an hour; if it's on the exam, I'll nail it."), rather than punishing ("I'm so stupid. Why didn't I keep up with the reading?").

11. _____ **Study with other students.** When you teach something to someone else, you must first learn it thoroughly yourself. Why not study with other students? You can take turns teaching one another, comparing class notes, and making practice exams for each other. For most of us, talking things through helps us figure them out as we go. But don't wait to be invited; take responsibility and start a study group yourself. And if you're concerned

that a study group of several students may degenerate into a social club, study with just one other person—find a study buddy and commit to doing the work.

12. _____ **Remind yourself of your long-term goals.** Why are you going to college? All this hard work is worth something or you wouldn't be doing it. Keep your sights on the finish line! Enjoy the feeling of accomplishing something now that contributes to your goal-oriented success later.

13. _____ **Arrive at the classroom early, but not too early.** Get there early enough to get a seat where the lighting is good and you won't be distracted by other students, but don't arrive so early that you build up excessive anxiety during a long wait.

14. _____ **Don't pop pills to stay awake.** You may know students who use Ritalin, Adderall, Vicodin, and OxyContin as study aids. This is a bad idea. When these drugs are used for the wrong reasons, they can help you stay awake for hours and enter a dreamy state. The potential side effects include insomnia, nausea or vomiting, dizziness, palpitations, headaches, tremors and muscle twitching, even seizures. With such horrible potential health risks staring you in the face, not to mention possible legal sanctions if you obtain these drugs without a prescription, why not make things simple? Just study.[3]

15. _____ **Don't let open-book or take-home tests lull you into a false sense of security.** What could be easier than an open-book test? What could be better than taking a test in the comfort of your own home? Actually, these two types of tests require more preparation than you'd expect. Time is the issue here. If you're unfamiliar with the material, flipping through pages of notes or skipping around in the textbook won't help. Create a reference guide or page tabs for yourself so that you can find various topics in your notes or textbook and use your time efficiently.

16. _____ **Don't mess with success.** If you're doing well and earning the grades you deserve, don't discard what is working for you. Honestly assess the efficiency and effectiveness of your current practices, and then decide what ideas from this chapter you should add to your test-taking preparation routine.

Cramming: Does "All or Nothing" Really Work?

Imagine yourself as the actor in the following scenarios. Compare these situations to cramming for tests.

> You haven't called your significant other since last year. Suddenly you appear at her door with candy, flowers, concert tickets, and dinner reservations at the most exclusive restaurant in town. You can't understand why she isn't happier to see you.

> You don't feed your dog for several months. When you finally bring him a plate loaded with ten T-bone steaks to make up for your neglect, you notice he's up and died on you. Oops!

Define—provide the meaning (usually requires a short answer)

Describe—give a detailed account, list characteristics or qualities

Discuss—describe a cause/effect relationship, the significance of something, the pros and cons, or the role played by someone or something

Enumerate—list qualities, characteristics, events, and so on

Explain—similar to discuss

Illustrate—give concrete examples

Interpret—comment on, give examples, provide an explanation for, discuss

Outline—describe the plot, main ideas, or organization of something

Prove—support an argument with evidence from the text or class notes

Relate—show the relationship or connection between two things

State—explain in precise terms

Summarize—give a condensed account of key points, reduce to the essential components

Trace—describe a process or the development of something

EXERCISE 10.3

Understanding "Verb-age"

What would you emphasize in your written response to these essay questions about this chapter, based on the verb used in each question? For each question, write the first several sentences of an answer to demonstrate how you might respond, just like the student's example in number 1.

1. **Critique** this chapter of FOCUS on taking tests.

   To me, this is the best chapter of FOCUS I've read so far. I never actually realized it before, but I have symptoms of all four aspects of text anxiety. Many students do. I usually think negatively about how well I'll do, feel frustrated, get fidgety, and get an upset stomach. To me, this one section of the chapter makes it worthwhile to read...

2. **Summarize** this chapter of FOCUS on taking tests.

3. **Outline** this chapter of FOCUS on taking tests.

4. **Analyze** this chapter of FOCUS on taking tests.

5. **Compare** this chapter of FOCUS with an earlier chapter.

> **Use terms from the course.** Perhaps more than any other type of exam, an essay test allows you room to truly display your knowledge. Use the opportunity! Reflect new terms you have learned, and tie your answer directly to course content.

> **Rifle your answer, don't shotgun.** Here's an analogy: A shotgun fires many small metal pellets. A rifle fires a single bullet. When writing an essay answer, some students write down everything they know, hoping that something will be correct. You may actually lose points by doing this. It's better to target your answer and be precise.

> **Generalize if you're unsure of small, exact details.** You can't quite remember, was it 1884 or 1894? The best idea is to write, "Toward the end of the nineteenth century" instead of choosing one of the two and being wrong.

> **Follow all the rules.** When answering an essay question, it's important to be as concise yet thorough as possible. Number your ideas ("There are *three* major . . . "). Avoid slang ("Wordsworth elaborated . . . " not "Wordsworth *jazzed up* the poem."). Refer to researchers or authors or noteworthy people by their last names ("Jung wrote . . . " not "Dr. Carl Jung wrote . . . ").

CONTROL: *YOUR LEARNING*

YOUR TOUGHEST TASK

In Class: Think about your most challenging class this term. Identify one key challenge you face in this class that relates to this chapter. Now develop a step-by-step action plan to deal with this one challenge. For example, Joe's algebra class was his most challenging. His action plan might look like this:

1. Reread the sections of the chapter on preparing for tests and test anxiety.
2. Meet with my instructor to discuss my problems in his class.
3. Show him this action plan, and ask for his suggestions.
4. Keep a journal of my progress to note improvement and meet with him four more times this term.

Now do the same for your most challenging class.

1. _____
   _____
2. _____
   _____
3. _____
   _____
4. _____
   _____

On the Job: Are you required to take tests on the job? Some jobs require that you undergo training and pass a proficiency test at the end. Or perhaps your supervisor "shadows" you from time to time to make sure you're doing things correctly. Although tests on the job may or may not be similar to the tests you take in your classes, find a suggestion in this chapter that does apply and note how you can benefit by trying out the information you've been reading about on the job.

> **Watch your grammar.** The reason why its important, to do this, is because many student's dont and there answers are marked wrong. They wish they would of done better afterwards. (You get the point.)

> **Write an answer that corresponds to how much the question is worth.** It's important to be concise, but generally, if one essay answer is worth 10 points and another is worth 25 points, your instructor will expect you to write more for the question that's worth more. A more detailed, thorough response is what is called for, but make sure you're adding content, not just padding your answer.

> **Put down what you do know.** If you see a question you didn't predict, don't panic. If you've studied, you know *something* that might help give you partial credit even if you don't know the answer in full.

> **Proofread and make sure your handwriting can be read.** While most instructors will count the number of points you covered and use specific standards, grading essays requires instructors to use their own judgment. A good essay answer is taken less seriously if it's littered with mistakes or a real mess to read. This is the real world; neatness counts. Anything you can do to create a positive impression may work in your favor.

> **If you run out of time, jot down any remaining points in the time that's left.** You may not get full credit, but partial credit is better than none.

> **Include a summary statement at the end.** Your essay answer should read like a real essay with an introduction, a body, and a conclusion. Don't just stop mid-sentence without wrapping things up.[26]

Don't Cheat Yourself!

What if you were in one of these situations? How would you respond?

> Many students in your math class get through the homework by sharing answers on their Facebook pages. The instructor doesn't know, and the course isn't all that interesting anyway.

> A friend of yours stores all the names and dates she'll need to know for her history exams on her cell phone. With just one click she can call up whatever information she needs. "Try it," she says. "Everyone else does it, and you'll feel cheated if you don't cheat. If you don't do what other students do, you'll graduate with so-so grades, and you'll never be able to compete for the jobs you've always wanted. Besides getting away with it here just helps prepare you for the business world where things are *really* cutthroat!"

> You hear about an entrepreneurial student who operates an underground paper-writing service. For $20 a page, he will guarantee you the grade you want (based on the grade you already have going in the course so

that your paper won't raise the instructor's suspicions), and he "doctors" each sentence so that the source can't be found on the Internet. You have four papers, a presentation, and an exam all due the same week, and one or two papers would only run you around $150 to $200. That's not all that much considering the tips you make as a server. Hmm....

For nothing can seem foul to those that win.

William Shakespeare, British poet and playwright (1564–1616)

How did you respond to these three scenarios? Are you aware of cheating schemes at your school? Could students you know be the ones these scenarios were written about? Notice that these students have practical-sounding reasons for what they are doing. If you want to cheat, it's not hard, and you can always blame someone else. What's the harm? You get better grades, your teachers think they're doing a good job, your school brags about the fine academic record of its students, and you pat yourself on your back for skillfully managing a very busy, demanding life. Everyone wins, right? Wrong.

According to some studies, fifty years ago, one in five college students admitted to cheating. Today's figures range from 75 to 90 percent. Here's some straight talk about cheating:[27]

1. **Remember that cheating snowballs.** What started as secretly pocketing some kid's CD or glancing at your neighbor's reading test in grade school turns into writing a math formula between your fingers or hiding the names of the constellations under your shirt cuff in middle school. Then these violations as a kid turn into full-fledged, sophisticated rule-breaking as students "download their workload" in high school and knowingly violate their school's Academic Integrity Policy in college. Where does it stop?

2. **Instead of saving time, cheating can take time.** Everyone is busy. Most students are working at jobs for pay in addition to taking classes. How can anyone get everything done that needs to get done? But instead of devising elaborate cheating schemes, which take time to design, why not just use that time to study?

3. **If you cheat now, you'll pay later.** Sooner or later, cheating will catch up with you. You may get past your math instructor this time, and you may

do about it. Are the skills related to emotional intelligence something *you* can work to improve?[10] And if so, how?

Seek honest input from others. It's hard to be objective about yourself. But it is possible to ask for the opinions of others who interact with you regularly. How do they see you? Use other people as coaches to help you see which aspects of your emotional intelligence need strengthening.

Find an EI mentor. A mentor on the job is someone who's older and more experienced than you are and can help you navigate your way through tough problems and manage your college or professional career. Mentors help, and an EI mentor—someone with EI skills you admire—can provide you with important advice about handling challenging emotional situations. Develop a personal relationship with someone whose wisdom you admire, be honest about your problems, and follow the guidance you get.

66

What's going on in the inside shows on the outside.

Earl Nightingale, success consultant

© Robert Recker/zefa/CORBIS

Complete an assessment tool. Other than just feeling up or down, or thinking back on on how you handled problems when they came up, is there a way to know more about your own emotional intelligence? The oldest and most widely used instrument to measure emotional intelligence is the Emotional Quotient Inventory, the EQ-i, from which the sample statements for the five scales we have been discussing come. The instrument asks you to respond to various statements by indicating that they are "very seldom true of me" to "very often true of me," and the results provide you with a self-assessment of your emotional intelligence on each of the five major scales and subscales within them.

As a part of the course for which you're using this textbook, you may have an opportunity to complete the EQ-i or a similar instrument. Check your college's Counseling Center, too, to see if it offers EI assessment tools for students. You can also locate plenty of informal instruments online. They may not be valid, however, so be cautious about fully trusting their results.

Work with a counselor to learn more. Some areas of emotional intelligence may be too challenging to develop on your own. You may need some in-depth, one-on-one counseling to work on areas that need enrichment. Recognize that doing so isn't a bad thing. Instead, you are taking advantage of the resources available on your campus and working toward the growth that can come during your college years.

Stressed Out?

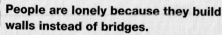

> **People are lonely because they build walls instead of bridges.**
>
> —JOSEPH F. NEWTON, WELL-KNOWN CROSS COUNTRY COACH AND AUTHOR

A famous Barbara Streisand song starts like this, "People, people who need people . . . are the luckiest people in the world." Don't we *all* need people? Building relationships is a critical part of our lives because many of our most basic needs can only be met by other people. It takes people to fulfill our need to belong, for example, and people to meet our need to be held in high esteem by others.

With that in mind, take a look at this formula: relationships ↓ = stress ↑. Do you agree? As much as we need healthy, productive relationships, they can be a big source of stress—perhaps precisely because we need them. The holidays are often portrayed as stressful times in movies because families have a little too much "together time." They start getting on each other's nerves, which can make for some great comedy on the silver screen. When things go wrong between us, we may obsess on questions like this: *"Should I have said that?" "Did he take that the wrong way?" "Why can't I stop thinking about the stupid fight we had last night?"* In one study of college students' sleeping habits, worrying about relationships was the reason most often cited for not getting enough sleep. And getting enough sleep is a key requirement for managing stress![11]

Devon Stephens/iStockphoto.com

TRY IT!

Think about the three most important relationships in your life—your romantic partner, your mom, your best friend, or your kid brother, for example. Fill in their names on the lines below. Put a + (things are great!), ✓ (things are okay), or – (this relationship needs work!) beside each entry. If any of the three relationships earned a minus sign, list three ways in which you may be contributing to the stress in the relationship—and what you can do to improve the relationship and thereby lower the stress in your life right now.

1) _____   2) _____   3) _____

a.   a.   a.

b.   b.   b.

c.   c.   c.

Be patient with yourself. Learning to become more sensitive to someone else's emotions in a close relationship isn't something you can get better at overnight, using cookbook techniques. Building emotional skills is a gradual process that involves becoming aware, acting on your new awareness, and noting the results over time.

Keep at it: Developing your emotional intelligence should be a long-term goal. It's safe to say that EI is something all of us can strengthen, if we're willing to work at it. Relationships that are important to us require the best of our emotional intelligence skills. In fact, studies show that the way in which we provide emotional support is strongly related to how satisfied we are with our relationships.[12]

bias against disabilities for 1 percent, and bias against ethnicity or national origin accounted for 13 percent.[50] People still harm one another out of hatred for differences they may not understand.

Diversity makes a difference, and as educator Adela A. Allen once wrote, "We should acknowledge differences, we should greet differences, until difference makes no difference anymore." What can we do about it? Raising awareness is a first step on the road to recognizing the reality and the richness of diversity.

What's Your CQ?

EXERCISE 11.8

Diagnosing Your Cultural Intelligence[51]

These statements reflect different aspects of cultural intelligence. For each set, add up your scores and divide by four to arrive at an average. As you answer, think about your answers in each category as they compare to the other two categories.

Rate how much you agree with each statement, using this scale:
1 = strongly disagree   2 = disagree   3 = neutral   4 = agree   5 = strongly agree

____ Before I interact with people from a new culture, I think about what I'm going to communicate.

____ If I come up against something unexpected in a new culture, I use the experience to think about how I should respond in other cultures in the future.

____ I plan how I'm going to relate to people from a different culture before I even meet them.

____ When I'm communicating in a new culture, I have a clear sense of whether things are going well or not.

____ **Total divided by 4 = ____ COGNITIVE CQ**

____ It's easy for me to change my body language (eye contact or posture, for example) to match that used by people from a different culture.

____ I can change my expression when I need to interact with people from another culture.

____ I can modify my speech (for example, accent or tone) when interacting with people from another culture.

____ I can easily change the way I act when a cross-cultural situation seems to require it.

____ **Total divided by 4 = ____ PHYSICAL CQ**

____ I have confidence that I can deal well with people from another culture.

____ I am certain that I can make friends with people from a culture that's different from mine.

____ I can adapt to the lifestyle of another culture when I need to fairly easily.

____ I am confident that I can deal with a cultural situation, even if it's unfamiliar.

____ **Total divided by 4 = ____ EMOTIONAL/MOTIVATIONAL CQ**

Generally, an average lower than three identifies an opportunity for improvement, and an average greater than 4.5 identifies a true CQ strength.

An advertisement for an international bank gets the point across well. It shows a picture of a grasshopper. Below the grasshopper are these three sentences that describe three different cultural views of grasshoppers: USA—Pest, China—Pet, Northern Thailand—Appetizer.[52] One insect, three cultural perspectives. Americans tend to shoo away pesky grasshoppers. But if you travel to China, be careful of stepping on one that may be someone else's beloved pet. And if you travel to Northern Thailand, try not to look disgusted when you see fried grasshoppers on the appetizer plate.

| America | China | Northern Thailand |

Just as individuals have emotional intelligence, they also have cultural intelligence. Some of us are more naturally sensitive to cultural differences, and we know how to handle ourselves. But all of us can grow our cultural intelligence with training and preparation. EQ relates to self-awareness and relationship skills; CQ relates to awareness and responses to other cultures (and subcultures of our own culture). EQ and CQ are linked.

Here's a definition: Cultural intelligence is an outsider's seemingly natural ability to interpret someone's unfamiliar and ambiguous gestures the way other people of that culture would.[53] CQ has three components that involve your head, your body, and your heart. All three work together to help you interact in a foreign culture—or a subculture that's new to you within your own larger culture. Think, for example, about taking a job in a new culture, either by transferring overseas or by entering an organization with different rules: "Casual Fridays," "Bring Your Dog to Work Day," "Follow Strict Communication Rules and Always Go Through Your Boss," or "Choose Your Own Project to Work on One Day a Week" (if you work for Google). These rules might be different for you, and you'd need good CQ skills to adapt. Or think about entering a subculture you're unfamiliar with: like being "straight" and having a gay best friend, or marrying someone of another ethnicity, like Kia and James did. CQ can be broken down into three parts, all of which work together:

1. **Cognitive quotient (head):** Do you understand the differences between another culture and your own? Before entering a new culture, do you think before you act? Do you learn about the culture in advance of interacting with its members so that you don't make embarrassing mistakes?

©Larry Harwood Photography. Property of Cengage Learning.

Stockbyte/Jupiter Ima

Ethan Cole

Constance Staley

O ne thing was certain: Ethan Cole was unsure. Unsure of his abilities, unsure of which major to choose, unsure of what he wanted to do with his life, unsure of himself. Unsure of almost everything.

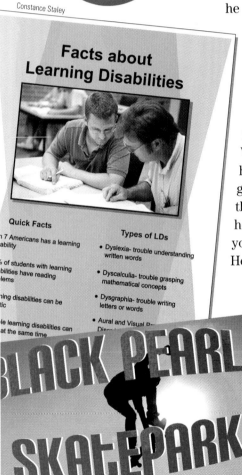

Facts about Learning Disabilities

Quick Facts

1 7 Americans has a learning ability

5 of students with learning bilities have reading lems

ning disabilities can be tic

le learning disabilities can at the same time

Types of LDs

• Dyslexia- trouble understanding written words

• Dyscalculia- trouble grasping mathematical concepts

• Dysgraphia- trouble writing letters or words

• Aural and Visual P— Diso—

BLACK PEARL SKATEPARK

GRAND CAYMAN

WORLD'S LARGEST CONCRETE SKATEPARK

A Jaye/Shutterstock.com, Konstantin Sutyagin/ Shutterstock.com

Ethan came from a good family, and he actually got along pretty well with his parents. They both had decent jobs, worked long hours, and overall they had been good to him. Compared with many of his friends, he came from a "happy home." But frankly, his parents weren't all that interested in the details of his life. When he announced one day as a high school senior that he wanted to go to the community college in town, they said, "What for?" When he said he didn't know, they replied, "Well, you'll figure it out." And that was that. He enrolled the next day.

The only thing Ethan was sure of was that skateboarding was his life right now. It's all he wanted to do and all he ever thought about. He'd look at a curve on a window frame or an arc in a picture and imagine what skating on it would feel like. All his friends were skateboarders, too, and he read skateboarder

magazines and dreamed of the day he might even go pro. He realized not many people make a living at it, but a few really talented athletes did, and maybe—just maybe—he'd be one of them. Recently, he'd found out about the largest concrete skatepark on the globe, Black Pearl in the Grand Cayman Islands—62,000 square feet! He'd made a promise to himself to skate there someday. *Life couldn't get much better than that*, he thought.

But school . . . that was a different story. Schoolwork had never captured his attention. In primary school, his physician had diagnosed Attention Deficit Disorder (ADD). *No wonder I don't like school*, he remembered thinking then. But finally knowing why he couldn't focus didn't change his attitude. He still hated sitting in a classroom.

Despite these challenges, his parents had always told him he was smart. "You can do anything you want to do," they'd said. "Look at you: you're a good-looking kid with plenty of

Manuel Fernandes/Shutterstock.com

TheSupe87/Shutterstock.com

talents. The world is your oyster!" *What a funny phrase*, he'd always thought when they said that. By the time he finally learned what it meant, he totally believed it. His life would become whatever he chose to make of it.

The problem was there were too many choices. How could anyone decide what he wanted to be when he was only nineteen? Ethan remembered liking geometry, he was good at creative writing, he played the drums like a real jazz musician, and he was an incredible artist. *But what do you do with* that *combination of skills?* he'd asked himself more than once. What possible college major and career would really fit him? He'd spent plenty of time on career websites to try and figure it out.

He'd managed to pull decent grades his first term—a B average—at the community college close to home. He'd taken Geography, Interpersonal Communication, Drawing 101, and Study Skills, and while he'd done well, none of the course material really sparked a genuine interest. His instructors didn't take much of an interest in him, either. His Study Skills instructor was friendly and tried to get him interested in class, and he knew the material could really help him. But frankly, Ethan just wasn't motivated when it came to school.

Instead, Ethan skateboarded every minute he could. He preferred skateboarding to studying any day of the week, and when it came to actually choosing a major—much less his classes for the next term—he was clueless. The one thing that did interest him was a certificate in entrepreneurship. It was all about starting a business of your own. Now that sounded intriguing. Ethan didn't quite fit any molds, and doing his own thing might just be "his thing!"

But, the more he thought about it, dropping out sounded like a good idea, too. He could get a job delivering pizzas, think about his life, and try to figure it all out. He'd have nobody to tell him what to do, nobody to hold him accountable, nobody to pressure him, nobody to force him into making decisions—and plenty of free time to skateboard.

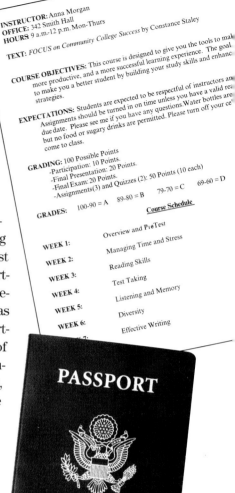

Study Skills (ID 102)
Course Syllabus

INSTRUCTOR: Anna Morgan
OFFICE: 342 Smith Hall
HOURS 9 a.m-12 p.m. Mon-Thurs

TEXT: *FOCUS on Community College Success* by Constance Staley

COURSE OBJECTIVES: This course is designed to give you the tools to mak more productive, and a more successful learning experience. The goal to make you a better student by building your study skills and enhanc strategies.

EXPECTATIONS: Students are expected to be respectful of instructors an Assignments should be turned in on time unless you have a valid rea due date. Please see me if you have any questions.Water bottles are but no food or sugary drinks are permitted. Please turn off your ce come to class.

GRADING: 100 Possible Points
-Participation: 10 Points.
-Final Presentation: 20 Points.
-Final Exam: 20 Points.
-Assignments(3) and Quizzes (2): 50 Points (10 each)

GRADES: 100-90 = A   89-80 = B   79-70 = C   69-60 = D

Course Schedule

WEEK 1:	Overview and PreTest
WEEK 2:	Managing Time and Stress
WEEK 3:	Reading Skills
WEEK 4:	Test Taking
WEEK 5:	Listening and Memory
WEEK 6:	Diversity
	Effective Writing

Never mistake knowledge for wisdom. One helps you make a living; the other helps you make a life.

Sandra Carey, consultant and lobbyist

Math is the fundamental language of *physics*, one branch of which studies atomic and subatomic particles. When atoms combine into molecules, such as carbon dioxide, the academic discipline involved is called *chemistry*. Chemicals combine to create living organisms studied in *biology* courses. Living organisms don't just exist, they think and behave, leading to the study of *psychology*. They also interact in groups, families, and societies, which you study in *sociology*. You can also study units of living beings throughout time and across cultures in the discipline of *anthropology*. These units—people—who live and work together are typically governed or govern themselves, leading to *political science*. Let's keep going.

When an account of peoples and countries and their rulers is recorded, you study *history*. These written accounts, sometimes factual or sometimes fictional (for pleasure or intrigue) comprise the study of *literature*.

Literature is one way to record impressions and provoke reactions—poetry is a good example—through the use of words. But images and symbols can do the same things—enter *art*. A particular question artists ask is "What is beauty?" otherwise known as aesthetics, which is also a particular topic of study in *philosophy*. Philosophy also includes another subspecialty called number theory, one of the earliest branches of pure mathematics. And now we're all the way around the Circle of Learning, arriving right back at *math*.

That's a quick rundown. Of course, many academic disciplines don't appear on this chart, but they could and should. The point isn't which disciplines are

CONTROL: *YOUR LEARNING*

YOUR TOUGHEST TASK

In Class: Think about your most challenging class this semester. Is it a general education course or one required for your major? If it's a general education course, make a list of all the ways this course can help you either to further your career or to become a well-educated person. If this course is one in your major, ask yourself why the challenge is so great. Do you understand the course content? Do you see how it connects with the content in other courses? Do you keep

up with readings and assignments? Can you follow your instructor's teaching style? Send your instructor in this class an e-mail indicating your specific efforts to do your best and detailing your progress.

On the Job: Assume your boss has just assigned you a challenging new task, one that will ask you to call on what you have learned in many different classes or disciplines. What might that task be? Describe it, along with knowledge you'd need from at least five academic disciplines.

represented. Instead, the Circle of Learning demonstrates that academic disciplines are interconnected because knowledge itself is interconnected. *Anthropology* (understanding people throughout time and across cultures) can provide an important foundation for *political science* (how people are governed or govern themselves), and *history* (a record of peoples and countries and rulers) can easily be the basis for *literature*. Using what you're learning in one discipline can lead to deeper understanding in another, and although some of your instructors will help you connect the dots, putting it all together is basically your responsibility.

In your career, you'll need to use knowledge without necessarily remembering in which course you learned it. You'll be thinking critically and creatively, solving problems, and calling upon all the skills you're developing in all the courses you're studying in college. The bottom line is that connections count. Recognize them, use them, and strengthen them to reinforce your learning.

"The self is not something that one finds. It's something one creates.

Thomas Szasz, Professor Emeritus in Psychiatry, State University of New York Health Science Center, Syracuse

How to Choose a Major and a Career

Like many students, you probably put value in how well college prepares you for a profession.[3] Choosing a college major and directing yourself toward a prospective career can be stressful. Many students feel pressure to make the right decision—and make it right now! You might hear conflicting advice from family members that put a high priority on financial success above other important factors, for example, and feel overwhelmed by the number of possibilities from which to choose.[4] You may know what you want to do with the rest of your life right now, but many of your classmates don't, and even if they *say*

How **FULL** is your plate?

" The laws of science do not distinguish between the past and the future. "
— STEVEN W. HAWKING

People talk about something being a real "slice of life." They mean that whatever they're talking about is a realistic snapshot in time. What did you do with today's slice of life? Were you realistic in what you expected of yourself? Did you pay attention to the things and people that are most important to you? Did you make progress toward the future you're trying to create?

Irafael/Shutterstock.com

TRY IT!

Keep track of how productively you "carve up" your time this week and be prepared to be accountable to your instructor and classmates next week. Keep a journal of each day's biggest accomplishment and most distracting obstacle, and see if you recognize patterns. Create one time management pointer of your own to share with your classmates.

they do, they may well change their minds. Yes, these decisions are important. But where do you start? The decision-making process should involve these critical steps. If you're still deciding, or even if you think you already have, consider how they apply to you.

Step 1: Follow Your Bliss

In an ideal world, which major and career would you choose? Don't think about anything except the actual content you'd be studying. Don't consider career opportunities, requirements, difficulty, or anything else that might keep you from making these choices in an ideal world. What are you passionate about? If it's skateboarding, think about which majors might apply. Majoring in physics would help you understand skateboard "flight paths," spin, and angles. Majoring in landscape architecture would allow you to design skateparks. Majoring in journalism would put you in a good position to write for a skateboarding magazine.

Like Ethan Cole from the "FOCUS Challenge Case," you may be wondering what to do with your life. Perhaps the *idealist* in you has one potential career in mind and the *realist* in you has another. The $300,000 salary you'd earn as a surgeon may look very compelling until you consider the years of medical school required after college, the time invested in an internship and residency, and the still further years of specialization. It takes long-term commitment, dedication, and resources—yours or borrowed ones—to make that dream come true. Do these factors lessen the appeal?

Perhaps there's conflict between your ideal career and someone else's idea of an ideal career for you. Comedian Robin Williams once said, "When I told my father I was going to be an actor, he said, 'Fine, but study welding just in case.'"

And perhaps you just don't know yet. If that's the case, don't panic. Despite the increased pressure these days to choose the right major because of rising tuition and a changeable economy, Ethan Cole is right: It's hard to have it all figured out from the start.[5]

One thing is certain: You'll be a happier, more productive person if you do what *you* want to do *and* pursue it vigorously. When it comes to success, ability (*Can* you do it?) and effort (Are you *willing* to invest what it takes?) go hand in hand. Whatever your motivation, remember this. It's unusual for people to become truly successful halfheartedly. There are undeniable emotional and psychological components involved in success. Wayne Gretzky, called the greatest player in the history of hockey, once said, "God gave me a special talent to play the game . . . maybe he didn't give me a talent, he gave me a *passion*."

© Bryan Allen/CORBIS

"Follow your bliss and be what you want to be. Don't climb the ladder of success only to find it's leaning against the wrong wall."

Dr. Bernie Siegel, physician and writer

Having said that, what if your "bliss" just isn't feasible? You'd give anything to play for the NBA, but you're five foot two and female. You dream of being a rock star, but you can't carry a tune. Then it may be time to set aside the dream and get real. Maybe then it's time to translate—or shift—your dreams into goals.

When the statistics are against you, achieving success isn't impossible, but it might take more than expert skill. It might also take some luck, very specific planning, and perseverance.

Step 2: Conduct Preliminary Research

Has it ever occurred to you that you may not have all the facts—accurate ones—about your ideal major? Do you know what it *really* takes? Have you gotten your information from qualified sources—or are you basing your opinion on your friend's reaction to one course he took?

Try an experiment. Choose three majors you're considering, one of which is your ideal major, and send yourself on a fact-finding mission. To find out if you're on target, get the answers to the following ten questions for each of the three possibilities. Go to the physical location (department) where each major is housed, and interview an instructor. The experiment requires legwork; don't just let your fingers do the clicking.

1. What is the major or certificate?

2. Who is the interviewee?

3. What is the name of the academic department where this major is housed? Where are the department offices physically located on campus?

4. Which introductory courses in this major would give you information about your interests and abilities?

5. Which specialized courses in this major interest you? (List three.)

6. What courses do you have to complete before you can major in the subject?

7. How many students major in this discipline on your campus?

8. Which required course in the major do students usually find most challenging? Which is most engaging? Which is most valued? Why?

9. How would the interviewee describe the reputation of this department on campus? What is it known for?

10. From the interviewee's perspective, why should a student major in this discipline?

After you complete your interviews, review the facts. Did you change any of your opinions based on what you learned?[6]

The privilege of a lifetime is being who you are.

Joseph Campbell, American professor and writer (1904–1987)

rank order the four parts of you listed in Figure 12.6, what would you put in first place? Second, third, and last? To get yourself thinking, ask these questions:

1. Do you find fulfillment by using your *head*? Do you enjoy solving complex problems or thinking through difficult situations? Do you like to reason things out, weigh evidence, and think critically? Someone working toward a paralegal certificate might fit this category.

2. Do you find it satisfying to work with matters of the *heart*? Are you the kind of person others come to with problems because you listen and care? Does trying to make others happy make you happy? A nursing major might be what students with this preference choose, for example.

3. Do you like to create things with your *hands*? Do you enjoy making art? Doing hands-on projects? Building things out of other things? A drafting major who designs and builds models might be what students with this preference choose, for example.

4. Do you excel at physical activities that involve your *whole body*? Are you athletic? Do you like to stay active, no matter what you're doing? A physical therapy major who goes on to work in a rehabilitation facility helping stroke victims relearn to walk might be what students with this preference choose, for example.

CAREER OUTLOOK: *Matt McClain, Entrepreneur*

Courtesy of Matt McClain.

Q1: Why did you decide to become an entrepreneur?
I decided I wanted to work for myself for a few reasons. One, I enjoy freedom–not only freedom to work how I want and when I want, but the freedom to bring my own ideas to life instead of someone else's. I've worked for a lot of people in my life and then one day I realized, "Hey, I can do that, too!" There is so much opportunity out there just waiting, and I felt that working for someone else was holding me back.

Q2: Beyond going to college, what else helped prepare you?
Before I decided to start my own production company, I spent six years working in television, two of which were spent interning. So, spending so much time in the field prepared me for the reality of doing it alone. I had a foundation of real world experience to build on. But beyond that, I'd say just networking. I'm constantly talking with other people in my field and comparing notes, sharing experi-

ences, and learning a lot. That's how I became involved in writing and directing the FOCUS TV episodes that go with this book.

Q3: What's the worst part of running your own business?
I'd say the lack of stability. When you're the boss, you have no one to rely on, no one to blame, no one to count on but yourself. You have to be constantly looking for jobs, marketing yourself, and being smart

with your money. You might have three good months and then two bad months, so you have to anticipate dry spells and be prepared. Oh, and not having health insurance is pretty tough.

Q4: What's your advice to college students who'd like to become entrepreneurs?
Well, I'd say do your homework, for sure. Make sure

FIGURE 12.6

What's Your Academic Anatomy?

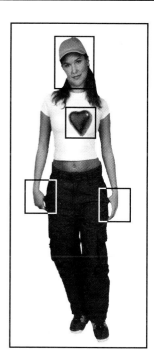

Another way of analyzing your preferences is by considering your "Academic Anatomy." What do you find most satisfying? Working with your

Head?
Heart?
Hands? or
Whole Body?

© Hemera Photo Objects

Now look at your academic anatomy rankings. Of course, the truth is that "all of you" is involved in everything you do. And achieving balance is important. But what are your priorities? This type of simple analysis can be one way of informing you about who you are and where you should be headed.

you know exactly what you're getting into and what to expect. And when choosing what type of business to start, make sure it's something you feel passionate about. Being your own boss requires a ton of discipline and motivation. It's hard to make yourself do something that you hate. And hire a good accountant who can help you navigate the waters of self employment. It can get pretty overwhelming, and it helps to have someone there to answer your questions.

HOW WOULD *YOU* LIKE IT?

Have you ever considered a career as an entrepreneur?

Facts to Consider[10]

Academic preparation required: Many community colleges now offer certificate programs in entrepreneurism that help you start up your own business. Entrepreneurs should have formal training in business and finance. A bachelor's degree may also be very helpful and depending on the size of your venture, a master's degree might be in order. Since starting a business typically involves getting investors to trust you, the more education you have the better.

Future workforce demand: With a continually changing economy and a constant need for innovation, there is no limit to entrepre-

neurial opportunities. It all comes down to how good your idea is and how well you execute it.

Work environment: Starting your own business usually starts first out of your own home with an idea. If it grows, it may lead to a larger space with more employees.

Essential skills: To be a successful entrepreneur, you need to be determined, confident, business savvy and most of all brave. A good idea is only as good as its execution.

Questions to Ponder

1. Do you have (or could you acquire) the skills this career requires?

2. Are you interested in a career like this? Why or why not?

For more career activities online, access the CourseMate via www.cengagebrain.com/shop/ISBN/0495906433 to do the Team Career exercises.

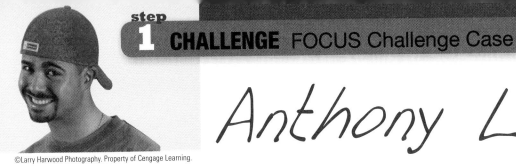

Anthony Lopez

©Larry Harwood Photography. Property of Cengage Learning.

A nthony Lopez was average in nearly every sense of the word. He played T-ball as a kid, but not particularly well. He didn't like school much, but he went when he felt like it. He didn't have many friends except for a few kids that lived in the eight city blocks that made up his neighborhood. He was even sandwiched between two older brothers and two younger sisters. His brothers were successful—one was an attorney and the other a doctor. Somehow, deep inside himself, Anthony knew that measuring up would be hard for him. Maybe that's why he decided to make his mark in his own way.

© Monkey Business Images, 2009. Used under license from Shutterstock.com; © Monkey Business Images, 2010. Used under license from Shutterstock.com; © Monkey Business Images, 2010. Used under copyright from Shutterstock.com.

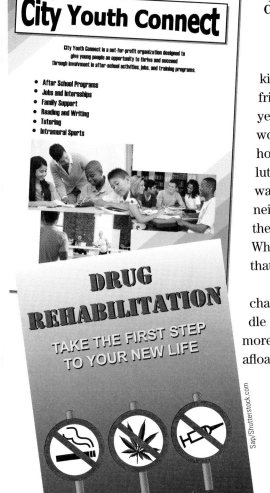

Sap/Shutterstock.com

You could say that Anthony's kid sister, Gina, was his closest friend. Even though she was four years younger, the two of them would pal around the neighborhood. They could laugh over absolutely anything, and their specialty was pulling pranks on all the other neighborhood kids. For a while, the two of them were inseparable. Whenever you saw Gina, you knew that Anthony was close by.

But as Anthony got older, things changed. The trouble started in middle school. His Mom, who worked more than one job to keep the family afloat, was worried that he was getting in with the wrong crowd. But Anthony wasn't worried. His friends knew where to get cigarettes and alcohol—even drugs. When he was with them, he imagined the other kids looked up to him and his tough-guy friends. By the time high school rolled around, Anthony already had a record. Eventually, he dropped out, left home, and basically lived on the streets. When he needed money, he snatched a purse or wallet. He lost contact with his family, and there seemed to be no turning back. Drugs were a way of life for him, and he began sinking deeper and deeper into a life that most people predicted wouldn't turn out well.

©Cengage Learning

Criminal Search- County		
Name: Lopez, Anthony	**DOB:** 7-10-1989	**SSN:** XXX-XX-XXXX

RESULT: RECORD FOUND

STATE/COUNTY:	VERIFIED INFORMATION

But that was then, and this was now. Anthony's life probably would have been headed in the wrong direction entirely, if it hadn't been for several wakeup calls, including seeing his little sister, Gina, on the street one day. He tried to talk with her, but she was so high that she didn't even recognize him. Anthony saw that she was repeating his worst mistakes, which troubled him deeply. The stark realization that he might be ruining her life in addition to his own shocked him back into reality.

Now Anthony was part of an inner-city youth organization for kids like him. The group's leader, Nicky Russo, had once been a gang member himself. He reached out to Anthony, and Anthony responded. Anthony was on a mission to find Gina and get her into the group. Anthony's life was changing, and his life's goal was becoming clear: to help other people like him. He decided to earn his GED and enroll in the best community college he could find to earn an associate's degree in social services. And that's exactly what he did.

As he sat in his favorite class, Urban Social Issues, Anthony realized that he had made the right choice. So much of what he heard his instructor lecturing about had been a part of his own past. As he got deeper into the associate's program, Anthony learned that an associate's degree in social services was a general degree that prepared graduates for many types of jobs. But what if he wanted to be an actual social worker? He learned that the need for social workers was very high, working with young children to older adults. He was taking classes like Racial, Ethnic, and Minority Groups and Sociology of the Family.

Even though the classes were hard, it wasn't long before Anthony was totally engrossed, and he knew he wanted to continue his education. With an associate's degree in social services, he could certainly work more knowledgeably alongside Nicky in the inner city. But what if he transferred to a four-year school for a bachelor's degree in sociology? What if he wanted to earn a master's degree in social work to specialize and become a school or hospital social worker? What if he wanted to conduct research and teach, like his community college instructors? What would getting a Ph.D. require, and should he even be thinking that far ahead? A million questions were forming in his mind.

What did the future hold for Anthony? Right now, he couldn't answer that question. But he did know that his future would be different from the future he might have had without college. What had always been true about Anthony was now true in the best possible sense: Anthony would make his mark.

Sociology Program C Comparison

	Bachelor's Degree
Ethnic Relations	
City in a Global Society	
Societal Change and Development	
Environmental Sociology	
Global Sociology	
Sociological Analysis	
Classical Theories of Society	
Contemporary Theories of Society	
Sociological Field Methods	
Gender and Society	
Global Sociology	
Quantitative Methods	
Regression and Multivariate Data Analysis	
Policy Issues in Education	
Economics of Educational Policy	
Public Policy	
Demographic Analysis	
Evaluation of Educational Programs	
Race and Class in American Cities	
Masters Thesis Project	
Qualitative Research	
Sociological Analysis	
Inter...	

Experience Sociology...
WITH A WIDE RANGE OF RESOURCES
AVAILABLE FROM WADSWORTH

KLENIEWSKI

CITIES,
CHANGE &
CONFLICT

CITIES, CHAN

A Political Econ

SOCIOLOGY
ASSOCIATE OF ARTS DEGREE

The AA degree with an emphasis in Sociology is designed to provide a better understanding of how humans act and interact in social settings. The program offered provides an excellent foundation for students seeking to continue their education in Sociology, either pursuing a Bachelor's or Master's degree.

First Semester		3
ENGL 101	English Composition I	3
SOC 101	Introduction to Sociology	3
	Science Elective	3
	Humanities Elective	12
	Total Credits	

Second Semester		3

Launching a Career: Plan Your Work and Work Your Plan

Career Auction

Assume you have $100,000 to spend on the following items. In a few minutes, your instructor will begin a real-live auction, putting one item at a time up for auction. Before the auction begins, budget your money in the first column. You may select as many items as you wish to bid on, but you may not place all your money on any single item. As the group auction proceeds, fill in the appropriate amounts that are actually spent by members of the class for each item.

	BUDGETED AMOUNT	WINNING BID
1. Becoming the CEO of a leading Fortune 500 company	_____	_____
2. Being a top earner in your career field	_____	_____
3. Being the number-one expert in your profession	_____	_____
4. Having good friends on the job	_____	_____
5. Being your own boss	_____	_____
6. Creating a good balance between productive work and a happy family life	_____	_____
7. Having opportunities for travel and adventure in your job	_____	_____
8. Doing work you find fully satisfying	_____	_____
9. Working in a beautiful setting	_____	_____
10. Being a lifelong learner so that your career can develop and change over time	_____	_____

Let's assume, for now, that you decide to go straight into your chosen career field after community college. You've been focused all along, earned your degree, and now you're ready to find a job that fits your new skills, your personality—*you*! "Fit" is the key word in that last sentence. Where you choose to launch your career and who you work with will be critical factors in your job satisfaction.

The two questions posed early in this book resurface now: "Who are you?" and "What do you want?" Working your way through *FOCUS*, you have learned more about who you are (although this is a lifelong quest). In this final chapter, we'll deal with "What do you want?" The answer to that question can be just as important.

What do you really want from a career? What's important to you? Even though your views may change over time, it's important to start thinking about them now. In Exercise 13.1, item 4, "Having good friends on the job,"

may be a top priority now, but item 5, "Being your own boss," may be more appealing a few years down the road, after you have some additional work experience under your belt. Maybe you already prepared for a career once, but something has changed. The field you entered has transformed over time, so that you need to retool. Or a career that attracted you earlier turned out to be much less engaging than you expected. Or your family has grown and you need a career that brings in more resources. That's what community colleges are for. You may be older than the students sitting around you, but you deserve the same educational opportunities. Interestingly, according to research, the most important factor in job satisfaction isn't any of the ten items in Exercise 3.1. The number one contributor to job satisfaction, statistically speaking, is the quality of your relationship with your boss.[6] Here are some suggestions to help you launch the career you're aiming for.

Vasko Miokovic/iStockphoto.com

"I always wanted to be somebody, but I should have been more specific.

Lily Tomlin, comedian

Try on a Career for Size

If all your jobs thus far have been just that—*jobs*—to help you pay the bills, how do you know what you want in a *career*? A career is different from a job. It's a profession you've chosen and prepared for. Perhaps you've had more than a string of jobs, and your career is well underway, but now you'd like to go in a different direction. Or perhaps you haven't launched your career yet. Exactly how *do* you launch a new career? You have to start somewhere, so perhaps you'd search online or through actual newspaper want ads. There are plenty of career exploration websites online. Check out these career mega websites to explore some options:

> Careerbuilder.com
> Monster.com
> The Occupational Outlook Handbook (www.bls.gov/oco/)
> Americasjobexchange.com/
> Career-Journal.com
> Jobcentral.com
> USAJobs.gov
> TrueCareers.com
> AllJobSearch.com
> EmploymentWizard.com[7]

> It is not what we get but who we become, what we contribute . . . that gives meaning to our lives.

Anthony Robbins, motivational speaker and author

You can Google and surf to your heart's content.

But you may be likely to read something like this: "Opening in . . . (anything). Experience required." Isn't that the way it always goes? You have to *have* experience in order to get a job that will *give* you experience. This problem is one many people face. Sure, you have experience. It's just not the right kind. Perhaps you've bagged fries, mowed yards, bussed tables, and chauffeured pizzas up to this point. If that's not the kind of experience the posted opening is looking for, how do you get the right kind? Or perhaps you're in school to switch career fields. You have experience, but it won't help you go in a different direction.

The process of job-hunting includes many different steps. Here are some things for you to consider doing during your time in college. One important suggestion is to try a job on for size. Take a look at the three possibilities described in Figure 13.1.

These experiences help you in three ways. First, they allow you to test a potential career field. The actual day-to-day work may be exactly what you expected, or not. They show you whether that particular career field is one you'd really be interested in. *I had no idea this field was so cutthroat, hectic, dull . . . exciting, stimulating, invigorating. . . .* A thumbs-down can be just as informative as a thumbs-up. At least you can remove one option from your list. Second, internships, co-ops, and service-learning opportunities give you experience to list on your résumé. And third, they help you make connections with others in the field, and sometimes they even lead to employment.

The key to successful trial experiences such as internships is the relationship between you and your sponsor in the host organization. If you're not being given enough to do, or not allowed to test your skills in a particular area, speak up. The answer may be put in terms of company policy, or you're "not quite ready for prime time." Nevertheless, you must communicate about these kinds of important issues. No one can read your mind! As you work toward launching your career, keep up with the latest information. Read up on résumé writing and interviewing, networking, hot career fields, and the latest employment trends. Use the information in this chapter to pique your interest, and search further on your own.

	Description: What is a . . . ?	What kind of experience do I get?	Why would I want to do it?	How do I get involved?
Internships	An internship is an opportunity for you to work alongside a professional in a career field of interest to you, and to learn from him or her.	Your supervisor will mentor you, and you'll get a clearer picture of what the career field is like.	Some majors will require you to complete an internship as a part of your program, for licensure or certification, for example.	Internships may be offered through your academic major department, or through a central office on campus, or sometimes you can pursue one on your own through the Internet or personal connections.
Co-op Program	Co-op programs allow you to take classes and then apply what you've learned on the job, either after or while you take classes.	You may take classes for a term and then work full-time for a term. You can test a career field.	A potential employer can get a sense of your potential, and you can gain practical experience to put on your résumé.	Your advisor will be able to tell you if your program has co-op opportunities.
Service-Learning	Some classes contain service-learning experiences in which you volunteer your time.	A service-learning component built right into the syllabus can give you valuable, practical experience.	The emphasis is on hands-on learning and connecting what you're learning in class with what you're experiencing out of class. If you take a class on aging, for example, you may work with a senior citizen at an assisted living facility to apply what you're learning in class.	If you're particularly interested in hands-on learning, ask your advisor to recommend classes with service-learning components that will benefit you.

FIGURE 13.1

Three Ways to Try a Job on for Size

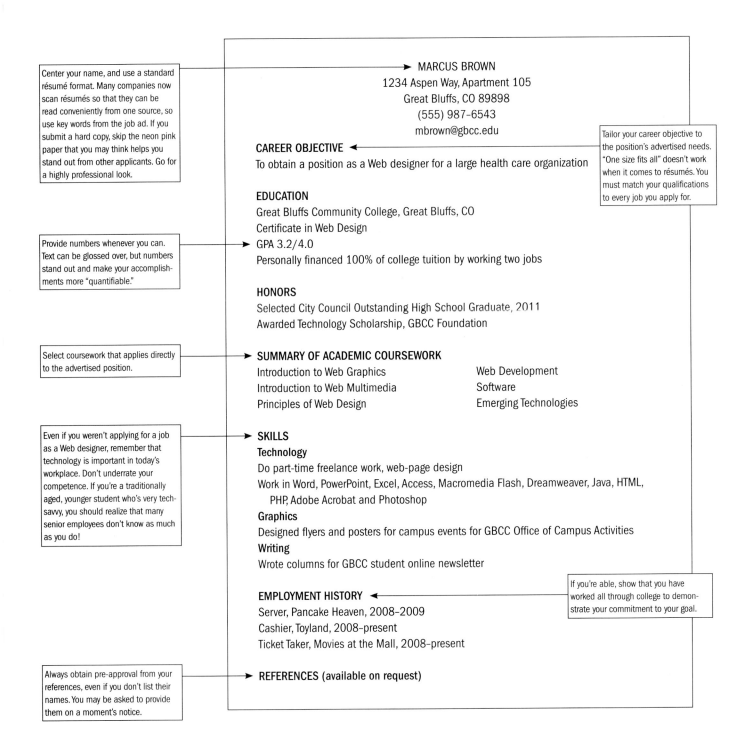

Center your name, and use a standard résumé format. Many companies now scan résumés so that they can be read conveniently from one source, so use key words from the job ad. If you submit a hard copy, skip the neon pink paper that you may think helps you stand out from other applicants. Go for a highly professional look.

Provide numbers whenever you can. Text can be glossed over, but numbers stand out and make your accomplishments more "quantifiable."

Select coursework that applies directly to the advertised position.

Even if you weren't applying for a job as a Web designer, remember that technology is important in today's workplace. Don't underrate your competence. If you're a traditionally aged, younger student who's very tech-savvy, you should realize that many senior employees don't know as much as you do!

Always obtain pre-approval from your references, even if you don't list their names. You may be asked to provide them on a moment's notice.

MARCUS BROWN
1234 Aspen Way, Apartment 105
Great Bluffs, CO 89898
(555) 987-6543
mbrown@gbcc.edu

CAREER OBJECTIVE
To obtain a position as a Web designer for a large health care organization

Tailor your career objective to the position's advertised needs. "One size fits all" doesn't work when it comes to résumés. You must match your qualifications to every job you apply for.

EDUCATION
Great Bluffs Community College, Great Bluffs, CO
Certificate in Web Design
GPA 3.2/4.0
Personally financed 100% of college tuition by working two jobs

HONORS
Selected City Council Outstanding High School Graduate, 2011
Awarded Technology Scholarship, GBCC Foundation

SUMMARY OF ACADEMIC COURSEWORK
Introduction to Web Graphics   Web Development
Introduction to Web Multimedia   Software
Principles of Web Design   Emerging Technologies

SKILLS
Technology
Do part-time freelance work, web-page design
Work in Word, PowerPoint, Excel, Access, Macromedia Flash, Dreamweaver, Java, HTML, PHP, Adobe Acrobat and Photoshop
Graphics
Designed flyers and posters for campus events for GBCC Office of Campus Activities
Writing
Wrote columns for GBCC student online newsletter

EMPLOYMENT HISTORY
Server, Pancake Heaven, 2008–2009
Cashier, Toyland, 2008–present
Ticket Taker, Movies at the Mall, 2008–present

If you're able, show that you have worked all through college to demonstrate your commitment to your goal.

REFERENCES (available on request)

It's likely that Marcus Brown is a traditionally aged college student. Notice that he has little experience in the field he'd like to work in after getting his certificate in Web Design. Contrast his résumé with the following one, where Jennifer Ortega has considerable experience working in the IT field. Rather than using a skills approach, her résumé uses a chronological approach that shows everything she's done that's related to the job she's applying for.

JENNIFER ORTEGA
789 Breckenridge Court, Apartment C
Great Bluffs, CO 89898
(555) 333-9999
jortega@gbcc.edu

CAREER OBJECTIVE
To obtain a position as a Web Designer in a large health care organization

EMPLOYMENT HISTORY

> Jennifer has had several jobs in the IT field. On her résumé, she lists what she did in each one that might be useful in the job she wants.

2009–present   Technology Helpdesk Manager, Central College
· Developed new phone answering system that increased the unit's responsiveness by 50%

> Numbers are important and memorable! Notice how they stand out.

· Oversaw a staff of 10 student technology experts
· Installed software and made troubleshooting visits to approximately 15 faculty offices per week

2008–2009   IT Supervisor, Great Bluffs School District 1
· Coordinated software maintenance in 12 elementary school administrative offices
· Managed a team of 8 technology employees
· Installed financial software to improve budget management at the K-6 level

2004–2008   Sales staff member, Tech 4 U, Great Bluffs, Colorado
· Earned Salesperson of the Quarter Award, Jan–Mar, 2008

> Notice that Jennifer gives specific dates and has listed a variety of things to discuss with an interviewer.

· Recognized with Sales and Service Award, June 2008
· Initiated store display rearrangement

EDUCATION
Great Bluffs Community College, Great Bluffs, CO
Certificate in Web Design
GPA 3.2/4.0
Personally financed 100% of college tuition

HONORS
Selected student representative to GBCC faculty government
Earned a place on the GBCC Dean's Honor Role each term

SUMMARY OF ACADEMIC COURSEWORK
Introduction to Web Graphics   Web Development
Introduction to Web Multimedia   Software
Principles of Web Design   Emerging Technologies

SKILLS
Technology
Do part-time freelance work, web-page design
Work in Word, PowerPoint, Excel, Access, Macromedia Flash, Dreamweaver, Java, HTML, PHP, Adobe Acrobat and Photoshop

> Notice that Jennifer starts each phrase with a verb to emphasize action, and that all verbs are in the same tense (past or present).

Graphics
Design brochures for local health care organizations as a freelancer:
    Forest Hills Rehabilitation Center, Mercy Hospital, and Sunnydale Senior Center
Writing
Write brochure content after consulting with management at these organizations

REFERENCES (available on request)

You may automatically assume that Jennifer has the advantage over Marcus, but the health care company with the opening may be looking for fresh, new talent, and Marcus should capitalize on his web design freelance work or get an actual internship with a professional web designer. Everyone has to start somewhere. Do your best with whichever approach fits you. Finally, remember that you can hire a professional to write a résumé for you, but if you read up on résumé writing and follow the suggestions here, you can do just fine on your own. Hiring a professional or going through an employment agency can be helpful, but they can also be expensive propositions. And if they promise you the moon ("You'll have a new job at the starting salary of your dreams in just one week!"), be wary.

EXERCISE 13.3

Cover Letter Critique

When you submit a résumé, either in person, through the mail, or online, you should send a well-written cover letter along with it that briefly outlines your qualifications for the job, expresses your interest, and gives the person who reviews your résumé some idea of who you are. Take a look at the following cover letter from Marcus Brown and critique it. What has he done right, and what has he done wrong?

---

15 September

To Whom It May Concenr,

I'd like to apply for your opening at Anderson-Wallace Healthcare Industries. I have heard a lot about your company and it sounds great. A friend of mine works there, and he said his starting salary was unbelieveable. What exactly do you do at your company? He's told me a few things, but I'm eager to learn more!

As you can see from my résumé, I don't have much experience. But I have just earned my web design certificate from GBCC, and I did pretty well. I want to start my career at a great company like yours.

I hope to hear from you soon.

Warmly,

Marcus Brown

After finding the mistakes Marcus made, rewrite this letter to bring to class or submit to your instructor.

Interview at Your Best

By now, you have probably already been interviewed several times to get a job. But when you're ready to launch your career, you'll be facing interviews for the new job you really want, the one you prepared for by earning a certificate or degree. Often interviewers aren't particularly skilled at asking questions. They haven't been trained on how to interview prospective employees, so they just ask whatever questions come to them. And often, interviewees don't quite know what they're doing either. Of course, you should always be honest, but there are various ways to communicate the same information. Telling an interviewer you "like to work alone" sounds antisocial. But if you say you "like to really focus

on what you're doing without distractions," you show dedication to your work ethic. You also need to be aware of real pitfalls to avoid. See what you think of these suggestions.

1. **Play up the positive, and downplay the negative.** A trap question interviewers sometimes ask is, "What's your worst fault?" While you may be tempted to say the first thing that comes to mind, that could be a big mistake. "Umm . . . sleeping too much! I really like to sleep in. Sometimes I sleep half the day away." Not good. But some faults you could identify might actually be seen as strengths: "I have a little too much nervous energy. I'm always on the go. I like to stay busy."

2. **Stay focused.** "Tell me about yourself" is a common question interviewers ask. How much time do you have? Most of us like to talk about ourselves, but it's important to stay on track. Think possible questions through in advance, and construct some hypothetical answers. Keep your answers job-focused: what your long-term career goals are, how this job can help you prepare, what you liked about your last job. You don't need to go into your family background or your personal problems. And it's always a bad idea to bash a previous job or former boss. The interviewer may worry that you'll bring whatever didn't work there with you to this new job.

3. **Don't just give answers, get some.** A job interview is like a first date. Find out what you need to know. If the job is one you're interested in long-term, ask questions such as these three key ones:

   > **What does this company value?** Listen to the answer. Hard work? New ideas? Communication skills? The answer will tell you about the personality of the company.

   > **What's a typical day like for you?** Ask the interviewer. An answer such as "I get up at 5:00 a.m., get here at 6:30 a.m., and go home around 7:00 p.m.—and then I do paperwork all evening" tells you something. This may—or may not—be the job or the company for you.

   > **What happened to the last person in this job?** If you find out he was promoted, that's one thing. But if you learn he was fired or quit, see if you can find out why. Maybe he had job performance problems, or maybe this is an impossible job that no one could do well. Listen to the interviewer. She may be looking for an opportunity to tell you things she thinks are important, too.

4. **Watch for questions that seem to come out of left field.** Some companies like to get creative with their interviewing. Microsoft, for example, is known for asking problem-solving questions, such as "If you could remove any of the fifty states, which would it be? Be prepared to give specific reasons why you chose the state you did." There is no right or wrong answer, although some answers are better than others. ("We should just nuke state X. I had a bad experience there once" would probably concern some people, and naming Washington state, where Microsoft is located, might be a bad choice.) The interviewer just wants to hear how you can think critically and give reasons for your answers.[10] Remember: Today's interviewers are looking for more than technical skills; they're looking for critical thinking skills, problem-solving skills, and creativity.[11]

5. **Don't start off with salary questions.** Make sure the first question out of your mouth isn't, "So tell me about the salary, again? Any way to notch that up a bit?" The last thing you want to do is give the interviewer the idea you're in it for the money. Of course, you are, but not just for that. More importantly, in every job you have, you'll gain experience and knowledge that will always better prepare you for every job that will be a part of your long-term career. Don't start negotiating a salary until you've actually been offered a job.

6. **Negotiate wisely.** If the interviewer asks you to name a salary figure, be careful. Saying "I could probably live on $30,000," when the actual figure the interviewer is authorized to start with is $38,000, has just given the employer the option to lower the salary based on your expectations. A good rule of thumb is: Never name a number. It's always best to ask the interviewer what the salary range for the job is. It's also good to research the salaries of similar jobs, and it's even better to have another job offer you're considering, so that you have choices. Otherwise, you're not negotiating, you're begging.[12]

7. **Know what you're dealing with.** One of the easiest ways to blow a job interview is by doing nothing. Candidates who don't do their homework usually don't pass an interview. If the interviewer asks "So what do you know about the company?" and you reply "Oh, not much, but I'm a fast learner," you'll be perceived to care very little about the outcome of the interview. Go online or read up about the place you'd like to work. Your knowledge, and therefore your interest, will show. And it goes without saying (although here it is, anyway) that you should arrive early, dress professionally, overprepare, and send a follow-up thank-you note or e-mail.[13]

Continuing Your Education

Like Anthony Lopez, perhaps you're exploring the idea of continuing your education. Typically, the more education you get, the more money you can make, the more you can do, and the more responsibility you have. Figure 13.2 sum-

FIGURE 13.2

Education Pays

Source: Bureau of Labor Statistics. ((27 May 2010). Available at http://www.bls.gov/emp/ep_chart_001.htm.

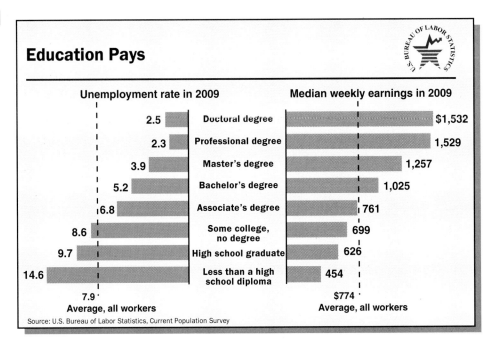

marizes both earnings and unemployment rates by educational level achieved, but the decision to continue is yours and yours alone. You know yourself and your interests best.

By the end of the "FOCUS Challenge Case," Anthony was considering four alternatives: an associate's degree, a bachelor's degree, a master's degree, and a Ph.D. Each level of these four educational paths has distinct differences he needs to know about. Anthony seems to have "found his bliss," and his heart is in the work. He is convinced that being a social worker is the right career field for him. He is motivated, engaged in what he's learning, and looking forward to a career of service. But at what level? Figure 13.3 lists some basic considerations for Anthony. Can you compare his choices to ones you may be considering?

FIGURE 13.3

An Educational Career Path[14]

	Associate's Degree in Social (Human) Services	Bachelor's Degree in Sociology (or a related field)	Master's of Social Work (MSW)	Ph.D. in Sociology (or Doctorate of Social Work)
Average Time to Complete:	2 years	4–5 years	2 years beyond a bachelor's degree	3–4 years beyond a master's degree
Average Number of Required Courses:	Approximately 20	Approximately 40	10 courses and 900 hours of supervised field experience or internship	10 (plus dissertation)
Type of Work:	Social Service Assistant or Aide, work with social workers, pharmacists, psychologists, etc. Varying levels of responsibility. Help people in need.	Social Worker (although an MSW is increasingly required), help clients cope with disabilities (like substance abuse or homelessness). Work in schools, public health agencies, hospitals, etc. and visit clients in their homes.	Social Worker clinical work, supervise other social workers, manage case loads. Must pass state licensure exam. May wish to go into private practice at least part-time. May specialize in such areas as • Child, family, or schools • Medical and public health • Mental health and substance abuse	Professor, High-level administrator, researcher. May teach at the college or university level, conduct research, or run a health-care or non-profit organization, for example.
Future Demand:	Much higher than average. Expected growth of 34 percent between 2006 and 2016.	Favorable (varies by type of specialization).	Favorable, much faster than average (varies by type of specialization).	Generally good for faculty positions (although varies by type of specialization and preference for full- or part-time work).
Median salary:	$27,280 (as of May, 2008)	$42,402 (as of May, 2008)	$45,790 and higher (as of May, 2008)	$58,830 (for all full-time college professors as of May, 2008)

Goals are the fuel in the furnace of achievement.

Brian Tracy, Eat that Frog

maker's history, what the company stands for, its vision and values, and the reputation it has earned from customers. It's easy to get tunnel vision and lose sight of the bigger picture.

3. **Prove you're a problem solver.** While taking your college classes, you learned problem-solving skills. Some of those problems were personal (who can I get to watch my kids at the last minute?), and some were academic (why *was* Edgar Allen Poe so "dark"?). On the job, everyone values the person who comes up with a workable solution when everyone else is stumped. And your boss will value you more if you come up with solutions yourself. Instead of, "What should I do about X?" say, "We're facing Problem X. Should I do A, B, or C?" You've proven that you've already thought about the problem and generated three possible solutions and demonstrated that you can think on your own.

4. **Speak and write well.** Your college career may have put more emphasis on these skills than any others. In today's world of abbreviated text messages (AYS = Are you serious?) and empty conversation ("And she's . . . like so . . . you know . . . whatever . . ."), you can become a super star on the job by just speaking and writing well. And in addition to speaking and writing, learn to listen to what's *really* being said and why. With practice, you can listen past the bravado or baloney and get to the *real* message. That's important!

CAREER OUTLOOK: *Laela Perkins, Social Worker*

Q1: Why did you decide to pursue a career in social work?
I was working for a magazine and was feeling like my job was very superficial. During that time, I was also volunteering in an after-school program for high school kids, and I realized that I was getting more fulfillment out of volunteering than from my job. So, I started to research different career paths that would

allow me to do something for other people, and I discovered that getting a degree in social work might be the avenue to take. In my research, I learned that social workers not only focus on helping individuals with personal issues, but they also address issues within our society and how they affect our lives. The profession teaches people to understand that an individual problem may actually be a social concern. I

decided that social work would give me an opportunity to have a career that was dedicated to helping others. I was into that.

Q2: Beyond going to college, what else helped prepare you?
Having job experience. I guess you could say that involving myself in the community and recognizing the need to make certain changes in society were both important.

Q3: What are the best and worst aspects of your career field?
The best aspect is knowing that you are in a career that is designed to help people. The worst aspect is that I live in New York, and it is difficult, especially at first, to make enough money to live.

5. **Polish your people skills.** Your college instructors may have assigned group projects in your classes to help you learn teamwork skills. Good teamwork skills are key to a successful career in anything! People can be difficult to work with, yet *people* are the way work gets done.

6. **Learn the rules of the game.** In school—and throughout your life—you have learned what's sometimes called "The Hidden Curriculum:" things everyone knows, more or less, but never learned formally. For example, most people know that it's not polite to tell off-color jokes to people you've just met or smack your gum while giving a speech. In the same way, on the job, the "grapevine" or informal network is important to understand. To be successful, you must be tuned in. Understand the culture of the organization you work for. What does it value? Who holds the power? Where do you fit in, and what can you contribute?

7. **Know how to gather information and use it.** In college, you're asked to develop your research skills. It's easy to think that each paper for a class is just another assignment to check off the list, when, actually, you're developing skills that will be critical to your success later. You don't just string together pieces of information when you do research for your college classes. You analyze research through the "eyes" of the problem you're trying to address and *your* perspective on it. You weave ideas together to make an argument.

8. **Understand that numbers count.** Unfortunately, math gets a bad rap. Many people approach math classes in college with "fear and loathing," when, actually, math is a key to success in the world of work. If you can understand spreadsheets or figure out the budget, you'll be ahead of the game. Some people de-emphasize the importance of financial skills by referring to them as "bean-counting" or "number crunching," but people who know how to apply math on the job are highly sought after.

©Larry Harwood Photography. Property of Cengage Learning.

> When one door closes, another opens. But often we look so long, so regretfully, upon the closed door that we fail to see the one that has opened for us.
>
> *Helen Keller, American author, activist, and lecturer (1880–1968)*

Q4: What's your advice to college students who'd like to become social workers?

Before going back to school and getting your master's degree, I would suggest getting a job first. Take some time to experience what it is like to work in the field before you jump back into school. Social work is a professional degree; therefore, it is important to have some professional experience in order to be able to do the job well.

HOW WOULD *YOU* LIKE IT?

Have you ever considered a career in social work?

Facts to Consider[18]

Academic preparation required: Most commonly, a bachelor's degree is the minimum requirement to become a social worker, but a degree in sociology, psychology, or a related field may be enough to get you an entry-level job.

Future workforce demand: Job opportunities in this field will increase in the coming years at a rate much faster than in other fields. With the growing elderly population and the aging baby boom generation, the demand for health and social services will increase dramatically over the next ten years.

Work environment: Social workers typically work in an office or residential facility, but may travel locally to visit clients, meet with service providers, or attend meetings.

Essential skills: Social workers need to be emotionally mature and be very understanding of their clients' problems. They should be caring and responsible as well as reliable individuals.

Questions to Ponder

1. Do you have (or could you acquire) the skills this career requires?
2. Are you interested in a career like this? Why or why not?

For more career activities online, access the CourseMate via www.cengagebrain.com/shop/ ISBN/0495906433 to do the Team Career exercises.

9. **Go for extra credit.** In some of your courses, your instructors may give extra credit. You could be allowed to do something extra, beyond the requirements on the syllabus, to raise your grade. But what's extra credit in terms of your career? On the job, you have "extra credit" when your abilities stand out. You speak German and no one else does, so when something needs translating, you're the go-to person. Or you're so exceptional at PowerPoint that you're affectionately referred to as the "PowerPoint King."

10. **Manage your time, your attention, and yourself.** College is about self-responsibility. You're in charge of your education; you call the shots. If you manage your time and money, you can focus as you should on your courses. If you "spend" unwisely—in either area—you lose your focus and your performance slips. In your career, the same will be true. Your ability to manage time, your attention, and yourself will affect your personal and professional future.[19]

What Ifs

Life is full of "what ifs?" isn't it? What if you had dated someone else? What if you took the other job? What if things were different?

What If College Isn't Right for You?

What if you decide, after a term or two, that college isn't right for you? Perhaps your heart just isn't in it, and neither is your head. If so, know that you aren't alone. That realization comes to many students. The important question to ask yourself is whether you're really making the right decision, not just getting discouraged if college seems too challenging. Remember that "College is a team sport," and use all of the campus resources available to you before you abandon your efforts. But something other than college may also be the right decision for you—right now at this particular point in your life.

What If You Can't Finish a Degree Now?

Even though you have dreams and goals, sometimes "life happens." A turn of events changes everything, a new job consumes all of your time and energy, or someone needs you. Don't feel like a failure if that happens. Take time off, regroup, and come back when you can. Going to college expands your thinking and gives you a whole new take on life. Beyond a certificate or diploma, the learning that takes place in college changes you forever—and it's worth the investment in your future.

> **Every adversity, every failure, every heartache carries with it the seed of an equal or greater benefit.**
>
> *Napoleon Hill, author,* Keys to Success: The 17 Principles of Personal Achievement *(1883–1970)*

©Larry Harwood Photography. Property of Cengage Learning.

My, How You've Grown! Goodbye and Good Luck!

Remember Aunt Ruth (or whatever her name was)? Every time she visited when you were a kid, she remarked about how much you'd grown. Or when you went to visit her, she'd measure you and mark a notch on the wall to compare your height now to the one from last year's visit. She loved watching you grow, and the fact that she noticed made you feel special.

There's no doubt about it. In this first term of college, you have grown. You have gained new perspectives, new insights, and new ways of thinking about things. Like Aunt Ruth, others may notice. If those close to you are threatened by these changes, reassure them that your newfound knowledge hasn't made you think less of them. Remember: "You should have education enough so that you won't have to look up to people; and then more education so that you will be wise enough not to look down on people." If they are proud of you and your accomplishments, and have supported you along the way, thank them!

The important thing is to keep learning and never stop. Continuing to learn—whether in college or in life—is what will determine who you are and what you will become. Learn new things, update your goals, and reinvent yourself. This book, and the course for which you're reading it, have begun that process. Now the rest is up to you!

> **"** People succeed in as many ways as there are people. Some can be completely fulfilled with destinations that are much closer to home and more comfortable. But if you long to keep going, then I hope you are able to follow my lead to the places I have gone. To within a whisper of your own personal perfection. To places that are sweeter because you worked so hard to arrive there. To places at the very edge of your dreams. **"**
>
> *Michael Johnson, American sprinter*

VARK Activity

Complete the activity recommended for your preferred VARK learning style and bring it to class (or follow your instructor's instructions).

Visual: Create a flowchart that shows long-term planning for how you want your life to go over the next ten years. For example:

Complete degree in → Launch career in → Get entry-level position as → Get promoted to → Continue on for degree in → Complete degree by

_____ _____ _____ _____ _____ _____

Aural: Interview someone in your intended career field. Be prepared to report back to class or e-mail your instructor the results. Access the CourseMate via www.cengagebrain.com/shop/ISBN/0495906433 to listen to the iAudio summary for this chapter.

Read/Write: Write up a paragraph for a possible item 11 for the section of the chapter called "Ten Things Employers Hope You Will Learn in College." Read your contribution to the class.

Kinesthetic: Identify a YouTube video that summarizes a lesson you learned from reading this chapter. Why did you choose it, and what is the lesson you learned?

At the beginning of this chapter, Anthony Lopez faced a series of challenges as a new college student. Now after learning from this chapter, would you respond differently to any of the questions you answered about the "FOCUS Challenge Case"? Using what you learned in the chapter, write a paragraph ending to Anthony's case study. What are some of the possible outcomes for Anthony?

1. Identify one new thing you learned in reading this chapter. Why did you select the one you've selected? How will it affect what you do in your college classes?

2. How will this chapter change how you approach your future, no matter which fork of the road you choose as a next step? What will be most challenging for you?

3. How do you plan to increase your skills in college so that you can be more successful in your next step?

REALITY CHECK · What did you **Learn?**

On a scale of 1 to 5, answer these questions now that you've completed this chapter.

1 = not very/not much/very little/low   5 = very/a lot/very much/high

How much do you know *now*?

Now rate your current level of knowledge about topics covered in this chapter.

Launching a career

        1 2 3 4 5

Writing a resume

        1 2 3 4 5

Continuing your education

        1 2 3 4 5

Knowing what employers really want

        1 2 3 4 5

How useful might the information in this chapter be to you?

How much do you think this information might affect your college success?

        1 2 3 4 5

How much do you think this information might affect your career success after college?

        1 2 3 4 5

How long did it actually take you to complete this chapter (both the reading and writing tasks)?

_____ Hour(s) _____ Minutes

  Challenge Yourself Online Quiz. To find out how much you've learned, access the CourseMate via www.cengagebrain.com/shop/ISBN/0495906433 to take the Challenge Yourself Online Quiz.

Compare these answers with your answers from the "Readiness Check" at the beginning of this chapter. How might the gaps between what you thought before starting the chapter and what you now think affect how you approach your next term of college?

FOCUS EXIT INTERVIEW

Although you have not quite completed your first term as a college student, we're interested in your reactions to college so far: how you have spent your time, what challenges you've experienced, and your general views about what college has been like. Please answer thoughtfully.

INFORMATION ABOUT YOU

Name _____

Student Number _____ Course/Section _____

Instructor _____

Gender _____ Age _____

INFORMATION ABOUT YOUR COLLEGE EXPERIENCE

1. **How did you find you learned best in college? (Check all that apply.)**

   _____ by looking at charts, maps, graphs   _____ by reading books

   _____ by looking at color-coded information   _____ by writing papers

   _____ by looking at symbols and graphics   _____ by taking notes

   _____ by listening to instructors' lectures   _____ by going on field trips

   _____ by listening to other students during an in-class discussion   _____ by engaging in activities

   _____ by talking about course content with friends or roommates   _____ by actually doing things

2. **For each of the following pairs of descriptors, which set sounds most like you based on what you've learned about yourself this term? (Please choose between the two options on each line and place a checkmark by your choice.)**

   _____ Extraverted and outgoing   or   _____ Introverted and quiet

   _____ Detail-oriented and practical   or   _____ Big-picture and future-oriented

   _____ Rational and truthful   or   _____ People-oriented and tactful

   _____ Organized and self-disciplined or   _____ Spontaneous and flexible

3. ***FOCUS* is about 13 different aspects of college life. Which did you find most interesting personally? Which contained information that you found to be most challenging to apply in your own life? (Check all that apply.)**

Most interested in	Most challenging to apply to myself		Most interested in	Most challenging to apply to myself
_____	_____ Getting the right start		_____	_____ Engaging, listening, and note-taking in class
_____	_____ Building dreams, setting goals		_____	_____ Developing your memory
_____	_____ Learning to learn		_____	_____ Reading and studying
_____	_____ Managing time and energy		_____	_____ Taking tests
_____	_____ Thinking critically and creatively		_____	_____ Building relationships, valuing diversity
_____	_____ Developing technology, research, and information literacy skills		_____	_____ Choosing a major and career
			_____	_____ Creating your future

4. **Which one of your classes was most challenging this term and why?**

   Which class? (course title *or* department and course number) _____

   Why?_____

   Did you succeed in this class? _____ yes _____ no

   Somewhat (please explain): _____

5. **How many total hours per week did you spend outside of class studying for your college courses this term?**

____ 0-5	____ 16-20	____ 31-35
____ 6-10	____ 21-25	____ 36-40
____ 11-15	____ 26-30	____ 40+

6. **Which of the following on-campus resources did you use once or more this term? (Please check all that apply.)**

____ library

____ campus learning centers (whatever is available on your campus, such as a Writing Center, Math Learning Center, etc.)

____ computer labs

____ the Student Success Center or New Student Center, if one is available

____ the Counseling Center, if one is available

____ instructors' office hours for individual meetings/conferences/help

____ student clubs or organizations

____ none

7. **For the following sets of opposite descriptive phrases, please put a checkmark on the line between the two that best represents your response.**

   My first term of college:

challenged me academically	____ ____ ____ ____ ____	was easy
was very different from high school	____ ____ ____ ____ ____	was a lot like high school
was exciting	____ ____ ____ ____ ____	was dull
was interesting	____ ____ ____ ____ ____	was uninteresting
motivated me to continue	____ ____ ____ ____ ____	discouraged me
was fun	____ ____ ____ ____ ____	was boring
helped me feel a part of this campus	____ ____ ____ ____ ____	made me feel alienated

8. **Please mark your *top three areas of concern* relating to your first term of college by placing 1, 2, and 3 next to the items you choose.**

____ I did not fit in.

____ I did have difficulty making friends.

____ I was not academically successful.

____ My performance disappointed my family.

____ My personal life interfered with my studies.

____ My studies interfered with my personal life.

____ I had financial difficulties.

____ My job(s) interfered with my studies.

____ My studies interfered with my job.

____ My social life interfered with my studies.

____ My studies interfered with my social life.

____ My instructors did not care about me as an individual.

____ I may not finish my degree.

____ I did not manage my time well.

____ I was bored in my classes.

____ I felt intimidated by my instructors.

____ I was overwhelmed by all I had to do.

____ other (please explain) _____

9. **Have you changed your thinking about selecting a major since entering college? Broadly speaking, now which area do you expect to major in?**

____ General Studies

____ An associate's degree in _____ .

____ A certificate in _____ _____ .

____ Other (please explain) _____

10. **How certain are you now of a chosen major (1 = totally sure, 5 = totally unsure)** ____

11. **How certain are you now that you will complete your degree or certificate? (1 = totally sure, 5 = totally unsure)** ____

12. **How certain are you now that you will complete your degree or certificate at this school? (1 = totally sure, 5 = totally unsure)** ____

13. **How certain are you now of your intended career choice? (1 = totally sure, 5 = totally unsure)** ____

14. **How certain are you now about whether you'll transfer to a four-year school? (1 = totally sure, 5 = totally unsure)** ____

15. **What will your grade point average to be at the end of your first term of college?**

    _____ A+   _____ B+   _____ C+   _____ D or lower

    _____ A   _____ B   _____ C

    _____ A−   _____ B−   _____ C−

16. **Which of the following sources of information about college turned out to be most accurate? (Mark your top three information sources with 1, 2, and 3.)**

    _____ TV and movies

    _____ friends/siblings who have already gone to college

    _____ discussions with teachers/counselors in high school

    _____ information I received from colleges in the mail

    _____ talks with my family

    _____ talks with my friends who are also now starting college

    _____ the Internet

    _____ other (please explain) _____

17. **How confident are you in yourself in each of the following areas now? (1 = very confident, 5 = not at all confident)**

    _____ overall academic ability   _____ technology skills

    _____ mathematical skills   _____ physical well being

    _____ leadership ability   _____ writing skills

    _____ reading skills   _____ social skills

    _____ public speaking skills   _____ emotional well being

    _____ study skills   _____ teamwork skills

18. **Why did you decide to go to college? Now that you've experienced your first term of college, how would you respond? (Check all that apply)**

    _____ Because I want to build a better life for myself.

    _____ Because I want to build a better life for my family.

    _____ Because I want to be very well off financially in the future.

    _____ Because I need a college education to achieve my dreams.

    _____ Because my friends were going to college.

    _____ Because my family encouraged me to go.

    _____ Because it was expected of me.

    _____ Because I was recruited for athletics.

    _____ Because I want to continue learning.

    _____ Because the career I am pursuing requires a degree.

    _____ Because I was unsure of what I might do instead.

    _____ other (please explain) _____

19. **Looking ahead, how satisfied do you expect to be with your decision to attend this school?**

    _____ very satisfied   _____ somewhat dissatisfied

    _____ satisfied   _____ very dissatisfied

    _____ not sure

20. **Did you achieve the outcomes you were hoping to achieve at the beginning of this term? Why or why not?** _____

_____

21. **What was the biggest difference between what you thought college would be like and what it was actually like for you?** _____

_____

APPENDIX

Additional Time Monitors

7:00 A.M. _____	3:00 _____	11:00 _____
7:30 _____	3:30 _____	11:30 _____
8:00 _____	4:00 _____	12:00 A.M. _____
8:30 _____	4:30 _____	12:30 _____
9:00 _____	5:00 _____	1:00 _____
9:30 _____	5:30 _____	1:30 _____
10:00 _____	6:00 _____	2:00 _____
10:30 _____	6:30 _____	2:30 _____
11:00 _____	7:00 _____	3:00 _____
11:30 _____	7:30 _____	3:30 _____
12:00 P.M. _____	8:00 _____	4:00 _____
12:30 _____	8:30 _____	4:30 _____
1:00 _____	9:00 _____	5:00 _____
1:30 _____	9:30 _____	5:30 _____
2:00 _____	10:00 _____	6:00 _____
2:30 _____	10:30 _____	6:30 _____

7:00 A.M. _____	3:00 _____	11:00 _____
7:30 _____	3:30 _____	11:30 _____
8:00 _____	4:00 _____	12:00 A.M. _____
8:30 _____	4:30 _____	12:30 _____
9:00 _____	5:00 _____	1:00 _____
9:30 _____	5:30 _____	1:30 _____
10:00 _____	6:00 _____	2:00 _____
10:30 _____	6:30 _____	2:30 _____
11:00 _____	7:00 _____	3:00 _____
11:30 _____	7:30 _____	3:30 _____
12:00 P.M. _____	8:00 _____	4:00 _____
12:30 _____	8:30 _____	4:30 _____
1:00 _____	9:00 _____	5:00 _____
1:30 _____	9:30 _____	5:30 _____
2:00 _____	10:00 _____	6:00 _____
2:30 _____	10:30 _____	6:30 _____

7:00 A.M.	_____	3:00	_____	11:00	_____
7:30	_____	3:30	_____	11:30	_____
8:00	_____	4:00	_____	12:00 A.M.	_____
8:30	_____	4:30	_____	12:30	_____
9:00	_____	5:00	_____	1:00	_____
9:30	_____	5:30	_____	1:30	_____
10:00	_____	6:00	_____	2:00	_____
10:30	_____	6:30	_____	2:30	_____
11:00	_____	7:00	_____	3:00	_____
11:30	_____	7:30	_____	3:30	_____
12:00 P.M.	_____	8:00	_____	4:00	_____
12:30	_____	8:30	_____	4:30	_____
1:00	_____	9:00	_____	5:00	_____
1:30	_____	9:30	_____	5:30	_____
2:00	_____	10:00	_____	6:00	_____
2:30	_____	10:30	_____	6:30	_____

7:00 A.M.	_____	3:00	_____	11:00	_____
7:30	_____	3:30	_____	11:30	_____
8:00	_____	4:00	_____	12:00 A.M.	_____
8:30	_____	4:30	_____	12:30	_____
9:00	_____	5:00	_____	1:00	_____
9:30	_____	5:30	_____	1:30	_____
10:00	_____	6:00	_____	2:00	_____
10:30	_____	6:30	_____	2:30	_____
11:00	_____	7:00	_____	3:00	_____
11:30	_____	7:30	_____	3:30	_____
12:00 P.M.	_____	8:00	_____	4:00	_____
12:30	_____	8:30	_____	4:30	_____
1:00	_____	9:00	_____	5:00	_____
1:30	_____	9:30	_____	5:30	_____
2:00	_____	10:00	_____	6:00	_____
2:30	_____	10:30	_____	6:30	_____

NOTES

CHAPTER 1

1. Paulson, K., & Boeke, M. (2006). *Adult learners in the United States: A national profile*. Washington, DC: American Council on Education.

2. Carey, K. (2007). America's best community colleges: Why they're better than some of the "best" four-year universities. *Washington Monthly*. Available at http://www.washingtonmonthly.com/features/2007/0709 .careyessay.html.

3. Knowles' Andragogy. Available at http://www.learningandteaching.info/ learning/knowlesa.htm.

4. Barrier busters: *Community college students...by the numbers. Lumina Foundation Focus*. From The American Association of Community Colleges, based on material in the National Profile of Community Colleges: Trends & Statistics, Phillippe & Patton, 2000. Available at http://www .luminafoundation.org/publications/focus archive/winter_2006/cc _students.html; (2007, July 20). Documentary shows struggles of non-traditional community college students. Available at http://newsroom .ucr.edu/news_item.html?action=page&id=1634; Matthews, D. (2009, February). A stronger nation through higher education. *A Special Report from Lumina Foundation for Education*. Available at http:// www.luminafoundation.org/publications/A_stronger_nation_through _higher_education.pdf; CCSSE, 2006 findings. *Act on fact: Using data to improve student success*. Available at http://www.ccsse.org/publications/ CCSSENationalReport2006.pdf.

5. Balderrama, A. (2009, May 1). The ten best jobs requiring two-year degrees. Available at http://www.careerbuilder.com/Article/CB-1366 -Job-Search-10-Best-Jobs-Requiring-Two-Year-Degrees/?ArticleID =1366&cbRecursionCnt=1&cbsid=960a4ed9fa914960bc395ac15340 70d9-322921368-w0-6&ns_siteid=ns_us_g_percentage_of_jobs_re_.

6. Crosby, O. (2002–2003, Winter). Associate degree: Two years to a career or jump start to a bachelor's degree. *Occupational Outlook Quarterly*, 2–13. Available at http://www.bls.gov/opub/ooq/2002/winter/art01.pdf.

7. What's the Difference between an Associate Degree and a Certificate? *Brookhaven College*. Available at http://www.brookhavencollege.edu/ studentsvcs/counseling/faq.aspx#q18.

8. Certificate program vs. associate's degree—What's the difference? *Top Colleges Blog*. Available at http://www.top-colleges.com/blog/ 2007/04/11/certificate-program-vs-associates-degree/.

9. (2007, January/February) Different paths for different majors. Datanotes: *Achieving the Dream*. Available at http://www.achievingthedream .org/_pdfs/datanotes/datanotes-janfeb-2007.pdf.

10. Marchand, A. (2010, 29 March). 6 strategies can help entering community-college students succeed. *The Chronicle of Higher Education*. Available at http://chronicle.com/article/6-Strategies-Can-Help -Entering/64871.

11. Hart Research Associates. (2010, January 20). *Raising the bar: Employers' views on college learning in the wake of the economic downturn*. Available at http://www.aacu.org/leap/documents/2009_Employer Survey.pdf.

12. Shoenberg, R. (2005). *Why do I have to take this course? A student guide to making smart educational choices*. Association of American Colleges and Universities. Washington, DC: AAC&U.

13. Linda Foltz and the Student Success Center advisors at the University of Colorado at Colorado Springs; Jennifer Sengenberger and Wayne Artis, Pikes Peak Community College; Kocel, K. C., (2008, March 12). Advising first-generation college students for continued success. Kocel, K. (2008, March 12). *The Mentor: An Academic Advising Journal*. Available at http://www.psu.edu/dus/mentor/080312kk .htm; Knight, T. M. (2000, May 17). Planting the seeds of success: Advising college students with disabilities. *The Mentor: An Academic Advising Journal*. Available at http://psu.edu/dus/mentor/000517tk .htm.

14. The challenges of remedial education: Views of 3 presidents (2006, October 27). *The Chronicle of Higher Education*. Available at http:// chronicle.com/article/The-Challenges-of-Remedial/32361/.

15. (2006, September/October). Developmental education and student success. *Datanotes: Achieving the Dream*. Available at http://www.achieving thedream.org/_pdfs/DataNotes/DataNotes-SeptOct-2006.pdf.

16. Crews, D. M., & Aragon. S. R. (2004). Influence of a community college developmental education writing course on academic performance. *Community College Review, 32*(2), 1–18.

17. Dweck, C. S. (2006). *Mindset: The new psychology of success*. New York: Random House. pp. 104–105.

18. Employment Projections—2008–2018 Summary. Available at http://www .bls.gov/news.release/ecopro.nr0.htm.

19. Rampell, C. (2009, July 13). Preparing today's workers or tomorrow's jobs. *The New York Times*. Available at http://economix.blogs.nytimes .com/2009/07/13/preparing-todays-workers-for-tomorrows-jobs/.

20. (2006, July). Fact Sheet. Community Colleges: Challenges and Benefits. *Achieving the Dream*. Available at http://www.lee.edu/atd/pdf/FS -ChallengeBenefit.pdf.

21. Ibid.

22. Omara-Otunnu, E. (2006, July 24). Conference examines transition from high school to college. University of Connecticut *Advance*. Available at http://advance.uconn.edu/2006/060724/06072407.htm.

23. Hoachlander, G., Sikora, A. C., Horn, L., & Carroll, C. D. (2003, June). Community college students: Goals, academic preparation and outcomes. *National Center for Education Statistics*. Available at http:// nces.ed.gov/pubs2003/2003164.pdf.

24. Pascarella, E. T., Pierson, C. T., Wolniak, G. C., and Terenzini, P. T. (2004). First-generation college students: Additional evidence on college experiences and outcomes. *Journal of Higher Education, 75*(3), 249–284.

25. Tyler, M. D., Johns, K Y. (2009). From First-Generation College Student to First Lady. *Diverse Issues in Higher Education Psychology, 25*(25). Available at http://diverseeducation.com/article/12184/.

26. Community college: Myth vs. reality. The College Board. Available at http://www.collegeboard.com/student/csearch/where-to-start/150494 .html; (2000, August 17). These famous people of color got their start at a community college. *Black Issues in Higher Education*. Available at http://findarticles.com/p/articles/mi_m0DXK/is_ai_65229406; 2006); Notable alumni. American Association of Community Colleges. Available at http://www.aacc.nche.edu/Content/NavigationMenu/About CommunityColleges/OutstandingAlumni/Notable_Alumni.htm.

27. Bal, F. T., Zhang, S., & Tachlyama, G. T. (2008). Effects of a self-regulated learning course on the academic performance and graduation rate of college students in an academic support program. *Journal of College Reading and Learning, 39*(1), 54–73; O'Gara, L., Karp, M. M., & Hughes, K. L. (2009). Student success courses in the community college: An exploratory study. *Community College Review, 36*(3), 195–218.

CHAPTER 2

1. Multi-tasking adversely affects brain's learning, UCLA psychologists report. (2006, July 26). *ScienceDaily*. Available: http://www.science daily.com/releases/2006/07/060726083302.htm; Hamilton, J. (2008, October 9). Multitasking teens may be muddling their brains. *NPR Morning Edition*. Available at http://www.npr.org/templates/story/story .php?storyId=95524385; Gorlick, A. (2009, August 24). Media multitaskers pay mental price, Stanford study shows. *Stanford University News*.

Available at http://news.stanford.edu/news/2009/august24/multitask-research-study-082409.html; Tugend, A. (2008, October 24). Multitasking can make you . . . lose . . . um . . . focus. *The New York Times*. Available at http://www.nytimes.com/2008/10/25/business/yourmoney/25shortcuts.html; Pennebaker, R. (2009, August 30). The mediocre multitasker. *The New York Times*. Available at http://www.nytimes.com/2009/08/30/weekinreview/30pennebaker.html; Glenn, D. (2010, February 28). Divided attention. *The Chronicle of Higher Education*. Available at http://chronicle.com/article/Scholars-Turn-Their-Attention/63746/.

2. Spielberg finally to graduate. (2002, May 15). *BBC News*. Available at http://news.bbc.co.uk/2/hi/entertainment/1988770.stm.

3. Staley, C. (2003). *50 ways to leave your lectern*, "Spending Time," p. 54.

4. Davis, J. R. (1993), *Better teaching, more learning*. Phoenix, AZ: Oryx Press.

5. French, B. F., & Oakes, W. (2003). Measuring academic intrinsic motivation in the first year of college: Reliability and validity evidence for a new instrument. *Journal of the First-Year Experience, 15*(1), 83–102; French, B. F. Executive summary of instruments utilized with system-wide first-year seminars. Policy Center on the First Year of College; French, B. F., Immerkus, J. C., & Oakes, W. C. (2005). An examination of indicators of engineering students' success and persistence. *Journal of Engineering Education, 94*(4), 419–425.

6. For more information, see U.S. Department of Labor, Bureau of Labor Statistics, *Occupational Outlook Handbook, 2010–2011 Edition*. Also available at http://www.bls.gov/oco/ocos291.htm#related; http://www.bls.gov/oco/ocos023.htm.

7. Based on Harrell, K. (2003). *Attitude is everything: 10 life-changing steps to turning attitude into action*. New York: HarperBusiness.

8. Dweck, C. S. (2000). *Self-theories: Their role in motivation, personality, and development*. New York: Psychology Press, p. 1.

9. Berglas, S. & Jones, E. E. (1978). Drug choice as a self-handicapping strategy in response to noncontingent success. *Journal of Personality and Social Psychology, 36*, 405–417; Jones, E. E. & Berglas, S. (1978). Control of attributions about the self through self-handicapping strategies: The appeal of alcohol and the role of underachievement. *Personality and Social Psychology Bulletin, 4*, 200–206; Dweck, C. S. (2006). *Mindset: The new psychology of success*. New York: Random House.

10. Dweck, C. S. (2000). *Self-theories: Their role in motivation, personality, and development*. New York: Psychology Press; Dweck, *Mindset*.

11. Robins, R. W., & Pals, J. (2002). Implicit self-theories of ability in the academic domain: A test of Dweck's model. *Self and Identity, 1*, 313–336.

12. Mangels, J. A., Butterfield, B., Lamb, J., Good, C. D., & Dweck, C. S. (2006). Why do beliefs about intelligence influence learning success? A social cognitive neuroscience model. *Social Cognitive and Affective Neuroscience, 1*(2), 75–86.

13. Bauer, A. R., Grant, H., & Dweck, C. S. (2006). *Personal goals predict the level and impact of dysphoria*. Unpublished manuscript.

CHAPTER 3

1. Leamnson, R. (1999). *Thinking about teaching and learning: Developing habits of learning with first year college and university students*. Sterling, VA: Stylus.

2. Caine, R. N., & Caine, G. (1994). *Making connections: Teaching and the human brain*. Menlo Park, CA: Addison Wesley.

3. Shuster, W. G. (2001). *Less stress? Yes! Jewelers' Circular Keystone, 172*(2), 98.

4. Jozefowicz, C. (2004, June). Sweating makes you smart. *Psychology Today*, 56–58.

5. Csikszentmihalyi, M. (2006). *Flow: The psychology of optimal experience*. New York: Academic Internet Publishers; Csikszentmihalyi, M. (1997). *Creativity: Flow and the psychology of discovery and invention*. New York: Harper Perennial; Gross, R. (1999). *Peak learning*. New York: Tarcher.

6. Caine & Caine, *Making connections*; Jensen, E. (2000). *Different brains, different learners*. San Diego: The Brain Store.

7. Brandt, R. (1998). *Powerful learning*. Alexandria, VA: Association for Supervision and Curriculum Development, p. 29.

8. Campbell, B. (1992). Multiple intelligences in action. *Childhood Education, 68*(4), 197–201; Gardner, H., & Hatch, T. (1989). Multiple intelligences go to school: Educational implications of the theory of multiple intelligences. *Educational Researcher, 18*(8), 4–9; Gardner, H. (1983). *Frames of Mind: The Theory of Multiple Intelligences*. New York: Basic Books.

9. Armstrong, T. (2000). *MI and cognitive skills*. Available at http://www.ascd.org/publications/books/100041/chapters/MI_and_Cognitive_Skills.aspx.

10. Law of Supply and Demand. *Wikipedia*. Available at http://en.wikipedia.org/wiki/Supply_and_demand.

11. Also available at http://www.bls.gov/oco/ocos160.htm.

12. Davis, B. (2009). *Tools for teaching*, second edition. San Francisco: Jossey-Bass, p. 273.

13. Fleming, N. D. (1995). I'm different; not dumb: Modes of presentation (VARK) in the tertiary classroom. In A. Zeimer (Ed.), *Research and Development in Higher Education, Proceedings of the 1995 Annual Conference of the Higher Education and Research Development Society of Austral-asia (HERDSA), HERDSA, 18*, 308–313; Fleming, N. D., & Mills, C. (1992). Not another inventory, rather a catalyst for reflection. *To Improve the Academy, 11*, 137–149. Available at http://www.ntlf.com/html/lib/suppmat/74fleming.htm.

14. Fleming, I'm different; not dumb.

15. Fleming, N. D. (2005). *Teaching and learning styles: VARK strategies*. Christchurch, NZ: Microfilm Limited.

16. Based on DiTiberio, J. K., & Hammer, A. L. (1993). *Introduction to type in college*. Palo Alto, CA: Consulting Psychologists Press.

CHAPTER 4

1. Austin, C. (2010). Go with the flow: Fresh ideas for managing time. *Prezi.com*. Available at http://prezi.com/7gypurup9uke/go-with-the-flow/.

2. Eade, D. M. (1998). Energy and success: Time management. *Clinician News*, July/August. Available at http://www.adv-leadership-grp.com/articles/energy.htm.

3. Loehr, J., & Schwartz, T. (2003). *The power of full engagement: Managing energy, not time, is the key to high performance and personal renewal*. New York: Free Press.

4. Bittel, L. R. (1991). *Right on time! The complete guide for time-pressured managers*. New York: McGraw-Hill, p. 16.

5. DeMaio, S. (2009, March 25). The art of the self-imposed deadline. *Harvard Business Review*. Available at http://blogs.hbr.org/demaio/2009/03/the-art-of-the-selfimposed-dea.html.

6. Bittel, *Right on time!* p. 16.

7. Astin, A. W., Astin, H. S., Lindholm, J. A., & Bryant, A. N. (2005). *The spiritual life of college students: A national study of college students' search for meaning and purpose*. Los Angeles: Higher Education Research Institute, UCLA; http://spirituality.ucla.edu/; Crosby, J. (2010, April 4). College students struggle with religion and spirituality. *Cape Cod Times*. Available at http://www.capecodonline.com/apps/pbcs.dll/article?AID=/20100404/LIFE/4040307/-1/NEWSMAP.

8. Loehr, *The power of full engagement*.

9. Nathan, R. (2005). *My freshman year: What a professor learned by becoming a student*. Ithaca, NY: Cornell University Press.

10. Also available at http://www.bls.gov/oco/ocos001.htm.

11. Based on Covey, S. R., Merrill, A. R., & Merrill, R. R. (1996). *First things first: To live, to love, to learn, to leave a legacy.* New York: Free Press, 37.

12. Fortino, M. (2001). *E-mergency.* Groveland, CA: Omni Publishing. Also see The American Time Use Survey results at http://www.bls.gov/news .release/atus.nr0.htm.

13. Hobbs, C. R. (1987). *Time power.* New York: Harper & Row, pp. 9–10.

14. Based on Berglas, S. (2004, June). Chronic time abuse. *Harvard Business Review*, 90–97.

15. Solomon, L. J., & Rothblum, E. D. (1984). Academic procrastination: Frequency and cognitive-behavioral correlates. *Journal of Counseling Psychology, 31,* 503–509.

16. Hoover, E. (2005, December 9). Tomorrow I love ya! *The Chronicle of Higher Education, 52*(16), A30–32.

17. Ferrari, J. R., McCown, W. G., & Johnson, J. (2002). *Procrastination and task avoidance: Theory, research, and treatment.* New York: Springer Publishing.

18. Hoover, Tomorrow I love ya!.

19. Sandholtz, K., Derr, B., Buckner, K., & Carlson, D. (2002). *Beyond juggling: Rebalancing your busy life.* San Francisco: Berrett-Koehler Publishers.

20. Adapted from Sandholtz et al., *Beyond juggling.*

21. Farrell, E. F. (2005, February 4). More students plan to work to help pay for college. *The Chronicle of Higher Education, 51*(22), A1. Available online at http://chronicle.com/weekly/ v51/i22/22a00101.htm.

22. McFaddon, L. (2009, August 20). 8 major benefits of new credit card law. *Bankrate.com.* Available at http://www.bankrate.com/finance/ credit-cards/8-major-benefits-of-new-credit-card-law-1.aspx.

23. Norvilitis, J. M., & Santa Maria, P. (2002). Credit card debt on college campuses: Causes, consequences, and solutions. *College Student Journal, 36*(3), 356–364.

24. Choosing a credit card. The Federal Reserve Board. Available at http:// www.federalreserve.gov/pubs/shop/default.htm.

25. Muller, K. New credit card laws (2009) and students. *ezine@rticles.com.* Available at http://ezinearticles.com/?New-Credit-Card-Laws-(2009)-And -Students&id=2410035; Miranda. (2009, May 21). Credit CARD Act of 2009: How it affects you. *Personaldividends.*com. Available at http://personal dividends.com/money/miranda/credit-card-act-of-2009-how-it-affects-you.

26. Kantrowitz, M. (2007). *FAQs about financial aid.* FinAid: The Smart Student Guide to Financial Aid. Available at http://www .finaid.org/questions/faq.html.

CHAPTER 5

1. Halx, M. D., & Reybold, E. (2005). A pedagogy of force: Faculty perspective of critical thinking capacity in undergraduate students. *The Journal of General Education, 54*(4), 293–315.

2. Walkner, P., & Finney, N. (1999). Skill development and critical thinking in higher education. *Teaching in Higher Education, 4*(4), 531–548.

3. Diestler, S. (2001). *Becoming a critical thinker: A user friendly manual.* Upper Saddle River, NJ: Prentice Hall.

4. Perry, J. (1995–2008). *Procrastination and perfectionism. Philosophy Talk @Stanford.* Available at http://www.structuredprocrastination .com/light/perfectionism.php.

5. Falcione, P. A. (1998). *Critical thinking: What it is and why it counts.* Millbrae, CA: California Academic Press.

6. Twale, D., & Sanders, C. S. (1999). Impact of non-classroom experiences on critical thinking ability. *NASPA Journal, 36*(2), 133–146.

7. Thomas, C., & Smoot, G. (1994, February/March). Critical thinking: A vital work skill. *Trust for Educational Leadership, 23,* 34–38.

8. Kaplan-Leiserson, E. (2004). Workforce of tomorrow: How can we prepare *all* youth for future work success? *Training & Development, 58*(4), 12–14. 13. Based in part on Brookfield, S. D. (1987). *Developing critical thinkers: Challenging adults to explore alternative ways of thinking and acting.* San Francisco: Jossey-Bass.

9. Van den Brink-Budgen, R. (2000). *Critical thinking for students.* (3rd ed.). Oxford: How to Books; Ruggiero, V. R. (2001). *Becoming a critical thinker.* (4th ed.). Boston: Houghton Mifflin.

10. Also available at http://www.bls.gov/oco/ocos114.htm.

11. Blakey, E., & Spence, S. (1990). Developing metacognition. *ERIC Digest.* Available at http://www.eric.ed.gov/PDFS/ED327218.pdf.

12. Florida, R. (2002). *The rise of the creative class: And how it's transforming work, leisure, community and everyday life.* New York: Basic Books, xii.

13. Sternberg. R. J. (2004). Teaching college students that creativity is a decision. *Guidance & Counseling, 19*(4), 196–200.

14. Rowe, A. J. (2004). *Creative intelligences: discovering the innovative potential in ourselves and others.* Upper Saddle, NJ: Pearson Education, pp. 3–6, 34.

15. Michalko, M. (2001). *Cracking creativity: The secrets of creative genius.* Berkeley, CA: Ten Speed Press.

16. Adapted from Adler, R., & Proctor, R. F. II (2011). *Looking out/Looking in.* (13th ed.) New York: Holt, Rinehart, and Winston, pp. 110–116.

17. Douglas, J. H. (1977). The genius of everyman (2): Learning creativity. *Science News, 111*(8), 284–288.

18. Harris, R. (1998). Introduction to creative thinking. *VirtualSalt.* Available at http://www.virtualsalt.com/crebook1.htm.

19. Eby, D. Creativity and flow psychology. Available at http://talentdevelop .com/articles/Page8.html.

CHAPTER 6

1. Guess, A. (2007, September 17). Students' "Evolving" use of technology. *Inside Higher Ed.* Available at http://www.insidehighered.com/ layout/set/print/news/2007/09/17/it; (2007, September). Key findings: The ECAR study of undergraduate students and information technology, 2007. *Educause.* Available at http://net.educause.edu/ir/library/pdf/ ERS0706/ekf0706.pdf; Smith, S. D., Salalway, G., & Caruso, J. B. (2009, October). Key findings: The ECAR study of undergraduate students and information technology, 2009. *Educause.* Available at http://net .educause.edu/ir/library/pdf/EKF/EKF0906.pdf.

2. Roach, R. (2004). Survey unveils high-tech ownership profile of American college students. *Black Issues in Higher Education, 21*(16), 37.

3. Jones, S., & Madden, M. (2002, September 15). The Internet goes to college: How students are living in the future with today's technology. *Pew Internet.* Available at http://www.pewinternet.org/PPF/r/71/report _display.asp.

4. *Internet World Stats.* Available at http://www.internetworldstats.com/ stats.htm.

5. Billout, G. (2008, July/August). Is Google making us stupid? *The Atlantic.com.* Available at http://www.theatlantic.com/magazine/print/ 2008/07/is-google-making-us-stupid/6868/.

6. (2010, June). Social insecurity. *Consumer Reports: Best and worst computers,* 24–27.

7. Holson, L. M. (2010, May 8). Tell-all generation learns to keep things offline. *The New York Times.* Available at http://www.nytimes .com/2010/05/09/fashion/09privacy.html.

8. (2010, June). Social insecurity. *Consumer Reports: Best and worst computers*, pp. 24–27.

9. Cohen, C. (2009, April 23). 5 clues that you are addicted to Facebook. CNN News. Available at http://www.cnn.com/2009/HEALTH/04/23/ep.facebook.addict/index.html.

10. Facebook addiction is needless, yet compelling. *The Volante Online*. Available at http://media.www.volanteonline.com/media/storage/paper468/news/2005/10/05/Opinion/Facebook.Addiction.Is.Needless.Yet.Compelling-1008873.shtml.

11. Greenfield, D. N. (1999). *Virtual addiction*. Oakland, CA: New Harbinger Publications; Yair, E., & Hamburger, A. (2005). *The social net*. Oxford: Oxford University Press; Young, K. S. (1998). *Caught in the net*. New York: John Wiley.

12. Guess, A. (2007, September 17). Students' "Evolving" use of technology. *Inside Higher Ed*. Available at http://www.insidehighered.com/layout/set/print/news/2007/09/17/it; Caruso, J. B., & Salaway, G. (2007, September). Key findings: The ECAR study of undergraduate students and information technology, 2007. *Educause*. Available at http://net.educause.edu/ir/library/pdf/ERS0706/ekf0706.pdf.

13. Caruso, J. B., & Salaway, G. (2007, September). Key findings: The ECAR study of undergraduate students and information technology, 2007. *Educause*. Available at http://net.educause.edu/ir/library/pdf/ERS0706/ekf0706.pdf.

14. Kelly, W. E., Kelly, K. E. & Clanton, R. C. (2001). The relationship between sleep length and grade-point average among college students. *College Student Journal, 35*(1), 84–86; Stein, R. (2005, October 9). Scientists finding out what losing sleep does to a body. *The Washington Post*. Available at http://www.washingtonpost.com/wp-dyn/content/article/2005/10/08/AR2005100801405.html; Frisinger, C. (2009, October 24). Not getting enough sleep is more serious than you think. *The News Argus*. Available at http://www.thenewsargus.com/2.5246/not-getting-enough-sleep-is-more-serious-than-you-might-think-1.799912.

15. http://compnetworking.about.com/od/dns_domainnamesystem/a/domain-name-tld.htm; http://lists.econsultant.com/top-10-domain-name-extensions.html;http://webfoot.com/advice/email.domain.php.

16. Sullivan, D. (2007, March 28). Major search engines and directories. *SeachEngineWatch.com*. Available at http://searchenginewatch.com/showPage.html?page=2156221; (2008). Recommended search engines. *UC Berkeley Library*. Regents of the University of California. Available at http://www.lib.berkeley.edu/TeachingLib/Guides/Internet/SearchEngines.html.

17. Caruso, J. B., & Salaway, G. (2007, September). Key findings: The ECAR study of undergraduate students and information technology, 2007. *Educause*. Available at http://net.educause.edu/ir/library/pdf/ERS0706/ekf0706.pdf.

18. Trunk, P. (2008, July/August). Show me the blog. *Wild Blue Yonder*, p. 44.

19. Jaschik, S. (2008, April 7). Distance ed continues rapid growth at community colleges. *Inside Higher Ed*. Available at http://www.insidehighered.com/news/2008/04/07/distance.

20. For more information, see U.S. Department of Labor, Bureau of Labor Statistics, *Occupational Outlook Handbook*, 2010–2011 Edition.

21. Bollet, R. M., & Fallon, S. (2002). Personalizing e-learning. *Educational Media International, 39*(1), 39–45.

22. (1998). What is research? Available at http://danroh89.wordpress.com/2010/01/19/research-methodology-2---reading-1/ (from *Practical Research* by P. D. Leedy and J. D. Ormrod).

23. Fitzgerald, M. A. (2004). Making the leap from high school to college. *Knowledge Quest, 32*(4), 19–24; Ehrmann, S. (2004). Beyond computer literacy: Implications of technology for the content of a college education. *Liberal Education*. Available at http://www.aacu.org/liberal education/le-fa04/le-fa04feature1.cfm; Thacker, P. (2006, November 15). Are college students techno idiots? *Inside Higher Ed*. Available at http://www.insidehighered.com/news/2006/11/15/infolit.

24. Ableson, H. Ledeen, K., & Lewis, H. (2008). *Blown to bits: your life, liberty, and happiness after the digital explosion*. Boston, MA: Pearson Education, Inc.

25. Thacker, P. (2006, November 15). Are college students techno idiots? *Inside Higher Ed*. Available at http://www.insidehighered.com/news/2006/11/15/infolit.

26. Ibid.

27. De Vos, I. (1988, October). Getting started: How expert writers do it. *Training & Development Journal*, 18–19.

28. Bean, J. C. (1996). *Engaging ideas: The professor's guide to integrating writing, critical thinking and active learning in the classroom*. San Francisco: Jossey-Bass.

29. Based on Wood, G. (2004, April 9). Academic original sin: Plagiarism, the Internet, and librarians. *The Journal of Academic Librarianship, 30*(3), 237–242.

CHAPTER 7

1. Burchfield, C. M., & Sappington, J. (2000). Compliance with required reading assignments. *Teaching of Psychology, 27*(1), 58–60; Hobson, E. H. (2004). *Getting students to read: Fourteen tips*. IDEA Paper No. 40, Manhattan, KS: Kansas State University, Center for Faculty Evaluation and Development; Maleki, R. B., & Heerman, C. E. (1992). *Improving student reading*. IDEA Paper No. 26, Manhattan, KS: Kansas State University, *Center for Faculty Evaluation and Development*. Most Idea Center papers available at http://www.idea.ksu.edu/.

2. Marburger, D. R. (2001). Absenteeism and undergraduate exam performance. *Journal of Economic Education, (32)*, 99–109; Romer, D. 1993. Do students go to class? Should they? *Journal of Economic Perspectives 7* (Summer), 167–74.

3. Perkins, K. K., & Wieman, C. E. (2005). The surprising impact of seat location on student performance. *The Physics Teacher, 43*(1), 30–33. Available at http://scitation.aip.org/journals/doc/PHTEAH-ft/vol_43/iss_1/30_1.html.

4. Armbruster, B. B. (2000). Taking notes from lectures. In R. F. Flippo & D. C. Caverly (Eds.), *Handbook of college reading and study strategy research*. Mahwah, NJ: Erlbaum, pp. 175–199.

5. Hughes, C. A., & Suritsky, S. K. (1993). Notetaking skills and strategies for students with learning disabilities. *Preventing School Failure, 38*(1).

6. Staley, C. C., & Staley R. S. (1992). *Communicating in business and the professions*. Mahwah, NJ: Erlbaum, pp. 229–236.

7. Kiewra, K. A., Mayer, R. E., Christensen, M., Kim, S., & Risch, N. (1991). Effects of repetition on recall and note-taking: Strategies for learning from lectures. *Journal of Educational Psychology, 83*, 120–123.

8. Brock, R. (2005, October 28). Lectures on the go. *The Chronicle of Higher Education, 52*(10), A39–42; French, D. P. (2006). iPods: Informative or invasive? *Journal of College Science Teaching, 36*(1), 58–59; Hallett, V. (2005, October 17). Teaching with tech. *U.S. News & World Report, 139*(14), 54–58; *The Horizon Report*. (2006). Stanford, CA: The New Media Consortium.

9. Adapted from Mackie, V., & Bair, B. Tips for improving listening skills; *International Student and Scholar Services*. University of Illinois at Urbana–Champaign. Available at http://isss.illinois.edu/students/englang.shtml#listen.

10. Based on Staley, C. (2003). *50 ways to leave your lectern*. Belmont, CA: Wadsworth, pp. 80–81.

4. Segerstrom, S. C., & Miller, G. E. (2004). Psychological stress and the human immune system: A meta-analytic study of 30 years of inquiry. *Psychological Bulletin, 130*(4), 601–630. Available at http://www.apa .org/pubs/journals/releases/bul-1304601.pdf; (2004, July 4). Stress affects immunity in ways related to stress type and duration, as shown by nearly 300 studies. *APA Press Release.* Available at http://www.apa .org/news/press/releases/2004/07/stress-immune.aspx.

5. Brinthaupt, T. M., & Shin, C. M. (2001). The relationship of academic cramming to flow experience. *College Student Journal, 35*(3), 457–472.

6. Tigner, R. B. (1999). Putting memory research to good use: Hints from cognitive psychology. *Journal of College Teaching, 47*(4), 149–152.

7. Small, G. (2002). *The memory bible.* New York: Hyperion.

8. (2010). Test anxiety. *University of Oregon Counseling and Testing Center.* Available at http://counseling.uoregon.edu/dnn/SelfhelpResources/ StressandAnxiety/TestAnxiety/tabid/337/Default.aspx.

9. Tozoglu, D., Tozoglu, M. D., Gurses, A., & Dogar, C. (2004). The students' perceptions: Essay versus multiple-choice type exams. *Journal of Baltic Science Education, 2*(6), 52–59.

10. Schutz, P. A., & Davis, H. A. (2000). Emotions and self-regulation during test taking. *Educational Psychologist, 35*(4), 243–256.

11. Coren, *Sleep thieves.*

12. Perina, K. (2002). Sum of all fears. *Psychology Today.* Available at http://www.psychologytoday.com/articles/pto-20021108-000001.html.

13. Perry, A. B. (2004). Decreasing math anxiety in college students. *College Student Journal, 38*(2), 321–324.

14. Perry, Decreasing math anxiety in college students.

15. Jonides, J., Lacey, S. C., & Nee, D. E. (2005). Processes of working memory in mind and brain. *Current Directions in Psychological Science, 14*(1), 2–5.

16. Ashcraft, M. H., & Kirk, E. P. (2001). The relationships among working memory, math anxiety, and performance. *Journal of Experimental Psychology: General. 130*(2), 224–237.

17. Beilock, S. L., Kulp, C. A., Holt, L. E., & Carr, T. H. (2004). More on the fragility of performance: Choking under pressure in mathematical problem solving. *Journal of Experimental Psychology: General, 133*(4), 584–600.

18. Mundell, E. J. (2005, March 9). Test pressure toughest on smartest. *Healingwell.com.* Available at http://news.healingwell.com/index .php?p=news1&id=524405.

19. Arem, C. (2003). *Conquering math anxiety,* second edition. Belmont, CA: Brooks/Cole.

20. Glenn, D. (2010, February 7). How students can improve by studying themselves. *The Chronicle of Higher Education.* Available at http:// chronicle.com/article/Struggling-Students-Can-Imp/64004/.

21. Firmin, M., Hwang, C., Copella, M., & Clark, S. (2004). Learned helplessness: The effect of failure on test-taking. *Education, 124*(4), 688–693.

22. Heidenberg, A. J., & Layne, B. H. (2000). Answer changing: A conditional argument. *College Student Journal, 34*(3), 440–451.

23. Also available at http://www.bls.gov/oco/ocos153.htm.

24. See http://news.bbc.co.uk/2/hi/uk_news/scotland/glasgow_and_west/ 4755297.stm.

25. Preparing for tests and exams. (2007). York University. Available at http://www.yorku.ca/cdc/lsp/skillbuilding/exams.html#Multiple.

26. Taking exams. Brockport High School. Available at http://www .frontiernet.net/~jlkeefer/takgexm.html. Adapted from Penn State University; On taking exams. University of New Mexico. Available at http://www.unm.edu/~quadl/college_learning/taking_exams.html;

Lawrence, J. (2006). Tips for taking examinations. Lawrence Lab Homepage. Available at http://cobamide2.bio.pitt.edu/testtips.htm; The multiple choice exam. (2003). Counselling Services, University of Victoria. Available at http://www.coun.uvic.ca/learning/exams/ multiple-choice.html; General strategies for taking essay tests. *GWired.* Available at http://gwired.gwu.edu/counsel/asc/index.gw/Site_ID/46/ Page_ID/14565/; Test taking tips: Guidelines for answering multiple-choice questions. *Arizona State University.* Available at http:// neuer101.asu.edu/additionaltestingtips.htm; Landsberger, J. (2007). True/false tests. *Study Guides and Strategies.* Available at http://www .studygs.net/tsttak2.htm; Landsberger, J. (2007). Multiple choice tests. *Study Guides and Strategies.* Available at http://www.studygs.net/ tsttak3.htm; Landsberger, J. (2007). The essay exam. *Study Guides and Strategies.* Available at http://www.studygs.net/tsttak4.htm; Landsberger, J. (2007). Short answer tests. *Study Guides and Strategies.* Available at http://www.studygs.net/tsttak5.htm; Landsberger, J. (2007). Open book tests. *Study Guides and Strategies.* Available at http://www .studygs.net/tsttak7.htm; Rozakis, L. (2003). *Test-taking strategies and study skills for the utterly confused.* New York: McGraw-Hill; Meyers, J. N. (2000). *The secrets of taking any test.* New York: Learning Express; Robinson, A. (1993). *What smart students know.* New York: Crown Trade Paperbacks.

27. *Plagiarism.org.* Available at http://www.plagiarism.org/facts.html; A cheating crisis in America's schools. (2007, 29 April). ABC News. Available at http://abcnews.go.com/Primetime/story?id=132376&page=1.

28. Young, J. R. (2010, March 28). High tech cheating abounds, and professors bear some blame. *The Chronicle of Higher Education.* Available at http:// chronicle.com/article/High-Tech-Cheating-on-Homew/64857/; Gabriel, T. (2010, August 1). Plagiarism lines blur for students in digital age. *The New York Times.* Available at http://www.nytimes.com/2010/08/02/ education/02cheat.html?_r=1&src=me&ref=homepage.

29. Caught cheating. (2004, April 29). *Primetime Live,* ABC News Transcript. Interview of college students by Charles Gibson; Zernike, K. (2002, November 2). With student cheating on the rise, more colleges are turning to honor codes. *The New York Times,* p. Q10, column 1, National Desk; Warren, R. (2003, October 20). Cheating: An easy way to cheat yourself. The Voyager via U-Wire. *University Wire (www.uwire.com)*; Thomson, S. C. (2004, February 13). Heyboer, K. (2003, August 23). Nearly half of college students say Internet plagiarism isn't cheating. *The Star-Ledger Newark, New Jersey*; Kleiner, C., & Lord, M. (1999).

CHAPTER 11

1. Some situation topics suggested at Hay Group Transforming Learning EI Quiz. *Haygroup.com.* Available at http://www.haygroup.com/ leadershipandtalentondemand/Demos/EI_Quiz.aspx.

2. Gardner, H. (1993). *Multiple intelligences: The theory in practice.* New York: Basic Books; Checkley, K. (1997). The first seven . . . and the eighth: A conversation with Howard Gardner. Expanded Academic ASAP (online database). Original Publication: *Education,* 116.

3. Parker, J. D. A., Duffy, J. M., Wood, L. M., Bond, B. J., & Hogan, M. J. (2005). Academic achievement and emotional intelligence: Predicting the successful transition from high school to university. *Journal of the First Year Experience & Students in Transition 17*(1), 67–78; Schutte, N. S., & Malouff, J. (2002). Incorporating emotional skills content in a college transition course enhances student retention. *Journal of the First Year Experience & Students in Transition 14*(1), 7–21.

4. EQ-i:S™ Post Secondary, Multi-Health Systems, Inc. North Tonawanda, NY. Available at http://www.mhs.com. Used with permission.

5. Turning lemons into lemonade: Hardiness helps people turn stressful circumstances into opportunities. (2003, December 22). *Psychology Matters.* Available at *APA Online* at http://www.apa.org/research/ action/lemon.aspx; Marano, H. E. (2003). The art of resilience. *Psychology Today.* Available at http://www.psychologytoday.com/articles/ pto-20030527-000009.html; Fischman, J. (1987). Getting tough: Can people learn to have disease-resistant personalities? *Psychology Today, 21,* 26–28; Friborg, O., Barlaug, D., Martinussen, M., Rosenvinge, J. H.,

& Hjemdal, O. (2005). Resilience in relation to personality and intelligence. *International Journal of Methods in Psychiatric Research, 14*(1), 29–42; Schulman, P. (1995). Explanatory style and achievement in school and work. In G. M. Buchanan & M. E. P. Seligman (Eds.), *Explanatory style* (pp. 159–171). Hillsdale, NJ: Lawrence Erlbaum; American Psychological Association. (1997). Learned optimism yields health benefits. *Discovery Health.* Available at http://health.discovery.com/centers/mental/articles/optimism/optimism.html.

6. Cherniss, C. (2000). *Emotional Intelligence: What it is and why it matters.* Paper presented at the Annual Meeting of the Society for Industrial and Organizational Psychology, New Orleans, LA. Available at http://www.eiconsortium.org/research/what_is_emotional_intelligence.htm.

7. Ibid.

8. Goleman, D. (2002, June 16). Could you be a leader? *Parade Magazine,* pp. 4–6.

9. Boyatzis, R. E., Cowan, S. S., & Kolb, D. A. (1995). *Innovations in professional education: Steps on a journey from teaching to learning.* San Francisco: Jossey-Bass.

10. Saxbe, D. (2004, November/December). The socially savvy. *Psychology Today.* Available at http://www.psychologytoday.com/articles/pto-3636.html.

11. Kelly, W. E. (2003). Worry content associated with decreased sleep length among college students: Sleep deprivation leads to increased worrying. *College Student Journal, 37,* 93–95.

12. Cramer, D. (2004). Satisfaction with a romantic relationship, depression, support and conflict. *Psychology and Psychotherapy: Theory, Research and Practice, 77*(4), 449–461.

13. Cramer, D. (2004). Satisfaction with a romantic relationship, depression, support and conflict. *Psychology and Psychotherapy: Theory, Research and Practice, 77*(4), 449–461.

14. Fisher, H. (2004). *Why we love.* New York: Henry Holt.

15. Beach, S. R. H., & Tesser, A. (1988). Love in marriage; a cognitive account. In R. J. Sternberg & M. L. Barnes (Eds.), *The Psychology of Love.* 330–355 New Haven, CT: Yale University Press; Hatfield, E., & Walster, G. W. (1978). *A new look at love.* Lanham, MD: University Press of America.

16. Rath, T., & Clifton, D. O. (2004). *How full is your bucket?* New York: Gallup Press.

17. Parker-Popel, T. (2009, April 20). What are friends for? A longer life. *The New York Times.* Available at http://www.nytimes.com/2009/04/21/health/21well.html?_r=1; Ybarra, O., Burnstein, E., Winkielman, P., Keller, M. C., Manis, M. Chan, E., & Rodriguez, J. (2008). Mental exercising through simple socializing: Social interaction promotes general cognitive functioning. *Personality and Social Psychology Bulletin, 34,* 248–259.

18. Knox, D., Schacht, C., & Zusman, M. E. (1999, March). Love relationships among college students. *College Student Journal, 33*(1), 149–154. Available at http://findarticles.com/p/articles/mi_m0FCR/is_1_33/ai_62894068/.

19. Schwartz, P. (2003, May–June). Love is not all you need. *Psychology Today.* Available at http://www.psychologytoday.com/articles/200302/love-is-not-all-you-need.

20. Bach, G. R., & Goldberg, H. (1974). *Creative aggression: The art of assertive living.* Garden City, NJ: Doubleday; Bach, G. R, & Wyden, P. (1972). *The intimate enemy: How to fight fair in love and marriage.* New York: Avon; Bach, G. R., Deutsch, R. M., (1985). *Stop! You're driving me crazy.* New York: Berkley Publishing Group; Tucker-Ladd, C. E. (1996–2006); *Driving each other crazy.* Psychological self-help. Available at http://psychologicalselfhelp.org/Chapter9/chap9_90.html.

21. Fisher, *Why we love.*

22. Fisher, R., & Brown, S. (1988). *Getting together: Building a relationship that gets to yes.* Boston: Houghton Mifflin, p. xi.

23. Wilmot, W. W., & Hocker, J. L. (2010). *Interpersonal conflict* (8th ed.). New York: McGraw Hill.

24. Based in part on Marano, H. (2002). Relationship rules. *Psychology Today.* Available at http://www.psychologytoday.com/articles/200410/relationship-rules.

25. Dakss, B. (2006, March 3). Study: Bad relationships bad for heart. *CBS News.* Available at http://www.cbsnews.com/stories/2006/03/03/early show/contributors/emilysenay/main1364889.shtml. (2005, December 5) Unhappy marriage: bad for your health. *WebMD.* Available at http://www.webmd.com/sexrelationships/news/20051205/unhappy-marriage-bad-for-your-health. Based on Keicolt-Glaser, J. (2005). *Archives of general psychiatry, 62,* 1377–1384.

26. Dusselier, L., Dunn, B., Wang, Y., Shelley, M. C., & Whalen, D. F. (2005). Personal, health, academic, and environmental predictors of stress for residence hall students. *Journal of American College Health, 54*(1), 15–24; Hardigg, V., & Nobile, C. (1995). Living with a stranger. *U.S. News & World Report, 119*(12), 90–91. Available at http://www.usnews.com/usnews/edu/articles/950925/archive_032964_print.htm; Nankin, J. (2005). Rules for roomies. *Careers & Colleges, 25*(4), 29.

27. Thomas, K. (1977). Conflict and conflict management. In M. D. Dunnette (Ed.), *Handbook of industrial and organizational psychology,* 889–935 Chicago: Rand McNally; Kilmann, R., & Thomas, K. W. (1975). Interpersonal conflict handling behavior as reflections of Jungian personality dimensions. *Psychological Reports, 37,* 971–980; Rahim, M., & Magner, N. R. (1995). Confirmatory factor analysis of the styles of handling interpersonal conflict: First-order factor model and its invariance across groups. *Journal of Applied Psychology, 80,* 122–132; Wilmot, W. W., & Hocker, J. L. (2001). *Interpersonal conflict* (6th ed.). New York: McGraw Hill. Kilmann, R. H., and K. W. Thomas. (1977). Developing a Forced Choice Measure of Conflict-Handling Behavior: The MODE Instrument, *Educational and psychological measurement, 37*(2), 309 325.

28. Miller, G. R., & Steinberg, M. (1975). *Between people: A new analysis of interpersonal communication.* Chicago: Science Research Associates.

29. Staley, C. (2003). *50 Ways to Leave Your Lectern,* Belmont, CA: Wadsworth, p. 32.

30. Fulbeck, K. (2010). *Mixed: Portraits of multiracial kids.* San Francisco: Chronicle Books.

31. *Race, the power of an illusion. PBS.* California Newsreel. Available at http://www.pbs.org/race/000_General/000_00-Home.htm.

32. Based on "Sorting People" activity at http://www.pbs.org/race/002_SortingPeople/002_00-home.htm.

33. Wyer, K. (2007). Today's college freshmen have family income 60% above national average, UCLA survey reveals. *UCLA News.* Available at http://www.heri.ucla.edu/PDFs/PR_TRENDS_40YR.pdf.

34. Humphrey, D., & Davenport, A. (2004, Summer/Fall). What really matters in college: How students view and value liberal education. *Liberal Education.* Excerpt: Diversity and civic engagement outcomes ranked among least important. Available at http://www.diversityweb.org/Digest/vol9no1/humphreys.cfm.

35. Laird, T. F. (2005). College students' experiences with diversity and their effects on academic self-confidence, social agency, and disposition toward critical thinking. *Research in Higher Education, 46*(4), 365–387.

36. Bucher, R. D. (2004). *Diversity consciousness: Opening our minds to people, cultures, and opportunities* (2nd ed.). Upper Saddle River, NJ: Pearson Education.

37. Moore, D. G. (2003, November 14). Toward a single definition of college. *The Chronicle of Higher Education, 50*(12), B7; Diversity defines new generation of college students. (2009, June 18). *The Chronicle of Higher Education.* Available at http://www.phoenix.edu/colleges_divisions/office-of-the-president/articles/diversity-defines-new-generation-college-students.html.

38. Pusser, B., Breneman, D. W., Gansneder, B. M., Kohl, K. J., Levin, J. S., Milam, J. H., & Turner, S. E. (2007). *Returning to learning: Adults' success in college is key to America's future.* Lumina Foundation. Available at http://www.luminafoundation.org/publications/Returntolearning April2007.pdf.

39. Gomstyn, A. (2003, October 17). Minority enrollment in colleges more than doubled in past 20 years, study finds. *The Chronicle of Higher Education, 50*(8), A25; Schmidt, P. (2003, 28 November). Academe's Hispanic future. *The Chronicle of Higher Education, 50*(14), A8.

40. Jaschik, S. (2007, November 28). Growth and consolidation of minority enrollments. *Inside Higher Ed.* Available at http://www.insidehighered.com/news/2007/11/28/minority.

41. Staley, C. (2003). *50 ways to leave your lectern.* Belmont, CA: Wadsworth, p. 67. Based on Defining "Diversity." (1995). In B. Pike & C. Busse, *101 games for trainers* (p. 11). Minneapolis: Lakewood Books.

42. Carnes, M. C. (2005). Inciting speech. *Change, 37*(2), 6–11.

43. Based on Nilsen, L. B. (1998). The circles of awareness. *Teaching at Its Best.* Bolton, MA: Anker Publishing; Bucher, R. D. (2008). *Building cultural intelligence. Nine megaskills.* Upper Saddle River, NJ: Pearson.

44. Lyons, P. (2005, April 15). The truth about teaching about racism. *The Chronicle of Higher Education, 51*(32), B5.

45. Epstein, G. (2005, June 5) More women advance, but sexism persists. *College Journal from the Wall Street Journal.* Women CEOs. CNNMoney.com. Available at http://money.cnn.com/magazines/fortune/fortune500/2008/womenceos/.

46. Wessel, D. (2003, September 9). Race still a factor in hiring decisions. *College Journal from the Wall Street Journal.* Available at http://usearch.mnscu.edu/news/fw/fw4522FutureWork.html.

47. Beilke, J. R., & Yssel, N. (1999). The chilly climate for students with disabilities in higher education. *College Student Journal, 33*(3), 364–372.

48. Parker, P. N. (2006, March–April). Sustained dialogue: How students are changing their own racial climate. *About Campus, 11*(1), 17–23.

49. Gortmaker, V. J., & Brown, R. D. (2006). Out of the college closet: Differences in perceptions and experiences among out and closeted lesbian and gay students. *College Student Journal, 40*(3), 606–619.

50. Incidences and Statistics. (2005). *Hate crime statistics 2005.* Department of Justice, Uniform Crime Reporting Program. Available at http://www.fbi.gov/ucr/hc2005/incidentsoffenses.htm; *FBI Hate Crime Statistics.* Available at http://www.fbi.gov/ucr/hc2007/table_01.htm.

51. Based on Earley, P. C., & Mosakowski, E. (2004, October). Cultural intelligence. *Harvard Business Review*, p. 143.

52. Earley, P. C., & Mosakowski, E. (2004, October). Cultural intelligence. *Harvard Business Review*, 139–146; Early, C. P., Ang, S., & Tan, J. (2006) *CQ: Developing Cultural Intelligence at Work.* Stanford, CA: Stanford University Press; Osborn, T. N., (2006). *"CQ": Another aspect of emotional intelligence.* Available at http://www.teaminternational.net/resources/docs/cultural%20intelligence.pdf.

53. Earley, P. C., & Mosakowski, E. (2004, October). Cultural intelligence. *Harvard Business Review*, 139–146.

54. Also available at http://www.bls.gov/oco/ocos083.htm.

55. Bucher, R. D. (2004). *Diversity consciousness: Opening our minds to people, cultures, and opportunities* (2nd ed.). Upper Saddle River, NJ: Pearson Education.

56. Dwyer, T., & Flannigan, K. (2001). Web globalization: Write once, Deploy worldwide. Available amazon.com; see http://www.internetworldstats.com/stats.htm.

57. http://www.compact.org/.

58. Zlotkowski, E. (1999). Pedagogy and engagement. In R. G. Bringle, R. Games, & E. A. Malloy (Eds.). (1999). *Colleges and Universities as Citizens* (pp. 96–120). Needham Heights, MA: Allyn & Bacon.

59. Honnet, E. P., & Poulsen, S. J. (1989). *Principles of good practice for combining service and learning: A Wingspread special report.* Racine, WI: The Johnson Foundation. Available at http://servicelearning.org/filemanager/download/Principles_of_Good_Practice_for_Combining _Service_and_Learning.pdf.

60. Eyler, J., Giles, Jr., D. E., & Schmiede, A. (1996). *A practitioner's guide to reflection in service learning: Student voices and reflections.* Nashville, TN: Vanderbilt University Press.

CHAPTER 12

1. Gregory, M. (2003, September 12). A liberal education is not a luxury. *The Chronicle of Higher Education, 50*(3), B16.

2. Staley, R. S., II. (2003). In C. Staley, *50 ways to leave your lectern* (pp. 70–74). Belmont, CA: Wadsworth.

3. Farrell, E. F. (2006, December 12). Freshmen put high value on how well college prepares them for a profession, survey finds. *The Chronicle of Higher Education.* Farrell, E. F. (2007, January 5). Report says freshmen put career prep first. *The Chronicle of Higher Education, 53*(18), A32. Available at http://chronicle.com/article/Report-Says-Freshmen -Put-Ca/19260/. Bok, D. (2010, January 31). College and the well-lived life. *The Chronicle of Higher Education.* Available at http://chronicle.com/article/Collegethe-Well-Lived-/63789/.

4. Associated Press (2007, January 22). Polls say wealth important to youth. WBZTV.com. Available at http://wbztv.com/national/wealth .youth.money.2.277926.html; Schwartz, B. (2004, January 23). The tyranny of choice. *The Chronicle of Higher Education, 50*(20), B6.

5. Koeppel, D. (2004, December 5). Choosing a college major: For love or for the money? *The New York Times*, section 10, p. 1, column 4. Available at http://www.nytimes.com/2004/12/05/jobs/05jmar.html?ex=125998920 0&en=51dcc14fa52a65e7&ei=5090&partner=rssuserland; Dunham, K. J. (2004, March 2). No ivory tower: College students focus on career. *Wall Street Journal* (Eastern Edition), pp. B1, B8. Available at http://online.wsj.com/article/SB107818521697943524.html.

6. Based in part on Gordon, V. N., & Sears, S. J. (2004). *Selecting a college major: Exploration and decision making,* 5th edition. Upper Saddle River, NJ: Pearson Education.

7. Based on Hansen, R. S., & Hansen, K. *Using a SWOT analysis in your career planning.* Quintessential Careers. Available at http://www.quint careers.com/SWOT_Analysis.html.

8. Rowh, M. (2003, February–March). Choosing a major. *Career World, 31*(5), 21–23.

9. Ezarik, M. M. (2007, April-May). A major decision. *Career World, 35*(6), 20–22.

10. See, for example, http://www.princetonreview.com/Careers.aspx?cid=60; http://www.studydiscussions.com/career-choice-as-an-entrepreneur/; http://www.jobdiagnosis.com/myblog/how-to-become-a-successful -entrepreneur.htm.

11. Rask, K. N., & Bailey, E. M. (2002). Are faculty role models? Evidence from major choice in an undergraduate institution. *The Journal of Economic Education, 33*(2), 99–124.

12. Based on Staley, *50 ways to leave your lectern,* p. 82.

CHAPTER 13

1. Levine, M. (2005). *Ready or not, here life comes.* New York: Simon & Schuster, p. 4; Levine, M. (2005, February 18). College graduates aren't ready for the real world. *The Chronicle of Higher Education, 51*(24), B11.

2. *Dictionary of occupational titles.* (1991). Washington, DC: Bureau of Labor Statistics. Or see *O*Net Online* (Occupational Information Network) at http://online.onetcenter.org/find/.

3. Schwartz, B. (2004, January 23). The tyranny of choice. *The Chronicle of Higher Education, 50*(20), B6.

4. See J. K. Rowling Biography at http://www.biography.com/search/article.jsp?aid=9465815&page=2&search=.

5. Levine, *Ready or not, here life comes.*

6. Goldhaber, G. M. (1986). *Organizational communication* (4th ed.). Dubuque, IA: Wm. C. Brown, p. 236. In Staley, R. S., II, & Staley, C. C. (1992). *Communicating in business and the professions: The inside word.* Belmont, CA: Wadsworth.

7. See Top Job Search Websites at http://www.quintcareers.com/top_10_sites.html.

8. Staley, *50 ways to leave your lectern*, p. 33. Based on "Group Resume." (1995). In M. Silberman, *101 ways to make training active* (pp. 49–50). Johannesburg: Pfeiffer.

9. McConnon, A. (2007, September 7). innetworks: Social networking is graduating—and hitting the job market. *BusinessWeek.* pp. IN 4, IN 6.

10. *Job interviews get creative.* (2003, August 22). NPR. Available at http://www.npr.org/templates/story/story.php?storyId=1405340.

11. Vance, E. (2007, February 2). College graduates lack key skills, report says. *The Chronicle of Higher Education, 53*(22), A30.

12. Ashler, D. (2004). *How to get any job with any major.* Berkeley, CA: Ten Speed Press.

13. Pollak, L. (2007). *Getting from college to career.* New York: HarperCollins.

14. Occupational Outlook Handbook, 2008–2009. Available at http://www.bls.gov/oco/ocos059.htm and http://www.bls.gov/oco/ocos060.htm.

15. Cedja, B. D., Kaylor, A. J., & Rewey, K. L. (1998). Transfer shock in an academic discipline: The relationship between students' majors and their academic performance. *Community College Review, 26*(3), 1–13.

16. Thurmond, K. Transfer shock: Why is a term forty years old still relevant? National Academic Advising Association (NACADA). Available at http://www.nacada.ksu.edu/clearinghouse/AdvisingIssues/Transfer-Shock.htm; Rhine, T. J., Milligan, D. M., & Nelson, L. R. (2000). Alleviating transfer shock: Creating an environment for more successful transfer students. *Community College Journal of Research and Practice, 24,* 443–452.

17. Idea from Wallace, P. C. (2005). *Life 101.* New York: iUniverse, Inc., p. 3.

18. For more information, see U.S. Department of Labor, Bureau of Labor Statistics, *Occupational Outlook Handbook*, 2008–2009 Edition.

19. Coplin, B. (2003). *10 things employers want you to learn in college.* Berkeley, CA: Ten Speed Press.

Index

A

A-B-C method, 88–89
Ability, effort vs., 38–40
Absentmindedness, memory and, 202
Absolutes, defined, 251
Academic, defined, 4
Academic advisor, 12–13, 332
Academic anatomy, 309–313
Academic disciplines, defined, 300–303
Academic Intrinsic Motivation Scale (AIMS), 32–36
Academic Search Premier, 144
Academic success, 76
Accountability, defined, 238
Accountant, career as, 86–87
Accuracy, in information literacy, 147
Acronyms, defined, 198
Action
    in CRIA system, 31
    plan of, 121
Active-learning lecturer, defined, 166
Actors, memory and, 199
Adaptability skills, 270
Adequacy, defined, 111
Advisor, academic, 12–13, 332
Affordability, of Internet, 131
Age diversity, 284
AIMS. See Academic Intrinsic Motivation Scale (AIMS)
Alertness, relaxed, 52
All-over-the-map lecturer, defined, 166, 170
Alternating, time/energy and, 95–96
American mosaic, 287–290
American Psychological Association (APA), 152
Analogy, defined, 192
Analysis, SWOT, 306–308
Analytical decision making, 120
Analyze, defined, 255
Anthropology, defined, 302, 303
Antivirus program, 141
Anxiety, tests and, 243–247
APA. See American Psychological Association (APA)
Aptitude, defined, 36
Arguments
    analyzing, 109–111
    bad, 113
    deductive, 110
    inductive, 110
Art, defined, 302
Ask, defined, 137
Assertions, defined, 255
Associate's degree, 7, 10, 20, 331, 332
Assumptions, 111–112, 114

B

Attendance, 159
Attention management, 76, 336
Attention span, 227
Attitude
    goals and, 36–38
    learning and, 54
    tests and, 240
Audiovisual resources, 144
Aural learning strategy, 63, 67, 169. See also VARK
Author, 213–214
Authority, in information literacy, 147
Availability, on Internet, 131

Bachelor's degree, 7, 10, 331
Balance, 95, 97
Behavioral aspects, of test anxiety, 244, 245
Behavioral decision making, 120
Benedict Arnolds, defined, 278
Bias, defined, 203
Biology, defined, 302
Blamers, defined, 278
Blessings, attitude and, 37
Blocking, 202
Blogs, defined, 137
Bodily-kinesthetic intelligence, 60, 61, 62
Body, major/career and, 310, 311, 312
Body language, 160
Bookmark, defined, 146
Book(s)
    buying, 18
    note-taking by, 177
Boss, relationship with, 321
Brain
    learning and, 50–51, 52, 53
    memory and, 192
    mind maps and, 174
Bundling, 96
Business Source Premier, 144

C

Calculator, 246
Campus resources, 17–19, 336
Campus Security, 19
Card catalog, defined, 143–144
Career
    as accountant, 86–87
    in AIMS, 35, 36, 40
    choosing, 303–313, 332
    as computer assisted draftsman, 192–193
    as concierge, 216–217
    as day care owner, 182–183
    defined, 35, 36

as entrepreneur, 310–311
as fashion merchandiser, 34–35
interview for, 328
job vs., 321
launching, 320–330, 333
as legal assistant, 118–119
as nurse, 292–293
as police officer, 60–61
as social worker, 334–335
as teacher's assistant, 248–249
as web designer, 140–141
Career center, 18
Cell phone, 160
Certificates, 7, 20
C-Factors, 36, 40
Challenge reaction insight action system (CRIA) system, 29–31, 36
Challenge(s)
    in AIMS, 35, 36, 40
    constructive responses to, 37
    in CRIA system, 30
    focusing as, 28
    learning and, 29, 31, 39, 52, 226
    to not procrastinate, 92
    successful people and, 38, 76
Cheating, 258–261
Chemistry, defined, 302
Chew on, defined, 166
Chicago Manual of Style, 152
Child care, 18
Choices
    attitude and, 37
    conflict and, 280
    to engage, 161
    learning and, 55, 70
Chronological approach, for résumé, 325
Chunking, memory and, 193, 199
Circle of Learning, 301–303
Claims, 112
Class time, 8
Classmates, relationships with, 276
Classrooms/classes
    diversity in, 287
    online, 139–142
C-learning, 139–142
Cognition, defined, 224
Cognitive aspects, of tests anxiety, 244
Cognitive quotient (CQ), 291
College
    benefits of, 20–22
    community (See Community college)
    obstacles in, 20–22
Commentary, defined, 214
Communicating
    emotional connections and, 80
    in relationships, 275–279

Community college
    convenience of, 17
    educational goals and, 21
    people attending, 6, 22
    reasons for, 4–6
    variety in, 14
Community, learning, 141
Compare, defined, 255
Compare and contrast format,
    defined, 148
Comprehension, tests and, 246
Computer assisted draftsman, career
    as, 192–193
Computer help desk, 18
Concentration, defined, 10
Conceptual decision making, 120
Concierge, career as, 216–217
Conclusion, hasty, 114
Concreteness, in FOCUS, 44
Conflict, in relationships, 279–282
Confusion, learning and, 54
Connecting, memory and, 197
Conscientious, defined, 238
Conscientiously, defined, 8
Conscious learning, 55
Constructive responses, defined, 37
Contemplate, defined, 166
Content-intensive lecturer, defined, 166
Context, reading and, 214, 220
Continuing education, 330–331
Contradictory, defined, 110
Contrast, defined, 255
Control/controlling
    in AIMS, 35, 36, 40
    managing vs., 28
    online classes and, 140
    of procrastination, 93
    of spending, 100
    time management and, 91
Co-ops, 322, 323
Core, defined, 10
Cornell system, 173–174, 176, 177
Counselor, 12, 17–18, 272. See also
    Advisor
Course management systems,
    defined, 137
Coursework, planning, 9–11
Cover letter, 328
Coverage, in information literacy, 147
Cramming, 196, 232
"Crazymaking," defined, 278
Creative style, 123
Creative thinking, 106, 122–125
Creativity, 122–125
Credit Card Act of 2009, 99
Credit cards, 99–100
Credit history, 100
Credit reports, 100
Credits, advisor and, 12–13
CRIA system. See Challenge reaction ins
    ight action system (CRIA) system

Criteria, defined, 239
Critic, defined, 106
Critical searching skills, 146
Critical thinking
    becoming better at, 121–122
    defined, 106, 107
    four-part model of, 108–121
    importance of, 108
    information literacy and, 146
Critical Thinking Pyramid, 112,
    113, 123
Criticize, defined, 255
Critique, defined, 255
Cultural intelligence, 290–292
Cultural literacy, defined, 214
Curiosity, in AIMS, 35, 36, 40
Currency
    defined, 131
    in information literacy, 147

D

Databases, defined, 144
Day care owner, career as, 182–183
Deadlines, 87, 231
Decision making
    analytical, 120
    behavioral, 120
    conceptual, 120
    directive, 120
    major/career and, 304, 306
Deductive arguments, 110
Deep learner, defined, 31
Deep-level processing, 204
Define
    defined, 256
    in information literacy, 145–146
Degree
    associate's, 7, 10, 20, 331, 332
    bachelor's, 7, 10, 331
    finishing, 336
    master's, 331
    two-year, 7
Degree plan, 9–11
Demonstration, reading and, 216
Describe, defined, 256
Details
    information literacy and, 148
    studying and, 226–227
    tests and, 257
Developmental, defined, 14
Dewey Decimal system, 144
Dictionary, 220
Directions, 249
Directive decision making, 120
Disability, learning, 18, 192, 223
Discrimination
    defined, 286
    persistence of, 289–290
    racial, 286
Discuss, defined, 256
Distance education, defined, 139

Diversity, 283–294
    age, 284
    in classrooms, 287
    gender, 284
    geographic, 284
    media and, 286
    physical, 284
    relationships and, 268–269
    religious, 284
    sexual orientation, 284
    success and, 268–269
Drawings, memory and, 201
Dreams
    goals and (See Goals)
    major/career and, 305
Dropping a class, 17

E

Earning potential, 20
"Easy" listening, 161–162
Echoic memory, 191
Editing, defined, 151
Education
    continuing, 330–332
    distance, 139
Educational Resources Information
    Center (ERIC), 144
Effort, ability vs., 38–40
Either/or thinking, 114
Elaborative rehearsal, 196
E-learning, 139–142
Emotional appeal, 114
Emotional aspects, of test anxiety,
    244–245
Emotional energy, 78, 80–81
Emotional intelligence, 269–273
Emotional quotient (EQ), 269, 291, 292
Emotional Quotient Inventory (EQ-i), 272
Emotions. See also Feelings
    learning and, 54
    memory and, 197
    relationships and, 273
Employers, 324, 333–336
Employment, 322
Energy
    emotional, 78, 80–81
    mental, 78, 81
    physical, 78, 79
    as resource, 77–81
    spiritual, 78, 80, 81
    tests and, 240, 242
Energy management, 78
Engagement/engaging, 158–161
English, reading and, 218–220
English as a Second Language (ESL),
    164, 219
Entrepreneur, career as, 310–311
Enumerate, defined, 256
Environment
    concerns for, 293
    learning, 141–142

lecturer styles and, 166
   online classes and, 139, 141–142
EQ. *See* Emotional quotient (EQ)
EQ-i. *See* Emotional Quotient
   Inventory (EQ-i)
ERIC. *See* Educational Resources
   Information Center (ERIC)
ESL. *See* English as a Second
   Language (ESL)
Essay questions, 255, 261
Essay tests, 244, 254, 255–258
Ethical standards, defined, 260
Ethnicities, defined, 286
Evaluate, defined, 255
Evidence
   defined, 109
   evaluating, 112
   on note-taking, 169
   reading and, 221
   tests and, 255
Examples
   note-taking and, 170
   reading and, 221
   tests and, 255
Experience, 309, 322
Experts, defined, 51
Explain, defined, 256
External forces, defined, 308
Extra credit, 336
Extrinsic motivation
   defined, 33, 34
   learning and, 52

F

Facebook, 131, 132, 325
Facilitators, defined, 165
Facts, defined, 112
Faculty member, 12. *See also* Advisor
Fading, memory and, 202
False authority, 114
False cause and effect, 113
Family members, relationships with, 276
Fashion merchandiser, career as, 34–35
Faulty reasoning, 113–114
Feedback, learning and, 55, 56
Feelings. *See also* Emotions
   learning and, 54
   memory and, 197
Fees, for credit cards, 100
Fill in the blank questions, 261
Fill in the blank tests, 254–255
Financial aid, 100–101
Fine print, for credit cards, 100
First-year seminar course, 22
Fit, in FOCUS, 44
Flash cards, 232, 247
Flow, defined, 53
FOCUS, defined, 44
Focus
   engagement and, 160
   memory and, 191–192
   time management and, 76

Focused listening, 161–162
Focused thinking, defined, 106, 107
Focusing, 28–29
Four I's, 319
Four-part model of critical thinking,
   108–121
Free time, 81–82
Friends, relationships with, 275–276

G

GED. *See* General education
   development (GED)
Gender diversity, 284
General education courses, 7
General education development (GED),
   defined, 4
Generalization, reading and, 221
Geographic diversity, 284
Gestures, 162
Goal setting, memory and, 199
Goals
   ability and, 38–40
   attitude and, 36–38
   CRIA system and, 29–31
   defined, 41
   developing, 28–29
   dreams *vs.*, 42–45
   effort and, 38–40
   future and, 318
   learning and, 68
   long-term, 44, 45, 241, 273
   major/career and, 305
   motivation and, 32–36
   personal, 332
   portfolio and, 324
   schedule and, 87
   short-term, 44, 45
   values and, 41–42
Go-beyond-the-text lecturer,
   defined, 166
Google, 137, 145, 146
Grade point averages (GPAs),
   defined, 13–14
Grading scale, 14
Grammar, tests and, 258
Groups, 9
Guided notes, 176
Gunnysackers, defined, 278

H

Handouts, 170, 175–176
Hands, major/career and, 310, 311, 312
Haptic memory, 191
Hard listening skills, defined, 163
Hardiness, 270
Hasty conclusion, 114
Head, major/career and, 310, 311, 312
Health, engagement and, 160
Health services, 18
Heart, major/career and, 310, 311, 312
High school, college transition after, 4–5
High school diploma, 20

History
   credit, 100
   defined, 302, 303
Hit and run fighters, defined, 278
Humor, 201–202
Hunger, 160

I

Iconic memory, 191
Illustrate, defined, 256
Imaginative creative style, 123
Impending, defined, 180
Inaccuracy, of Internet, 131
Inductive arguments, 110
Inferences, defined, 220–221
Information, learning and, 63–68
Information Age, 146
Information literacy, 144–151
Injustice, defined, 289
Inner direction, 319
Innovative creative style, 123
Insight
   as benefit of college, 21
   in CRIA system, 31
   learning and, 68
Inspiration creative style, 123
Instructors, relationships with, 276
Instrumentation, 319
Intelligence
   ability/effort and, 39, 40
   bodily-kinesthetic, 60, 61, 62
   cultural, 290–292
   defined, 59
   emotional, 269–273
   interpersonal, 60, 62, 269
   intrapersonal, 61, 62, 269
   kinesthetic, 269
   linguistic, 60, 61, 62, 269
   logical-mathematical, 61, 62, 269
   multiple, 57–63, 269
   musical, 61, 62, 269
   naturalistic, 61, 62, 269
   spatial, 60, 61, 62, 269
Intelligence quotient (IQ), 269
Intelligence-oriented study techniques,
   61–62
Intentional learners, 225–227, 231
Intentional plagiarism, 152
Interaction, 319
Interactivity, on Internet, 131
Interference, memory and, 197
Internal forces, defined, 308
Internet
   critical searching on, 147
   information literacy and, 145
   pros/cons of, 130–134
Internet domain extensions, defined, 137
Internships, 322, 323
Interpersonal intelligence, 60, 62, 269
Interpersonal skills, 270
Interpret, defined, 256
Interpretation, 319

Interviews, 305, 328–330
Intrapersonal intelligence, 61, 62, 269
Intrapersonal skills, 270
Intrinsic motivation
    defined, 33–34, 35, 36
    learning and, 52
Intuitive creative style, 123
Inventing, 203
IQ. *See* Intelligence quotient (IQ)

J

Job growth, 20
Job preferences, 306
Jobs, defined, 321
Journals, 144
Judgments, 162

K

Key terms, 253
Key words, 170
Kinesthetic intelligence, 269
Kinesthetic learning strategy, 64, 67, 169.
    See also VARK
Knowledge
    learning and, 51, 55
    major/career and, 301, 303, 307, 309
    memory and, 196, 197
    studying and, 232
    on tests, 238–239

L

Language
    attitude and, 37
    body, 160
    reading and, 215
Law of averages, 252
Laziness, Internet and, 131–132
Learned optimism, defined, 270
Learners
    deep, 31
    defined, 39, 40
    intentional, 225–227, 231
Learning
    brain and, 50–51
    C-, 139–142
    cheating and, 260
    Circle of, 301–303
    conditions for, 51–56
    conscious, 55
    E-, 139–142
    employers and, 333–334
    engagement and, 160
    importance of, 337
    information and, 63–68
    intelligence and, 40
    lifelong, 21
    memory and, 189
    note-taking and, 176
    passive, 55
    personality and, 68–71
    self-regulated, 247
    service-, 294, 322, 323

successful people and, 38
tests and, 260, 261–262
to think, 106
unconscious, 55
VARK and, 63–68
Learning center, 17, 18
Learning community, defined, 141
Learning curve, defined, 9
Learning disability, 18, 192, 223
Learning environment, 141–142
Learning points, attitude and, 37
Learning strategy, 63, 67. *See also* VARK
Learning style
    defined, 63
    listening and, 164
    MBTI and, 69, 70
    memory and, 195
    note-taking and, 170–171
    tests and, 244
Lecture notes, 181
Lecture styles, 165–166, 167
Legal assistant, career as, 118–119
Library, 143–144, 146
Library of Congress, 144
Lifelong learning, 21
Linguistic intelligence, 60, 61, 62, 269
LinkedIn, 325
Linking mnemonic, 199
Listening
    "easy," 161–162
    ESL and, 164
    with focus, 161–167
    focused, 161–162
    note-taking skills and, 168–169, 176
Listening skills, 168–169
Listening styles, 165–166
Literacy
    cultural, 214
    information, 144–151
Literature, defined, 302, 303
Locate, in information literacy, 146
Loci mnemonic system, 198
Logic, 110
Logical-mathematical intelligence,
    61, 62, 269
Long-term goals, 44, 45, 241, 273
Long-term memory, 190, 194, 240

M

Magazines, 144
Main idea, defined, 170, 221
Main points, note-taking and, 170
Maintenance rehearsal, 196
Major, choosing, 12, 18, 303–313
Management
    attention, 76, 336
    energy, 78
    money, 97–101
    time (*See* Time management)
Managing
    of conflict, 279–282
    controlling *vs.*, 28

of personal life, 95–97
of stress, 273
Manipulating, 181, 200–201
Marginal notes, 214
Marketplace of ideas, defined, 5
Master study plan, 225–227, 231
Master's degree, 331
Matching tests, 254–255
Math, defined, 301, 302
Math anxiety, 245–247
MBTI. *See* Myers-Briggs Type Indicator®
    (MBTI)
Meaning, memory and, 199
Media, diversity and, 286
Memorization, tests and, 246
Memory, 59–60
    deepen your, 204
    echoic, 191
    failure of, 202–204
    haptic, 191
    humor in, 201–202
    iconic, 191
    long-term, 190, 194, 240
    manipulating, 200–201
    mastering, 195–202
    mnemonic devices for, 198–200
    note-taking and, 173, 174
    questions and, 249
    sensory, 190, 191–192
    short-term, 190, 192, 240, 246 (*See
        also* Working memory)
    testing, 188–190, 201
    tests and, 240
    three R's of remembering and,
        190–195
    working, 190, 192–194, 196, 246
Mental energy, 78, 81
Mentor, 272
Metacognition
    defined, 121
    reading and, 224–225
    studying and, 224–225
Microsoft Excel, defined, 137
Microsoft Powerpoint, defined, 137
Microsoft Word, defined, 137
Mind maps, 174–175, 178, 201
Mindreaders, defined, 278
Mistakes, math anxiety and, 247
Mistaking, 203
MLA. *See* Modern Language Association
    (MLA)
Mnemonic devices, 198–200
Modern Language Association (MLA),
    152
Money management, 97–101
Moods
    EI and, 270
    tests and, 244–245
Motivation, 32–36, 52, 304
Motivational quotient, 292. *See also*
    Emotional quotient (EQ)
Moving, memory and, 199

Multimodal, defined, 68–69
Multiple intelligences, 57–63, 269
Multiple-choice questions, 249, 261
Multiple-choice tests, 244, 251–254
Multitasking, 179
    defined, 28–29, 77
    "focused," 179
Musical intelligence, 61, 62, 269
Myers-Briggs Type Indicator® (MBTI),
    69–70
MySpace, 132, 325

N

Naturalistic intelligence, 61, 62, 269
Negative forces, defined, 308
Negatives, defined, 251
Netiquette, 138–139
Networking, 132, 325
Newspapers, 144
Notes
    guided, 176
    information literacy and, 148–149
    lecture, 181
    marginal, 214
    online classes and, 141
    reading and, 158, 214
    tests and, 255
Note-taking
    by book, 177
    Cornell system of, 173–174
    guided notes for, 176
    on instructor-provided handouts,
        175–176
    lecture notes for, 181
    listening skills and, 168–169
    mind maps for, 174–175
    outlining as, 172–173
    parallel, 176
    PowerPoint miniatures for, 175–176
    by system/subject, 169–178
Note-taking 4-M, 182
Note-taking skills, 168–169
Novice, defined, 51
Number theory, defined, 302
Nurse, career as, 292–293

O

Objective questions, 249
Objective tests, 250–255
Objectivity, defined, 147
Online classes, 139–142
Online research, 144
Online tests, 250
Open-book tests, 241
Opportunities, defined, 307
Optimism, learned, 270
Orators, defined, 165
Organizational chart, 201
Organizational pattern, 170
Organize, in information literacy,
    147–148
Outlining/outline, 172–173, 200, 256

Outsourcing, 96
Overdependence, of Internet, 132
Overgeneralization, critical thinking
    and, 114
Overlearning, memory and, 196
Oversimplification, critical thinking
    and, 114
Ownership, in FOCUS, 44
Oxymoron, defined, 201

P

Paragraph analysis, 222–223
Parallel note-taking, 176
Paraphrasing, 152, 181
Passive learning, 55
Patterns
    learning and, 54
    organizational, 170
PDF files, defined, 138
Peer pressure, 250
Peg system, 200
People pleasers, 91, 92
People skills, 335
Perceive, defined, 63
Perceptions, defined, 284
Perfectionists, 91, 92
Performers, defined, 39, 40
Persistence, defined, 203
Personal attack, 114
Personal life, managing, 95–97
Personal meaning, learning and, 54
Personality, 68–71
Ph.D, 331
Philosophy, defined, 302
Phishing, 132
Physical activity, tests and, 245
Physical diversity, 284
Physical energy, 78, 79
Physical factors, for reading, 213
Physical quotient, 292
Physical state, learning and, 52
Physics, defined, 302
Physiological aspects, of test anxiety,
    244, 245
Pillow Method, 124
Plagiarism, 151–153
Plan of action, 121
Planner, 86, 87, 88
Planning ahead, advisor and, 12
Planning strategies, 226–227, 231
Podcasts, defined, 138
Police officer, career as, 60–61
Political science, defined, 302, 303
Pontificating, defined, 166
Portfolio, 324
Positive forces, defined, 308
Posture, 160
Powerpoint miniatures, 175–176
Powerpoint presentation, 137, 150, 324
Practice, tests and, 246
Predictors, defined, 21
Preemptives, 91, 92

Prefixes, 218
Prejudice, defined, 287
Prep time, 162
Preparation
    engagement and, 158–160
    for tests, 239–247
Prerequisites, defined, 12, 52
Present, in information literacy, 148–149,
    151
Prewriting, 149
Primary sources, defined, 211
Priority
    defined, 8
    developing, 89
Proactive, defined, 286
Problem solving, 116–119, 334
Problem-solution format, defined, 148
Process, defined, 169, 280
Process of elimination, 252
Processing
    deep-level, 204
    memory and, 204
    surface-level, 204
Procrastinating, 12
Procrastination, 92–95
Procrastinators, 91, 92
Product, defined, 169, 280
Productive skills, 113
Proofreading, 151
Proposition, defined, 110
Prove, defined, 256
Psychological factors, for reading, 213
Psychology, defined, 302
PsycInfo, 144
Public Safety Office, 19

Q

Qualifiers, defined, 251
Quality, energy and, 78
Quantity, energy and, 78
Questions
    asking, 9, 51, 54, 179–180
    essay, 255, 261
    fill in the blank, 261
    interview, 329, 330
    listening and, 162
    major/career and, 305
    metacognition and, 225
    multiple-choice, 249, 261
    note-taking and, 174
    objective, 249
    reading and, 158
    in SQ3R, 215
    subjective, 249
    on tests (See Time per item (TPI))
    tests and, 249
    true-false, 249, 253, 261

R

Race, 285
Racial discrimination, 286
Racism, 285, 289

Rapid-fire lecturer, defined, 165, 169–170
Reaction, in CRIA system, 30–31
Reading
    engagement and, 158–159
    ESL and, 219
    importance of, 210–211
    knowledge about, 211–216
    LD and, 223
    lecture styles and, 166
    master study plan and, 225–227, 231
    memory and, 200
    metacognition and, 224–225
    note-taking and, 176
    paragraph analysis for, 222–223
    in SQ3R, 215
    stress and, 211
    studying and, 224–225, 228–232
    tests and, 239
Reading log, 212
Reading skills, 211, 217–223
Reading style, 213
Read/write learning strategy, 64, 67, 169.
    See also VARK
Reasoning, 109–116
Recall, learning information to, 189
Receptive skills, 113
Reciting, in SQ3R, 215
Recognize, learning information to, 189
Recording, 190, 192–194, 195
Rehearsal, 196
Relate, defined, 256
Relationships
    American mosaic and, 287–290
    with boss, 321
    communicating in, 275–279
    conflict in, 279–282
    EI and, 269–273
    with friends, 275–276
    love, 274
    romantic, 277–279
    stress and, 273
Relaxation training, 245
Relaxed alertness, defined, 52
Relearning, defined, 181
Relevancy, 111
Religious diversity, 284
Remediation, 14–15
Remembering, three R's of, 190–195
Repetition, learning and, 51
Research
    on ability, 39
    on attention span, 227
    conducting, 142
    defined, 142, 143
    on degrees, 332
    on effort, 39
    on EI, 269
    evaluation during, 146–147
    information literacy and, 145, 149
    on job satisfaction, 321
    major/career and, 305–308
    on memory, 197, 240

    online, 144
    on reading, 213
    on relationships, 275–276
    on salaries, 330
    scholarly, 211
    on sleep, 79
    on stress, 53
    on studying, 231
Research skills, 142–144, 335
Resilience, defined, 270
Resource(s)
    audiovisual, 144
    campus, 17–19, 336
    energy as, 77–81
Responsibility
    attitude and, 37
    listening and, 162
Résumé, 322, 324, 325–328
Retaining, 190, 194, 195
Retrieving, 190, 194, 195
Review/reviewing
    note-taking and, 181
    online classes and, 142
    in SQ3R, 215
    studying and, 227
    tests and, 240, 250
Review-the-text lecturer, defined, 166
Revision, defined, 149, 151
Rewriting, 149, 151
Romantic relationships, 277–279
Ruminate, defined, 166

S

Salaries, 330
Schedule
    study, 240
    studying and, 226
    success and, 83–88
Scholarly research, defined, 211
Scope, defined, 131
Search engines, defined, 137
Select, in information literacy, 146–147
Self-concept, 125
Self-criticism, 125
Self-discipline, defined, 29
Self-handicapping, defined, 39
Self-regulated learning, 247
Senses
    defined, 63
    studying and, 232
Sensory memory, 190, 191–192
Sensory preferences, 66–68
Serial-position effect, 197
Service-learning, 294, 322, 323
Sexism, 289
Sexual orientation diversity, 284
Shallow rehearsal, 196
Shifting the burden of proof, 114
Short-answer tests, 254–255
Short-hand system, in note-taking,
    171–172
Short-term goals, 44, 45

Short-term memory, 190, 192, 240, 246.
    See also Working memory
Simplifying, 96–97
Skills approach, for résumé, 325
Sleep, 79, 135
Slow-go lecturer, defined, 166
Social worker, career as, 334–335
Sociology, defined, 302
Soft listening skills, defined, 163
Software, defined, 137
Sounds, reading and, 218, 221
Sources, citing, 152
Spam, 132
Spatial intelligence, 60, 61, 62, 269
Speaking, 153
Speech patterns, 162
Spellcheck, 151, 218
Spelling
    reading and, 218
    writing and, 151
Spiritual energy, 78, 80, 81
Spyware, 132
SQ3R, 215
Stacks, defined, 144
State, defined, 256
Statistics
    reading and, 221
    tests and, 255
Stereotypes
    defined, 286
    persistence of, 289–290
Straw man, 114
Strengths, defined, 306
Stress
    choice and, 84
    emotional intelligence and, 270
    learning and, 52, 53
    reading and, 211
    relationships and, 273
    sleep and, 135
    spirituality and, 80
    tests and, 242, 245
    time management and, 97
Stress management skills, 270
Stretch, in FOCUS, 44
Study breaks, 227
Study buddy, 227
Study plan, master, 225–227, 231
Study schedule, 240
Study techniques, 227
Studying
    disciplined, 228–230
    explanation of, 231–232
    metacognition and, 224–225
    reading and, 224–225, 228–232
    tests and, 240–241
Style
    creative, 123
    learning (See Learning style)
    lecture, 165–166, 167
    listening, 165–166
    reading, 213

Subject, note-taking by, 177–178
Subjective essay tests, 255–258
Subjective questions, 249
Substance, learning and, 54
Success
    academic, 76
    defined, 20, 23
    EI and, 269, 271
    information literacy and, 144–151
    major/career and, 304
    relationships/diversity and, 268–269
    research skills and, 142–144
    schedule and, 83–88
    tests and, 241, 245
Suffixes, 218
Summarize, defined, 145, 256
Summarizing, 172, 181
Summary, defined, 172
Summary statement, 258
Supplementary materials, defined, 165
Support centers, 17
Surface-level processing, 204
Survey, in SQ3R, 215
Sustainability, defined, 293
SWOT analysis, 306–308
Syllables, reading and, 218, 221
Syllabus, 15–16, 158

T

Take stock, defined, 31
Take-home tests, 241
Tangent, defined, 180
Teacher's assistant, career as, 248–249
Teamwork, 9
Techflexing, 96
Technology
    campus resources and, 18
    cheating and, 260
    plagiarism and, 152
    time management and, 96
Technology ownership, 135
Technology skills, 130–142
Technology use, 135
Television, 80
"Term on a Page" calendar, 84–85, 87
Test anxiety, 243–247
Test scores, increasing, 245–247
Testimony
    reading and, 221
    tests and, 255
Tests
    before, 239–247
    during, 247–250
    after, 261–262
    cheating on, 258–261
    essay, 244, 254, 255–258
    fill in the blank, 254–255
    matching, 254–255
    multiple-choice, 244, 251–254
    objective, 250–255
    online, 250

    open-book, 241
    short-answer, 254–255
    showing knowledge on, 238–239
    subjective essay, 255–258
    take-home, 241
    true-false, 250–251, 252
Textbook websites, defined, 137
Themes, 162
Thesis statement
    defined, 255
    for essay tests, 255
    reading and, 221
Thinking
    creative, 106, 122–125
    critical (See Critical thinking)
    defined, 106
    either/or, 114
    focused, 106, 107
    reading and, 210
    rethinking, 106–107
    tests and, 244
Threats, defined, 307
Three R's of remembering, 190–195
Time
    assignments and, 8
    cheating and, 259
    class, 8
    dreams/goals and, 31
    free, 81–82
    memory and, 196
    prep, 162
    studying and, 227, 231, 232
    tests and, 241, 242, 255, 258
Time management, 76–77, 81–97, 98, 142,
    163, 203, 333, 336
Time per item (TPI), 252
Tip of the Tongue (TOT) phenomenon,
    202
To-do list, 88
Tolerance, defined, 286
Topical format, defined, 148
TOT phenomenon. See Tip of the Tongue
    (TOT) phenomenon
TPI. See Time per item (TPI)
Trace, defined, 256
Training, relaxation, 245
Trappers, defined, 278
Trojan horses, defined, 138
True-false questions, 249, 253, 261
True-false tests, 250–251, 252
Turning points, attitude and, 37
Tutor, 17
Two-way inferences, 221
Two-year degree, 7

U

Unconscious learning, 55
Understanding, reading and, 212, 226
Unemployment rates, 20
Unintentional plagiarism, 152
Unwarranted assumption, 114

Urgency, defined, 89
Usefulness, in FOCUS, 44

V

Values, 41–42. See also Goals
Variety
    in community college, 14
    studying and, 227
VARK, learning and, 63–68, 70, 71
Verb, tests and, 255–256
Virtual Private Network (VPN),
    defined, 138
Viruses, 132, 138, 141
Visual learning strategy, 63, 67, 169.
    See also VARK
Vocabulary, reading and, 218, 220
VPN. See Virtual Private Network (VPN)

W

Weaknesses, defined, 307
Web 2.0, defined, 138
Web designer, career as, 140–141
Web logs, defined, 137
Websites
    for careers, 321, 324
    evaluation of, 146–147
    textbook, 137
What ifs, 336
Wikipedia, 131, 145
Wikis, defined, 137
WilsonWeb OmniFile Full Text
    Mega, 144
Wisdom, as benefit of college, 21
Words
    attitude and, 37
    reading and, 221
Work
    learning and, 55
    managing, 95–97
    online classes and, 141
Work ethic, 333
Working memory, 190, 192–194, 196, 246
Worms, defined, 138
Write learning strategy. See Read/write
    learning strategy
Writing
    in information literacy, 148–151
    memory and, 200
    note-taking and, 170, 176
    plagiarism and, 153
Writing skills, 211, 324

Y

Yahoo, defined, 137
YouTube, defined, 137

August 2011–December 2013

MONTHLY PLANNER

AUGUST 2011

MONDAY	TUESDAY	WEDNESDAY
1	2	3
8	9	10
15	16	17
22	23	24
29	29	30

July 2011

M	T	W	T	F	S/S
				1	2/3
4	5	6	7	8	9/10
11	12	13	14	15	16/17
18	19	20	21	22	23/24
25	26	27	28	29	30/31

September 2011

M	T	W	T	F	S/S
			1	2	3/4
5	6	7	8	9	10/11
12	13	14	15	16	17/18
19	20	21	22	23	24/25
26	27	28	29	30	

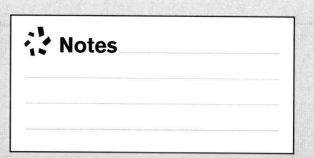

Notes

_____

_____

_____

_____

THURSDAY	FRIDAY	SATURDAY/SUNDAY
4	5	6
		7
11	12	13
		14
18	19	20
		21
25	26	27
		28
31		

SEPTEMBER 2011

MONDAY	TUESDAY	WEDNESDAY
		1
5 *Labor Day*	**6**	**7**
12	**13**	**14**
19	**20**	**21**
26	**27**	**28**

August 2011

M	T	W	T	F	S/S
1	2	3	4	5	6/7
8	9	10	11	12	13/14
15	16	17	18	19	20/21
22	23	24	25	26	27/28
29	30	31			

October 2011

M	T	W	T	F	S/S
					1/2
3	4	5	6	7	8/9
10	11	12	13	14	15/16
17	18	19	20	21	22/23
24/31	25	26	27	28	29/30

Notes

THURSDAY	FRIDAY	SATURDAY/SUNDAY
1	2	3
		4
8	9	10
		11
15	16	17
		Patriot Day 18
22	23 *Autumn begins*	24
		25
29 *Rosh Hashanah begins at sundown*	30	

cengage.com

OCTOBER 2011

MONDAY	TUESDAY	WEDNESDAY
3	**4**	**5**
10 *Columbus Day Observed*	**11**	**12**
17	**18**	**19**
24 *United Nations Day* *Halloween* **31**	**25**	**26**

September 2011

M	T	W	T	F	S/S
			1	2	3/4
5	6	7	8	9	10/11
12	13	14	15	16	17/18
19	20	21	22	23	24/25
26	27	28	29	30	

November 2011

M	T	W	T	F	S/S
	1	2	3	4	5/6
7	8	9	10	11	12/13
14	15	16	17	18	19/20
21	22	23	24	25	26/27
28	29	30			

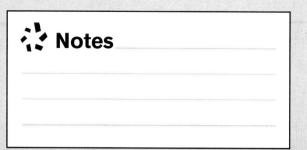 **Notes**

THURSDAY	FRIDAY	SATURDAY/SUNDAY
		1
		2
6	7	8
		9
13	14	15
		16
20	21	22
		23
27	28	29
		30

NOVEMBER 2011

MONDAY	TUESDAY	WEDNESDAY
	1	**2**
7	**8** *Election Day*	**9**
14	**15**	**16**
21	**22**	**23**
28	**29**	**30**

October 2011

M	T	W	T	F	S/S
				1	1/2
3	4	5	6	7	8/9
10	11	12	13	14	15/16
17	18	19	20	21	22/23
24/31	25	26	27	28	29/30

December 2011

M	T	W	T	F	S/S
			1	2	3/4
5	6	7	8	9	10/11
12	13	14	15	16	17/18
19	20	21	22	23	24/25
26	27	28	29	30	31

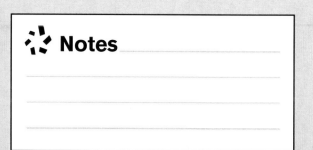

Notes

_____

_____

_____

THURSDAY	FRIDAY	SATURDAY/SUNDAY
3	**4**	**5**
		6 Daylight Saving ends
10	**11** Veterans Day	**12**
		13
17	**18**	**19**
		20
24 Thanksgiving Day	**25**	**26**
		27

cengage.com

DECEMBER 2011

MONDAY	TUESDAY	WEDNESDAY
5	6	7
12	13	14
19	20	21 *Hanukkah/Chanukah begins*
26 *Kwanzaa begins*	27	28

November 2011

M	T	W	T	F	S/S
	1	2	3	4	5/6
7	8	9	10	11	12/13
14	15	16	17	18	19/20
21	22	23	24	25	26/27
28	29	30			

January 2012

M	T	W	T	F	S/S
					/1
2	3	4	5	6	7/8
9	10	11	12	13	14/15
16	17	18	19	20	21/22
23/30	24/31	25	26	27	28/29

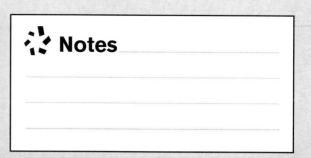

Notes

THURSDAY	FRIDAY	SATURDAY/SUNDAY
1	**2**	**3**
		4
8	**9**	**10**
		11
15	**16**	**17**
		18
22 *Winter begins*	**23**	**24** *Christmas Eve*
		Christmas Day **25**
29	**30**	**31** *New Years Eve*

JANUARY 2012

MONDAY	TUESDAY	WEDNESDAY
2	3	4
9	10	11
16	17	18
23 / 30	24 / 31	25

December 2011						
M	T	W	T	F	S/S	
			1	2	3/4	
5	6	7	8	9	10/11	
12	13	14	15	16	17/18	
19	20	21	22	23	24/25	
26	27	28	29	30	31/	

February 2012						
M	T	W	T	F	S/S	
			1	2	3	4/5
6	7	8	9	10	11/12	
13	14	15	16	17	18/19	
20	21	22	23	24	25/26	
27	28	29				

Notes

THURSDAY	FRIDAY	SATURDAY/SUNDAY
		New Year's Day **1**
5	**6**	**7** / **8**
12	**13**	**14** / **15**
19	**20**	**21** *Martin Luther King Jr. Day* / **22**
26	**27**	**28** / **29**

FEBRUARY 2012

MONDAY	TUESDAY	WEDNESDAY
		1
6	**7**	**8**
13	**14** *Valentine's Day*	**15**
20 *Presidents' Day*	**21**	**22** *George Washington's Birthday* *Ash Wednesday*
27	**28**	**29**

	January 2012					
M	**T**	**W**	**T**	**F**	**S/S**	
					/1	
2	3	4	5	6	7/8	
9	10	11	12	13	14/15	
16	17	18	19	20	21/22	
23/30	24/31	25	26	27	28/29	

	March 2012					
M	**T**	**W**	**T**	**F**	**S/S**	
			1	2	3/4	
5	6	7	8	9	10/11	
12	13	14	15	16	17/18	
19	20	21	22	23	24/25	
26	27	28	29	30	31/	

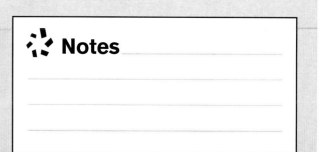

Notes

THURSDAY	FRIDAY	SATURDAY/SUNDAY
2 *Groundhog Day*	**3**	**4** **5**
9	**10**	**11** *Lincoln's Birthday* **12**
16	**17**	**18** **19**
23	**24**	**25** **26**

MARCH 2012

MONDAY	TUESDAY	WEDNESDAY
	1	2
5	6	7
12	13	14
19	20 *Spring begins*	21
25	26	27

February 2012

M	T	W	T	F	S/S
		1	2	3	4/5
6	7	8	9	10	11/12
13	14	15	16	17	18/19
20	21	22	23	24	25/26
27	28	29			

April 2012

M	T	W	T	F	S/S
					/1
2	3	4	5	6	7/8
9	10	11	12	13	14/15
16	17	18	19	20	21/22
23/30	24	25	26	27	28/29

Notes

THURSDAY	FRIDAY	SATURDAY/SUNDAY
1	**2**	**3**
		4
8	**9**	**10**
		Daylight Saving begins **11**
15	**16**	**17** *St. Patrick's Day*
		18
22	**23**	**24**
		27
28	**29**	**30**

cengage.com

APRIL 2012

MONDAY	TUESDAY	WEDNESDAY
2	3	4
9	10	11
16	17	18
23 / 30	24	25

March 2012

M	T	W	T	F	S/S
			1	2	3/4
5	6	7	8	9	10/11
12	13	14	15	16	17/18
19	20	21	22	23	24/25
26	27	28	29	30	31

May 2012

M	T	W	T	F	S/S
	1	2	3	4	5/6
7	8	9	10	11	12/13
14	15	16	17	18	19/20
21	22	23	24	25	26/27
28	29	30	31		

Notes

THURSDAY	FRIDAY	SATURDAY/SUNDAY
		Palm Sunday **1**
5	**6** *Good Friday*	**7** *Passover begins at sundown* / *Easter* **8**
12	**13** *Passover ends at sundown*	**14** / **15**
19	**20**	**21** / *Earth Day* **22**
26	**27**	**28** / **29**

MAY 2012

MONDAY	TUESDAY	WEDNESDAY
	1	2
7	8	9
14	15	16
21	22	23
28 *Memorial Day*	29	30

April 2012

M	T	W	T	F	S/S	
				1	2/1	
2	3	4	5	6	7/8	
9	10	11	12	13	14/15	
16	17	18	19	20	21/22	
23/30	24	25	26	27	28/29	

June 2012

M	T	W	T	F	S/S	
				1	2/3	
4	5	6	7	8	9/10	
11	12	13	14	15	16/17	
18	19	20	21	22	23/24	
25	26	27	28	29	30/	

Notes

THURSDAY	FRIDAY	SATURDAY/SUNDAY
3	4	5 *Cinco de Mayo*
		6
10	11	12
		Mother's Day 13
17	18	19
		20
24	25	26
		27
31		

JUNE 2012

MONDAY	TUESDAY	WEDNESDAY
4	5	6
11	12	13
18	19	20 *Summer begins*
25	26	27

May 2012

M	T	W	T	F	S / S
	1	2	3	4	5/6
7	8	9	10	11	12/13
14	15	16	17	18	19/20
21	22	23	24	25	26/27
28	29	30	31		

July 2012

M	T	W	T	F	S / S
					/1
2	3	4	5	6	7/8
9	10	11	12	13	14/15
16	17	18	19	20	21/22
23/30	24/31	25	26	27	28/29

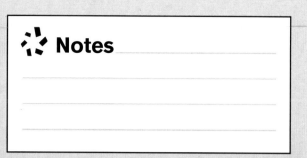

Notes

THURSDAY	FRIDAY	SATURDAY/SUNDAY
	1	**2** / **3**
7	**8**	**9** / **10**
14 *Flag Day*	**15**	**16** / **17** *Father's Day*
21	**22**	**23** / **24**
28	**29**	**30**

cengage.com

JULY 2012

MONDAY	TUESDAY	WEDNESDAY
2	3	4 *Independence Day*
9	10	11
16	17	18
23	24	25
30	31	

June 2012

M	T	W	T	F	S / S
				1	2/3
4	5	6	7	8	9/10
11	12	13	14	15	16/17
18	19	20	21	22	23/24
25	26	27	28	29	30/

August 2012

M	T	W	T	F	S / S
		1	2	3	4/5
6	7	8	9	10	11/12
13	14	15	16	17	18/19
20	21	22	23	24	25/26
27	28	29	30	31	

Notes

THURSDAY	FRIDAY	SATURDAY/SUNDAY
		1
5	6	7 / 8
12	13	14 / 15
19	20	21 / 22
26	27	28 / 29

AUGUST 2012

MONDAY	TUESDAY	WEDNESDAY
		1
6	7	8
13	14	15
20	21	22
27	28	29

July 2012						
M	**T**	**W**	**T**	**F**	**S**	**/ S**
						/1
2	3	4	5	6	7	/8
9	10	11	12	13	14	/15
16	17	18	19	20	21	/22
23/30	24/31	25	26	27	28	/29

September 2012						
M	**T**	**W**	**T**	**F**	**S**	**/ S**
						1/2
3	4	5	6	7	8	/9
10	11	12	13	14	15	/16
17	18	19	20	21	22	/23
24	25	26	27	28	29	/30

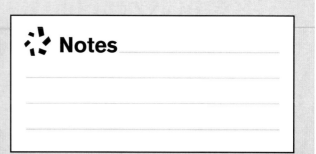

Notes

THURSDAY	FRIDAY	SATURDAY/SUNDAY
2	3	4
		5
9	10	11
		12
16	17	18
		19
23	24	25
		26
30	31	

SEPTEMBER 2012

MONDAY	TUESDAY	WEDNESDAY
3 *Labor Day*	**4**	**5**
10	**11**	**12**
17	**18**	**19**
24	**25**	**26** *Yom Kippur begins at sundown*

August 2012

M	T	W	T	F	S/S
1	2	1	2	3	4/5
6	7	8	9	10	11/12
13	14	15	16	17	18/19
20	21	22	23	24	25/26
27	28	29	30	31	

October 2012

M	T	W	T	F	S/S
1	2	3	4	5	6/7
8	9	10	11	12	13/14
15	16	17	18	19	20/21
22	23	24	25	26	27/28
29	30	31			

Notes

_____

_____

_____

_____

THURSDAY	FRIDAY	SATURDAY/SUNDAY
		1
6	7	8 — 2
13	14	15 — *Patriot Day* 9
20	21	22 — *Rosh Hashanah begins at sundown* 16
27	28	29 — *Autumn begins* 23
		30

OCTOBER 2012

MONDAY	TUESDAY	WEDNESDAY
1	**2**	**3**
8 *Columbus Day Observed*	**9**	**10**
15	**16**	**17**
22	**23**	**24** *United Nations Day*
29	**30**	**31** *Halloween*

September 2012

M	T	W	T	F	S/S
					¹/₂
3	4	5	6	7	⁸/₉
10	11	12	13	14	¹⁵/₁₆
17	18	19	20	21	²²/₂₃
24	25	26	27	28	²⁹/₃₀

November 2012

M	T	W	T	F	S/S
			1	2	³/₄
5	6	7	8	9	¹⁰/₁₁
12	13	14	15	16	¹⁷/₁₈
19	20	21	22	23	²⁴/₂₅
26	27	28	29	30	

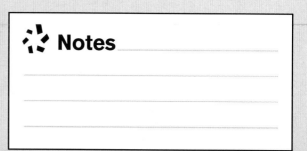

Notes

THURSDAY	FRIDAY	SATURDAY/SUNDAY
4	**5**	**6** / **7**
11	**12**	**12** / **14**
18	**19**	**20** / **21**
25	**26**	**27** / **28**

NOVEMBER 2012

MONDAY	TUESDAY	WEDNESDAY
5	**6** *Election Day*	**7**
12 *Veterans Day*	**13**	**14**
19	**20**	**21**
26	**27**	**28**

October 2012

M	T	W	T	F	S/S
1	2	3	4	5	6/7
8	9	10	11	12	13/14
15	16	17	18	19	20/21
22	23	24	25	26	27/28
29	30	31			

December 2012

M	T	W	T	F	S/S
				1	2	1/2
3	4	5	6	7	8/9
10	11	12	13	14	15/16
17	18	19	20	21	22/23
24/31	25	26	27	28	29/30

✳ Notes _____

THURSDAY	FRIDAY	SATURDAY/SUNDAY
1	**2**	**3**
		4 *Daylight Saving ends*
8	**9** *Veterans Day*	**10**
		11
15	**16**	**17**
		18
22 *Thanksgiving Day*	**23**	**24**
		25
29	**30**	

DECEMBER 2012

MONDAY	TUESDAY	WEDNESDAY
3	4	5
10	11	12
17	18	19
24 *Christmas Eve*	25 *Christmas Day*	26 *Kwanzaa begins*
New Year's Eve 31		

November 2012

M	T	W	T	F	S/S
			1	2	3/4
5	6	7	8	9	10/11
12	13	14	15	16	17/18
19	20	21	22	23	24/25
26	27	28	29	30	

January 2013

M	T	W	T	F	S/S
	1	2	3	4	5/6
7	8	9	10	11	12/13
14	15	16	17	18	19/20
21	22	23	24	25	26/27
28	29	30	31		

Notes

THURSDAY	FRIDAY	SATURDAY/SUNDAY
		1
6	**7**	**8** **2**
		Hanukkah/Chanukah begins **9**
13	**14**	**15** **16**
20	**21** *Winter begins*	**22** **23**
27	**28**	**29** **30**

cengage.com

JANUARY 2013

MONDAY	TUESDAY	WEDNESDAY
	1 *New Year's Day*	**2**
7	**8**	**9**
14	**15**	**16**
21 *Martin Luther King, Jr. Day*	**22**	**23**
28	**29**	**30**

DECEMBER 2012

M	T	W	T	F	S/S
					1/2
3	4	5	6	7	8/9
10	11	12	13	14	15/16
17	18	19	20	21	22/23
24/31	25	26	27	28	29/30

FEBRUARY 2013

M	T	W	T	F	S/S
				1	2/3
4	5	6	7	8	9/10
11	12	13	14	15	16/17
18	19	20	21	22	23/24
25	26	27	28		

Notes _____

_____

_____

_____

THURSDAY	FRIDAY	SATURDAY/SUNDAY
3	4	5
		6
10	11	12
		13
17	18	19
		20
24	25	26
		27
31		

FEBRUARY 2013

MONDAY	TUESDAY	WEDNESDAY
4	**5**	**6**
11	**12** *Lincoln's Birthday*	**13** *Ash Wednesday*
18 *President's Day*	**19**	**20**
25	**26**	**27**

JANUARY 2013

M	T	W	T	F	S/S
	1	2	3	4	5/6
7	8	9	10	11	12/13
14	15	16	17	18	19/20
21	22	23	24	25	26/27
28	29	30	31		

MARCH 2013

M	T	W	T	F	S/S
				1	2/3
4	5	6	7	8	9/10
11	12	13	14	15	16/17
18	19	20	21	22	23/24
25	26	27	28	29	30/31

Notes _____

THURSDAY	FRIDAY	SATURDAY/SUNDAY
	1	2 Groundhog Day
		3
7	8	9
		10
14 Valentine's Day	15	16
		17
21	22 Washington's Birthday	23
		24
28		

cengage.com

MARCH 2013

MONDAY	TUESDAY	WEDNESDAY
4	**5**	**6**
11	**12**	**13**
18	**19**	**20** *Spring begins*
25	**26** *Passover begins*	**27**

FEBRUARY 2013					
M	T	W	T	F	S/S
				1	2/3
4	5	6	7	8	9/10
11	12	13	14	15	16/17
18	19	20	21	22	23/24
25	26	27	28		

APRIL 2013					
M	T	W	T	F	S/S
1	2	3	4	5	6/7
8	9	10	11	12	13/14
15	16	17	18	19	20/21
22	23	24	25	26	27/28
29	30				

Notes _____

_____

_____

_____

THURSDAY	FRIDAY	SATURDAY/SUNDAY
		1 / **2**
		3
7	**8**	**9**
		Daylight Saving begins **10**
14	**15**	**16**
		St. Patrick's Day **17**
21	**22**	**23**
		Palm Sunday **24**
28	**29** *Good Friday*	**30**
		Easter **31**

cengage.com

APRIL 2013

MONDAY	TUESDAY	WEDNESDAY
1 *Passover ends*	**2**	**3**
8	**9**	**10**
15	**16**	**17**
22 *Earth Day*	**23**	**24**
29	**30**	

MARCH 2013					
M	T	W	T	F	S/S
				1	2/3
4	5	6	7	8	9/10
11	12	13	14	15	16/17
18	19	20	21	22	23/24
25	26	27	28	29	30/31

MAY 2013					
M	T	W	T	F	S/S
		1	2	3	4/5
6	7	8	9	10	11/12
13	14	15	16	17	18/19
20	21	22	23	24	25/26
27	28	29	30	31	

Notes _____

_____

_____

_____

THURSDAY	FRIDAY	SATURDAY/SUNDAY
4	5	6 / 7
11	12	13 / 14
18	19	20 / 21
25	26	27 / 28

MAY 2013

MONDAY	TUESDAY	WEDNESDAY
		1
6	**7**	**8**
13	**14**	**15**
20	**21**	**22**
27 *Memorial Day*	**28**	**29**

APRIL 2013					
M	T	W	T	F	S/S
1	2	3	4	5	6/7
8	9	10	11	12	13/14
15	16	17	18	19	20/21
22	23	24	25	26	27/28
29	30				

JUNE 2013					
M	T	W	T	F	S/S
					1/2
3	4	5	6	7	8/9
10	11	12	13	14	15/16
17	18	19	20	21	22/23
24	25	26	27	28	30/31

Notes _____

_____

_____

_____

THURSDAY	FRIDAY	SATURDAY/SUNDAY
2	3	4
		Cinco de Mayo 5
9	10	11
		Mother's Day 12
16	17	18
		19
23	24	25
		26
30	31	

JUNE 2013

MONDAY	TUESDAY	WEDNESDAY
3	4	5
10	11	12
17	18	19
24	25	26

MAY 2013					
M	T	W	T	F	S/S
		1	2	4	5/6
7	8	9	10	11	12/13
14	15	16	17	18	19/20
21	22	23	24	25	26/27
28	29	30	31		

JULY 2013					
M	T	W	T	F	S/S
1	2	3	4	5	6/7
8	9	10	11	12	13/14
15	16	17	18	19	20/21
22	23	24	25	26	27/28
29	30	31			

Notes _____

_____

_____

_____

THURSDAY	FRIDAY	SATURDAY/SUNDAY
		1 / **1**
		2
6	**7**	**8**
		9
13	**14** *Flag Day*	**15**
		Father's Day **16**
20	**21** *Summer begins*	**22**
		23
27	**28**	**29**
		30

cengage.com

JULY 2013

MONDAY	TUESDAY	WEDNESDAY
1	2	3
8	9	10
15	16	17
22	23	24
29	30	31

JUNE 2013

M	T	W	T	F	S/S
					1/2
3	4	5	6	7	8/9
10	11	12	13	14	15/16
17	18	19	20	21	22/23
24	25	26	27	28	29/30

AUGUST 2013

M	T	W	T	F	S/S
			1	2	3/4
5	6	7	8	9	10/11
12	13	14	15	16	17/18
19	20	21	22	23	24/25
26	27	28	29	30	31/

Notes _____

_____

_____

_____

THURSDAY	FRIDAY	SATURDAY/SUNDAY
4 *Independence Day*	**5**	**6** **7**
11	**12**	**13** **14**
18	**19**	**20** **21**
25	**26**	**27** **28**

cengage.com

AUGUST 2013

MONDAY	TUESDAY	WEDNESDAY
5	6	7
12	13	14
19	20	21
26	27	28

JULY 2013

M	T	W	T	F	S/S
1	2	3	4	6	/1
2	3	4	5	6	7/8
9	10	11	12	13	14/15
16	17	18	19	20	21/22
23/30	24/31	25	26	27	28/29

SEPTEMBER 2013

M	T	W	T	F	S/S
					/1
2	3	4	5	6	7/8
9	10	11	12	13	14/15
16	17	18	19	20	21/22
23/30	24	25	26	27	28/29

Notes _____

_____

_____

_____

THURSDAY	FRIDAY	SATURDAY/SUNDAY
1	2	3
		4
8	9	10
		11
15	16	17
		18
22	23	24
		25
29	30	31

SEPTEMBER 2013

MONDAY	TUESDAY	WEDNESDAY
2 *Labor Day*	**3**	**4**
9	**10**	**11** *Patriot Day*
16	**17**	**18**
23 **30**	**24**	**25**

AUGUST 2013					
M	T	W	T	F	S/S
			1	2	3/4
5	6	7	8	9	10/11
12	13	14	15	16	17/18
19	20	21	22	23	24/25
26	27	28	29	30	31/

OCTOBER 2013					
M	T	W	T	F	S/S
	1	2	3	4	5/6
7	8	9	10	11	12/13
14	15	16	17	18	19/20
21	22	23	24	25	26/27
28	29	30	31		

Notes _____

_____

_____

_____

THURSDAY	FRIDAY	SATURDAY/SUNDAY
		1
		1
5 *Rosh Hashanah*	**6**	**7**
		8
12	**13**	**14** *Yom Kippur*
		15
19	**20**	**21**
		Autumn begins **22**
26	**27**	**28**
		29

OCTOBER 2013

MONDAY	TUESDAY	WEDNESDAY
	1	2
7	8	9
14 *Columbus Day*	15	16
21	22	23
28	29	30

SEPTEMBER 2013

M	T	W	T	F	S/S
					/1
2	3	4	5	6	7/8
9	10	11	12	13	14/15
16	17	18	19	20	21/22
23/30	24	25	26	27	28/29

NOVEMBER 2013

M	T	W	T	F	S/S
			1	2/3
4	5	6	7	8	9/10
11	12	13	14	15	16/17
18	19	20	21	22	23/24
25	26	27	28	29	30/

Notes _____

_____

_____

_____

THURSDAY	FRIDAY	SATURDAY/SUNDAY
3	**4**	**5** / **6**
10	**11**	**12** / **13**
17	**18**	**19** / **20**
24 *United Nations Day*	**25**	**26** / **27**
31 *Halloween*		

NOVEMBER 2013

MONDAY	TUESDAY	WEDNESDAY
4	**5** *Election Day*	**6**
11 *Veterans Day*	**12**	**13**
18	**19**	**20**
25	**26**	**27**

OCTOBER 2013						
M	T	W	T	F	S/S	
	1	2	3	4	5/6	
7	8	9	10	11	12/13	
14	15	16	17	18	19/20	
21	22	23	24	25	26/27	
28	29	30	31			

DECEMBER 2013						
M	T	W	T	F	S/S	
					/1	
2	3	4	5	6	7/8	
9	10	11	12	13	14/15	
16	17	18	19	20	21/22	
23/30	24/31	25	26	27	28/29	

Notes _____

_____

_____

_____

THURSDAY	FRIDAY	SATURDAY/SUNDAY
1	**1**	**2**
		Daylight Saving ends **3**
7	**8**	**9**
		10
14	**15**	**16**
		17
21	**22**	**23**
		24
28 *Thanksgiving Day* *Hannukkah/Chanukah begins*	**29**	**30**

cengage.com

DECEMBER 2013

MONDAY	TUESDAY	WEDNESDAY
2	3	4
9	10	11
16	17	18
23	24 *Christmas Eve*	25 *Christmas Day*
30	*New Years Eve* 31	

NOVEMBER 2013

M	T	W	T	F	S/S
				1	2/3
4	5	6	7	8	9/10
11	12	13	14	15	16/17
18	19	20	21	22	23/24
25	26	27	28	29	30/

JANUARY 2014

M	T	W	T	F	S/S
		1	2	3	4/5
6	7	8	9	10	11/12
13	14	15	16	17	18/19
20	21	22	23	24	25/26
27	28	29	30	31	

Notes _____

_____

_____

_____

THURSDAY	FRIDAY	SATURDAY/SUNDAY
		1
5	6	7 / 8
12	13	14 / 15
19	20	21 *Winter begins* / 22
26 *Kwanza begins*	27	28 / 29

2012

JANUARY 2012
M	T	W	T	F	S/S
					/1
2	3	4	5	6	7/8
9	10	11	12	13	14/15
16	17	18	19	20	21/22
23/30	24/31	25	26	27	28/29

FEBRUARY 2012
M	T	W	T	F	S/S
		1	2	3	4/5
6	7	8	9	10	11/12
13	14	15	16	17	18/19
20	21	22	23	24	25/26
27	28	29	30	31	

MARCH 2012
M	T	W	T	F	S/S
			1	2	3/4
5	6	7	8	9	10/11
12	13	14	15	16	17/18
19	20	21	22	23	24/25
26	27	28	29	30	31/

APRIL 2012
M	T	W	T	F	S/S
					/1
2	3	4	5	6	7/8
9	10	11	12	13	14/15
16	17	18	19	20	21/22
23/30	24	25	26	27	28/29

MAY 2012
M	T	W	T	F	S/S
	1	2	3	4	5/6
7	8	9	10	11	12/13
14	15	16	17	18	19/20
21	22	23	24	25	26/27
28	29	30	31		

JUNE 2012
M	T	W	T	F	S/S
				1	2/3
4	5	6	7	8	9/10
11	12	13	14	15	16/17
18	19	20	21	22	23/24
25	26	27	28	29	30/

JULY 2012
M	T	W	T	F	S/S
					/1
2	3	4	5	6	7/8
9	10	11	12	13	14/15
16	17	18	19	20	21/22
23/30	24/31	25	26	27	28/29

AUGUST 2012
M	T	W	T	F	S/S
		1	2	3	4/5
6	7	8	9	10	11/12
13	14	15	16	17	18/19
20	21	22	23	24	25/26
27	28	29	30	31	

SEPTEMBER 2012
M	T	W	T	F	S/S
					1/2
3	4	5	6	7	8/9
10	11	12	13	14	15/16
17	18	19	20	21	22/23
24	25	26	27	28	29/30

OCTOBER 2012
M	T	W	T	F	S/S
1	2	3	4	5	6/7
8	9	10	11	12	13/14
15	16	17	18	19	20/21
22	23	24	25	26	27/28
29	30	31			

NOVEMBER 2012
M	T	W	T	F	S/S
			1	2	3/4
5	6	7	8	9	10/11
12	13	14	15	16	17/18
19	20	21	22	23	24/25
26	27	28	29	30	

DECEMBER 2012
M	T	W	T	F	S/S
					1/2
3	4	5	6	7	8/9
10	11	12	13	14	15/16
17	18	19	20	21	22/23
24/31	25	26	27	28	29/30

2013

JANUARY 2013
M	T	W	T	F	S/S
	1	2	3	4	5/6
7	8	9	10	11	12/13
14	15	16	17	18	19/20
21	22	23	24	25	26/27
28	29	30	31		

FEBRUARY 2013
M	T	W	T	F	S/S
				1	2/3
4	5	6	7	8	9/10
11	12	13	14	15	16/17
18	19	20	21	22	23/24
25	26	27	28		

MARCH 2013
M	T	W	T	F	S/S
				1	2/3
4	5	6	7	8	9/10
11	12	13	14	15	16/17
18	19	20	21	22	23/24
25	26	27	28	29	30/31

APRIL 2013
M	T	W	T	F	S/S
1	2	3	4	5	6/7
8	9	10	11	12	13/14
15	16	17	18	19	20/21
22	23	24	25	26	27/28
29	30				

MAY 2013
M	T	W	T	F	S/S
	1	2	3	4/5	
6	7	8	9	10	11/12
13	14	15	16	17	18/19
20	21	22	23	24	25/26
27	28	29	30	31	

JUNE 2013
M	T	W	T	F	S/S
					1/2
3	4	5	6	7	8/9
10	11	12	13	14	15/16
17	18	19	20	21	22/23
24	25	26	27	28	29/30

JULY 2013
M	T	W	T	F	S/S
1	2	3	4	5	6/7
8	9	10	11	12	13/14
15	16	17	18	19	20/21
22	23	24	25	26	27/28
29	30	31			

AUGUST 2013
M	T	W	T	F	S/S
			1	2	3/4
5	6	7	8	9	10/11
12	13	14	15	16	17/18
19	20	21	22	23	24/25
26	27	28	29	30	30/

SEPTEMBER 2013
M	T	W	T	F	S/S
					/1
2	3	4	5	6	7/8
9	10	11	12	13	14/15
16	17	18	19	20	21/22
23/30	24	25	26	27	28/29

OCTOBER 2013
M	T	W	T	F	S/S
	1	2	3	4	5/6
7	8	9	10	11	12/13
14	15	16	17	18	19/20
21	22	23	24	25	26/27
28	29	30	31		

NOVEMBER 2013
M	T	W	T	F	S/S
				1	2/3
4	5	6	7	8	9/10
11	12	13	14	15	16/17
18	19	20	21	22	23/24
25	26	27	28	29	30/

DECEMBER 2013
M	T	W	T	F	S/S
					/1
2	3	4	5	6	7/8
9	10	11	12	13	14/15
16	17	18	19	20	21/22
23/30	24/31	25	26	27	28/29